Success in America

Success in America

Edited by

JAMES J. CLARK
San Jose State College

ROBERT H. WOODWARD
San Jose State College

Wadsworth Publishing Company, Inc., Belmont, California

For Jeanne and Carol

L.C. Cat. Card No.: 66–17715
Printed in the United States of America

PREFACE

This collection of studies of the American concept of success and of literary selections illustrating the many ways in which the concept has been reflected in America's literature is designed primarily for use as a controlled-research textbook. Unlike the more usual book of this type, which is limited to a single author, a single literary work, a single literary genre, or a single event in history, this book focuses upon a single theme. Because this theme—the concept of success in America—has through the more than three centuries of its existence defied exact definition, we have carefully avoided the temptation to impose our own definition or to organize the book in such a way as to argue a thesis; the student will, however, find sufficient material to allow him to formulate and to document his own definition or argument.

Even though we have sought to avoid imposing our own interpretation of the material, we have nevertheless felt compelled to order the material in such a way as to suggest a direction of study. The first section, "Perspectives," provides several authoritative and critical assessments of the theme. They make generalizations and observations that can be supported, or argued, by the following groups of primarily literary selections that comprise the larger body of the book. The second section illustrates a few representative expressions of the promise of success. The third section explores the features of American society and thought that have resulted in the changes in the types of figures representing success, and the fourth section consists of major statements by writers who have not shared the public concepts of success. The single story in the final section suggests the current ambiguous status of the American concept of success. We have been acutely aware of space limitations, which have forced us to limit the anthology primarily to literary expressions of the success theme and to keep at a minimum documents that focus directly upon its economic, social, and psychological aspects. A few of the selections (e.g., those by Horace Greeley, Russell H. Conwell, Horatio Alger, Jr., Andrew

Carnegie, and Norman Vincent Peale) are included not because of their literary value but because they are perhaps better representatives of attitudes of their times than the purely literary selections. Only a few poems are included, for we believe that the prose writers have been better able than the poets to express the complexities and subtleties of the theme of success.

We have kept to a minimum the editorial additions. The introductions to the main divisions of the book are intended to provide only a brief overview of the selections and ideas that follow. At the end of the book is a group of questions designed to lead the student into the selections and to help him discover their relevance to the theme of success. Some of the questions, on specific points, will suggest topics for short papers. Other questions, on relationships between two or more selections, will be suitable topics for longer papers. The volume concludes with suggestions for further reading and with brief notes on the authors.

To facilitate use of the book for the controlled-research paper, we have used standard texts and have provided complete bibliographical data for each selection, including original pagination. The bracketed number before the virgule (/) indicates the end of the original page; the number after it signals the beginning of a new page.

It is a pleasure for us to express our appreciation to Professors William F. Irmscher of the University of Washington, Glenn Reed and Graham C. Wilson of San Jose State College, and, especially, Maurice Beebe of Purdue University, for their helpful suggestions and criticisms, and to Dorothy Ohliger and Richard Kuhn of Wadsworth Publishing Company for their editorial acumen and encouragement.

J. J. C.
R. H. W.

CONTENTS

vii

1. PERSPECTIVES

AN EMINENT OBSERVER OF AMERICAN SOCIETY, C. WRIGHT MILLS, HAS RE-
marked that "'Success' in America has been a widespread fact, an
engaging image, a driving motive and a way of life." A concept that is
simultaneously fact, image, motive, and way of life for a nation surely
does not lend itself to exact definition; but in all of its facets, according
to Professor Mills, the concept focuses upon a common center: "the
heraldry of American success has been the greenback." It is partially
this concept of money success with which the critical and literary
documents in this volume are concerned, but success in America must
also be seen in terms of the vision of the people—"the dim outline of
a mountain summit," to use Henry Adams's metaphor, "rising high
above the mist and mud of American democracy."

The five essays that follow, written by professional observers of
the American phenomenon of success, provide various perspectives for
the interpretation and meaning of the literary documents that comprise
the main body of this book. Collectively, the five essays trace the
development of the American concept of success from its historical and
democratic origins, examine its alliance with the Protestant or Puritan
ethic, and describe its nineteenth-century and twentieth-century transformations during the eras of the entrepreneur and the bureaucrat.

Even though personal ambition is recognized as something a man
in any country may feel, American ambition must be considered a
product of forces that went into the exploration and settlement of the
continent. The favorable economic conditions of the new world and
the ideals of freedom and equality in an emerging democracy led many
Americans, wise and foolish, to accept the condition of unlimited opportunities as a natural human condition, an inalienable right to
accompany their freedoms and equalities. Popular slogans even into
the present century persistently reminded both the native and the
newly arrived immigrant of the wealth of free land, of the chances for
money in independent ventures, of the increasing number and variety

1

of jobs for all who cared to work, of unprecedented possibilities for the poor man. A man seeking fame and fortune was acutely aware of those who had capitalized on these opportunities—of the small-town merchant, for instance, who had begun his successful career as a driver of a delivery cart. As Henry Adams shows in his essay on "American Ideals," America was the proper setting for the dream of success, which subtly touched the lives of Americans on every economic and social level.

In addition, early Puritanism brought to the wilderness a set of religious beliefs and a code of behavior appropriate to the demands of individual aspirations in a mercantile environment; the Protestant ethic—the Puritan businessman's paradoxical, but energetic, struggle for worldly success while abjuring the world itself—was the logical offspring of the union of piety and trade. Two of the following essays examine this ethic. The German economist Max Weber theorizes that the rise of capitalism in Europe was accompanied by a change in ethical and religious standards—a change that gave respectability and spiritual sanction to man's concern for worldly wealth. In a study of the views of three colonial American Puritans on the subject of prosperity, A. Whitney Griswold examines the effect of this Protestant ethic on American thought and values. He concludes that the gospel equating sanctity and wealth has had a lasting effect on American life, particularly in the fact that the Puritans "laid down a code of living the followers of which believed that God desired Americans to be rich."

The frontier atmosphere, the early effects of democracy, the Protestant ethic—all influenced in some degree the original concept of success in America, a concept which remained more or less stable to the time of the Civil War. There were skeptics who scorned material success, it is true, but their dissenting voices were heard very faintly in an atmosphere of progress.

By the later nineteenth century, however, the moral foundations of success had changed. Earlier, the praise of the man of wealth customarily included a romantic, rags-to-riches assumption, a variation of the Abraham Lincoln legend, which affirmed the prerequisite of a virtuous life or, at the very least, of humble beginnings and early days of hard work. But naturalistic determinism introduced a new way to look at morality; and Theodore Dreiser's amoral financier Frank Cowperwood, who saw only strength and weakness, not good and evil, is one result. Cowperwood, his characterization a curious amalgam of romantic and deterministic traits, was representative of only one attitude, however. In many of the fictional characterizations of the independent capitalist after 1900, the type was severely criticized, shown either to be morally culpable or destructive or simply ridiculous in his pretensions. Max Lerner, in "The Rise and Decline of the Titan," discusses the financier—or "titan"—as the figure dramatizing the concept of success during this period.

About 1900, with the rise of large financial institutions, the individual's opportunity to achieve material success appreciably narrowed. But despite economic realities, in the first half of the twentieth century the public image of success seems to have been affected little. There still remained—as myth—the Puritan equation that virtue guarantees success, and the public still retained faith that anyone, with a little luck, could achieve success. The heritage of the frontier, of the Puritans, of the Lincoln legend had fused into a myth of success. The major writers of the twentieth century have criticized this myth because of its materialistic foundation and its invitation to social hypocrisy, because it invites the conclusion that wealth means virtue and because it has too often failed to conform to reality. Most modern writers observe that man achieves success within prescribed limits and that morality is no longer the crucial issue. Professor Mills, for example, in his analysis of "the new entrepreneur"—a phenomenon of bureaucracy—describes the limits that the corporate society imposes on the twentieth-century American in his quest for success.

Embodied in the American concept of success is the individual's optimistic belief in his own unlimited potentialities, in his freedom of will and action, and in his rejection of the need for outside forces in realizing these potentialities. It is a secular expression, for though it does not deny belief in a higher being, it accepts this being as an instrument to accomplish the natural law of cause and effect, effort and reward. It is peculiarly American because in America democratic and religious conditions caused it to assume a specific form and exert a special kind of influence. A new being in a new world, the American had no dominant tradition to guide him in his religious and philosophic thinking and no extreme of dogma, aristocratic or proletarian, to dictate rules of behavior. The expanse of undeveloped continent encouraged a simple, graspable philosophy for this American, and such the concept of success has proved to be. But in the realities of a changing world it has become something more than simple. The American's attempt to adapt to the concept as well as to the reality of success has created a unique body of literature.

American Ideals

HENRY ADAMS

NEARLY EVERY FOREIGN TRAVELLER WHO VISITED THE UNITED STATES during these early years, carried away an impression sober if not sad. A thousand miles of desolate and dreary forest, broken here and there by settlements; along the sea-coast a few flourishing towns devoted to commerce; no arts, a provincial literature, a cancerous disease of negro slavery, and differences of political theory fortified within geographical lines,—what could be hoped for such a country except to repeat the story of violence and brutality which the world already knew by heart, until repetition for thousands of years had wearied and sickened mankind? Ages must probably pass before the interior could be thoroughly settled; even Jefferson, usually a sanguine man, talked of a thousand years with acquiescence, and in his first Inaugural Address, at a time when the Mississippi River formed the Western boundary, spoke of the country as having "room enough for our descendants to the hundredth and thousandth generation." No prudent person dared to act on the certainty that when settled, one government could comprehend the whole; and when the day of separation should arrive, and America should have her Prussia, Austria, and Italy, as she [156/157] already had her England, France, and Spain, what else could follow but a return to the old conditions of local jealousies, wars, and corruption which had made a slaughter-house of Europe?

The mass of Americans were sanguine and self-confident, partly by temperament, but partly also by reason of ignorance; for they knew little of the difficulties which surrounded a complex society. The Duc de Liancourt, like many critics, was struck by this trait. Among other instances, he met with one in the person of a Pennsylvania miller, Thomas Lea, "a sound American patriot, persuading himself that nothing good is done, and that no one has any brains, except in America; that the wit, the imagination, the genius of Europe are

From Henry Adams, *History of the United States of America during the Administration of Thomas Jefferson* (New York: Albert and Charles Boni, 1930), I, 156–184. Originally published 1889–1891.

already in decrepitude"; and the duke added: "This error is to be found in almost all Americans,—legislators, administrators, as well as millers, and is less innocent there." In the year 1796 the House of Representatives debated whether to insert in the Reply to the President's Speech a passing remark that the nation was "the freest and most enlightened in the world,"—a nation as yet in swaddling-clothes, which had neither literature, arts, sciences, nor history; nor even enough nationality to be sure that it was a nation. The moment was peculiarly ill-chosen for such a claim, because Europe was on the verge of an outburst of genius. Goethe and Schiller, Mozart and Haydn, Kant and Fichte, Cavendish and Herschel were making way for Walter Scott, Wordsworth, and [157/158] Shelley, Heine and Balzac, Beethoven and Hegel, Oersted and Cuvier, great physicists, biologists, geologists, chemists, mathematicians, metaphysicians, and historians by the score. Turner was painting his earliest landscapes, and Watt completing his latest steam-engine; Napoleon was taking command of the French armies, and Nelson of the English fleets; investigators, reformers, scholars, and philosophers swarmed, and the influence of enlightenment, even amid universal war, was working with an energy such as the world had never before conceived. The idea that Europe was in her decrepitude proved only ignorance and want of enlightenment, if not of freedom, on the part of Americans, who could only excuse their error by pleading that notwithstanding these objections, in matters which for the moment most concerned themselves Europe was a full century behind America. If they were right in thinking that the next necessity of human progress was to lift the average man upon an intellectual and social level with the most favored, they stood at least three generations nearer than Europe to their common goal. The destinies of the United States were certainly staked, without reserve or escape, on the soundness of this doubtful and even improbable principle, ignoring or overthrowing the institutions of church, aristocracy, family, army, and political intervention, which long experience had shown to be needed for the safety of society. Europe might be right in thinking that without such safeguards society must come to an end; [158/159] but even Europeans must concede that there was a chance, if no greater than one in a thousand, that America might, at least for a time, succeed. If this stake of temporal and eternal welfare stood on the winning card; if man actually should become more virtuous and enlightened, by mere process of growth, without church or paternal authority; if the average human being could accustom himself to reason with the logical processes of Descartes and Newton!—what then?

Then, no one could deny that the United States would win a stake such as defied mathematics. With all the advantages of science and capital, Europe must be slower than America to reach the common goal. American society might be both sober and sad, but except for negro slavery it was sound and healthy in every part. Stripped for the hardest work, every muscle firm and elastic, every ounce of brain ready for use, and not a trace of superfluous flesh on his nervous and supple body, the American stood in the world a new order of man. From Maine to Florida, society was in this respect the same, and was so organized as to use its human forces with more economy than could be approached by any society of the world elsewhere. Not only were artificial barriers carefully removed, but every influence that could appeal to ordinary ambition was applied. No brain or appetite active enough to be conscious of stimulants could fail to answer the intense incentive. Few human beings, however sluggish, could long resist the [159/160] temptation to acquire power; and the elements of power were to be had in America almost for the asking. Reversing the old-world system, the American stimulant increased in energy as it reached the lowest and most ignorant class, dragging and whirling them upward as in the blast of a furnace. The penniless and homeless Scotch or Irish immigrant was caught and consumed by it; for every stroke of the axe and the hoe made him a capitalist, and made gentlemen of his children. Wealth was the strongest agent for moving the mass of mankind; but political power was hardly less tempting to the more intelligent and better-educated swarms of American-born citizens, and the instinct of activity, once created, seemed heritable and permanent in the race.

Compared with this lithe young figure, Europe was actually in decrepitude. Mere class distinctions, the *patois* or dialect of the peasantry, the fixity of residence, the local costumes and habits marking a history that lost itself in the renewal of identical generations, raised from birth barriers which paralyzed half the population. Upon this mass of inert matter rested the Church and the State, holding down activity of thought. Endless wars withdrew many hundred thousand men from production, and changed them into agents of waste; huge debts, the evidence of past wars and bad government, created interests to support the system and fix its burdens on the laboring class; courts, with habits of extravagance that shamed common-sense, helped to consume private [160/161] economics. All this might have been borne; but behind this stood aristocracies, sucking their nourishment from industry, producing nothing themselves, employing little or no active capital or intelligent labor, but pressing on the energies and ambition of society with the weight of an incubus. Picturesque and entertaining as these social anomalies were, they were better fitted for the theatre or for a museum of historical costumes than for an active workshop preparing to compete with such machinery as America would soon command. From an economical point of view, they were as incongruous as would have been the appearance of a mediæval knight in helmet and armor, with battle-axe and shield, to run the machinery of Arkwright's cotton-mill; but besides their bad economy they also

tended to prevent the rest of society from gaining a knowledge of its
own capacities. In Europe, the conservative habit of mind was fortified
behind power. During nearly a century Voltaire himself—the friend of
kings, the wit and poet, historian and philosopher of his age—had
carried on, in daily terror, in exile and excommunication, a protest
against an intellectual despotism contemptible even to its own sup-
porters. Hardly was Voltaire dead, when Priestley, as great a man if
not so great a wit, trying to do for England what Voltaire tried to do
for France, was mobbed by the people of Birmingham and driven to
America. Where Voltaire and Priestley failed, common men could not
struggle; the weight of society stifled their thought. In America [161/
162] the balance between conservative and liberal forces was close;
but in Europe conservatism held the physical power of government. In
Boston a young Buckminster might be checked for a time by his
father's prayers or commands in entering the path that led toward freer
thought; but youth beckoned him on, and every reward that society
could offer was dangled before his eyes. In London or Paris, Rome,
Madrid, or Vienna, he must have sacrificed the worldly prospects of his
life. . . . [162/170]

Possibly the view of Wordsworth and Moore, of Weld, Dennie,
and Dickens was right. The American democrat possessed little art of
expression, and did not watch his own emotions with a view of uttering
them either in prose or verse; he never told more of himself than the
world might have assumed without listening to him. Only with diffi-
dence could history attribute to such a class of men a wider range of
thought or feeling than they themselves cared to proclaim. Yet the
difficulty of denying or even ignoring the wider range was still greater,
for no one questioned the force or the scope of an emotion which
caused the poorest peasant in Europe to see what was invisible to poet
and philosopher,—the dim outline of a mountain-summit across the
ocean, rising high above the mist and mud of American democracy. As
though to call attention to some such difficulty, European and American critics, while affirming that Americans were a race without illusions
or enlarged ideas, declared in the same breath that Jefferson was a
visionary whose theories would cause the heavens to fall upon them.
Year after year, with endless iteration, in every accent of contempt,
rage, and despair, [170/171] they repeated this charge against Jefferson. Every foreigner and Federalist agreed that he was a man of
illusions, dangerous to society and unbounded in power of evil; but if
this view of his character was right, the same visionary qualities
seemed also to be a national trait, for every one admitted that Jefferson's opinions, in one form or another, were shared by a majority of the
American people.

Illustrations might be carried much further, and might be drawn
from every social class and from every period in national history. Of all
presidents, Abraham Lincoln has been considered the most typical

representative of American society, chiefly because his mind, with all its practical qualities, also inclined, in certain directions, to idealism. Lincoln was born in 1809, the moment when American character stood in lowest esteem. Ralph Waldo Emerson, a more distinct idealist, was born in 1803. William Ellery Channing, another idealist, was born in 1780. Men like John Fitch, Oliver Evans, Robert Fulton, Joel Barlow, John Stevens, and Eli Whitney were all classed among visionaries. The whole society of Quakers belonged in the same category. The records of the popular religious sects abounded in examples of idealism and illusion to such an extent that the masses seemed hardly to find comfort or hope in any authority, however old or well established. In religion as in politics, Americans seemed to require a system which gave play to their imagination and their hopes. [171/172]

Some misunderstanding must always take place when the observer is at cross-purposes with the society he describes. Wordsworth might have convinced himself by a moment's thought that no country could act on the imagination as America acted upon the instincts of the ignorant and poor, without some quality that deserved better treatment than poignant scorn; but perhaps this was only one among innumerable cases in which the unconscious poet breathed an atmosphere which the self-conscious poet could not penetrate. With equal reason he might have taken the opposite view,—that the hard, practical, money-getting American democrat, who had neither generosity nor honor nor imagination, and who inhabited cold shades where fancy sickened and where genius died, was in truth living in a world of dream, and acting a drama more instinct with poetry than all the avatars of the East, walking in gardens of emerald and rubies, in ambition already ruling the world and guiding Nature with a kinder and wiser hand than had ever yet been felt in human history. From this point his critics never approached him,—they stopped at a stone's throw; and at the moment when they declared that the man's mind had no illusions, they added that he was a knave or a lunatic. Even on his practical and sordid side, the American might easily have been represented as a victim to illusion. If the Englishman had lived as the American speculator did,—in the future,—the hyperbole of enthusiasm would have seemed less monstrous. "Look [172/173] at my wealth!" cried the American to his foreign visitor. "See these solid mountains of salt and iron, of lead, copper, silver, and gold! See these magnificent cities scattered broadcast to the Pacific! See my cornfields rustling and waving in the summer breeze from ocean to ocean, so far that the sun itself is not high enough to mark where the distant mountains bound my golden seas! Look at this continent of mine, fairest of created worlds, as she lies turning up to the sun's never-failing caress her broad and exuberant breasts, overflowing with milk for her hundred million children! See how she glows with youth, health, and love!" Perhaps it was not altogether unnatural that the foreigner, on being asked to see

what needed centuries to produce, should have looked about him with
bewilderment and indignation. "Gold! cities! cornfields! continents!
Nothing of the sort! I see nothing but tremendous wastes, where sickly
men and women are dying of home-sickness or are scalped by savages!
mountain-ranges a thousand miles long, with no means of getting to
them, and nothing in them when you get there! swamps and forests
choked with their own rotten ruins! nor hope of better for a thousand
years! Your story is a fraud, and you are a liar and swindler!"

Met in this spirit, the American, half perplexed and half defiant,
retaliated by calling his antagonist a fool, and by mimicking his heavy
tricks of manner. For himself he cared little, but his dream was his
[173/174] whole existence. The men who denounced him admitted
that they left him in his forest-swamp quaking with fever, but clinging
in the delirium of death to the illusions of his dazzled brain. No class of
men could be required to support their convictions with a steadier
faith, or pay more devotedly with their persons for the mistakes of
their judgment. Whether imagination or greed led them to describe
more than actually existed, they still saw no more than any inventor or
discoverer must have seen in order to give him the energy of success.
They said to the rich as to the poor, "Come and share our limitless
riches! Come and help us bring to light these unimaginable stores of
wealth and power!" The poor came, and from them were seldom heard
complaints of deception or delusion. Within a moment, by the mere
contact of a moral atmosphere, they saw the gold and jewels, the
summer cornfields and the glowing continent. The rich for a long time
stood aloof,—they were timid and narrow-minded; but this was not
all,—between them and the American democrat was a gulf.

The charge that Americans were too fond of money to win the
confidence of Europeans was a curious inconsistency; yet this was a
common belief. If the American deluded himself and led others to their
death by baseless speculations; if he buried those he loved in a gloomy
forest where they quaked and died while he persisted in seeing there a
splendid, healthy, and well-built city,—no one could deny that he
sacrificed [174/175] wife and child to his greed for gain, that the
dollar was his god, and a sordid avarice his demon. Yet had this been
the whole truth, no European capitalist would have hesitated to make
money out of his grave; for, avarice against avarice, no more sordid or
meaner type existed in America than could be shown on every 'Change
in Europe. With much more reason Americans might have suspected
that in America Englishmen found everywhere a silent influence,
which they found nowhere in Europe, and which had nothing to do
with avarice or with the dollar, but, on the contrary, seemed likely at
any moment to sacrifice the dollar in a cause and for an object so
illusory that most Englishmen could not endure to hear it discussed.
. . . [175/180]

Yet even then one part of the American social [180/181] system was proving itself to be rich in results. The average American was more intelligent than the average European, and was becoming every year still more active-minded as the new movement of society caught him up and swept him through a life of more varied experiences. On all sides the national mind responded to its stimulants. Deficient as the American was in the machinery of higher instruction; remote, poor; unable by any exertion to acquire the training, the capital, or even the elementary textbooks he needed for a fair development of his natural powers,—his native energy and ambition already responded to the spur applied to them. Some of his triumphs were famous throughout the world; for Benjamin Franklin had raised high the reputation of American printers, and the actual President of the United States, who signed with Franklin the treaty of peace with Great Britain, was the son of a small farmer, and had himself kept a school in his youth. In both these cases social recognition followed success; but the later triumphs of the American mind were becoming more and more popular. John Fitch was not only one of the poorest, but one of the least-educated Yankees who ever made a name; he could never spell with tolerable correctness, and his life ended as it began,—in the lowest social obscurity. Eli Whitney was better educated than Fitch, but had neither wealth, social influence, nor patron to back his ingenuity. In the year 1800 Eli Terry, another Connecticut Yankee of the same class, took into his [181/182] employ two young men to help him make wooden clocks, and this was the capital on which the greatest clock-manufactory in the world began its operations. In 1797 Asa Whittemore, a Massachusetts Yankee, invented a machine to make cards for carding wool, which "operated as if it had a soul," and became the foundation for a hundred subsequent patents. In 1790 Jacob Perkins, of Newburyport, invented a machine capable of cutting and turning out two hundred thousand nails a day; and then invented a process for transferring engraving from a very small steel cylinder to copper, which revolutionized cotton-printing. The British traveller Weld, passing through Wilmington, stopped, as Liancourt had done before him, to see the great flour-mills on the Brandywine. "The improvements," he said, "which have been made in the machinery of the flour-mills in America are very great. The chief of these consist in a new application of the screw, and the introduction of what are called elevators, the idea of which was evidently borrowed from the chain-pump." This was the invention of Oliver Evans, a native of Delaware, whose parents were in very humble life, but who was himself, in spite of every disadvantage, an inventive genius of the first order. Robert Fulton, who in 1800 was in Paris with Joel Barlow, sprang from the same source in Pennsylvania. John Stevens, a native of New York, belonged to a more favored class, but followed the same impulses. All these men were the outcome of typical American society, and all their [182/183] inventions transmuted the democratic instinct into a practical and tangible shape. Who would undertake to say that there was a limit to the fecundity of this teeming source? Who that saw only the narrow, practical, money-getting nature of these devices could venture to assert that as they wrought their end and raised the standard of millions, they would not also raise the creative power of those millions to a higher plane? If the priests and barons who set their names to Magna Charta had been told that in a few centuries every swine-herd and cobbler's apprentice would write and read with an ease such as few kings could then command, and reason with better logic than any university could then practise, the priest and baron would have been more incredulous than any man who was told in 1800 that within another five centuries the ploughboy would go a-field whistling a sonata of Beethoven, and figure out in quaternions the relation of his furrows. The American democrat knew so little of art that among his popular illusions he could not then nourish artistic ambition; but leaders like Jefferson, Gallatin, and Barlow might without extravagance count upon a coming time when diffused ease and education should bring the masses into familiar contact with higher forms of human achievement, and their vast creative power, turned toward a nobler culture, might rise to the level of that democratic genius which found expression in the Parthenon; might revel in the delights of a new Buonarotti and a richer Titian; might create for [183/184] five hundred million people the America of thought and art which alone could satisfy their omnivorous ambition.

Whether the illusions, so often affirmed and so often denied to the American people, took such forms or not, these were in effect the problems that lay before American society: Could it transmute its social power into the higher forms of thought? Could it provide for the moral and intellectual needs of mankind? Could it take permanent political shape? Could it give new life to religion and art? Could it create and maintain in the mass of mankind those habits of mind which had hitherto belonged to men of science alone? Could it physically develop the convolutions of the human brain? Could it produce, or was it compatible with, the differentiation of a higher variety of the human race? Nothing less than this was necessary for its complete success. [184]

The Spirit of Capitalism

MAX WEBER

IN THE TITLE OF THIS STUDY IS USED THE SOMEWHAT PRETENTIOUS PHRASE, the *spirit* of capitalism. What is to be understood by it? The attempt to give anything like a definition of it brings out certain difficulties which are in the very nature of this type of investigation.

If any object can be found to which this term can be applied with any understandable meaning, it can only be an historical individual, i.e. a complex of elements associated in historical reality which we unite into a conceptual whole from the standpoint of their cultural significance.

Such an historical concept, however, since it refers in its content to a phenomenon significant for its unique individuality, cannot be defined according to the formula *genus proximum, differentia specifica*, but it must be gradually put together out of the individual parts which are taken from historical reality to make it up. Thus the final and definitive concept cannot stand at the beginning of the investigation, but must come at the end. We must, in other words, work out in the course of the discussion, as its most important result, the best conceptual formulation of what we here understand by the spirit of capitalism, that is the best from the point of view which interests us here. This point of view (the one of which we shall speak later) is, further, by no means the only possible one from which the historical phenomena we are investigating can be analysed. Other standpoints would, for this as for every [47/48] historical phenomenon, yield other characteristics as the essential ones. The result is that it is by no means necessary to understand by the spirit of capitalism only what it will come to mean to *us* for the purposes of our analysis. This is a necessary result of the nature of historical concepts which attempt for their methodological purposes not to grasp historical reality in abstract general formulæ, but

Reprinted with the permission of Charles Scribner's Sons from *The Protestant Ethic and the Spirit of Capitalism*, pp. 47–58, by Max Weber, translated by Talcott Parsons. (Charles Scribner's Sons, 1930.) Originally published 1904–1905. The following selection is the first part of Chapter 2 of the book. Weber's footnotes have not been included.

in concrete genetic sets of relations which are inevitably of a specifically unique and individual character.

Thus, if we try to determine the object, the analysis and historical explanation of which we are attempting, it cannot be in the form of a conceptual definition, but at least in the beginning only a provisional description of what is here meant by the spirit of capitalism. Such a description is, however, indispensable in order clearly to understand the object of the investigation. For this purpose we turn to a document of that spirit which contains what we are looking for in almost classical purity, and at the same time has the advantage of being free from all direct relationship to religion, being thus, for our purposes, free of preconceptions.

"Remember, that *time* is money. He that can earn ten shillings a day by his labour, and goes abroad, or sits idle, one half of that day, though he spends but sixpence during his diversion or idleness, ought not to reckon *that* the only expense; he has really spent, or rather thrown away, five shillings besides.

"Remember, that *credit* is money. If a man lets his money lie in my hands after it is due, he gives me the interest, or so much as I can make of it during that [48/49] time. This amounts to a considerable sum where a man has good and large credit, and makes good use of it.

"Remember, that money is of the prolific, generating nature. Money can beget money, and its offspring can beget more, and so on. Five shillings turned is six, turned again it is seven and threepence, and so on, till it becomes a hundred pounds. The more there is of it, the more it produces every turning, so that the profits rise quicker and quicker. He that kills a breeding-sow, destroys all her offspring to the thousandth generation. He that murders a crown, destroys all that it might have produced, even scores of pounds."

"Remember this saying, *The good paymaster is lord of another man's purse.* He that is known to pay punctually and exactly to the time he promises, may at any time, and on any occasion, raise all the money his friends can spare. This is sometimes of great use. After industry and frugality, nothing contributes more to the raising of a young man in the world than punctuality and justice in all his dealings; therefore never keep borrowed money an hour beyond the time you promised, lest a disappointment shut up your friend's purse for ever.

"The most trifling actions that affect a man's credit are to be regarded. The sound of your hammer at five in the morning, or eight at night, heard by a creditor, makes him easy six months longer; but if he sees you at a billiard-table, or hears your voice at a tavern, when you should be at work, he sends for his money the next day; demands it, before he can receive it, in a lump.

"It shows, besides, that you are mindful of what you [49/50] owe;

it makes you appear a careful as well as an honest man, and that still increases your credit.

"Beware of thinking all your own that you possess, and of living accordingly. It is a mistake that many people who have credit fall into. To prevent this, keep an exact account for some time both of your expenses and your income. If you take the pains at first to mention particulars, it will have this good effect: you will discover how wonderfully small, trifling expenses mount up to large sums, and will discern what might have been, and may for the future be saved, without occasioning any great inconvenience.

"For six pounds a year you may have the use of one hundred pounds, provided you are a man of known prudence and honesty.

"He that spends a groat a day idly, spends idly above six pounds a year, which is the price for the use of one hundred pounds.

"He that wastes idly a groat's worth of his time per day, one day with another, wastes the privilege of using one hundred pounds each day.

"He that idly loses five shillings' worth of time, loses five shillings, and might as prudently throw five shillings into the sea.

"He that loses five shillings, not only loses that sum, but all the advantage that might be made by turning it in dealing, which by the time that a young man becomes old, will amount to a considerable sum of money."

It is Benjamin [Franklin] who preaches to us in these sentences, the same which Ferdinand Kürnberger [50/51] satirizes in his clever and malicious *Picture of American Culture* as the supposed confession of faith of the Yankee. That it is the spirit of capitalism which here speaks in characteristic fashion, no one will doubt, however little we may wish to claim that everything which could be understood as pertaining to that spirit is contained in it. Let us pause a moment to consider this passage, the philosophy of which Kürnberger sums up in the words, "They make tallow out of cattle and money out of men." The peculiarity of this philosophy of avarice appears to be the ideal of the honest man of recognized credit, and above all the idea of a duty of the individual toward the increase of his capital, which is assumed as an end in itself. Truly what is here preached is not simply a means of making one's way in the world, but a peculiar ethic. The infraction of its rules is treated not as foolishness but as forgetfulness of duty. That is the essence of the matter. It is not mere business astuteness, that sort of thing is common enough, it is an ethos. *This* is the quality which interests us.

When Jacob Fugger, in speaking to a business associate who had retired and who wanted to persuade him to do the same, since he had made enough money and should let others have a chance, rejected that as pusillanimity and answered that "he (Fugger) thought otherwise, he wanted to make money as long as he could," the spirit of his statement is evidently quite different from that of Franklin. What in the former case was an expression of commercial daring and a personal inclination morally neutral, in the latter takes on the character of an ethically coloured maxim [51/52] for the conduct of life. The concept spirit of capitalism is here used in this specific sense, it is the spirit of modern capitalism. For that we are here dealing only with Western European and American capitalism is obvious from the way in which the problem was stated. Capitalism existed in China, India, Babylon, in the classic world, and in the Middle Ages. But in all these cases, as we shall see, this particular ethos was lacking.

Now, all Franklin's moral attitudes are coloured with utilitarianism. Honesty is useful, because it assures credit; so are punctuality, industry, frugality, and that is the reason they are virtues. A logical deduction from this would be that where, for instance, the appearance of honesty serves the same purpose, that would suffice, and an unnecessary surplus of this virtue would evidently appear to Franklin's eyes as unproductive waste. And as a matter of fact, the story in his autobiography of his conversion to those virtues, or the discussion of the value of a strict maintenance of the appearance of modesty, the assiduous belittlement of one's own deserts in order to gain general recognition later, confirms this impression. According to Franklin, those virtues, like all others, are only in so far virtues as they are actually useful to the individual, and the surrogate of mere appearance is always sufficient when it accomplishes the end in view. It is a conclusion which is inevitable for strict utilitarianism. The impression of many Germans that the virtues professed by Americanism are pure hypocrisy seems to have been confirmed by this striking case. But in fact the matter is not by any means so simple. Benjamin Franklin's own character, as it appears in [52/53] the really unusual candidness of his autobiography, belies that suspicion. The circumstance that he ascribes his recognition of the utility of virtue to a divine revelation which was intended to lead him in the path of righteousness, shows that something more than mere garnishing for purely egocentric motives is involved.

In fact, the *summum bonum* of this ethic, the earning of more and more money, combined with the strict avoidance of all spontaneous enjoyment of life, is above all completely devoid of any eudaemonistic, not to say hedonistic, admixture. It is thought of so purely as an end in itself, that from the point of view of the happiness of, or utility to, the single individual, it appears entirely transcendental and absolutely irrational. Man is dominated by the making of money, by acquisition as the ultimate purpose of his life. Economic acquisition is no longer subordinated to man as the means for the satisfaction of his material needs. This reversal of what we should call the natural relationship, so irrational from a naïve point of view, is evidently as definitely a leading principle of capitalism as it is foreign to all peoples not under capitalistic influence. At the same time it expresses a type of feeling which is closely connected with certain religious ideas. If we thus ask, *why* should "money be made out of men," Benjamin Franklin himself, although he was a colourless deist, answers in his autobiography with a quotation from the Bible, which his strict Calvinistic father drummed into him again and again in his youth: "Seest thou a man diligent in his business? He shall stand before kings" (Prov. xxii. 29). The earning of money within the modern economic order is, so long [53/54] as it is done legally, the result and the expression of virtue and proficiency in a calling; and this virtue and proficiency are, as it is now not difficult to see, the real Alpha and Omega of Franklin's ethic, as expressed in the passages we have quoted, as well as in all his works without exception.

And in truth this peculiar idea, so familiar to us to-day, but in reality so little a matter of course, of one's duty in a calling, is what is most characteristic of the social ethic of capitalistic culture, and is in a sense the fundamental basis of it. It is an obligation which the individual is supposed to feel and does feel towards the content of his professional activity, no matter in what it consists, in particular no matter whether it appears on the surface as a utilization of his personal powers, or only of his material possessions (as capital).

Of course, this conception has not appeared only under capitalistic conditions. On the contrary, we shall later trace its origins back to a time previous to the advent of capitalism. Still less, naturally, do we maintain that a conscious acceptance of these ethical maxims on the part of the individuals, entrepreneurs or labourers, in modern capitalistic enterprises, is a condition of the further existence of present-day capitalism. The capitalistic economy of the present day is an immense cosmos into which the individual is born, and which presents itself to him, at least as an individual, as an unalterable order of things in which he must live. It forces the individual, in so far as he is involved in the system of market relationships, to conform to capitalistic rules of action. The manufacturer who in the long [54/55] run acts counter to these norms, will just as inevitably be eliminated from the economic scene as the worker who cannot or will not adapt himself to them will be thrown into the streets without a job.

Thus the capitalism of to-day, which has come to dominate economic life, educates and selects the economic subjects which it needs through a process of economic survival of the fittest. But here one can easily see the limits of the concept of selection as a means of historical explanation. In order that a manner of life so well adapted to the peculiarities of capitalism could be selected at all, i.e. should come to dominate others, it had to originate somewhere, and not in isolated individuals alone, but as a way of life common to whole groups of men. This origin is what really needs explanation. Concerning the doctrine of the more naïve historical materialism, that such ideas originate as a reflection or superstructure of economic situations, we shall speak more in detail below. At this point it will suffice for our purpose to call attention to the fact that without doubt, in the country of Benjamin Franklin's birth (Massachusetts), the spirit of capitalism (in the sense we have attached to it) was present before the capitalistic order. There were complaints of a peculiarly calculating sort of profit-seeking in New England, as distinguished from other parts of America, as early as 1632. It is further undoubted that capitalism remained far less developed in some of the neighbouring colonies, the later Southern States of the United States of America, in spite of the fact that these latter were founded by large capitalists for business motives, while the New England colonies were founded by preachers [55/56] and seminary graduates with the help of small bourgeois, craftsmen and yeomen, for religious reasons. In this case the causal relation is certainly the reverse of that suggested by the materialistic standpoint.

But the origin and history of such ideas is much more complex than the theorists of the superstructure suppose. The spirit of capitalism, in the sense in which we are using the term, had to fight its way to supremacy against a whole world of hostile forces. A state of mind such as that expressed in the passages we have quoted from Franklin, and which called forth the applause of a whole people, would both in ancient times and in the Middle Ages have been proscribed as the lowest sort of avarice and as an attitude entirely lacking in self-respect. It is, in fact, still regularly thus looked upon by all those social groups which are least involved in or adapted to modern capitalistic conditions. This is not wholly because the instinct of acquisition was in those times unknown or undeveloped, as has often been said. Nor because the *auri sacra fames*, the greed for gold, was then, or now, less powerful outside of bourgeois capitalism than within its peculiar sphere, as the illusions of modern romanticists are wont to believe. The difference between the capitalistic and pre-capitalistic spirits is not to be found at this point. The greed of the Chinese Mandarin, the old Roman aristocrat, or the modern peasant, can stand up to any comparison. And the *auri sacra fames* of a Neapolitan cab-driver or *barcaiuolo*, and certainly of Asiatic representatives of similar trades, as well as of the craftsmen of southern European or Asiatic countries, is, as anyone can find out for himself, very much more [56/57] intense, and especially more unscrupulous than that of, say, an Englishman in similar circumstances.

The universal reign of absolute unscrupulousness in the pursuit of selfish interests by the making of money has been a specific characteristic of precisely those countries whose bourgeois-capitalistic development, measured according to Occidental standards, has remained backward. As every employer knows, the lack of *coscienziosità* of the labourers of such countries, for instance Italy as compared with Germany, has been, and to a certain extent still is, one of the principal obstacles to their capitalistic development. Capitalism cannot make use of the labour of those who practise the doctrine of undisciplined *liberum arbitrium,* any more than it can make use of the business man who seems absolutely unscrupulous in his dealings with others, as we can learn from Franklin. Hence the difference does not lie in the degree of development of any impulse to make money. The *auri sacra fames* is as old as the history of man. But we shall see that those who submitted to it without reserve as an uncontrolled impulse, such as the Dutch sea-captain who "would go through hell for gain, even though he scorched his sails," were by no means the representatives of that attitude of mind from which the specifically modern capitalistic spirit as a mass phenomenon is derived, and that is what matters. At all periods of history, wherever it was possible, there has been ruthless acquisition, bound to no ethical norms whatever. Like war and piracy, trade has often been unrestrained in its relations with foreigners and those outside the group. The double ethic has permitted here what was forbidden in dealings among brothers. [57/58]

Capitalistic acquisition as an adventure has been at home in all types of economic society which have known trade with the use of money and which have offered it opportunities, through *commenda,* farming of taxes, State loans, financing of wars, ducal courts and office-holders. Likewise the inner attitude of the adventurer, which laughs at all ethical limitations, has been universal. Absolute and conscious ruthlessness in acquisition has often stood in the closest connection with the strictest conformity to tradition. Moreover, with the break-down of tradition and the more or less complete extension of free economic enterprise, even to within the social group, the new thing has not generally been ethically justified and encouraged, but only toler-ated as a fact. And this fact has been treated either as ethically indifferent or as reprehensible, but unfortunately unavoidable. This has not only been the normal attitude of all ethical teachings, but, what is more important, also that expressed in the practical action of the average man of pre-capitalistic times, pre-capitalistic in the sense that the rational utilization of capital in a permanent enterprise and the rational capitalistic organization of labour had not yet become domi-nant forces in the determination of economic activity. Now just this attitude was one of the strongest inner obstacles which the adaptation of men to the conditions of an ordered bourgeois-capitalistic economy has encountered elsewhere. [58]

Three Puritans on Prosperity

ALFRED WHITNEY GRISWOLD

"... they ... believed that God desired Americans to be rich. ..."

I

SINCE THE GERMAN ECONOMIST MAX WEBER FIRST CALLED SERIOUS ATtention to the relationship of Protestantism and capitalism, various scholars have become intrigued with the idea.[1] Some have taken issue with Weber on minor points, but most have accepted his general conclusions. R. H. Tawney, in particular, has elaborated the thesis, and integrated it with the history of the Reformation.[2] Ernst Troeltsch has shown its development in sectarian ethics.[3] Yet so far, no one has sought to demonstrate the forms in which this relationship has manifested itself in American history.

For three centuries, Americans have been taught to admire material success: the "frontier," perhaps, provided the economic basis for the lesson. The growing sense of nationalism, the democratic levelling

A. Whitney Griswold, "Three Puritans on Prosperity," *The New England Quarterly*, VII (1934), 475–493. Reprinted with the permission of *The New England Quarterly*.

[1] Weber's work first appeared in *Archiv für Sozialwissenschaft und Sozialpolitik*, 1904–1905. It was published as a book in Germany in 1920 and afterwards translated into English and published as *The Protestant Ethic and the Spirit of Capitalism* (London, 1930).

[2] In *Religion and the Rise of Capitalism* (London, 1929). For an excellent review of both Weber and Tawney, see Georgia Harkness, *John Calvin, the Man and His Ethics* (New York, 1931), 187–191. These, and other critics of Weber, have picked minor flaws in his argument, such as his over-simplification of Calvinism and his neglect of the social and economic origins of capitalism. They point out that before Luther and Calvin, Thomas Aquinas bestowed a rather negative sanction upon the virtue of thrift. But they uphold as sound Weber's main thesis, that since the Reformation, Protestantism has supplied both inspiration and ethical basis for the capitalist economy.

[3] In *The Social Teaching of the Christian Churches* (London, 1931). See also Preserved Smith, *The Age of the Reformation* (New York, 1920), and Reinhold Niebuhr, "Puritanism and Prosperity," in the *Atlantic Monthly*, CXXXVII, 721.

of social barriers, immense natural resources have combined to make us a nation of "rugged individualists," intent upon getting rich. In addition, we have been harangued, severally and individually, on the virtue of making money by a race of success-prophets indigenous [475/476] to our soil. It is with three early members of that race that this paper deals.

It is worth while, by way of orientation, to review, in brief, the essence of Weber's theory. Because no one has done this so concisely as Professor Morison, let us borrow from his *Builders of the Bay Colony:*

Max Weber, a German economist of the last century, propounded the interesting theory that Calvinism released the business man from the clutches of the priest, and sprinkled holy water on economic success. According to him, John Calvin defended the taking of interest on loans, which the medieval church had condemned under the name of usury. Since God would not justify reprobates by prosperity, so the argument goes, the successful business man was probably one of God's elect; hence the Puritan sought success as evidence of his election to eternal bliss.

This is the theory to which Tawney, Troeltsch, and others have given added currency. Not so Mr. Morison. He rejects it on the grounds that "in none of the scores of funeral sermons which I have read, is it hinted 'Our departed friend was successful, so he must be in Heaven.' " Further, Mr. Morison proceeds to the conclusion of Professor Clive Day that "the economic ideas of the New England Puritans were medieval; and so far as their church had political power, it regulated rather than stimulated business enterprise."[4]

With the economic implications of the criticism of Messrs. Morison and Day, we are not specifically concerned. Yet their suggestion that "the economic ideas of the New England Puritans were medieval"[5] needs considerable qualification. In spite of the evidence offered by Mr. Day in support of this contention,[6] we can not overlook the failure of the collectivist experiment at Plymouth. It is incorrect to deny that at least [476/477] the seeds of rugged individualism came over on the *Mayflower.* Later they grew so luxuriantly as to shut collectivism completely out of the Puritan sun. In partial proof of this we offer the sermons of our three Puritans.

Mr. Morison's criticism of the rational process suggested by Weber holds more water. Weber would have us believe that the New England farmer of Calvinist persuasion sought to make money not in order to secure the approval of God, but to prove to himself that God already had bestowed His approval, that he was already a member of

---

[4] S. E. Morison, *Builders of the Bay Colony* (Boston, 1930), 160.

[5] The words are Professor Morison's.

[6] Clive Hart Day, "Capitalistic and Socialistic Tendencies in the Puritan Colonies," *Annual Report of the American Historical Association . . . 1920* (Washington, 1925), 225–235.

the elect. The notion is over-subtle. Doubtless it has been entertained by wealthy merchants of the Back Bay and Salem; but, whether through inadvertence or shame, none seems to have committed it to writing. This does not justify the conclusion that Weber is entirely wrong. The fact is that God did "sprinkle holy water on economic success." Only He did it in a much more forthright manner, which the masses could understand, and which neither the Teutonic intellect of Herr Weber nor the sharp wit of Mr. Morison would have missed had they been citizens of that Puritan world. The three Puritans will speak for themselves. They are far from the old-world seats of learning. They address frontier audiences. They have no use for subtleties. They deal in plain truths for plain men.

II

Cotton Mather dealt most specifically with the relationship of business and religion in *Two Brief Discourses, one Directing a Christian in his General Calling; another Directing him in his Personal Calling*, a document of 1701 published in Boston the same year. Mather has become a much-quoted authority for the Weber thesis. Weber himself hastens over this document. It may profit us to turn its pages more leisurely. As its explicit title implies, the work deals with the relation of a man's business to his religion. There is a "calling" for each. The "general calling" is "to serve the Lord Jesus [477/478] Christ," the "personal calling" "a certain Particular Employment by which his *Usefulness* in his neighborhood is distinguished."[7] Each is a matter of the utmost seriousness. A godly man must worship the Lord punctiliously. At the same time he should contract to do no business he "cannot comfortably venture to pray over." And he must have a business. Worshipping the Lord in prayer and hymn is not enough. Contemplation of the good means nothing without accomplishment of the good. A man must not only be pious; he must be useful.

Now it follows also, that a man must not only be useful but likewise successful. The Lord had made provision for that, too. One should "be careful about the point: *What call from God have I to be in this place and at this work? Am I now where my Lord Jesus Christ would have me to be?*" After assuming this propitious attitude, he might safely trust in God "for the *Success* of all our *Business*, all the day long." But if he refused so to do, failure would be his lot, for "At no time of the Day, may we expect that our Business will succeed without *God's Blessing.*"[8]

In Mather's congregation there must have been some logicians, especially among the business men. It was a comfort for them to hear their occupations sanctified. If they were to undertake no business they

---

[7] Mather, *Two Brief Discourses*, 37.
[8] Mather, *Two Brief Discourses*, 22–23.

could not "comfortably venture to pray over," might they not calm
uneasy consciences by praying harder? Might not the prayer draw up
the business to its own level? We are not surprised to find Puritan
merchants mentioning God prominently in their invoices—thanking
Him for profit gained, or ascribing losses to *His* greater glory.[9] Neither
are we at pains to discover one source of a typically American habit.
Mention business to a business man, and he pulls a long face and
assumes an air of mystery. [478/479] This is not all pedantry. For
business to Americans has been more than a struggle for existence,
more than a career: it has been a "calling."

As for success in that calling, we need not depend on logic to be
informed of what Mather thought of it. "A Christian, at his *Two
Callings*," he elaborated, "is a man in a Boat, Rowing for Heaven; the
House which our Heavenly Father hath intended for us. If he mind but
one of his *Callings*, be it which it will, he pulls the *oar*, but on one side
of the Boat, and will make but a poor dispatch to the Shoar of Eternal
Blessedness." Let a man pray with might and main, he can not get to
Heaven unless he attends well to his personal calling, "some *Settled
Business*, wherein a Christian should for the most part spend most of
his time [the words which follow are significant] and this, that so he
may glorify God, by doing of *Good* for *others*, and getting of *Good* for
himself."[10]

The meaning of these words is clear enough. We may have
difficulty in reconciling the principles of "doing of *Good* for *others*,"
and "getting of *Good* for *himself*"; but that is the paradox which
pervades the ethics of Protestantism. As we shall find in the pages
which follow, it is sometimes hard to determine where the greater
emphasis lies: whether upon a man's impersonal social usefulness, or
on his own individual economic success. Cotton Mather did not forget
the welfare of society. He reminded his listeners that their occupations
should not be anti-social, that they should "have a tendency to the
Happiness of Mankind."[11] Yet we submit that Cotton Mather was
thinking primarily as an individual, and that he was laying the true
moral foundations for rugged American individualism.

The further he purses his subject, the more specific become his
rules of conduct.

Would a man *Rise* by his Business? I say, then let him *Rise* to his
Business. It was foretold. Prov. 22.29, *Seest thou a man Diligent* [479/480]
in his Business? He shall stand before Kings; He shall come to preferment.
And it was instanced by him who foretold it; 1 Kings 11.28. *Solomon, seeing that the young man was industrious, he made him a Ruler.* I tell you,
with *Diligence* a man may do marvallous [*sic*] things. *Young* man, work

[9] William B. Weeden, *Economic and Social History of New England, 1620–
1789* (Boston and New York, 1890), I, 250.

[10] Mather, *Two Brief Discourses*, 38. The italics are Mather's.

[11] Mather, *Two Brief Discourses*, 49.

hard while you are *Young:* You'l Reap the effects of it when you are *Old.* Yea, How can you Ordinarily enjoy any Rest at *Night,* if you have not been well at work in the *Day?* Let your *Business* engross the most of your time.[12] . . . Let every man have the *Discretion* to be well instructed in, and well acquainted with, all the mysteries of his *Occupation.* Be a master of your trade; count it a disgrace to be no workman.[13]

It may well have been that Mather himself thought of individual prosperity as an instrument of social welfare. But he presented it to his congregation first and foremost as both the temporal and spiritual reward for a life spent in industrious enterprise. Individuals should achieve salvation individually. Because industry tended to rally the Christian virtues within a man, industry should be encouraged. Thus the material fruits of industry were blessed in the sight of God.

In Mather's system of the two complementary callings, God had the material success of individuals entirely at his disposal. Piety, therefore, was an instrument in achieving it. Practise the Christian virtues; kneel daily in prayer, and "all your *Business* will go on the better, all the day, for your being thus faithful to God."[14] The individual could be reassured by this. It meant that however he might lack in native ability, piety would repair the deficiency. He had Mather's word for it, for the latter said, "with the *Help of God* never fear, but your Hands will be sufficient for you."[15] To the democratic implications of this system we shall return directly. For the moment we may see in it another manifestation of God's concern for the individual prosperity of Puritan business men. [480/481]

So far, it may be objected, we have judged Mather by only one sermon. Although of all his writings it is the one which deals most specifically with our subject, let us see if he afterwards changed his mind. Twenty years elapse, and he returns to the old theme in "The Vain Presumption of Living and Thriving in the World; which does too often possess and poison the *Children of* this *World.*"[16] A large congregation has assembled to hear him preach. The title gives a clue to the content. In 1720 too many people seem to have been finding economic success possible without piety. They have, as it were, been rowing themselves around in circles with the oar of "personal calling" and consequently are drifting away from the "Shoar of Eternal Blessedness." Mather pleads with them:

Acknowledge thy *Dependence* on the glorious God, for thy *Thriving* in the World. It is what we are minded of; Deut. VIII.18. *Thou shalt remember*

12 Mather, *Two Brief Discourses*, 48.
13 Mather, *Two Brief Discourses*, 53.
14 Mather, *Two Brief Discourses*, 67.
15 Mather, *Two Brief Discourses*, 69.

16 Cotton Mather, *Sober Sentiments,* funeral sermon, *Produced by the Premature and Much-lamented Death of Mr. Joshua Lamb* (Boston, 1722).

the Lord thy God; for it is He that gives thee Power to get wealth. Be sensible of this; *Riches* not always to them who are sharpest at inventing the most probable Methods of coming at it. Be sensible of this; The way to succeed in our Enterprizes, *O Lord, I know the way of man is not in himself!* Be sensible of this; In our *Occupation* we spread our *Nets;* but it is God who brings unto our *Nets* all that comes into them.[17]

One pictures a worldly congregation, some of which was no doubt thinking about other things than the sermon—of clever ways to outwit English customs-officers. Others, more serious, might have been wondering if God filled even smugglers' nets.

Mather has changed his emphasis but not his doctrine. God is still vitally interested in man's economic lot. He still desires that to be successful. Moreover, according to the great divine, God had vouchsafed success to the poorest mortals, to men [481/482] of the humblest parts. For wealth was "not always to them who are sharpest at inventing the most probable methods of coming at it." The social ethics embodied in Mather's preaching were reflected in the exigencies of frontier life—or did the ethics reflect the frontier? It is often asserted that religion generally sanctions the customs of society. What of the Puritanism of Cotton Mather? The most eminent spiritual leader of the Puritans for half a century, he held up to them an ideal of success to be achieved for the glory of God. Conditions on the frontier made collectivism difficult: at Plymouth it was tried and abandoned. Servants were lured away by the opportunity to acquire farms of their own for nothing. Wages, in several colonies, became so exorbitant as to necessitate statutory limits. Most obvious of all, one had to work in the wilderness, or die. Conditions demanded precisely the same moral qualities of industry, perseverance, sobriety, thrift, and prudence, as did Cotton Mather. They stressed, likewise, individual enterprise. Indeed, we might suppose that the frontier would have created a system of social ethics closely resembling Mather's if America had never heard of Luther and Calvin, were it not for one phrase which lingers: Wealth "not always to them who are sharpest at inventing the most probable methods of coming at it." This was the perfervid hope which the Puritanism of Cotton Mather held out to the common man. It meant, in humble ken, that God had made provision for all men to succeed.

As worldliness crept into the Puritan religion, occasioning the desperate effort of Jonathan Edwards to revive the fire and brimstone of primitive Calvinism, the social ethics preached by Mather did not die. American Protestants became divided into hostile sects: Methodists, Baptists, Unitarians. Some called themselves Deists. But as a general rule, their business remained a vital part of their religion, a calling. God continued to fill the nets of individual enterprise. Call it rationalization, hypocrisy, inspiration, or what you will, Puritans clung

[17] Mather, *Sober Sentiments*, 25.

to the doctrine that God would point the way to [482/483] individual prosperity, and would be pleased at its achievement.

Cotton Mather did not invent this doctrine: he merely gave it expression. His utterances are of interest to us not so much for the persuasive influence they may have had upon his contemporaries, as because they represent the mind of orthodox Puritanism two centuries ago. They indicate that thinking men were casting about in their minds for a moral sanction for money-making, and that they found that sanction in the ethical system originally propounded by Martin Luther and John Calvin. Thus, in a sense, Cotton Mather deserves recognition as one of the first to teach American business men to serve God by making money.

III

One day in 1724 Cotton Mather received a young caller at his home in Boston. It was a sober youth of eighteen years who presented himself. Benjamin Franklin had returned from Philadelphia for a brief visit to his native town, and had stopped to pay his respects to the great Puritan, whom he much admired. Franklin's later account of the visit indicates that it made some impression on him. Mather

. . . received me in his library [he wrote] and on my taking leave showed me a shorter way out of the house, through a narrow passage, which was crossed by a beam overhead. We were talking as I withdrew, he accompanying me behind, and I turning partly towards him, when he said hastily, "Stoop, stoop!" I did not understand him till I felt my head hit against the beam. He was a man that never missed any occasion of giving instruction, and upon this he said to me: "You are young, and have the world before you; STOOP as you go through it, and you will miss many hard thumps." This advice, thus beat into my head, has frequently been of use to me, and I often think of it when I see pride mortified and misfortunes brought upon people by carrying their heads too high.[18] [483/484]

Was this all that Mather had to offer his visitor; or was there a real spiritual bond between the two?

The God in which Franklin consistently professed belief was far more genial than Cotton Mather's stern Jehovah. Out of a vast "Chorus of Worlds" He was merely "that particular Wise and good God, who is the author and owner of our System."[19] His greatest gift to man was reason, by which man might discover his true function in the scheme of things. So glaring are the inconsistencies in Franklin's life that we take whatever he said with many grains of salt. We should not, for example, attach too much importance to the "Articles of Faith and Acts of Religion" which he drew up, with solemn precocity at the age of twenty-two. His life proclaims him too palpable a *citoyen du monde* to warrant much attention to his theology. Yet by virtue of this fact, it is

[18] Benjamin Franklin, *Complete Works* (New York, 1887), VIII, 484–485.
[19] Franklin, *Works*, I, 308.

all the more intriguing that he should have subscribed to a system of ethics identical to Cotton Mather's. In his life Franklin was a Deist, if not an out-and-out agnostic; in his writings, he was the soul of Puritanism. Why was this?

To be sure, Franklin had been born a Puritan in Puritan society. In childhood he heard his father admonish him over and over again on the inestimable value of all the Puritan virtues. But neither heredity nor environment can wholly account for Dr. Franklin. Was there some spiritual kinship, then, some intellectual contact with Puritan philosophers? Franklin himself says there was. The books which he precociously read numbered among them Pilgrim's Progress, Plutarch, and the works of Daniel Defoe. But it was from none of these that the spark of Franklin's Puritanism flashed. If we are to take him at his word, we must consider rather a small volume entitled *Essays to Do Good* by the Reverend Cotton Mather. This, he says in the *Autobiography*, "perhaps gave me such a turn of thinking that had an influence on some of the principle future events of my life."[20] And in 1784, from [484/485] the terminus of his great career, he wrote Cotton Mather's son renewing the acknowledgment. The *Essays* had given him "such a turn of thinking, as to have an influence on my conduct through life, for I have always set a greater value on the character of a *doer of good*, than on any other kind of reputation; and if I have been, as you seem to think, a useful citizen, the public owes the advantage of it to that book."[21]

Before rejecting Franklin's compliments as insincere, let us see what Mather had to say to him. Let us pause, for a moment, over the strange intellectual kinship of the author of *The Wonders of the Invisible World*, and the man who "discovered" electricity. The central theme of the *Essays to Do Good* is that of the sermons: personal salvation achieved through good works. The two callings receive lengthy treatment; and there is a categorical exposition of methods of doing good. Ministers, school teachers, lawyers, physicians all have their specific functions. But the greatest opportunity awaits persons of wealth. To them Mather has something special to say:

Sirs, you cannot but acknowledge that it is the sovereign God who has bestowed upon you the riches which distinguish you. A devil himself, when he saw a rich man, could not but make this acknowledgement to the God of heaven: "Thou hast blessed the work of his hands, and his substance is increased in the land."[22]

But the divine esteem enjoyed by the man of property does not diminish his obligations to society. The Lord has made him His "steward." He has charged him with a sacred trust, charity. Moreover, God

[20] Franklin, *Works*, I, 44: this was written in 1771.

[21] Franklin, *Works*, VIII, 484.

[22] Mather, *Essays to Do Good*: American Tract Society (Boston, 1710), 86–87.

in His infinite wisdom has made charity an attractive sacrifice, for if we are to believe Cotton Mather, the charitable

. . . very frequently . . . have been rewarded with remarkable success in their affairs, and increase of their property; and even [485/486] in this world have seen the fulfillment of those promises: "Cast thy bread upon the waters—thy grain into the moist ground—and thou shalt find it after many days." "Honor the Lord with thy substance; so shall thy barns be filled with plenty." History has given us many delightful examples of those who have had their *decimations* followed and rewarded by a surprising prosperity of their affairs. Obscure mechanics and husbandmen have risen to estates, of which once they had not the most distant expectation.[23]

So spoke the Reverend Cotton Mather to young Ben Franklin. His words are at once corroborative and prophetic. They are further evidence of his belief in the piety of individual prosperity, and they whisper of the future when thousands of "obscure mechanics and husbandmen" would rise (as millions would aspire) "to estates of which they had not the most distant expectation."

It would be interesting to lay the texts of Mather's *Essays* and Franklin's *Autobiography* side by side, so much is the former reflected in the latter. The purpose in recording his own rise "from the poverty and obscurity in which I was born and bred, to a state of affluence and some degree of reputation in the world,"[24] Franklin declares, is to allow others to profit by his example. He himself thought it "fit to be imitated" and therefore he would write a book about it. But first he desired "with all humility to acknowledge that I owe the mentioned happiness of my past life to [God's] kind providence, which led me to the means I used and gave them success."[25] How like a Puritan to attribute to the Lord "a state of affluence and some degree of reputation in the world." The *Autobiography* is filled with similar professions of humility and piety. To the uncritical reader, the sermon it preached must have seemed even more convincing than Mather's, for it had received from its author the pragmatic [486/487] sanction of successful practice. So he declared, at any rate. He had found it helpful as a young printer's apprentice to draw up a chart of the virtues necessary for complete moral perfection, and then to score himself daily on progress made—or not made. Mather himself could not have improved the list. It included temperance, silence, order, resolution, frugality, industry, sincerity, justice, moderation, cleanliness, tranquility, chastity, and humility. Of these, industry was most important. "Lose no time," he said to himself, "be always employed in something useful; cut off all unnecessary actions."[26]

But it is *Poor Richard* who sings the loudest praise of industry.

23 Mather, *Essays to Do Good*, 89–90.
24 Franklin, *Works*, I, 29.
25 Franklin, *Works*, I, 30–31.
26 Franklin, *Works*, I, 176.

Luck, says he, is of no account. Americans need only work hard and never trouble themselves about luck, for *"Diligence is the Mother of good luck,* and *God gives all things to industry."* *Poor Richard* likewise knows all about the calling: *"He that hath a trade hath an estate, and he that hath a calling hath an office of profit and honor."*[27] In fact the way to wealth was, in his own words, "as plain as the way to market" to Benjamin Franklin.

It depends chiefly on two words, *industry* and *frugality*—that is, waste neither *time* nor *money,* but make the best use of both. Without industry and frugality nothing will do, and with them everything. He that gets all he can and saves all he can . . . will certainly become rich, if that Being who governs the world, to whom all should look for a blessing on their honest endeavors, doth not, in his wise providence, otherwise determine.[28]

Did Franklin learn all this from Cotton Mather? It is authentic Puritanism. Mather had, at times, stooped low enough to commend charity as a profitable business venture. Franklin certainly knew Mather and read his works. Yet the man who paraphrased classic aphorisms for simple Americans feared no Puritan God. The thunderbolt which was the [487/488] angry voice of Jehovah to Mather trickled harmlessly off a wet kite-string into Franklin's Leyden jar. *Poor Richard's* wisdom is savory with business acumen. Whence, therefore, the piety? Was it an after-thought?

It makes little difference where Franklin got his Puritanism. Very likely Mather made substantial contributions. Yet the piety, in all probability, was no after-thought. It was put there with deliberate intent. Let us not forget that Benjamin Franklin was a journalist and publisher by trade. *Poor Richard's Almanac,* like the most of his other publications, was distinctly a money-making venture. Its shrewd author knew his trade; and what was more, he knew his public. Any publisher knows that catering to a public's taste is profitable, and that is precisely what Franklin did. He understood Puritanism well enough to realize that it offered assurances of material prosperity to all who followed its code of morals. Piety was inexpensive, and so although he himself was worlds apart from orthodoxy, he preached Puritan ethics as good as Mather's. From an unmoral point of view he perceived that the Puritan virtues had immense utilitarian value. And, skeptic though he was, he doubtless thought it wise to be on the safe side, to propitiate whatever God there might be. However that may be, he knew his public would think so.

The popularity of his writings bears witness to Frankin's shrewdness. The *Autobiography* became a famous American success story. Let its author be accused of hypocrisy in affecting the moral austerity of Puritanism. His public must have been delighted to find that he, a

---

[27] Franklin, *Works,* I, 444.

[28] Franklin, *Works,* II, 120–121.

scientist, a patriot, a man who had in actuality risen to "a state of affluence and some degree of reputation in the world" endorsed the same democratic virtues as their ministers. It must have relieved them to have such a man turn thumbs down on chance, as it rejoiced them to hear him re-affirm the sanctity of individual prosperity. Benjamin Franklin not only commended prosperity; he dramatized it. [488/489]

IV

While Cotton Mather represents the mind of orthodox Puritanism, and Franklin a secularized version of the same, Timothy Dwight is the soul of Puritanism revivalism. Unlike the other two, Dwight was never really a national figure. His fame and his influence are localized in Connecticut, over the spiritual destinies of which he presided as Congregational "Pope." Although a persevering student and a teacher of some accomplishment, Dwight was scarcely a profound thinker. His preaching is of interest to us because it embodies the latter-day Puritanism revived in the outward form of Congregationalism. In a new age, in a new church, Dwight taught the old ethics of his spiritual fathers; and out of them he evolved a primitive social philosophy which became a national religion. The sermons of Timothy Dwight are Puritan documents. As might be expected, they deplored the seven deadly sins; they dealt uncompromisingly with Satan, and they lauded the Christian virtues. In them we find the same doctrine of good works and the calling, the same especial praise for industry. Only Dwight, being somewhat of a scholar, adduced the wisdom of classical antiquity as well as that of the Old Testament to drive home his points. "The diligent hand maketh rich" he balanced with "Diligentia vincit omnia."[29] And speaking for himself, he declared that idleness was "not only a gross vice in itself, but the highway to all the other vices."[30]

Like Cotton Mather, the man of God, and Benjamin Franklin, the man of the world, Dwight believed that individuals must save their own souls first, the soul of society afterwards. He, too, felt that the Puritan virtues were, and ought to be, individualistic. His exposition of the calling is proof of this. Each man has a soul, he said, and [489/490]

. . . the value of that soul is inconceivable. It is infinite. The world, nay the universe, weighed against it is nothing. . . . It claims, therefore, it deserves, all your attention, all your labours, all your prayers. . . . At the same time your earthly concerns are not to be forgotten. They, too, have their importance.

So far, we might be listening to Cotton Mather. But in the words which follow a more specific relationship is established between busi-

29 Timothy Dwight, *Sermons* (Edinburgh, 1828), I, 308.
30 *The Charitable Blessed* (New Haven, 1810), 19.

ness and religion than any we have yet observed. It shows that Dwight had begun to look at the whole ethical problem objectively, and was trying to find a rational place for it in American life. Spiritual and earthly concerns, he resumed, are not incompatible.

Happily for you the attention which they really demand is in no degree inconsistent with the effectual promotion of your eternal welfare. The same sobriety of mind, which is so useful to the advancement of your heavenly interests, is the direct means of your earthly prosperity.[31]

This was a splendid way to popularize "sobriety of mind" among worldly folk, prosperity among the religious.

In a sense, however, Dwight was a child of a new era. A throw-back in his religion, he was a citizen of a new nation. Thus, in addition to commending material prosperity on religious grounds, he did so also on patriotic. If Mather's sermons were at least in part rationalizations of frontier life, Dwight had begun to think in terms of nationalism. The United States was now an independent democracy. Constitutionally it was now easier than ever for "obscure mechanics and husbandmen" to rise "to estates, of which they had not the most distant expectation." Although entirely out of sympathy with those very elements in the rabble of Jefferson's followers, Dwight inconsistently proclaimed the sanctity of industry, and the kindred Puritan virtues which enabled them to rise. He further encouraged them, moreover, in bestowing upon prosperity a patriotic, as well as a religious sanction. [490/491]

Timothy Dwight was an observer of American society as well as a minister of the gospel. In his extensive travels through New York and New England, he noted with a critical eye the habits of the people in those sections. At Boston, in 1810, he found that "a man, who is not believed to follow some useful business, can scarcely acquire, or retain, even a decent reputation."[32] Proceeding into Vermont, he paid close attention to the social evolution in progress on that frontier. The frontiersman came in for searching analysis in Dwight's note-book, affording him case history by which to substantiate a social theory which he now evolved. It was not a new theory. He merely carried the familiar Puritan ethics to their logical conclusion, expressed in terms of American society.

The frontier, to Dwight, was a line of least resistance, the fron-tiersman a shiftless lover of "this irregular, adventurous, half-working and half-lounging life." He was a painful contrast to the farmer, upon whose "sober industry and prudent economy" rested civilization itself. Dwight painted a dreary picture of his subject. In Vermont, he wrote,

they are obliged to work, or starve. They accordingly cut down some trees, and girdle others; they furnish themselves with an ill-built log house, and a worse barn; and reduce a part of the forest into fields, half-enclosed, and

---

[31] Dwight, *Sermons*, II, 24–25.

[32] *Travels in New England and New York* (New Haven, 1821), I, 507.

half-cultivated. The forests furnish browse; and their fields yield a stinted herbage.[33]

A dreary picture, indeed, but an historic picture. For what Dwight saw in Vermont he might have seen at Plymouth in an earlier age, or in Michigan at a later. It was American society in its primitive state. That he should hold it in contempt is indication, among other things, of the progress of civilization in the United States. The frontiersman could send his sons to the college of Timothy Dwight to be educated. But first he had to settle the country.

The great Congregationalist did not, however, despair of [491/ 492] frontiersmen. He conceded that they were not entirely lost, for even they could "become sober, industrious citizens, merely by the acquisition of property." This led him immediately to the conclusion that "The love of property to a certain degree seems indispensable to the existence of sound morals."[34] It was, therefore, the duty of those who had the welfare of the state at heart to encourage its individual members to make money.

The possession of this money removes, perhaps for the first time, the despair of acquiring property; and awakens the hope, and the wish, to acquire more. The secure possession of property demands, every moment, the hedge of law; and reconciles a man, originally lawless, to the restraints of government. Thus situated, he sees that reputation, also, is within his reach. Ambition forces him to aim at it; and compels him to a life of sobriety, and decency. That his children may obtain this benefit, he is obliged to send them to school, and to unite with those around him in supporting a schoolmaster. His neighbours are disposed to build a church, and settle a minister. A regard to his own character, to the character and feelings of his family, and very often to the solicitations of his wife, prompts him to contribute to both these objects; to attend, when they are compassed, upon the public worship of God; and perhaps to become in the end a religious man.[35]

Thus was the common man instructed by Timothy Dwight. Prosperity was the touchstone by which the savage might be civilized, the heathen made Christian.

V

So spoke three Puritans at various moments in our early history: Cotton Mather from the mysterious universe of Jehovah, Benjamin Franklin from the commercial capital of a new world, Timothy Dwight from the pulpit of revivalism. As their lives overlapped each other, so did their [492/493] thoughts. And from their several vantage points they came into clear agreement that individual prosperity was a highly desirable thing.

[33] Dwight, *Travels*, II, 459–460.
[34] Dwight, *Travels*, II, 462.
[35] Dwight, *Travels*, II, 462–463.

How much influence their teaching may have had it is difficult to say. Possibly it is more than a coincidence that in New England, where business was a calling, and wealth both a sign of heavenly approval and a bulwark of civilization, the Federalists should have their principal strength. When one is told in church that property is sacred, its acquisition a duty, its charitable distribution profitable, it is not strange that he should vote for that same "hedge of law" which Timothy Dwight and Alexander Hamilton thought so essential. Neither is it strange, on the other hand, that a religious gospel promising material success to all who served the Puritans' God should find many adherents among the self-made men who followed Jefferson. One thing is certain, however. Insofar as Cotton Mather, Benjamin Franklin, and Timothy Dwight represent the various facets of American Puritanism, they laid down a code of living the followers of which believed that God desired Americans to be rich. [493]

The Rise and Decline of the Titan

MAX LERNER

"THE TYCOON IS DEAD" WAS THE WAY *Fortune,* THE BEST SPOKESMAN FOR the American business mind, phrased the basic change that has come over the structure of American business. In what sense was this true?

Every civilization has its characteristic flowering in some civilization type, the *persona* of the social mask on which the ordinary man in the civilization models himself. In the Athenian civilization the *persona* was the leisure-class citizen with a turn for art and philosophy; with the Jews it was the lawgiver-prophet, in the Roman Empire the soldier-administrator, in the Middle Ages the cleric dreaming of sainthood, in the Chinese civilization the mandarin-scholar, in the Indian the ascetic, in the Italian Renaissance the patron-*condottiere,* at the height of French power the courtier, at the height of British power the merchant-adventurer and empire builder; in German and Japanese history it was

From Max Lerner, *America as a Civilization* (New York: Simon and Schuster, 1957), pp. 274–284. Copyright © 1957 by Max Lerner. Reprinted by permission of Simon and Schuster, Inc.

the elite soldier of the *Junker* and *samurai* classes, with the Communists today it is the worker-commissar.

The *persona* of the American civilization has been the businessman—the "Titan," as Dreiser called him; the "Tycoon," as *Fortune* called him. Where other civilization types have pursued wisdom, beauty, sanctity, military glory, predacity, asceticism, the businessman pursues the magnitudes of profit with a similar single-minded drive. When confronted in business by appeals to nonpecuniary values, his comment is likely to be that he is not in business for his health. "The business of America," as Calvin Coolidge put it, "is business." The survivors in the fierce competitive struggle were those who most clearly embodied the businessman's single-mindedness of purpose. They were men like "Jupiter" Morgan, Vanderbilt, Jay Gould, Daniel Drew, John D. Rockefeller, Jay Cooke, "Bet-a-Million" Gates, Andrew Carnegie, Charles T. Yerkes, Solomon Guggenheim, Henry Ford, Irénée Du Pont. Some have been honest according to the standards of business honesty, some have not hesitated to use force, guile, and bribery. All have been unsentimental [274/275] and hard in business, even when they have been pious in the church, devoted in the home, and softhearted in friendship.

The business spirit was not indigenous to America. It grew out of the history of European capitalism, and by the time of the American Revolution it had already found expression in Italy, England, and Holland. During the first half century of American national life the American business spirit lagged behind the European. While there were land speculators, a shipbuilding and commercial group, an incipient factory system, and (as John Taylor used to put it) an "aristocracy of paper and credit," the type-figure of America well into the Jacksonian era was the farmer-turned-artisan or the artisan-turned-farmer.

De Tocqueville gave only the briefest mention to the new "aristocracy of manufactures" in America, although his few pages are perceptive. He noted that "the number of large fortunes there is small, and capital is still scarce," and called America "a nation which contains, so to speak, no rich men"—compared, that is, with the great fortunes and landed families of Europe. Yet even in this early stage De Tocqueville saw that "the Americans carry their businesslike qualities and their trading passions" into all their pursuits, including farming. In other words, he saw the beginnings of that business civilization which has almost obscured every other aspect of American life. When he wrote, there was as yet no consciousness of American businessmen as a class. Yet he saw that the best talents were being attracted to business pursuits, and that the gap between employer and workers was widening.

When Charles Dickens made his second journey through America several decades later he found a hard materialist spirit everywhere.

The events of the next quarter century burst the bounds of confinement which De Tocqueville had seen around the business spirit. The spread of a railway network in the 1850s, the triumph of Northern capitalism over the Southern plantation system in the 1860s, the rise of investment banking and the process of rapid capital formation in the 1870s, the trust movement of the 1880s, the harvests of money and power reaped from the Big Technology throughout this period: all these combined to make of America a Paradise for the new business fortunes and a stamping ground for the business spirit.

The result was the emergence of the Big Money and the Big Businessman. In a single decade between the election of McKinley and the Panic of 1907—the decade of the great "consolidations"—there were Harriman and Hill building railroad fortunes as well as railroads, with Harriman dreaming of a world railroad empire, like some daring Sidonia such as Disraeli had imagined; out of the steel industry were forged the fortunes of Gary, Schwab, Gates, Carnegie, Morgan; oil [275/276] spouted forth a whole tribe of Rockefellers; farm machinery clattered away like the roaring of a McCormick; street railways, with their clinking nickels, built the fortunes of Widener, Whitney, Ryan, Yerkes. The armies of finance wheeled and maneuvered, attacked and retreated.

There was a time when the Titan was treated with unctuous servility. In the 1870s James Parton, a sort of American Samuel Smiles, had edited a volume of Sketches of Men of Progress, and the chapter by the Reverend Mr. McClintock on Daniel Drew had spoken of his "affording an example of industry, energy, and business talents of the highest order, combined with a sense of personal honor and unimpeachable integrity.... May he be long spared to enjoy the fruits of his industry, and to share in advancing the kingdom of Christ on earth, not merely by his Christian use of the large wealth of which God has made him steward, but also ... by his living example of peaceful but active piety." Alas, Charles Francis Adams and Henry Adams, in their Chapters of Erie, gave a different picture of Drew, as well as of Gould and Vanderbilt, as men who cheated and tricked one another, acquired railroads and wrecked them, built paper structures of securities and unloaded them on a gullible public. By the turn of the century, after the work of the muckrakers, the mood of the press and the reading public became more realistic. By the time of the first World War the Titan had caught the imagination of the novelists as well as the populace, and for the press and magazines he became a legendary figure in a manner different from the sugar-loaf legends of the early admirers.

Americans needed no fire-breathing imperialist swaggerers to express their sense of national importance. The Titan was all the symbol they needed. Wherever he went there was a planetary turmoil and a sense of construction, and the big money poured around him. Even when the muckrakers excoriated him for corrupting legislatures, buying up city governments, and betraying the original democratic premise, they left little doubt that their target was indeed a Titan. The magazine readers glimpsed the outlines of the heroic in the subjects of the biographical exposés and felt more envy than indignation.

Some of this may be found in the novelists as well. Mark Twain, himself a businessman and absorbed in money-making schemes, wrote a blistering indictment in *The Gilded Age* of the methods by which the big fortunes were built up. William Dean Howells was torn between an admiration for honest businessmen like Silas Lapham and the anger against the men of "the Accumulation" which he set down in *A Traveler from Altruria*. Henry James recoiled from trade yet, like Scott Fitzgerald after him, he was obsessed with money and its aura. In the James tradition the Edith Wharton novels come to life, in *The House [276/277] of Mirth* and *The Custom of the Country*, when she deals with her money-driven women, her female counterparts of single-minded businessmen. The muckrakers themselves, as they dug around in the archives of business methods and corporate finance, were moved by a complex *odi et amo* feeling about their subjects. Even the novelists who attacked the Titan most drastically, like Frank Norris and Theodore Dreiser, were (as Kenneth Lynn has pointed out in the *Dream of Success*) covertly admirers of his greatness and sharers of his values.

Dreiser's portrait of Frank Algernon Cowperwood—which he took from Charles Tyson Yerkes, the Philadelphia and Chicago traction king—shows most clearly the combined fascination-and-recoil which, until the Great Depression, most Americans felt for the power and the ruthless drive of the business Titans. Dreiser did his studies of Cowperwood-Yerkes while he was brooding over the Darwinian doctrine that the survivors must be the fittest, and over the beyond-good-and-evil and will-to-power ideas of Nietzsche. The term he used for Cowperwood—"the Titan"—was a Lucretian image, implying that these men who operated far above the groundlings and held themselves superior to human law were not so much immoral as amoral. He wrote about Cowperwood with the sympathy of an Indiana boy out of the Midwestern climate of striving and dreaming from which so many of the business Titans came. Plebeian that he was, he was himself half in love with the symbol of the plebeian-turned-plutocrat that he portrayed. He shows Cowperwood growing up in Philadelphia like a boy with his nose pressed against a shopwindow, looking in at the wealth that spells power and is crowned by the need of beauty. The class lines in such a society had to be sharp, yet not too sharp; resistant enough to apply the spur to the hungering youthful will, yet mobile enough so that one could master them. The process of mastery involved for Cowperwood a term in a Philadelphia jail, the betrayal of his friends, the corruption of city councils and legislatures, the destruction of those closest to him.

Yet he lived out his willed dream, and as he did so his prowess and predacity hardened. He piled up wealth and power, crushed the men who stood in his way, combined with those he could not crush; he won a mastery over women as well—especially *their* women—the daughters of those who had been the symbols of his dream of success and the obstacles in his path. In the end he failed and got religion (in the third volume of the trilogy, *The Stoic*), but this was an afterthought of the later Dreiser.

As Dreiser and many others saw him, the Titan was half conqueror, half child. He had a daring vision and made reckless use of his resources to gain his ends; he had a quick sense for estimating and using people and an ability to see his lucky chance and grasp it. Yet with all this, [277/278] there was a restless search for novelty, as with a child; a love of big things because they are big, almost as if his great projects had become only toys. There was in him a joy in the creation of means but an obtuseness about ends. Most of all, there was a quality of tenacious single-mindedness of purpose which was preindustrial in the American character, and the symbolic theme of Captain Ahab's unrelenting pursuit of the whale of *Moby Dick*.

There is one division which cuts across most of the Titans of the earlier prewar era of America—the split between the Puritan and the magnifico. J. Pierpont Morgan, the greatest of all the Titans, was a magnifico in the sense that he operated on a scale of magnificence. So also were Hill, Gates, Gould, several of the early Du Ponts, and Yerkes himself. There was a lustiness and a grandeur of scope in their private as in their business lives. They bet and gambled, lived conspicuously, gave parties, sailed yachts, were seen in the European capitals; there were legends of the stables of women they kept; they built palatial homes and crammed them with art treasures rifled from the museums and collections of Europe. There was a native optimism in them; in business as in private life they were "bullish"; their motto was Morgan's "never sell America short"; their fortunes were made on the upward arc of an expanding American economy. They saw far enough ahead to see the expansion and contributed to it their boldness and their measure of vision.

There was another strain, however, represented by Daniel Drew, the Rockefellers, Henry Ford: not the strain of magnificence but of the taut Puritan qualities. These men came out of the small towns and remained at home in small-town America. They were abstemious, church-going, taught Sunday-school classes. They spent little on themselves, and what they did they spent quietly. Like Rockefeller, they handed out shiny dimes; like Ford, they plowed everything back into the business. They had the eccentricities in which men can indulge when they sit on top of a pyramid of power. They were apt to be gloomy men and presented a stern visage to the world, at once unsmiling and unrelenting. Yet they were probably closer than the magnificos to the theological roots of capitalism: the demonstration of virtue through success, the doctrine of calling, the gospel of work and thrift.

Together these two strains condense the appeal of business enterprise as a way of life. To the middle-class mind the appeal is to the Puritan virtues of austerity and acquisitiveness; to the Faustian spirit of the imaginative it is that of movers and shakers and of empire builders. One stresses efficacy in the sight of God, the other power in the sight of man. One moves step by step, the other by bold leaps. One [278/279] is the accumulative spirit, the other the gambling spirit. One operates best in the realm of production and managerial organization, the other in the realm of promotion and finance. Neither is complete without the other, and while in every Titan one or the other had predominated, no Titan has lacked elements of both. Their combined appeal has been powerful since even the groundlings, who could not live the life of the Titan, could identify themselves with his economic efficacy and share vicariously in his magnitudes.

As De Tocqueville noted even before the Civil War, the old European sense that there was something degrading about business quickly vanished in America, and the talented young people turned to business pursuits. The legend of the Titan attracted them almost as much as the Big Money itself. For while the formal goal of business enterprise is profit, the psychic rewards of the businessman's way of life came to consist as much in the pursuit of power as in the accumulation of money. There was a sense of risk and excitement in Big Enterprise. And while it was possible for many of the businessmen to pursue profit and power with a meanness of spirit and impoverished intellectual and emotional resources, this was not true of the outstanding figures. Unlike the worker chained to the machine, and the small businessman embittered by his struggle with his competitors and workers, the Titan often showed himself to have a spacious and creative mind.

Something happened to the Titan in the two decades after World War I. Before that time the indictment against him had stressed the enormity of his power, the charge being that he used it to betray the early ideals of the Republic. John Chamberlain has suggested that the reason for the persistent "belittling" of the Big Businessman by American novelists was their rebellion against their fathers and their search for a different kind of father symbol on the Left. Sometimes this was so, but I suspect that most of them wrote what they wrote out of the disillusionment that overcame them at the chasm between the Jeffersonian dream of a spacious and egalitarian American democracy, and the actual power of Big Business. They were protesting against the wasteland of American moral and cultural life between the time of Grant's Presidency and that of Wilson.

What happened in the Great Depression changed the image of the

Titan more drastically. Big Business of the 1920s, certain that it had
found the secret of perpetual prosperity, claimed the right to the policy-
making decisions not only in the economy but in the government. But
the economic collapse of 1929 resulted in a disillusionment with the
Titan: the Big Money of the boom of the 1920s came clamoring to the
[279/280] White House for extreme unction in the 1930s. Those who
had seemed to be the "Lords of Creation" were stripped of a good deal
of their stature and grandeur.

The businessman began to lose stature even before the Great
Depression. After Dreiser's Cowperwood, Sinclair Lewis's Babbitt was
a letdown. Babbitt is the biggest real-estate dealer in the minor
universe of Zenith, Ohio, whose life revolves around his house, car,
service clubs, lodge, and church; who mouths platitudes about business
ethics but sees nothing wrong in pulling a real-estate squeeze play on a
small butcher: Babbitt is no Titan, neither a great creator nor a great
destroyer, but the fag end of business enterprise as a way of life. Lewis
did what was in some ways a moving portrait of him, yet gave him
none of the quiet dignity and sense of craftsmanship that Howells gave
the painting-firm hero of *The Rise of Silas Lapham*: and the shift from
the portrait of the 1890s marks the running down of a tradition.

Some of the other novelists showed an even sharper disenchantment. *U.S.A.*, the novel trilogy by John Dos Passos, applies to fiction
some of the elements of Veblen's savage critique of American business
enterprise. Charlie Anderson, who plays an important role in *The Big
Money*, is the embodiment of constructive drives which have been
corrupted by the manic passions of promotion. In a less intentional
way Scott Fitzgerald's *The Great Gatsby*—the buccaneer who was part
phony promoter, part racketeer, the man seemingly from nowhere
whose shimmering appearance is woven out of the cloudless fabric of
nothing—is also a figure of disenchantment. In Thomas Wolfe's *You
Can't Go Home Again* the head of the "Company" is obsessed with
finding new advertising slogans; and Wolfe portrays the squeezing of
every sales executive in the lower rank by the one above him in the
panicky sales hierarchy of the "Company." The emphasis was shifting
from the figure of production and finance to that of promotion and
sales, from the man who made the goods to the man who knew the
magic of extracting something from nothing; from the major legendary
figures like Morgan to the minor legends of the rising sales curve and
the "hucksters" of the advertising legions. The portrait of business
reached its furthest remove from the Titan in the description, in
Faulkner's *The Hamlet* and *The Town*, of the locust invasion of his
Mississippi county by the swarming Snopes family, which moved with
mercantile ardor into all the crevices left by the crack-up of precapital-
ist Southern society.

But the crucial transformation of the Titan was wrought not so
much by the Great Depression, nor by the invasion of the groundlings,

but by the corporation. The type-figure who carved out the great industrial [280/281] empires was almost submerged in the impersonality of the corporate form. In every area of life the winning of power has always required bolder and more vigorous talents than its consolidation. In the new and highly specialized technology, experts took over every phase of the corporation's activity—engineering, financing, production, promotion, advertising, salesmanship, personnel relations. In place of the heroic adventurism of the Titans came a group of "managerial skills" that required talent and judgment in the art of management but seemed earth-creeping by comparison. The increasing division of labor built up business hierarchies in which the aggressive mind of the Titan was less at home than the corporate bureaucratic mind. Once the regime of high-salaried managers was created it took on a life of its own, crowding out the life of the Titan. He ceased to be the giant in whose shadow the business institutions were shaped and became himself the shadow of the institution, taking his stature from the corporation. The corporation as instrument grew in importance while the men wielding it shrank. Those who were once considered barbarian invaders now became absorbed in the structure of the power they themselves created. The conquerors were conquered.

Does this mean that the Titan "reformed"? The big fact about the "Robber Barons" (the phrase was Matthew Josephson's) was not their personal ethics, although to a moralistic generation of reformers it may have seemed so. When Commodore Vanderbilt made his famous "public be damned" remark he was expressing a generalized sense of swaggering power. In broad perspective the ethics of the Big Businessmen were, taken as a group, no worse than the ethics of any other historical group of conquerors. Comparing how America was industrialized with the methods by which Germany, Japan, and Russia were later industrialized, the American record seems like a Sunday picnic or a huddle of innocents. Even the worst of the Robber Barons—men like Gould, Fisk, and Yerkes—were men of virtue compared with the Gauleiter and commissars who performed a similar task in their own countries. The real point is not that the Titan has "reformed," for he was never truly evil. It is rather that he has grown less colorful, less swaggering, more sophisticated; he has had to take his place in a bureaucracy in which his predecessors would have felt stifled; he has had to cope with the regulatory demands of a welfare state and the power of a labor movement; he has had to worry less about his competitors than about "business conditions," domestic and world politics, advertising, consumer demand, and the securities market. He must always feel the pulse of public opinion and be wary of alienating it. Wherever he goes he is accompanied by survey makers, "human-relations" technicians, public-opinion analysts, public-relations experts. [281/282]

Once known primarily as a man of action (*furor Americanus* is what Aldous Huxley called the American cult of action), the business-man still remains that. But the areas of significant action have changed. They are no longer concerned with the crushing of competitors, the piling up of big fortunes, and the carving out of family dynastic power. The old competitive system has been replaced by a system of "imper-fect competition" in which the corporations compete with one another less in prices than in brands and in "products"—that is, in alternative materials for achieving the same results. As for the big fortunes, a more drastic tax system than any continental European can envisage has made them archaic. The heads of the corporate empires no longer get their sense of fulfillment from personal accumulation, nor is their prime quality that of acquisitiveness. They are still movers and shakers, but for a different reason than before. The new Titan is still the creator and consolidator of corporate structures, the guiding mind of monopolies and cartels, the organizer of business "peak-associations." The men who run Metropolitan Life or General Motors, General Electric or U.S. Steel, Alcoa or A.T.&T., are men of power not because of their great fortunes or talents but because they have powerful instruments at their command. They have control of enormous blocks of investment and power. For income-tax purposes the new Titans allow the corporate profits to remain inside the corporation and then declare stock divi-dends. They create "charitable trusts" as legal fictions, and "founda-tions" as ways of escaping the ax of the inheritance tax. But where they once sought profit, they now seek the retention of the power over their capital investments. Their prime concern is the figure they can cut in America and the world as proconsuls administering their huge aggre-gates of power.

This requires and has developed a new personality profile for the Titan—that of a corporate statesman. He reads more than he used to, goes to college, makes speeches and statements (alas, too many and too platitudinous), is seen at public conferences. His suavity is more evident than his ruthlessness. He knows something of the workings of the economy and the government, and of world affairs. I am speaking, of course, not of the run-of-mill corporate vice-president, nor of the sales manager or advertising manager who may be only a contempo-rary Babbitt, but of the small group of sophisticated holders of business power who embody business creativeness. He has even had to take a hand in developing the idea of the welfare state itself, as Wendell Willkie did; or administering its controls over business, as Charles E. Wilson did; or in supervising the American economic aid to Europe, as Paul Hoffman did. [282/283]

The Big Businessman has had to come up squarely against the problems of the survival of the economy and the organization of a transformed society. This new type of businessman—represented, for example, by the members of the Committee for Economic Develop-ment—is still not accepted by the mediocre but stubborn men who remember the old catchwords of the free-market economy and strike out blindly against any innovating doctrine. These men act sometimes like the defenders of a besieged city, a League of Frightened Men who in their panic are bent on searching out heresy in their own ranks. Once the new businessman makes clear his premise that the productivity which is the source of profits is more important than any particular profit, that an expanding economy may require the co-operative action of the welfare corporation and the welfare state, he runs the danger of being branded as a maverick and cast out of the herd.

The image of the old Titan still remains in the popular mind and colors the dreams that the young men dream. But the effective figure is a new one, in a new setting, the result of the complex and powerful transforming process of the past half century of American society.

It may be significant that no one has yet found a name for him that will stick, as "Titan" and "Tycoon" did to his predecessor. He is often called a "business statesman" by those who stand in awe of him and feel there must be some appellation of a dignity that parallels his massive business power—also sometimes his wealth. Such men as Alfred Sloan, Charles E. Wilson, and Harlow Curtice of General Motors are considered a cut above the old-fashioned, profit-seeking, money-grasping Titans. As a result they have been called on to speak as oracles not only on industrial matters but on the welfare of the nation, and sometimes have convinced themselves (often with public approval) that the country is only an enlarged image of the company and that they have the right to make decisions about what is good for both.

Perhaps the simplest name for them is what their employees tend to call them—"Mr. Big"—carrying with it a half affectionate, half scornful set of overtones. In conversation the ordinary American will say of one of these new corporate moguls that he is the "head" of such-and-such a corporate empire. These are indeed the "head men" of American life, and what gives the name some aptness is that it refers less to the stature or personality of the man himself than to his position at the head of a hierarchy of function and power. When one head man goes, another arrives to take his place. What is crucial, as in the hierarchy of the Middle Ages, is not so much the individual as the status. In fact, a number of writers have noted that these American head men are emerging as corporate seigneurs, and that their position and power have much in common with the frame of medieval society. [283/284]

Yet what strikes the popular mind is their power and ruthlessness as they contend for place with the most modern of weapons—promotion schemes, mergers, corporate reorganizations. During the 1950s, a new type of novel about the businessman emerged, in which the problems of authority and ethical codes were posed. In Cameron

Hawley's *Executive Suite* the tradition set up by the corporate founder, which seemed archaic to the new managerial group, finally triumphed, and with it the idea that the heart of corporate enterprise is what it can do for the workers, the community, and the values of craftsmanship. In the same author's *Cash McCall* there is a skillful delineation of the new Napoleons of corporate finance who march and wheel their chess pieces across the board without much concern for what any particular corporation is producing: here again, once the ethical problem has been posed, it is resolved (as in the case of religious conversion) by a saving insight into the productive values that transcend the merely financial ones. In a TV and movie story called *Patterns* the resolution is not so simple: the "head man" is depicted in almost Nietzschean terms as driven by an urge to stretch himself and his associates to the utmost of their powers, beyond the human. But Nietzsche never foresaw that in the American case the effort to reach to the godlike would apply to the creation not of the Superman but of Super-corporation. And the hero of this story, while seeing the evil and ruthlessness of the head man, is himself at the end half caught up in his fervor and asks only for a chance to be more ruthless himself and to make a victim of the man who has made victims of others—all in the name of the Corporation.
[284]

The New Entrepreneur

C. WRIGHT MILLS

BALZAC CALLED BUREAUCRACY 'THE GIANT POWER WIELDED BY PYGMIES,' but actually not all the men who wield bureaucratic control are appropriately so termed. Modern observers without first-hand or sensitive experience in bureaucracies tend, first, to infer types of bureaucrats from the ideal-type definition of bureaucracy, rather than to examine the various executive adaptations to the enlarged enterprise and centralized bureau; and, second, to assume that big businesses are strictly bureaucratic in form. Such businesses are, in fact, usually mixtures, especially as regards personnel, of bureaucratic, patrimonial, and entrepreneurial forms of organization. This means, in brief, that

From C. Wright Mills, *White Collar: The American Middle Classes* (New York: Oxford University Press, 1956), pp. 91–100. Copyright 1951 by Oxford University Press, Inc. Reprinted by permission.

'politics' (as well as administration) is very much at work in selecting and forming types of managers.

There are in the modern enterprise men who fulfil the bureaucratic formula; in brief, here is how they look and act:

They follow clearly defined lines of authority, each of which is related to other lines, and all related to the understood purposes of the enterprise as a going concern. Their activities and feelings are within delimited spheres of action, set by the obligations and requirements of their own 'expertese.' Their power is neatly seated in the office they occupy and derived only from that office; all their relations within the enterprise are thus impersonal and set by the formal hierarchical structure. Their expectations are on a thoroughly calculable basis, and are enforced by the going rules and explicit sanctions; their appointment is by examination, or, at least, on the basis of trained-for competencies; and they are vocationally secure, with expected life tenure, and a regularized promotion scheme.

Such a description is, of course, a rational caricature, although useful as a guide to observation. There are, in fact, two sorts of managers whose personal adaptations most closely approximate the 'bureaucratic' type. At the top of some hierarchies, one often notices personalities who are calm and sober and unhurried, but who betray a lack of confidence. They are often glum men who display a great importance of manner, seemingly have little to do, and act with slow deliberation. They reduce the hazards of personal decision by carefully following the rules, and are heavily burdened by anxiety if decisions not covered by previous rule are forced upon them. They are carefully protected from the world-to-be-impressed by subordinates and secretaries who are working around them; they are men who have things done for them. Liking the accoutrements of authority, they are always in line with the aims of the employer or other higher ups; the ends of the organization become their private ends. For they are selected by and act for the owners or the political boss, [92/93] as safe and sound men with moderate ambitions, carefully held within the feasible and calculable lines of the laid-out career. That is why they are at the top and that is the point to be made about them: they are cautiously selected to represent the formal interest of the enterprise and its organizational integrity: they serve that organization and, in doing so, they serve their own personal interests. Among all the apparatus, they sit cautiously, and after giving the appearance of weighty pondering usually say No.

Often identical with this bureaucratic type, but usually lower down the hierarchy of safety, are 'the old veterans.' They are men who say they started in the business when it was small, or in some other small business now a division of the big one. They follow instructions, feeling insecure outside the bounds of explicit orders, keeping out of the limelight and passing the buck. Usually they feel a disproportion between their abilities and their experience, and having come to feel that competition is without yield, often become pedantic in order to get a much-craved deference. Carefully attending to formalities with their co-workers and with the public, they strive for additional deference by obedience to rule. They sentimentalize the formal aspects of their office and feel that their personal security is threatened by anything that would detach them from their present setting.

But there are other types of managers who are adapted to bureaucratic life, but who are by no means bureaucrats in the accepted image. The bureaucratic ethos is not the only content of managerial personalities. In particular, bureaucracies today in America are vanguard forms of life in a culture still dominated by a more entrepreneurial ethos and ideology. Among the younger managers, two types display a blend of entrepreneurial and bureaucratic traits. One is the 'live-wire' who usually comes up from the sales or promotion side of the business, and who represents a threat to those above him in the hierarchy, especially the old veterans, although sometimes also to the glum men. It may be that in due course the live-wire will settle down; occasionally one does settle down, becomes somebody's 'bright boy,' somebody else's live-wire who is then liked [93/94] and favored by those whom he serves. If his loyalty is unquestionable, and he is careful not to arouse anxieties by his brightness, he is on the road to the top.

Some live-wires, however, do not readily become somebody's bright boy: they become what we may call New Entrepreneurs, a type that deserves detailed discussion.

The dominating fact of the new business setting is the business bureaucracy and the managerial supplementation, or even replacement, of the owner-operator. But bureaucratization has not completely replaced the spirit of competition. While the agents of the new style of competition are not exactly old-fashioned heroes, neither are conditions old-fashioned. Initiative is being put to an unexampled test.

In a society so recently emerged from the small-entrepreneur epoch, still influenced by models of success congruent with that epoch's ideology, it is not likely that the sober-bureaucratic type can readily become dominant. Yet the structure of the society will not permit the traditional way of amassing personal wealth. The nineteenth-century scene of competition was one of relatively equal powers and the competition was between individual businessmen or firms. The twentieth-century scene contains huge and powerful units which compete not so much with one another but as a totality with the consuming public and sometimes with certain segments of the government. The new entrepreneur represents the old go-getting competition in the new setting.

The general milieu of this new species of entrepreneur is those areas that are still uncertain and unroutinized. The new entrepreneur is very much at home in the less tangible of the 'business services'—

commercial research and public relations, advertising agencies, labor relations, and the mass communication and entertainment industries. His titles are likely to be 'special assistant to the president,' 'counsel for the general manager,' 'management counsellor and engineering adviser.' For the bright, young, educated man, these fields offer limitless opportunities, if he only has the initiative and the know-how, and if only the anxieties of the bureaucratic chieftains hold up. [94/95] The new entrepreneur may in time routinize these fields, but, in the process of doing so, he operates in them.

The areas open to the new entrepreneur, usually overlapping in various ways, are those of great uncertainties and new beginnings: (1) adjustments between various business bureaucracies, and between business and government; (2) public relations, the interpretative justification of the new powers to the underlying outsiders; and (3) new industries that have arisen in the last quarter-century, especially those —for example, advertising—which involve selling somewhat intangible services.

The old entrepreneur succeeded by founding a new concern and expanding it. The bureaucrat gets a forward-looking job and climbs up the ladder within a pre-arranged hierarchy. The new entrepreneur makes a zig-zag pattern upward within and between established bureaucracies. In contrast to the classic small businessman, who operated in a world opening up like a row of oysters under steam, the new entrepreneur must operate in a world in which all the pearls have already been grabbed up and are carefully guarded. The only way in which he can express his initiative is by servicing the powers that be, in the hope of getting his cut. He serves them by 'fixing things,' between one big business and another, and between business as a whole and the public.

He gets ahead because (1) men in power do not expect that things can be done legitimately; (2) these men know fear and guilt; and (3) they are often personally not very bright. It is often hard to say, with any sureness, whether the new entrepreneur lives on his own wits, or upon the lack of wits in others. As for anxiety, however, it is certain that, although he may be prodded by his own, he could get nowhere without its ample presence in his powerful clients.

Like Balzac's des Lupeaulx, thrown up by the tide of political events in France in the first quarter of the nineteenth century, who had discovered that 'authority stood in need of a charwoman,' the American new entrepreneur is an 'adroit climber ... to his professions of useful help and go-between he added a third—he gave gratuitous advice on the internal diseases of power.... He bore the brunt of the first explosion of despair or anger; he laughed and mourned with his chief. ... It was his [95/96] duty to flatter and advise, to give advice in the guise of flattery, and flattery in the form of advice.'

The talent and intelligence that go with the new entrepreneurship are often dangerous in the new society. He who has them but lacks power must act as if those in power have the same capacities. He must give credit for good ideas to his superiors and take the rap himself for bad ones. The split between the executive who judges and the intelligence that creates is sharp and finds a ready justification: 'So I write a show? Or produce one?' asks an account executive in one of the recent tales of unhappiness among the new entrepreneurs. 'And I take it down to [the] sponsor. And he asks me, in your judgment should I spend a million dollars a year on this show you've created? See, Artie? Actually, I'd have no judgment. I wouldn't be in a position to criticize. In short, I wouldn't be an executive.'

As a competitor, the new entrepreneur is an agent of the bureaucracy he serves, and what he competes for is the good will and favor of those who run the system; his chance exists because there are *several* bureaucracies, private and public, in complicated entanglements. Unlike the little white-collar man, he does not often stay within any one corporate bureaucracy; his path is within and between bureaucracies, in a kind of uneasy but calculated rhythm. He makes a well-worn path between big business and the regulatory agencies of the Federal Government, especially its military establishment and political parties.

On the higher managerial levels there is a delicate balance of power, security, and advancement resting upon a sensitive blend of loyalty to one's firm and knowledge of its intimately valuable secrets—secrets which other firms or governments would like to know. Not 'secrets' in any hush-hush sense, although there have been simple sellouts, but secrets in the sense of what is inaccessible to those who have not operated in the context. In a bureaucratic world, the individual's experience is usually controlled; the clever executive squashes entrepreneurial tendencies by using his formal power position to monopolize contacts with important clients. It is a characteristic of the new entrepreneur that he manages to gain experience without being controlled.

There are many instances of men who learn the secrets and procedures of a regulatory agency of government to which they [96/97] are not loyal in a career sense. Their loyalties are rather to the business hierarchy to which they intend to return. This is the structure of one type of twentieth-century opportunity. The curriculum of such 'businessmen in government' is familiar: they have been in and out of Washington since the NIRA days, serving on advisory boards, in commerce department committees and war production boards, retaining contact with a middle- or large-scale business enterprise. In this interlinked world, there has been genuine opportunity for big success over the last fifteen years.

The openings have been on all levels. On the lower levels, a chief clerk of an OPA board may set up a business service—an OPA buffer—for firms dealing with OPA, and slowly grow into a management counselling service. At the center, however, operations have gone on in a big way during and after the war. Surplus-property disposal, for example, became so complicated that 'the government' wasn't sure just what it was doing. The surface has only been scratched, but evidence has been published of millions being made from investments of thousands; of expediters buying surplus tools from the government and selling them back again; of buying from the Navy and immediately selling to the Army, et cetera. A few smaller fry have been caught; the big fixers probably never will be, for they were only carrying on business as usual during wartime and with the government.

Perhaps the Number One figure in the short history of the new entrepreneur has been Thomas Gardner ('Tommy-the-Cork') Corcoran, who for two terms was one of President Roosevelt's 'principal advisers and . . . trouble shooters. . . . He possessed that rare asset, either inside or outside of the Federal Government, of knowing the whole, intricate mechanism of the Washington establishment.' A free-ranging talent scout for the administration, he was, as John H. Crider of the *New York Times* puts it, 'personally responsible for putting literally scores of men in key positions throughout the Federal organization. . . . He has more pipelines into the Government than probably any other individual on the outside. . . . He always operated for the President behind the scenes, having had several titles during his government employment, including counsel . . . assistant . . . special [97/98] assistant.' Leaving the government service which paid him only $10,000 a year, he earned as lawyer and expeditor $100,000 plus.

For the 'fixer,' who lives on the expectation that in the bureaucratic world things cannot be accomplished quickly through legitimate channels, bargaining power and sources of income consist of intangible contacts and 'pipe-lines' rather than tangible assets. Yet he is no less an entrepreneur in spirit and style of operation than the man of small property; he is using his own initiative, wile, and cunning to create something where nothing was before. Of course, he does not have the security that property ownership once provided; that is one thing that makes Sammy run. Yet, for the successful, the risks are not incommensurate with the returns.

Sometimes, of course, the new entrepreneur does become a member of the propertied rich. He can scatter his property in various stocks in a sensible attempt to spread risks and concentrate chances of success. If he does not invest capital, his success is all the greater measure of his inherent worth, for this means that he is genuinely creative. Like the more heroic businessmen of old, he manages to get something for very little or nothing. And like them, he is a man who never misses a bet.

The power of the old captain of industry purportedly rested upon his engineering ability and his financial sharp dealing. The power of the ideal bureaucrat is derived from the authority vested in the office he occupies. The power of the managerial chieftain rests upon his control of the wealth piled up by the old captain and is increased by a rational system of guaranteed tributes. The power of the new entrepreneur, in the first instance at least, rests upon his personality and upon his skill in using it to manipulate the anxieties of the chieftain. The concentration of power has thus modified the character and the larger meaning of competition. The new entrepreneur's success or failure is decided not so much by the 'supply and demand' of the impersonal market as by the personal anxieties and decisions of intimately known chieftains of monopoly.

The careers of both the new entrepreneur and the ordinary white-collar worker are administered by powerful others. But there is this difference: the toadying of the white-collar employee is small-scale and unimaginative; he is a member of the stable corps of the bureaucracy, and initiative is regimented out of his [98/99] life. The new ulcered entrepreneur operates on the guileful edges of several bureaucracies.

With his lavish expense account, the new entrepreneur sometimes gets into the public eye as a fixer—along with the respectable business-man whose work he does—or even as an upstart and a crook: for the same public that idolizes initiative becomes incensed when it finds a grand model of success based simply and purely upon it. For one Murray Garsson caught how many others were there? The Garssons ran a letterhead corporation title into a profit of 78 million dollars out of war contracts, and the same public that honors pluck and success and the Horatio Alger story became angry. In an expanding system, profits seem to coincide with the welfare of all; in a system already closed, profits are made by doing somebody in. The line between the legitimate and the illegitimate is difficult to draw because no one has set up the rules for the new situation. Moreover, such moral questions are decisively influenced by the size of the business and the firmness and reliability of contacts.

Part of the new entrepreneur's frenzy perhaps is due to apprehension that his function may disappear. Many of the jobs he has been doing for the chieftains are now a standardized part of business enterprise, no longer requiring the entrepreneurial flair, and can be handled by cheaper and more dependable white-collar men. Increasingly, big firms hire their own talent for those fields in which the new entrepreneurs pioneered. In so far as this is so, the new entrepreneurs become bright boys and, as salaried employees, are stable members of the managerial cadre.

In the more strictly bureaucratic setting, the value of contacts a given manager has and the secrets he learns are definitely lessened. Rationalization of the managerial hierarchy decreases the chance for any one man down the line to get a view of the whole. It is the Tommy Corcoran *without* a definite bureaucratic role who learns the whole, and serves his chief—and in due course himself—by telling selected others about it. In the General Somervell type of managership, the executive's control section monopolizes the chance to see things whole, and tells what it will once each month to all executives. [99/100]

Rationalization prohibits a total view: by rationalizing the organization via rotation systems and control sections, top bureaucrats can guide the vision of underlings. The 'entrepreneurial type' who does not play ball can be excluded from inside information. Like the commodity market before it, the top level of the personality market may well become an object to be administered, rather than a play of free forces of crafty wile and unexampled initiative. [100]

2. THE PROMISE OF SUCCESS

SINCE CAPTAIN JOHN SMITH FIRST DESCRIBED FOR PROSPECTIVE COLONISTS the opportunities available in America, the promise of success in America has found expression by many writers. The selections in this section are but a sampling of a huge body of material, much of which is journalistic and rhetorical, voicing an enduring faith in the opportunity offered by America to the person who seeks to rise from obscurity to the pinnacle of worldly hopes—"success." From Crèvecoeur's description of America, extending hope to the poor of Europe at the end of the eighteenth century, to the rich imagery of Theodore Dreiser's portrait of the twentieth-century city, these selections reflect the vision known as the American dream of success.

In part the American promise of success is social, and in part political. From its beginnings America has been the land of opportunity, a country where poor laborers could, as Crèvecoeur observes, become men, with the blessings of "new laws, a new mode of living, a new social system." Under a government whose Constitution pledges to "promote the general welfare, and secure the blessings of liberty to ourselves and our posterity," both the immigrant and the native could feel that they counted for something, that they would receive the rewards of their own labor. "*He* is an American," Crèvecoeur says, "who, leaving behind him all his ancient prejudices and manners, receives new ones from the new mode of life he has embraced, the new government he obeys, and the new rank he holds." The new prejudices of the new American—the beliefs in opportunity, in self-determination, in the possibility of success—had the effect of creating in him a recognition of himself as a unique social and political being.

Although the promise of success has been an enduring one, through the years the actual expression of the promise has changed. Crèvecoeur wrote when the nation was a sparse settlement along the Eastern seaboard, opening to vast tracts of unsettled land to the West.

His expression of the promise focused on the contrast between the limited opportunities in Europe and the enlarged opportunities in America for the person with willing and capable hands. He saw the promise in primarily agrarian terms and envisioned a western movement of growing communities, agrarian in economy, continuing throughout the following century to offer opportunities for the farmer and the tradesman. But even as he was writing, America could not be called purely agrarian. Small industries had been developing in many of the seaboard towns. America was rapidly changing to an industrial nation. Although much of the western land was still open to homesteaders and speculators, manufacturing and commercial interests dominated the East. The journalist Horace Greeley offered advice to those moving westward as well as to those moving to the city. Like Benjamin Franklin before him and like Horatio Alger, Jr., who followed him, he stressed for both groups the Puritan virtues of thrift and industriousness. The appeal he made was similar to that of Crèvecoeur, for he spoke to the tradesman and the laborer. But the frontier was already clearing, and the opportunities that Crèvecoeur promised were disappearing. As if in recognition of this fact, the lecturer Russell H. Conwell, at the end of the nineteenth century, told millions of eager listeners that success was within reach, that diamonds—to use his metaphor—were always under foot. In the twentieth century the industrial and commercial centers, not the prairies, seem to hold the golden promise. But modern writers have realized the complex nature of this promise. In his description of "The City of My Dreams," Theodore Dreiser recognizes the siren call of the metropolis, which beckons many—some to success but others to defeat.

Viewed historically, any statement about America as a land of opportunity may be tinged with irony. Even at the time of Crèvecoeur, as Henry Adams has shown, some settlers in the new country lived out their days in unrelieved poverty. Many of the young men who followed Greeley's advice found that the West offered only defeat. As Conwell spoke of success available for all, the opportunities for his listeners were in effect being restricted by the large industrialists and financiers. Dreiser himself expresses the irony in his essay describing New York.

Still, however it may have changed with a changing America, the promise has endured. There have been enough examples of the rise from poverty to wealth and power in actual life to make the promise of success a valid one. Horace Greeley's often-quoted advice to the young man has become hackneyed, but the promise it expresses has remained central to the American character for over three hundred years.

What Is an American?

MICHEL-GUILLAUME JEAN DE CRÈVECOEUR

I WISH I COULD BE ACQUAINTED WITH THE FEELINGS AND THOUGHTS WHICH must agitate the heart and present themselves to the mind of an enlightened Englishman, when he first lands on this continent. He must greatly rejoice that he lived at a time to see this fair country discovered and settled; he must necessarily feel a share of national pride, when he views the chain of settlements which embellishes these extended shores. When he says to himself, this is the work of my countrymen, who, when convulsed by factions, afflicted by a variety of miseries and wants, restless and impatient, took refuge here. They brought along with them their national genius, to which they principally owe what liberty they enjoy, and what substance they possess. Here he sees the industry of his native country displayed in a new manner, and traces in their works the embryos of all the arts, sciences, and ingenuity which flourish in Europe. Here he beholds fair cities, substantial villages, extensive fields, an immense country filled with decent houses, good roads, orchards, meadows, and bridges, where an hundred years ago all was wild, woody, uncultivated! What a train of pleasing ideas this fair spectacle must suggest; it is a prospect which must inspire a good citizen with the most heartfelt pleasure. The difficulty consists in the manner of viewing so extensive a scene. He is arrived on a new continent; a modern society offers itself to his contemplation, different from what he had hitherto seen. It is not composed, as in Europe, of [39/40] great lords who possess everything, and of a herd of people who have nothing. Here are no aristocratical families, no courts, no kings, no bishops, no ecclesiastical dominion, no invisible power giving to a few a very visible one; no great manufacturers employing thousands, no great refinements of luxury. The rich and the poor are not so far removed from each other as they are in Europe. Some few towns excepted, we are all tillers of the earth, from

From Hector St. John de Crèvecoeur, *Letters from an American Farmer* (London: J. M. Dent & Sons; New York: E. P. Dutton & Co., Everyman's Library, 1912), pp. 39–44. Originally published 1782. Reprinted by permission of E. P. Dutton & Co., Inc.

Nova Scotia to West Florida. We are a people of cultivators, scattered over an immense territory, communicating with each other by means of good roads and navigable rivers, united by the silken bands of mild government, all respecting the laws, without dreading their power, because they are equitable. We are all animated with the spirit of an industry which is unfettered and unrestrained, because each person works for himself. If he travels through our rural districts he views not the hostile castle, and the haughty mansion, contrasted with the clay-built hut and miserable cabin, where cattle and men help to keep each other warm, and dwell in meanness, smoke, and indigence. A pleasing uniformity of decent competence appears throughout our habitations. The meanest of our log-houses is a dry and comfortable habitation. Lawyer or merchant are the fairest titles our towns afford; that of a farmer is the only appellation of the rural inhabitants of our country. It must take some time ere he can reconcile himself to our dictionary, which is but short in words of dignity, and names of honour. There, on a Sunday, he sees a congregation of respectable farmers and their wives, all clad in neat homespun, well mounted, or riding in their own humble waggons. There is not among them an esquire, saving the unlettered magistrate. There he sees a parson as simple as his flock, a farmer who does not riot on the labour of others. We have no princes, for whom we [40/41] toil, starve, and bleed: we are the most perfect society now existing in the world. Here man is free as he ought to be; nor is this pleasing equality so transitory as many others are. Many ages will not see the shores of our great lakes replenished with inland nations, nor the unknown bounds of North America entirely peopled. Who can tell how far it extends? Who can tell the millions of men whom it will feed and contain? for no European foot has as yet travelled half the extent of this mighty continent!

The next wish of this traveller will be to know whence came all these people? they are a mixture of English, Scotch, Irish, French, Dutch, Germans, and Swedes. From this promiscuous breed, that race now called Americans have arisen. The eastern provinces must indeed be excepted, as being the unmixed descendants of Englishmen. I have heard many wish that they had been more intermixed also: for my part, I am no wisher, and think it much better as it has happened. They exhibit a most conspicuous figure in this great and variegated picture; they too enter for a great share in the pleasing perspective displayed in these thirteen provinces. I know it is fashionable to reflect on them, but I respect them for what they have done; for the accuracy and wisdom with which they have settled their territory; for the decency of their manners; for their early love of letters; their ancient college, the first in this hemisphere; for their industry; which to me who am but a farmer, is the criterion of everything. There never was a people, situated as they are, who with so ungrateful a soil have done more in so short a time. Do you think that the monarchical ingredients which are more

prevalent in other governments, have purged them from all foul stains?
Their histories assert the contrary.

In this great American asylum, the poor of Europe have by some
means met together, and in consequence of [41/42] various causes; to
what purpose should they ask one another what countrymen they are?
Alas, two thirds of them had no country. Can a wretch who wanders
about, who works and starves, whose life is a continual scene of sore
affliction or pinching penury; can that man call England or any other
kingdom his country? A country that had no bread for him, whose
fields procured him no harvest, who met with nothing but the frowns
of the rich, the severity of the laws, with jails and punishments; who
owned not a single foot of the extensive surface of this planet? No!
urged by a variety of motives, here they came. Every thing has tended
to regenerate them; new laws, a new mode of living, a new social
system; here they are become men; in Europe they were as so many
useless plants, wanting vegetative mould, and refreshing showers; they
withered, and were mowed down by want, hunger, and war; but now
by the power of transplantation, like all other plants they have taken
root and flourished! Formerly they were not numbered in any civil lists
of their country, except in those of the poor; here they rank as citizens.
By what invisible power has this surprising metamorphosis been performed? By that of the laws and that of their industry. The laws, the
indulgent laws, protect them as they arrive, stamping on them the
symbol of adoption; they receive ample rewards for their labours; these
accumulated rewards procure them lands; those lands confer on them
the title of freemen, and to that title every benefit is affixed which men
can possibly require. This is the great operation daily performed by our
laws. From whence proceed these laws? From our government.
Whence the government? It is derived from the original genius and
strong desire of the people ratified and confirmed by the crown. This is
the great chain which links us all, this is the picture which every
province exhibits, Nova Scotia excepted. [42/43] There the crown has
done all; either there were no people who had genius, or it was not
much attended to: the consequence is, that the province is very
thinly inhabited indeed; the power of the crown in conjunction with
the musketos has prevented men from settling there. Yet some parts of
it flourished once, and it contained a mild harmless set of people. But
for the fault of a few leaders, the whole were banished. The greatest
political error the crown ever committed in America, was to cut off
men from a country which wanted nothing but men!

What attachment can a poor European emigrant have for a
country where he had nothing? The knowledge of the language, the
love of a few kindred as poor as himself, were the only cords that tied
him: his country is now that which gives him land, bread, protection,
and consequence: *Ubi panis ibi patria,* is the motto of all emigrants.
What then is the American, this new man? He is either an European,

or the descendant of an European, hence that strange mixture of blood, which you will find in no other country. I could point out to you a family whose grandfather was an Englishman, whose wife was Dutch, whose son married a French woman, and whose present four sons have now four wives of different nations. *He* is an American, who, leaving behind him all his ancient prejudices and manners, receives new ones from the new mode of life he has embraced, the new government he obeys, and the new rank he holds. He becomes an American by being received in the broad lap of our great *Alma Mater*. Here individuals of all nations are melted into a new race of men, whose labours and posterity will one day cause great changes in the world. Americans are the western pilgrims, who are carrying along with them that great mass of arts, sciences, vigour, and industry which began long since in the east; they will finish the [43/44] great circle. The Americans were once scattered all over Europe; here they are incorporated into one of the finest systems of population which has ever appeared, and which will hereafter become distinct by the power of the different climates they inhabit. The American ought therefore to love this country much better than that wherein either he or his forefathers were born. Here the rewards of his industry follow with equal steps the progress of his labour; his labour is founded on the basis of nature, *self-interest;* can it want a stronger allurement? Wives and children, who before in vain demanded of him a morsel of bread, now, fat and frolicsome, gladly help their father to clear those fields whence exuberant crops are to arise to feed and to clothe them all; without any part being claimed, either by a despotic prince, a rich abbot, or a mighty lord. Here religion demands but little of him; a small voluntary salary to the minister, and gratitude to God; can he refuse these? The American is a new man, who acts upon new principles; he must therefore entertain new ideas, and form new opinions. From involuntary idleness, servile dependence, penury, and useless labour, he has passed to toils of a very different nature, rewarded by ample subsistence.—This is an American. [44]

Advice to Young Men

HORACE GREELEY

To Aspiring Young Men

"I WANT TO GO INTO BUSINESS," IS THE ASPIRATION OF OUR YOUNG MEN: "can't you find me a place in the city?" their constant inquiry. "Friend," we answer to many, "the best business you can go into you will find on your father's farm or in his workshop. If you have no family or friends to aid you, and no prospect opened to you there, turn your face to the Great West, and there build up a home and fortune. But dream not of getting suddenly rich by speculation, rapidly by trade, or any how by a profession: all these avenues are choked by eager, struggling aspirants, and ten must be trodden down in the press where one can vault upon his neighbor's shoulders to honor or wealth. Above all, be neither afraid nor ashamed of honest industry; and if you catch yourself fancying anything more *respectable* than this, be ashamed of it to the last day of your life. Or, if you find yourself shaking more cordially the hand of your cousin the Congressman than of your uncle the blacksmith, *as such,* write yourself down an enemy to the principles of our institutions, and a traitor to the dignity of Humanity." [414/415]

To Young Mechanics

"It is the first step that costs." The main obstacle to saving is the lack of the habit. He who at twenty-two has saved a hundred dollars, earned by honest, useful effort during the first year of his self-control, will be very unlikely ever to be destitute thereafter. On the other hand, he who has saved nothing at the end of his first year of independence, will be pretty certain to carry a poor man's head on his shoulders while he lives.

Our young mechanics are not thrifty, because of the evil habits they have formed during their minority. . . . By-and-bye he marries, and retrenches some of his worst expenses, but too late—the increased

From J. Parton, *The Life of Horace Greeley* (New York: Mason Brothers, 1855), pp. 414–415.

demands of a growing family absorb every cent he can earn; and at fifty or sixty years of age you will see him emerging, seedy and sickly, from the groggery, whither he has repaired for his bitters or his eleven o'clock, enfeebled in body, and discouraged in spirit, out of humor with everything and everybody, and cursing the banks, or the land lords, the capitalists, or the speculators, as plunderers and enslavers of the poor.

Coming to the City

The young man fit to come to a city does not begin by importuning some relative or friend to find or make a place for him. Having first qualified himself, so far as he may, for usefulness here, he comes understanding that he must begin at the foot of the class, and work his way up. Having found a place to stop, he makes himself acquainted with those places where work in his line may be found, sees advertisements of "Wants" in the leading journals at an early hour each morning, notes those which hold out some prospect for him, and accepts the first place offered him which he can take honorably and fill acceptably. He who commences in this way is quite likely to get on. [415]

Acres of Diamonds

RUSSELL H. CONWELL

Friends.—This lecture has been delivered under these circumstances: I visit a town or city, and try to arrive there early enough to see the postmaster, the barber, the keeper of the hotel, the principal of the schools, and the ministers of some of the churches, and then go into some of the factories and stores, and talk with the people, and get into sympathy with the local conditions of that town or city and see what has been their history, what opportunities they had, and what they had failed to do—and every town fails to do something—and then go to the lecture and talk to those people about the subjects which applied to their locality. "Acres of Diamonds"—the idea—has continuously been precisely the same. The idea is

From Russell H. Conwell, *Acres of Diamonds* (New York and London: Harper & Brothers, 1915), pp. 2–28. Reprinted with the permission of Harper & Row, Publishers.

that in this country of ours every man has the opportunity to make more of himself than he does in his own environment, with his own skill, with his own energy, and with his own friends.   RUSSELL H. CONWELL [2/3]

When going down the Tigris and Euphrates rivers many years ago with a party of English travelers I found myself under the direction of an old Arab guide whom we hired up at Bagdad, and I have often thought how that guide resembled our barbers in certain mental characteristics. He thought that it was not only his duty to guide us down those rivers, and do what he was paid for doing, but also to entertain us with stories curious and weird, ancient and modern, strange and familiar. Many of them I have forgotten, and I am glad I have, but there is one I shall never forget. . . . [3/4]

Said he, "I will tell you a story now which I reserve for my particular friends." When he emphasized the words "particular friends," I listened, and I have ever been glad I did. . . . The old guide told me that there once lived not far from the River Indus an ancient Persian by the name of Ali Hafed. He said that Ali Hafed owned a very large farm, that he had orchards, grain-fields, and gardens; that he had money at interest, and was a wealthy and contented man. He was contented because he was wealthy, and wealthy because he was contented. One day there visited that old Persian farmer one of those ancient Buddhist priests, one of the wise men of the East. He sat down by the fire and told the old farmer how this world of ours was made. He said that this world was once a mere bank of fog, and that the Almighty thrust His finger into [4/5] this bank of fog, and began slowly to move His finger around, increasing the speed until at last He whirled this bank of fog into a solid ball of fire. Then it went rolling through the universe, burning its way through other banks of fog, and condensed the moisture without, until it fell in floods of rain upon its hot surface, and cooled the outward crust. Then the internal fires bursting outward through the crust threw up the mountains and hills, the valleys, the plains and prairies of this wonderful world of ours. If this internal molten mass came bursting out and cooled very quickly it became granite; less quickly copper, less quickly silver, less quickly gold, and, after gold, diamonds were made.

Said the old priest, "A diamond is a congealed drop of sunlight." Now that is literally scientifically true, that a diamond is an actual deposit of carbon from the sun. The old priest told Ali Hafed that if he had one diamond the size of his thumb he could purchase the county, and if he had a mine of diamonds he could place his children upon thrones through the influence of their great wealth.

Ali Hafed heard all about diamonds, how much they were worth, and went to his bed that night a poor man. He had not lost anything, but he was poor because he was discontented, and discontented because he feared he was poor. He said, "I want a mine of diamonds," and he lay awake all night. [5/6]

Early in the morning he sought out the priest. I know by experience that a priest is very cross when awakened early in the morning, and when he shook that old priest out of his dreams, Ali Hafed said to him:

"Will you tell me where I can find diamonds?"

"Diamonds! What do you want with diamonds?" "Why, I wish to be immensely rich." "Well, then, go along and find them. That is all you have to do; go and find them, and then you have them." "But I don't know where to go." "Well, if you will find a river that runs through white sands, between high mountains, in those white sands you will always find diamonds." "I don't believe there is any such river." "Oh yes, there are plenty of them. All you have to do is to go and find them, and then you have them." Said Ali Hafed, "I will go."

So he sold his farm, collected his money, left his family in charge of a neighbor, and away he went in search of diamonds. He began his search, very properly to my mind, at the Mountains of the Moon. Afterward he came around into Palestine, then wandered on into Europe, and at last when his money was all spent and he was in rags, wretchedness, and poverty, he stood on the shore of that bay at Barcelona, in Spain, when a great tidal wave came rolling in between the pillars of Hercules, and the poor, afflicted, suffering, dying man could not resist the awful temptation to cast himself into that incoming tide, and [6/7] he sank beneath its foaming crest, never to rise in this life again.

When that old guide had told me that awfully sad story he stopped the camel I was riding on and went back to fix the baggage that was coming off another camel, and I had an opportunity to muse over his story while he was gone. I remember saying to myself, "Why did he reserve that story for his 'particular friends'?" There seemed to be no beginning, no middle, no end, nothing to it. That was the first story I had ever heard told in my life, and would be the first one I ever read, in which the hero was killed in the first chapter. I had but one chapter of that story, and the hero was dead.

When the guide came back and took up the halter of my camel, he went right ahead with the story, into the second chapter, just as though there had been no break. The man who purchased Ali Hafed's farm one day led his camel into the garden to drink, and as that camel put its nose into the shallow water of that garden brook, Ali Hafed's successor noticed a curious flash of light from the white sands of the stream. He pulled out a black stone having an eye of light reflecting all the hues of the rainbow. He took the pebble into the house and put it on the mantel which covers the central fires, and forgot all about it.

A few days later this same old priest came in to visit Ali Hafed's successor, and the moment [7/8] he opened the drawing-room door he saw that flash of light on the mantel, and he rushed up to it, and shouted: "Here is a diamond! Has Ali Hafed returned?" "Oh no, Ali

Hafed has not returned, and that is not a diamond. That is nothing but a stone we found right out here in our own garden." "But," said the priest, "I tell you I know a diamond when I see it. I know positively that is a diamond."

Then together they rushed out into that old garden and stirred up the white sands with their fingers, and lo! there came up other more beautiful and valuable gems than the first. "Thus," said the guide to me, and, friends, it is historically true, "was discovered the diamond-mine of Golconda, the most magnificent diamond-mine in all the history of mankind, excelling the Kimberly itself. The Kohinoor, and the Orloff of the crown jewels of England and Russia, the largest on earth, came from that mine."

When that old Arab guide told me the second chapter of his story, he then took off his Turkish cap and swung it around in the air again to get my attention to the moral. Those Arab guides have morals to their stories, although they are not always moral. As he swung his hat, he said to me, "Had Ali Hafed remained at home and dug in his own cellar, or underneath his own wheat-fields, or in his own garden, instead of wretchedness, starvation, and death by suicide in a strange land, he would have had 'acres of diamonds.' [8/9] For every acre of that old farm, yes, every shovelful, afterward revealed gems which since have decorated the crowns of monarchs."

When he had added the moral to his story I saw why he reserved it for "his particular friends." But I did not tell him I could see it. It was that mean old Arab's way of going around a thing like a lawyer, to say indirectly what he did not dare say directly, that "in his private opinion there was a certain young man then traveling down the Tigris River that might better be at home in America." I did not tell him I could see that, but I told him his story reminded me of one, and I told it to him quick, and I think I will tell it to you.

I told him of a man out in California in 1847, who owned a ranch. He heard they had discovered gold in southern California, and so with a passion for gold he sold his ranch to Colonel Sutter, and away he went, never to come back. Colonel Sutter put a mill upon a stream that ran through that ranch, and one day his little girl brought some wet sand from the raceway into their home and sifted it through her fingers before the fire, and in that falling sand a visitor saw the first shining scales of real gold that were ever discovered in California. The man who had owned that ranch wanted gold, and he could have secured it for the mere taking. Indeed, thirty-eight millions of dollars has been taken out of a very few acres since then. . . . [9/10]

But a better illustration really than that occurred here in our own Pennsylvania. . . . There was a man living in Pennsylvania, not unlike some Pennsylvanians you have seen, who owned a farm, and he did with that farm just what I should do with a farm if I owned one in Pennsylvania—he sold it. But before he sold it he decided to secure employment collecting coal-oil for his cousin, who was in the business in Canada, where they first discovered oil on this continent. They dipped it from the running streams at that early time. So this Pennsylvania farmer wrote to his cousin asking for employment. You see, friends, this farmer was not altogether a foolish man. No, he was not. He did not leave his farm until he had something else to do. *Of all the simpletons the stars shine on I don't know of a worse one than the man who leaves one job before he has gotten another.* That has especial reference to my profession, and has no reference whatever to a man [10/11] seeking a divorce. When he wrote to his cousin for employment, his cousin replied, "I cannot engage you because you know nothing about the oil business."

Well, then the old farmer said, "I will know," and with most commendable zeal ... he set himself at the study of the whole subject. He began away back at the second day of God's creation when this world was covered thick and deep with that rich vegetation which since has turned to the primitive beds of coal. He studied the subject until he found that the drainings really of those rich beds of coal furnished the coal-oil that was worth pumping, and then he found how it came up with the living springs. He studied until he knew what it looked like, smelled like, tasted like, and how to refine it. Now said he in his letter to his cousin, "I understand the oil business." His cousin answered, "All right, come on."

So he sold his farm, according to the county record, for $833 (even money, "no cents"). He had scarcely gone from that place before the man who purchased the spot went out to arrange for the watering of the cattle. He found the previous owner had gone out years before and put a plank across the brook back of the barn, edgewise into the surface of the water just a few inches. The purpose of that plank at that sharp angle across the brook was to throw over to the other bank a [11/12] dreadful-looking scum through which the cattle would not put their noses. But with that plank there to throw it all over to one side, the cattle would drink below, and thus that man who had gone to Canada had been himself damming back for twenty-three years a flood of coal-oil which the state geologists of Pennsylvania declared to us ten years later was even then worth a hundred millions of dollars to our state, and four years ago our geologist declared the discovery to be worth to our state a thousand millions of dollars. The man who owned that territory on which the city of Titusville now stands, and those Pleasantville valleys, had studied the subject from the second day of God's creation clear down to the present time. He studied it until he knew all about it, and yet he is said to have sold the whole of it for $833, and again I say, "no sense." ... [12/15]

As I come here to-night and look around this audience I am seeing again what through these fifty years I have continually seen—men that are making precisely that same mistake. ... [15/16] I say to you that you have "acres of diamonds" in Philadelphia right where you now live. "Oh," but you will say, "you cannot know much about your city if you think there are any 'acres of diamonds' here."

I was greatly interested in that account in the newpsper of the young man who found that diamond in North Carolina. It was one of the purest diamonds that has ever been discovered, and it has several predecessors near the same locality. I went to a distinguished professor in mineralogy and asked him where he thought those diamonds came from. The professor secured the map of the geologic formations of our continent, and traced it. He said it went either through the underlying carboniferous strata adapted for such production, westward through Ohio and the Mississippi, or in more probability came eastward through Virginia and up the shore of the Atlantic Ocean. It is a fact that the diamonds were there, for they have been discovered and sold; and that they were carried down there during the drift [16/17] period, from some northern locality. Now who can say but some person going down with his drill in Philadelphia will find some trace of a diamond-mine yet down here? Oh, friends! you cannot say that you are not over one of the greatest diamond-mines in the world, for such a diamond as that only comes from the most profitable mines that are found on earth.

But it serves simply to illustrate my thought, which I emphasize by saying if you do not have the actual diamond-mines literally you have all that they would be good for to you. Because now that the Queen of England has given the greatest compliment ever conferred upon American woman for her attire because she did not appear with any jewels at all at the late reception in England, it has almost done away with the use of diamonds anyhow. All you would care for would be the few you would wear if you wish to be modest, and the rest you would sell for money.

Now then, I say again that the opportunity to get rich, to attain unto great wealth, is here in Philadelphia now, within the reach of almost every man and woman who hears me speak tonight, and I mean just what I say. I have not come to this platform even under these circumstances to recite something to you. I have come to tell you what in God's sight I believe to be the truth, and if the years of life have been of any value to me in the attainment of common sense, [17/18] I know I am right; that the men and women sitting here, who found it difficult perhaps to buy a ticket to this lecture or gathering to-night, have within their reach "acres of diamonds," opportunities to get largely wealthy. There never was a place on earth more adapted than the city of Philadelphia to-day, and never in the history of the world did a poor man without capital have such an opportunity to get rich quickly and honestly as he has now in our city. I say it is the truth, and I want you to accept it as such; for if you think I have come to simply recite something, then I would better not be here. I have no time to waste in any such talk, but to say the things I believe, and unless some of you get richer for what I am saying to-night my time is wasted.

I say that you ought to get rich, and it is your duty to get rich. How many of my pious brethren say to me, "Do you, a Christian minister, spend your time going up and down the country advising young people to get rich, to get money?" "Yes, of course I do." They say, "Isn't that awful! Why don't you preach the gospel instead of preaching about man's making money?" "Because to make money honestly is to preach the gospel." That is the reason. The men who get rich may be the most honest men you find in the community.

"Oh," but says some young man here to-night, "I have been told all my life that if a person has [18/19] money he is very dishonest and dishonorable and mean and contemptible." My friend, that is the reason why you have none, because you have that idea of people. The foundation of your faith is altogether false. Let me say here clearly, and say it briefly, though subject to discussion which I have not time for here, ninety-eight out of one hundred of the rich men of America are honest. That is why they are rich. That is why they are trusted with money. That is why they carry on great enterprises and find plenty of people to work with them. It is because they are honest men.

Says another young man, "I hear sometimes of men that get millions of dollars dishonestly." Yes, of course you do, and so do I. But they are so rare a thing in fact that the newspapers talk about them all the time as a matter of news until you get the idea that all the other rich men got rich dishonestly. . . . [19/20]

Money is power, and you ought to be reasonably ambitious to have it. You ought because you can do more good with it than you could without it. Money printed your Bible, money builds your churches, money sends your missionaries, and money pays your preachers, and you would not have many of them, either, if you did not pay them. I am always willing that my church should raise my salary, because the church that pays the largest salary always raises it the easiest. You never knew an exception to it in your life. The man who gets the largest salary can do the most good with the power that is furnished to him. Of course he can if his spirit be right to use it for what it is given to him.

I say, then, you ought to have money. If you can honestly attain unto riches in Philadelphia, it is your Christian and godly duty to do so. [20/21] It is an awful mistake of these pious people to think you must be awfully poor in order to be pious. . . . [21/27]

There are some over-pious Christian people who think if you take any profit on anything you sell that you are an unrighteous man. On the contrary, you would be a criminal to sell goods for less than they cost. You have no right to do that. You cannot trust a man with your money who cannot take care of his own. You cannot trust a man in your family that is not true to his own wife. You cannot trust a man in the world that does not begin with his own heart, his own character, and his own life. . . .

To live and let live is the principle of the gospel, and the principle of every-day common sense. Oh, young man, hear me; live as you go along. Do not wait until you have reached my years before you begin to enjoy anything of this life. If I had the millions back, or fifty cents of it, which I have tried to earn in these years, it [27/28] would not do me anything like the good that it does me now in this almost sacred presence to-night. Oh, yes, I am paid over and over a hundredfold to-night for dividing as I have tried to do in some measure as I went along through the years. I ought not speak that way, it sounds egotistic, but I am old enough now to be excused for that. I should have helped my fellow-men, which I have tried to do, and every one should try to do, and get the happiness of it. The man who goes home with the sense that he has stolen a dollar that day, that he has robbed a man of what was his honest due, is not going to sweet rest. He arises tired in the morning, and goes with an unclean conscience to his work the next day. He is not a successful man at all, although he may have laid up millions. But the man who has gone through life dividing always with his fellow-men, making and demanding his own rights and his own profits, and giving to every other man his rights and profits, lives every day, and not only that, but it is the royal road to great wealth. The history of the thousands of millionaires shows that to be the case. . . . [28]

The City of My Dreams

THEODORE DREISER

IT WAS SILENT, THE CITY OF MY DREAMS, MARBLE AND SERENE, DUE PER-haps to the fact that in reality I knew nothing of crowds, poverty, the winds and storms of the inadequate that blow like dust along the paths of life. It was an amazing city, so far-flung, so beautiful, so dead. There were tracks of iron stalking through the air, and streets that were as cañons, and stairways that mounted in vast flights to noble plazas, and

From *The Color of a Great City* by Theodore Dreiser. Copyright 1923 by Boni & Liveright, Inc. Copyright 1951 by Helen Dreiser. Published by arrangement with The World Publishing Company, Cleveland and New York.

steps that led down into deep places where were, strangely enough, underworld silences. And there were parks and flowers and rivers. And then, after twenty years, here it stood, as amazing almost as my dream, save that in the waking the flush of life was over it. It possessed the tang of contests and dreams and enthusiasms and delights and terrors and despairs. Through its ways and cañons and open spaces and underground passages were running, seething, sparkling, darkling, a mass of beings such as my dream-city never knew.

The thing that interested me then as now about New York—as indeed about any great city, but more definitely New York because it was and is so preponderantly large—was the sharp, and at the same time immense, contrast it showed between the dull and the shrewd, the strong [1/2] and the weak, the rich and the poor, the wise and the ignorant. This, perhaps, was more by reason of numbers and opportunity than anything else, for of course humanity is much the same everywhere. But the number from which to choose was so great here that the strong, or those who ultimately dominated, were so very strong, and the weak so very, very weak—and so very, very many.

I once knew a poor, half-demented, and very much shriveled little seamstress who occupied a tiny hall-bedroom in a side-street rooming-house, cooked her meals on a small alcohol stove set on a bureau, and who had about space enough outside of this to take three good steps either way.

"I would rather live in my hall-bedroom in New York than in any fifteen-room house in the country that I ever saw," she commented once, and her poor little colorless eyes held more of sparkle and snap in them than I ever saw there, before or after. She was wont to add to her sewing income by reading fortunes in cards and tea-leaves and coffee-grounds, telling of love and prosperity to scores as lowly as herself, who would never see either. The color and noise and splendor of the city as a spectacle was sufficient to pay her for all her ills.

And have I not felt the glamour of it myself? And do I not still? Broadway, at Forty-second Street, on those selfsame spring evenings when the city is crowded with an idle, sightseeing cloud of Westerners; when the doors of all shops are open, the windows of nearly all restaurants wide to the gaze of the idlest passer-by. Here [2/3] is the great city, and it is lush and dreamy. A May or June moon will be hanging like a burnished silver disc between the high walls aloft. A hundred, a thousand electric signs will blink and wink. And the floods of citizens and visitors in summer clothes and with gay hats; the street cars jouncing their endless carloads on indifferent errands; the taxis and private cars fluttering about like jeweled flies. The very gasoline contributes a distinct perfume. Life bubbles, sparkles; chatters gay, incoherent stuff. Such is Broadway.

And then Fifth Avenue, that singing, crystal street, on a shopping afternoon, winter, summer, spring or fall. What tells you as sharply of spring when, its windows crowded with delicate effronteries of silks and gay nothings of all description, it greets you in January, February and March? And how as early as November again, it sings of Palm Beach and Newport and the lesser or greater joys of the tropics and the warmer seas. And in September, how the haughty display of furs and rugs, in this same avenue, and costumes de luxe for ball and dinner, cry out of snows and blizzards, when you are scarcely ten days back from mountain or seaside. One might think, from the picture presented and the residences which line the upper section, that all the world was inordinately prosperous and exclusive and happy. And yet, if you but knew the tawdry underbrush of society, the tangle and mat of futile growth between the tall trees of success, the shabby chambers crowded with aspirants and climbers, the immense mansions barren of a single social affair, perfect and silent!

I often think of the. vast mass of underlings, boys and [3/4] girls, who, with nothing but their youth and their ambitions to commend them, are daily and hourly setting their faces New Yorkward, reconnoitering the city for what it may hold in the shape of wealth or fame, or, if not that, position and comfort in the future; and what, if anything, they will reap. Ah, their young eyes drinking in its promise! And then, again, I think of all the powerful or semi-powerful men and women throughout the world, toiling at one task or another—a store, a mine, a bank, a profession—somewhere outside of New York, whose one ambition is to reach the place where their wealth will permit them to enter and remain in New York, dominant above the mass, luxuriating in what they consider luxury.

The illusion of it, the hypnosis deep and moving that it is! How the strong and the weak, the wise and the fools, the greedy of heart and of eye, seek the nepenthe, the Lethe, of its something hugeness. I always marvel at those who are willing, seemingly, to pay any price— *the* price, whatever it may be—for one sip of this poison cup. What a stinging, quivering zest they display. How beauty is willing to sell its bloom, virtue its last rag, strength an almost usurious portion of that which it controls, youth its very best years, its hope or dream of fame, fame and power their dignity and presence, age its weary hours, to secure but a minor part of all this, a taste of its vibrating presence and the picture that it makes. Can you not hear them almost, singing its praises? [4]

3. SUCCESS IN A CHANGING AMERICA

THROUGHOUT THE YEARS OF AMERICA'S DEVELOPMENT FROM A LAND OF scattered agrarian communities into an urbanized nation, the forms that success has taken—the images held up for public emulation—have undergone many transformations. If generalizations can safely be made in this area, one can point to various professions that have attained prominence at various moments in our history: in Colonial New England, for instance, the minister and the magistrate were enviable figures, and ambitious boys of the time probably looked to the pulpit or the council chair when they dreamed of their future. In the South the truly respected man needed to be able to carry, or to assume as best he could, the marks of a gentleman. In Revolutionary times and the early decades of the nineteenth century the lawyer and the politician, at times the military leader, became figures of public esteem. In these early days the man of wealth and property was respected, of course; but the ideal of success was not then channeled as narrowly into the confines of money making as it was to be in the latter part of the nineteenth century.

During the eighteenth century, Benjamin Franklin and other practical philosophers of the time did much to change the people's attitudes toward money making by making the activity itself eminently respectable. Franklin's attitude toward money making was not dissimilar to the attitudes of his Puritan ancestors. Franklin inherited from the Puritans a serious, essentially moral attitude toward living in general. But for the Puritan the act of money making was colored with a tinge of piety, a man's daily occupation being a necessary part of the Lord's work; whereas for Franklin the act of money making was perhaps the most serious part of life's adventure, justified if not sanctified by the Puritan virtues of industriousness and thrift. This ethic of thrift and industriousness—the Protestant ethic or Puritan ethic as it has been variously called—was eminently satisfactory in a new world of opportunity and open trade. Moreover, by secularizing the definition of virtue into the convenient terms of thrift and industriousness, Franklin and his followers could include a dozen other more or less desirable character traits, such as acquisitiveness or ambition for power, and be assured that even possessing these traits, or maybe because they possessed them, they would be respectably rewarded, certainly on earth and possibly in heaven. The concept of success thus became inextricably interwoven into the heritage of Puritan morality. Its chief spokesmen in the nineteenth century were businessmen themselves, such as Andrew Carnegie, and writers like Horatio Alger, Jr., and Charles T. Adams ("Oliver Optic"), whose stories demonstrated that worldly success stems directly from self-denial, industriousness, and middle-class morality—with the help of a little well-deserved good luck. For many years after Puritanism ceased to be a dominant cultural force, this attitude toward industriousness remained.

Many twentieth-century writers, such as F. Scott Fitzgerald, have viewed the Puritan ethic as a private and social trap (Jay Gatsby, for instance, was pathetically trusting in his "general resolves" to better himself); for they have observed that hard work, even coupled with an acceptable morality, does not assure either personal or social fulfillment. It does not lead inevitably to success. The formulas, however, continue, though with necessary modifications. Whereas the Puritan interpreted the extent of his material success as evidence of the strength of his faith, the contemporary formula for success—as expressed by Norman Vincent Peale—builds from faith (or positive thinking) to psychic success and then, hopefully, to social success. According to this view, because the complexities of modern life are oppressive, the individual achieves a certain measure of success if he can only convince himself that the world is not positively against him.

The social phenomenon referred to as the Puritan ethic was only one of several social influences that have shaped the concept of success. Very quickly after colonization, and particularly after the democratizing effects of the Constitution were felt, the self-made man developed a public image of his own. Humble origin was of course the essential feature of this image. In certain areas of social and political activity the poverty of one's beginnings proved an indispensable asset. In the Presidential campaign of 1840, William Henry Harrison displayed log cabins and coonskin caps to remind the voters of his lowly origin in his successful bid to defeat the patrician Henry Clay. The rise of Abraham Lincoln from obscurity to the White House became an emblem of American success. A few decades later, "rags to riches" became a slogan to describe success opportunity. Horatio Alger, Jr., in the last half of the nineteenth century simply capitalized on a formula that had been serviceable for decades.

Implicit in the concept of the self-made man is the doctrine of "individualism." Individualism had always assumed importance for men who had considered the complex relationship of man against nature and society. The Puritan ethic, in particular, as modern sociologists have shown, was premised on the idea that each man and his conscience stand apart from society. But individualism, in the form of laissez-faire capitalism, became a formularized doctrine and slogan soon after the Civil War, when many men of business felt the need for unfettered freedom of action in their business affairs. In the 1880s and 1890s Darwinism provided sanction for individualism different from that of the Puritans. Darwinism, describing as it presumed to do an irrefutable law of nature, justified the strong individual in his actions even if his actions violated conventional Christian moral precepts. Naturalistic determinists like Theodore Dreiser thought that moral questions had an ambiguous place in a world of mechanistic forces. To the Darwinist, and to scientific determinists such as Dreiser, the person best able to adapt to the animal or mechanistic world is the strong-willed individual. Certain difficulties arose at times when moral considerations were weighed against the individualist's need for freedom of action, but with Dreiser and other Darwinian novelists the difficulties remained unresolved.

In the meantime social forces were at work to change the individual-centered equations of success. Soon after World War I, bureaucratic trends in the economic world tended to restrict individual freedom even while individualism was more stubbornly asserted as a necessary democratic virtue. In 1930 John Dewey, in *Individualism Old and New*, recognized the trend: "Even in high quarters, rugged individualism is praised as the glory in American life. But such words have little relation to the moving facts of that life." For the contemporary American money still calls the tune; but this time he is in a corporate society, which values social agility rather than individuality, executive ability rather than independent enterprise, and a willingness to subvert oneself to the goals and identity of the employing corporation. The man of success in the corporate society of today is a different man from the man of success, say, before the Civil War, or in the 1890s.

A. THE PURITAN ETHIC

Arriving at Moral Perfection

BENJAMIN FRANKLIN

IT WAS ABOUT THIS TIME I CONCEIV'D THE BOLD ARDUOUS PROJECT OF arriving at moral perfection. I wish'd to live without committing any fault at any time; I would conquer all that either natural inclination, custom, or company might lead me into. As I knew, or thought I knew, what was right and wrong, I did not see why I might not always do the one and avoid the other. But I soon found I had undertaken a task of more difficulty than I had imagined. While my care was employ'd in guarding against one fault, I was often surprised by another; habit took the advantage of inattention; inclination was sometimes too strong for reason. I concluded, at length, that the mere speculative conviction that it was our interest to be completely virtuous, was not sufficient to prevent our slipping; and that the contrary habits must be broken, and good ones acquired and established, before we can have any dependence on a steady, uniform rectitude of conduct. For this purpose I therefore contrived the following method.

In the various enumerations of the moral virtues I had met with in my reading, I found the catalogue more or less numerous, as different writers included more or fewer ideas under the same name. Temperance, for example, was by some confined to eating and drinking, while by others it was extended to mean the moderating every other pleasure, appetite, inclination, or passion, bodily or mental, even to our avarice and ambition. I propos'd to myself, for the sake of clearness, to use rather more names, with fewer ideas annex'd to each, than a few names with more ideas; and I included under thirteen names of virtues all that at that time occurr'd to me as necessary or desirable, and annexed to each a short precept, which fully express'd the extent I gave to its meaning.

These names of virtues, with their precepts, were: [82/83]

1. TEMPERANCE. Eat not to dullness; drink not to elevation.
2. SILENCE. Speak not but what may benefit others or yourself; avoid trifling conversation.

From Benjamin Franklin, *The Autobiography of Benjamin Franklin,* in *The Harvard Classics,* ed. Charles W. Eliot (New York: P. F. Collier & Son, 1909), I, 82–90.

3. ORDER. Let all your things have their places; let each part of your business have its time.

4. RESOLUTION. Resolve to perform what you ought; perform without fail what you resolve.

5. FRUGALITY. Make no expense but to do good to others or yourself; i.e., waste nothing.

6. INDUSTRY. Lose no time; be always employ'd in something useful; cut off all unnecessary actions.

7. SINCERITY. Use no hurtful deceit; think innocently and justly, and, if you speak, speak accordingly.

8. JUSTICE. Wrong none by doing injuries, or omitting the benefits that are your duty.

9. MODERATION. Avoid extreams; forbear resenting injuries so much as you think they deserve. [83/84]

10. CLEANLINESS. Tolerate no uncleanliness in body, cloaths, or habitation.

11. TRANQUILLITY. Be not disturbed at trifles, or at accidents common or unavoidable.

12. CHASTITY. Rarely use venery but for health or offspring, never to dullness, weakness, or the injury of your own or another's peace or reputation.

13. HUMILITY. Imitate Jesus and Socrates.

My intention being to acquire the *habitude* of all these virtues, I judg'd it would be well not to distract my attention by attempting the whole at once, but to fix it on one of them at a time; and, when I should be master of that, then to proceed to another, and so on, till I should have gone thro' the thirteen; and, as the previous acquisition of some might facilitate the acquisition of certain others, I arrang'd them with that view, as they stand above. Temperance first, as it tends to procure that coolness and clearness of head, which is so necessary where constant vigilance was to be kept up, and guard maintained against the unremitting attraction of ancient habits, and the force of perpetual temptations. This being acquir'd and establish'd, Silence would be more easy; and my desire being to gain knowledge at the same time that I improv'd in virtue, and considering that in conversation it was obtain'd rather by the use of the ears than of the tongue, and therefore wishing to break a habit I was getting into of prattling, punning, and joking, which only made me acceptable to trifling company, I gave *Silence* the second place. This and the next, *Order*, I expected would allow me more time for attending to my project and my studies. *Resolution*, once become habitual, would keep me firm in my endeavors to obtain all the subsequent [84/85] virtues; *Frugality* and Industry freeing me from my remaining debt, and producing affluence and independence, would make more easy the practice of Sincerity and Justice, etc., etc. Conceiving then, that, agreeably to the advice of Pythagoras in his Golden Verses, daily examination would be necessary, I contrived the following method for conducting that examination.

I made a little book, in which I allotted a page for each of the virtues. I rul'd each page with red ink, so as to have seven columns, one for each day of the week, marking each column with a letter for the day. I cross'd these columns with thirteen red lines, marking the beginning of each line with the first letter of one of the virtues, on which line, and in its proper column, I might mark, by a little black spot, every fault I found upon examination to have been committed respecting that virtue upon that day. . . . [85/86]

I determined to give a week's strict attention to each of the virtues successively. Thus, in the first week, my great guard was to avoid every the least offence against *Temperance*, leaving the other virtues to their ordinary chance, only marking every evening the faults of the day. Thus, if in the first week I could keep my first line, marked T, clear of spots, I suppos'd the habit of that virtue so much strengthen'd, and its opposite weaken'd, that I might venture extending my attention to include the next, and for the following week keep both lines clear of spots. Proceeding thus to the last, I could go thro' a course compleat in thirteen weeks, and four courses in a year. And like him who, having a garden to weed, does not attempt to eradicate all the bad herbs at once, which would exceed his reach and his strength, but works on one of the beds at a time, and, having accomplish'd the first, proceeds to a second, so I should have, I hoped, the encouraging pleasure of seeing on my pages the progress I made in virtue, by clearing successively my lines of their spots, till in the end, by a number of courses, I should be happy in viewing a clean book, after a thirteen weeks' daily examination. . . . [86/87]

The precept of *Order* requiring that *every part of my business should have its allotted time*, one page in my little book contain'd the following scheme of employment for the twenty-four hours of a natural day:

THE MORNING.	⌈ 5 ⌉	Rise, wash, and address *Powerful Goodness!* Contrive day's business,
Question. What good shall I do this day?	6	and take the resolution of the day; prosecute the present study, and
	⌊ 7 ⌋	breakfast.
	8	
	9	Work.
	10	
	11	
NOON.	⌈12⌉	Read, or overlook my accounts,
	⌊ 1 ⌋	and dine.
	2	
	3	Work.
	4	
	5	

EVENING.		6	Put things in their places. Supper.
		7	Music or diversion, or conversation.
Question. What good have		8	Examination of the day.
I done to-day?		9	
		10	
		11	
		12	
NIGHT.		1	Sleep.
		2	
		3	
		4	

[87/88]

I enter'd upon the execution of this plan for self-examination, and continu'd it with occasional intermissions for some time. I was surpris'd to find myself so much fuller of faults than I had imagined; but I had the satisfaction of seeing them diminish. To avoid the trouble of renewing now and then my little book, which, by scraping out the marks on the paper of old faults to make room for new ones in a new course, became full of holes, I transferr'd my tables and precepts to the ivory leaves of a memorandum book, on which the lines were drawn with red ink, that made a durable stain, and on those lines I mark'd my faults with a black-lead pencil, which marks I could easily wipe out with a wet sponge. After a while I went thro' one course only in a year, and afterward only one in several years, till at length I omitted them entirely, being employ'd in voyages and business abroad, with a multiplicity of affairs that interfered; but I always carried my little book with me. . . . [88/89]

It may be well my posterity should be informed that to this little artifice, with the blessing of God, their ancestor ow'd the constant felicity of his life, down to his 79th year, in which this is written. What reverses may attend the remainder is in the hand of Providence; but, if they arrive, the reflection on past happiness enjoy'd ought to help his bearing them with more resignation. To Temperance he ascribes his long-continued health, and what is still left to him of a good constitution; to Industry and Frugality, the early easiness of his circumstances and acquisition of his fortune, with all that knowledge that enabled him to be a useful citizen, and obtained for him some degree of reputation among the learned; to Sincerity and Justice, the confidence [89/90] of his country, and the honorable employs it conferred upon him; and to the joint influence of the whole mass of the virtues, even in the imperfect state he was able to acquire them, all that evenness of temper, and that cheerfulness in conversation, which makes his company still sought for, and agreeable even to his younger acquaintance. I hope, therefore, that some of my descendants may follow the example and reap the benefit. . . . [90]

First Lessons for Sam Barker

HORATIO ALGER, JR.

WHEN SUPPER WAS OVER SAM INQUIRED, "WHAT SHALL WE DO?"

"Suppose we take a walk?" suggested his companion.

"I'd rather go to the Old Bowery."

"I should like to go, but I can't afford it."

"You get five dollars a week, don't you?"

"Yes; but I need all of it for board, lodging and washing. So will you, too. I advise you to be careful about spending."

"What's the use of living if a fellow can't have a little fun?" grumbled Sam.

"There won't be much fun in going a day or two without anything to eat, Sam."

"We won't have to."

"Let me see about that. It costs a dollar and a quarter for the room, to begin with. Then our meals will cost us as much as forty or fifty cents a day, say three dollars a week. That will leave seventy-five cents for clothes and washing."

"It isn't much," Sam admitted.

"I should think not."

"I don't see how I am going to get any clothes."

"You certainly can't if you go to the theater."

"I used to go sometimes when I was a newsboy, and I didn't earn so much money then."

"Probably you didn't have a regular room then." [25/26]

"No, I didn't; and sometimes I only had one meal a day."

"That isn't a very nice way to live. You're so old now you ought to be considering what you'll do when you are a man."

"I mean to earn more than five dollars a week then."

"So do I; but if I were a street boy, picking up my living by blacking boots or selling papers, I shouldn't expect to. Now we have a chance to learn business, and improve."

From Horatio Alger, Jr., *Sam's Chance* (Racine, Wisconsin: Whitman Publishing Co., n.d.), pp. 25–31. Originally published 1876 as *Sam's Chance; or, How He Improved It*.

74

"Were you ever a street boy?" asked Sam, becoming interested in his companion's history.

"No, that is, not over a month. I was born in the country."

"So was I," said Sam.

"My father and mother both died, leaving nothing, and the people wanted to send me to the poorhouse; but I didn't like that, so I borrowed five dollars and came to New York. When I got here I began to think I should have to go back again. I tried to get a place and couldn't. Finally, I bought some papers and earned a little money selling them. It was better than nothing; but all the while I was hoping to get a place. One day, as I was passing the store where I am now, I saw some boys round the door. I asked them what was going on. They told me that Hamilton & Co. had advertised for an errand boy, and they were going to try for the place. I thought I might as well try, too, so I went in and applied. I don't know how it was, but out of about forty boys they took me."

"Did they give you five dollars a week right off?" [26/27]

"No; I only got three dollars the first year," answered Henry.

"You couldn't live on that, could you?"

"I had to."

"You didn't have the room you have now, did you?"

"I couldn't afford it. I lived at the 'Newsboys Lodge,' and took my breakfasts and suppers there. That cost me eighteen cents a day, or about a dollar and a quarter a week. Out of the rest I bought my dinners and clothes. So I got along till the second year, when my wages were raised to four dollars. At the beginning of the third year I got a dollar more."

"I suppose you'll get six dollars next year?"

"I hope so. Mr. Hamilton has promised to put me in the counting room then."

"It seems a long time to wait," said Sam.

"Yes, if you look ahead; but, after all, time goes fast. Next year I expect to lay up some money."

"Do you think you can?"

"I know I can, if I am well. I've got some money in the savings bank now."

"You have!" exclaimed Sam, pricking up his ears.

"Yes."

"How much?"

"Thirty dollars."

"Thirty dollars!" ejaculated Sam. "I'd feel rich if I was worth thirty dollars."

Henry smiled.

"I don't feel rich, but I am glad I've got it."

"You ain't saving up money now, are you?"

"I mean to, now that I pay fifty cents a week [27/28] less rent on account of your coming in with me. I am going to save all that."

"How can you?"

"I shall get along on two dollars and a half for meals. I always have, and I can do it now. You can do it, too, if you want to."

"I should starve to death," said Sam. "I've got a healthy appetite, and my stomach don't feel right if I don't eat enough."

"I don't like to stint myself any more than you, but if I am ever to be worth anything I must begin to save when I am a boy."

"Do you ever smoke?" asked Sam.

"Never, and I wouldn't if it didn't cost anything."

"Why not? It's jolly."

"It isn't good for a boy that is growing, and I don't believe it does men any good. Do you smoke?"

"When I get a chance," said Sam. "It warms a fellow up in cold weather."

"Well, it isn't cold weather now, and you'll find plenty of other ways to spend your money."

"I can't help it. If I don't go to the theater, I must have a cigar."

Sam stopped at a cigar store, and bought a cheap article for three cents, which he lighted and smoked with apparent enjoyment.

The conversation which has been reported will give a clew to the different characters of the two boys, who, after less than a day's acquaintance, have become roommates. Henry Martin was about Sam's age, but much more thoughtful and sedate. He had begun to think of the future, and to provide for it. This is always an encouraging sign, and an augury of [28/29] success. Sam had not got so far yet. He had been in the habit of living from day to day without much thought of the morrow. Whether he would be favorably affected by Henry's example remains to be seen.

After a walk of an hour or more the boys went back to their room.

"Are you going to bed, Henry?" asked Sam.

"Not yet."

"What are you going to do?"

"Study a little."

"Study!" exclaimed Sam, in astonishment. "Who's goin' to hear your lessons?"

"Perhaps you will," said Henry, with a smile.

"I! Why, I'm a regular know-nothing! What are you going to study?"

"To begin with, I'm going to do some sums."

Henry drew from under the bed a tattered arithmetic and a slate and pencil. He opened the arithmetic at interest, and proceeded to set down a problem on the slate.

"Have you got away over there?" asked Sam.

"Yes; I've been at work ever since last October. I don't get on very fast, because I have only my evenings."

"What do you do when you come to a tough customer?"

"I try again. There are some sums I have tried a half a dozen times."

"You must have a lot of patience," said Sam.

"I don't know about that. I always feel paid when I get the right answer at last."

"It must be dull work studyin' every night. I couldn't do it. It would make my head ache."

"Your head is tougher than you think for," said Henry. [29/30]

"Just let me see what sum you are tryin'."

His roommate handed him the books, and he read the following example:

"John Smith borrowed $546.75 at 7 per cent and repaid it at the end of two years, five months and six days. What amount was he required to pay?"

"Can you do that?" asked Sam.

"I think so; it isn't very hard."

"I never could do it; it's too hard."

"Oh, yes, you could, if you had gone over the earlier part of the arithmetic."

"What's the use of it, anyway?"

"Don't you see it's business? If you are going to be a business man, you may need to understand interest. I shouldn't expect to be promoted if I didn't know something about arithmetic. I am only an errand boy, now, and don't need it."

"I wish I knew as much as you. What else do you study?"

"I practice writing every evening. Here is my writing book."

Henry drew out, from under the bed, a writing book, which was more than half written through. He had evidently taken great pains to imitate the copy, and with fair success.

Sam was quite impressed.

"You can write as well as the teacher I went to up in the country," he said.

"You can write, can't you, Sam?"

"Not much. I haven't tried lately."

"Everybody ought to know how to read, and write a decent hand."

"I s'pose so," said Sam; "but there's a lot of work in it." [30/31]

He got into bed, and while he was watching Henry doing sums, he fell asleep. His roommate devoted an hour to arithmetic, and wrote a page in his copybook. Then he, too, undressed, and went to bed. [31]

The Road to Business Success: A Talk to Young Men

ANDREW CARNEGIE

IT IS WELL THAT YOUNG MEN SHOULD BEGIN AT THE BEGINNING AND occupy the most subordinate positions. Many of the leading business men of Pittsburg had a serious responsibility thrust upon them at the very threshold of their career. They were introduced to the broom, and spent the first hours of their business lives sweeping out the office. I notice we have janitors and janitresses now in offices, and our young men unfortunately miss that salutary branch of a business education. But if by chance the professional sweeper is absent any morning the boy who has the genius of the future partner in him will not hesitate to try his hand at the broom. The other day a fond fashionable mother in Michigan asked a young man whether he had ever seen a young lady sweep in a room so grandly as her Priscilla. He said no, he never had, and the mother was gratified beyond measure, but then said he, after a pause, "What I should like to see her do is sweep out a room." It does not hurt the newest comer to sweep [3/4] out the office if necessary. I was one of those sweepers myself, and who do you suppose were my fellow sweepers? David McCargo, now superintendent of the Alleghany Valley Railroad; Robert Pitcairn, Superintendent of the Pennsylvania Railroad, and Mr. Moreland, City Attorney. We all took turns, two each morning did the sweeping; and now I remember Davie was so proud of his clean white shirt bosom that he used to spread over it an old silk bandana handkerchief which he kept for the purpose, and we other boys thought he was putting on airs. So he was. None of us had a silk handkerchief.

Assuming that you have all obtained employment and are fairly started, my advice to you is, "aim high." I would not give a fig for the young man who does not already see himself the partner or the head of an important firm. Do not rest content for a moment in your thoughts

Andrew Carnegie, "The Road to Business Success: A Talk to Young Men," in *The Empire of Business* (New York: Doubleday, Page & Company, 1913), pp. 3–19. Originally delivered as an address in 1885.

as head clerk, or foreman, or general manager in any concern, no matter how extensive. Say each to yourself: "My place is at the top." *Be king in your dreams.* Make your vow that you will reach that position, with untarnished reputation, and make no other vow to distract your attention, except the very commendable one that when you are a member of the firm or before that, if you have been promoted two or three [4/5] times, you will form another partnership with the loveliest of her sex—a partnership to which our new partnership act has no application. The liability there is never limited.

Let me indicate two or three conditions essential to success. Do not be afraid that I am going to moralize, or inflict a homily upon you. I speak upon the subject only from the view of a man of the world desirous of aiding you to become successful business men. You all know that there is no genuine, praiseworthy success in life if you are not honest, truthful, fair-dealing. I assume you are and will remain all these, and also that you are determined to live pure, respectable lives, free from pernicious or equivocal associations with one sex or the other. There is no creditable future for you else. Otherwise your learning and your advantages not only go for naught, but serve to accentuate your failure and your disgrace. I hope you will not take it amiss if I warn you against three of the gravest dangers which will beset you in your upward path.

The first and most seductive, and the destroyer of most young men, is the drinking of liquor. I am no temperance lecturer in disguise, but a man who knows and tells you what observation has proved to him; and I say to you that you are more likely to fail in your career from acquiring the habit of drinking [5/6] liquor than from any, or all, the other temptations likely to assail you. You may yield to almost any other temptation and reform—may brace up, and if not recover lost ground, at least remain in the race, and secure and maintain a respectable position. But from the insane thirst for liquor escape is almost impossible. I have known but few exceptions to this rule. First, then, you must not drink liquor to excess. Better if you do not touch it at all—much better; but if this be too hard a rule for you, then take your stand firmly here: Resolve never to touch it except at meals. A glass at dinner will not hinder your advance in life or lower your tone; but I implore you hold it inconsistent with the dignity and self-respect of gentlemen, with what is due from yourselves to yourselves, being the men you are, and especially the men you are determined to become, to drink a glass of liquor at a bar. Be far too much of the gentleman ever to enter a bar-room. You do not pursue your careers in safety unless you stand firmly upon this ground. Adhere to it and you have escaped danger from the deadliest of your foes.

The next greatest danger to a young business man in this community I believe to be that of speculation. When I was a telegraph operator here we had no Exchanges in the city, but the men or firms who [6/7] speculated upon the Eastern Exchanges were necessarily known to the operators. They could be counted on the fingers of one hand. These men were not our citizens of first repute: they were regarded with suspicion. I have lived to see all of these speculators irreparably ruined men, bankrupt in money and bankrupt in character. There is scarcely an instance of a man who has made a fortune by speculation and kept it. Gamesters die poor, and there is certainly not an instance of a speculator who has lived a life creditable to himself, or advantageous to the community. The man who grasps the morning paper to see first how his speculative ventures upon the Exchanges are likely to result, unfits himself for the calm consideration and proper solution of business problems with which he has to deal later in the day, and saps the sources of that persistent and concentrated energy upon which depend the permanent success, and often the very safety, of his main business.

The speculator and the business man tread diverging lines. The former depends upon the sudden turn of fortune's wheel; he is a millionaire to-day, a bankrupt to-morrow. But the man of business knows that only by years of patient, unremitting attention to affairs can he earn his reward, which is the result, not of chance, but of well-devised means [7/8] for the attainment of ends. During all these years his is the cheering thought that by no possibility can he benefit himself without carrying prosperity to others. The speculator on the other hand had better never have lived so far as the good of others or the good of the community is concerned. Hundreds of young men were tempted in this city not long since to gamble in oil, and many were ruined; all were injured whether they lost or won. You may be, nay, you are certain to be similarly tempted; but when so tempted I hope you will remember this advice. Say to the tempter who asks you to risk your small savings, that if ever you decide to speculate you are determined to go to a regular and well-conducted house where they cheat fair. You can get fair play and about an equal chance upon the red and black in such a place; upon the Exchange you have neither. You might as well try your luck with the three-card-monte man. There is another point involved in speculation. Nothing is more essential to young business men than untarnished credit, credit begotten of confidence in their prudence, principles, and stability of character. Well, believe me, nothing kills credit sooner in any Bank Board than the knowledge that either firms or men engage in speculation. It matters not a whit whether gains or losses be the temporary result of [8/9] these operations. The moment a man is known to speculate, his credit is impaired, and soon thereafter it is gone. How can a man be credited whose resources may be swept away in one hour by a panic among gamesters? Who can tell how he stands among them? except that this is certain: he has given due notice that he may stand to lose all, so that those who credit him have themselves to blame. Resolve to be business men, but speculators, never.

The third and last danger against which I shall warn you is one which has wrecked many a fair craft which started well and gave promise of a properous voyage. It is the perilous habit of indorsing—all the more dangerous, inasmuch as it assails one generally in the garb of friendship. It appeals to your generous instincts, and you say, "How can I refuse to lend my name only, to assist a friend?" It is because there is so much that is true and commendable in that view that the practice is so dangerous. Let me endeavour to put you upon safe, honourable grounds in regard to it. I would say to you to make it a rule now, *never indorse;* but this is too much like never taste wine, or never smoke, or any other of the "nevers." They generally result in exceptions. You will as business men now and then probably become security for friends. Now, here is the line at which [9/10] regard for the success of friends should cease and regard for your own honour begin.

If you owe anything, all your capital and all your effects are a solemn trust in your hands to be held inviolate for the security of those who have trusted you. Nothing can be done by you with honour which jeopardizes these first claims upon you. When a man in debt indorses for another, it is not his own credit or his own capital he risks, it is that of his own creditors. He violates a trust. Mark you, then, never indorse until you have cash means not required for your own debts, and never indorse beyond those means.

Before you indorse at all, consider indorsements as gifts, and ask yourselves whether you wish to make the gift to your friend and whether the money is really yours to give and not a trust for your creditors.

You are not safe, gentlemen, unless you stand firmly upon this as the only ground which an honest business man can occupy.

I beseech you, avoid liquor, speculation, and indorsement. Do not fail in either, for liquor and speculation are the Scylla and Charybdis of the young man's business sea, and indorsement his rock ahead.

Assuming you are safe in regard to these your gravest dangers, the question now is how to rise from [10/11] the subordinate position we have imagined you in, through the successive grades to the position for which you are, in my opinion, and, I trust, in your own, evidently intended. I can give you the secret. It lies mainly in this: Instead of the question "What must I do for my employer?" substitute "What can I do?" Faithful and conscientious discharge of the duties assigned you is all very well, but the verdict in such cases generally is that you perform your present duties so well that you had better continue performing them. Now, young gentlemen, this will not do. It will not do for the coming partners. There must be something beyond this. We make Clerks, Bookkeepers, Treasurers, Bank Tellers of this class, and there they remain to the end of the chapter. The rising man must do something exceptional, and beyond the range of his special department. HE MUST ATTRACT ATTENTION. A shipping clerk, he may do so by discovering in an invoice an error with which he has nothing to do, and

which has escaped the attention of the proper party. If a weighing
clerk, he may save for the firm by doubting the adjustment of the
scales and having them corrected, even if this be the province of the
master mechanic. If a messenger boy, even he can lay the seed of
promotion by going beyond the letter of his instructions in order to
secure [11/12] the desired reply. There is no service so low and simple,
neither any so high, in which the young man of ability and willing
disposition cannot readily and almost daily prove himself capable of
greater trust and usefulness, and, what is equally important, show his
invincible determination to rise. Some day, in your own department,
you will be directed to do or say something which you know will prove
disadvantageous to the interest of the firm. Here is your chance. Stand
up like a man and say so. Say it boldly, and give your reasons, and thus
prove to your employer that, while his thoughts have been engaged
upon other matters, you have been studying during hours when
perhaps he thought you asleep, how to advance his interests. You may
be right or you may be wrong, but in either case you have gained the
first condition of success. You have attracted attention. Your employer
has found that he has not a mere hireling in his service, but a man; not
one who is content to give so many hours of work for so many dollars
in return, but one who devotes his spare hours and constant thoughts
to the business. Such an employee must perforce be thought of, and
thought of kindly and well. It will not be long before his advice is
asked in his special branch, and if the advice given be sound, it will
soon be asked and taken upon questions of broader bearing. This
[12/13] means partnership; if not with present employers, then with
others. Your foot, in such a case, is upon the ladder; the amount of
climbing done depends entirely upon yourself.

One false axiom you will often hear, which I wish to guard you
against: "Obey orders if you break owners." Don't you do it. This is no
rule for you to follow. Always break orders to save owners. There
never was a great character who did not sometimes smash the routine
regulations and make new ones for himself. The rule is only suitable
for such as have no aspirations, and you have not forgotten that you
are destined to be owners and to make orders and break orders. Do not
hesitate to do it whenever you are sure the interests of your employer
will be thereby promoted and when you are so sure of the result that
you are willing to take the responsibility. You will never be a partner
unless you know the business of your department far better than the
owners possibly can. When called to account for your independent
action, show him the result of your genius, and tell him that you knew
that it would be so; show him how mistaken the orders were. Boss your
boss just as soon as you can; try it on early. There is nothing he will
like so well if he is the right kind of boss; if he is not, he is not the man
for you to remain with—leave him whenever [13/14] you can, even at
a present sacrifice, and find one capable of discerning genius. Our

young partners in the Carnegie firm have won their spurs by showing that we did not know half as well what was wanted as they did. Some of them have acted upon occasion with me as if they owned the firm and I was but some airy New Yorker presuming to advise upon what I knew very little about. Well, they are not interfered with much now. They were the true bosses—the very men we were looking for.

There is one sure mark of the coming partner, the future millionaire: his revenues always exceed his expenditures. He begins to save early, almost as soon as he begins to earn. No matter how little it may be possible to save, save that little. Invest it securely, not necessarily in bonds, but in anything which you have good reason to believe will be profitable, but no gambling with it, remember. A rare chance will soon present itself for investment. The little you have saved will prove the basis for an amount of credit utterly surprising to you. Capitalists trust the saving young man. For every hundred dollars you can produce as the result of hard-won savings, Midas, in search of a partner, will lend or credit a thousand; for every thousand, fifty thousand. It is not capital that your seniors require, it is the man who has proved that he has the business habits [14/15] which create capital, and to create it in the best of all possible ways, as far as self-discipline is concerned, is by adjusting his habits to his means. Gentlemen, it is the first hundred dollars saved which tells. Begin at once to lay up something. The bee predominates in the future millionaire.

Of course there are better, higher aims than saving. As an end, the acquisition of wealth is ignoble in the extreme; I assume that you save and long for wealth only as a means of enabling you the better to do some good in your day and generation. Make a note of this essential rule: Expenditure always within income.

You may grow impatient, or become discouraged when year by year you float on in subordinate positions. There is no doubt that it is becoming harder and harder as business gravitates more and more to immense concerns, for a young man without capital to get a start for himself, and in this city especially, where large capital is essential, it is unusually difficult. Still, let me tell you for your encouragement, that there is no country in the world where able and energetic young men can so readily rise as this, nor any city where there is more room at the top. It has been impossible to meet the demand for capable, first-class bookkeepers (mark the adjectives); the supply has *never* been equal to the demand. Young men give all kinds of reasons why in their cases [15/16] failure was clearly attributable to exceptional circumstances which render success impossible. Some never had a chance, according to their own story. This is simply nonsense. No young man ever lived who had not a chance, and a splendid chance, too, if he ever was employed at all. He is assayed in the mind of his immediate superior, from the day he begins work, and, after a time, if he has merit, he is assayed in the council chamber of the firm. His ability, honesty, habits, associations, temper, disposition, all these are weighed and analyzed. The young man who never had a chance is the same young man who has been canvassed over and over again by his superiors, and found destitute of necessary qualifications, or is deemed unworthy of closer relations with the firm, owing to some objectionable act, habit, or association, of which he thought his employers ignorant.

Another class of young men attribute their failure to employers having relations or favourites whom they advance unfairly. They also insist that their employers dislike brighter intelligences than their own, and are disposed to discourage aspiring genius, and delight in keeping young men down. There is nothing in this. On the contrary, there is no one suffering so much for lack of the right man in the right place, nor so anxious to find him, as the owner. There is not a firm in Pittsburg today which is not [16/17] in the constant search for business ability, and every one of them will tell you that there is no article in the market at all times so scarce. There is always a boom in brains; cultivate that crop, for if you grow any amount of that commodity, here is your best market and you cannot overstock it, and the more brains you have to sell, the higher price you can exact. They are not quite so sure a crop as wild oats, which never fail to produce a bountiful harvest, but they have the advantage over these in always finding a market. Do not hesitate to engage in any legitimate business, for there is no business in America, I do not care what, which will not yield a fair profit if it receive the unremitting, exclusive attention and all the capital of capable and industrious men. Every business will have its season of depression—years always come during which the manufacturers and merchants of the city are severely tried—years when mills must be run, not for profit, but at a loss, that the organization and men may be kept together and employed, and the concern may keep its products in the market. But on the other hand, every legitimate business producing or dealing in an article which man requires is bound in time to be fairly profitable, if properly conducted.

And here is the prime condition of success, the great secret: concentrate your energy, thought, and [17/18] capital exclusively upon the business in which you are engaged. Having begun in one line, resolve to fight it out on that line, to lead in it; adopt every improvement, have the best machinery, and know the most about it.

The concerns which fail are those which have scattered their capital, which means that they have scattered their brains also. They have investments in this, or that, or the other, here, there, and everywhere. "Don't put all your eggs in one basket" is all wrong. I tell you "put all your eggs in one basket, and then watch that basket." Look round you and take notice; men who do that do not often fail. It is easy to watch and carry the one basket. It is trying to carry too many baskets that breaks most eggs in this country. He who carries three baskets must put one on his head, which is apt to tumble and trip him up. One fault of the American business man is lack of concentration.

To summarize what I have said: Aim for the highest; never enter a barroom; do not touch liquor, or if at all only at meals; never speculate; never indorse beyond your surplus cash fund; make the firm's interest yours; break orders always to save owners; concentrate; put all your eggs in one basket and watch that basket; expenditure always within revenue; lastly, be not impatient, for, as Emerson [18/19] says, "No one can cheat you out of ultimate success but yourselves."

I congratulate poor young men upon being born to that ancient and honourable degree which renders it necessary that they should devote themselves to hard work. A basketful of bonds is the heaviest basket a young man ever had to carry. He generally gets to staggering under it. We have in this city creditable instances of such young men, who have pressed to the front rank of our best and most useful citizens. These deserve great credit. But the vast majority of the sons of rich men are unable to resist the temptations to which wealth subjects them, and sink to unworthy lives. I would almost as soon leave a young man a curse as burden him with the almighty dollar. It is not from this class you have rivalry to fear. The partners' sons will not trouble you much, but look out that some boys poorer, much poorer than yourselves, whose parents cannot afford to give them the advantages of a course in this institute, advantages which should give you a decided lead in the race—look out that such boys do not challenge you at the post and pass you at the grand-stand. Look out for the boy who has to plunge into work direct from the common school and who begins by sweeping out the office. He is the probable dark horse that you had better watch. [19]

Gatsby's General Resolves

F. SCOTT FITZGERALD

IN A MOMENT MEYER WOLFSHIEM STOOD [171/172] SOLEMNLY IN THE doorway, holding out both hands. He drew me into his office, remarking in a reverent voice that it was a sad time for all of us, and offered me a cigar.

"My memory goes back to when first I met him," he said. "A

Reprinted with the permission of Charles Scribner's Sons from *The Great Gatsby*, pp. 171–176, by F. Scott Fitzgerald. Copyright 1925 Charles Scribner's Sons; renewal copyright 1953 Frances Scott Fitzgerald Lanahan.

young major just out of the army and covered over with medals he got
in the war. He was so hard up he had to keep on wearing his uniform
because he couldn't buy some regular clothes. First time I saw him was
when he came into Winebrenner's poolroom at Forty-third Street and
asked for a job. He hadn't eat anything for a couple of days. 'Come on
have some lunch with me,' I said. He ate more than four dollars' worth
of food in half an hour."

"Did you start him in business?" I inquired.

"Start him! I made him."

"Oh."

"I raised him up out of nothing, right out of the gutter. I saw right
away he was a fine-appearing, gentlemanly young man, and when he
told me he was an Oggsford I knew I could use him good. I got him to
join up in the American Legion and he used to stand high there. Right
off he did some work for a client of mine up to Albany. We were so
thick like that in everything"—he held up two bulbous fingers—"always together."

I wondered if this partnership had included the World's Series
transaction in 1919.

"Now he's dead," I said after a moment. "You were his closest
friend, so I know you'll want to come to his funeral this afternoon."

"I'd like to come."

"Well, come then." [172/173]

The hair in his nostrils quivered slightly, and as he shook his head
his eyes filled with tears.

"I can't do it—I can't get mixed up in it," he said.

"There's nothing to get mixed up in. It's all over now."

"When a man gets killed I never like to get mixed up in it in any
way. I keep out. When I was a young man it was different—if a friend
of mine died, no matter how, I stuck with them to the end. You may
think that's sentimental, but I mean it—to the bitter end."

I saw that for some reason of his own he was determined not to
come, so I stood up.

"Are you a college man?" he inquired suddenly.

For a moment I thought he was going to suggest a "gonnegtion,"
but he only nodded and shook my hand.

"Let us learn to show our friendship for a man when he is alive
and not after he is dead," he suggested. "After that my own rule is to
let everything alone."

When I left his office the sky had turned dark and I got back to
West Egg in a drizzle. After changing my clothes I went next door and
found Mr. Gatz walking up and down excitedly in the hall. His pride in
his son and in his son's possessions was continually increasing and now
he had something to show me.

"Jimmy sent me this picture." He took out his wallet with trembling fingers. "Look there."

It was a photograph of the house, cracked in the corners and dirty with many hands. He pointed out every detail to me eagerly. "Look there!" and then sought admiration from my eyes. He had shown it so often that I think it was more real to him now than the house itself. [173/174]

"Jimmy sent it to me. I think it's a very pretty picture. It shows up well."

"Very well. Had you seen him lately?"

"He came out to see me two years ago and bought me the house I live in now. Of course we was broke up when he run off from home, but I see now there was a reason for it. He knew he had a big future in front of him. And ever since he made a success he was very generous with me."

He seemed reluctant to put away the picture, held it for another minute, lingeringly, before my eyes. Then he returned the wallet and pulled from his pocket a ragged old copy of a book called *Hopalong Cassidy*.

"Look here, this is a book he had when he was a boy. It just shows you."

He opened it at the back cover and turned it around for me to see. On the last fly-leaf was printed the word SCHEDULE, and the date September 12, 1906. And underneath:

Rise from bed	6.00	A.M.
Dumbbell exercise and wall-scaling	6.15–6.30	"
Study electricity, etc.	7.15–8.15	"
Work	8.30–4.30	P.M.
Baseball and sports	4.30–5.00	"
Practice elocution, poise and how to attain it	5.00–6.00	"
Study needed inventions	7.00–9.00	"

GENERAL RESOLVES

No wasting time at Shafters or [a name, indecipherable]
No more smoking or chewing.
Bath every other day
Read one improving book or magazine per week
Save $5.00 [crossed out] $3.00 per week
Be better to parents [174/175]

"I come across this book by accident," said the old man. "It just shows you, don't it?

"Jimmy was bound to get ahead. He always had some resolves like this or something. Do you notice what he's got about improving his mind? He was always great for that. He told me I et like a hog once, and I beat him for it."

He was reluctant to close the book, reading each item aloud and then looking eagerly at me. I think he rather expected me to copy down the list for my own use.

A little before three the Lutheran minister arrived from Flushing, and I began to look involuntarily out the windows for other cars. So did Gatsby's father. And as the time passed and the servants came in and stood waiting in the hall, his eyes began to blink anxiously, and he spoke of the rain in a worried, uncertain way. The minister glanced several times at his watch, so I took him aside and asked him to wait for half an hour. But it wasn't any use. Nobody came.

About five o'clock our procession of three cars reached the cemetery and stopped in a thick drizzle beside the gate—first a motor hearse, horribly black and wet, then Mr. Gatz and the minister and I in the limousine, and a little later four or five servants and the postman from West Egg, in Gatsby's station wagon, all wet to the skin. As we started through the gate into the cemetery I heard a car stop and then the sound of some one splashing after us over the soggy ground. I looked around. It was the man with owl-eyed glasses whom I had found marvelling over Gatsby's books in the library one night three months before.

I'd never seen him since then. I don't know how he [175/176] knew about the funeral, or even his name. The rain poured down his thick glasses, and he took them off and wiped them to see the protecting canvas unrolled from Gatsby's grave.

I tried to think about Gatsby then for a moment, but he was already too far away, and I could only remember, without resentment, that Daisy hadn't sent a message or a flower. Dimly I heard some one murmur "Blessed are the dead that the rain falls on," and then the owl-eyed man said "Amen to that," in a brave voice.

We straggled down quickly through the rain to the cars. Owl-eyes spoke to me by the gate.

"I couldn't get to the house," he remarked.

"Neither could anybody else."

"Go on!" He started. "Why, my God! they used to go there by the hundreds."

He took off his glasses and wiped them again, outside and in.

"The poor son-of-a-bitch," he said. [176]

Positive Thinking

NORMAN VINCENT PEALE

BELIEVE IN YOURSELF! HAVE FAITH IN YOUR ABILITIES! WITHOUT A HUMBLE but reasonable confidence in your own powers you cannot be successful or happy. But with sound self-confidence you can succeed. A sense of inferiority and inadequacy interferes with the attainment of your hopes, but self-confidence leads to self-realization and successful achievement. Because of the importance of this mental attitude, this book will help you believe in yourself and release your inner powers.

It is appalling to realize the number of pathetic people who are hampered and made miserable by the malady popularly called the inferiority complex. But you need not suffer from this trouble. When proper steps are taken, it can be overcome. You can develop creative faith in yourself—faith that is justified.

After speaking to a convention of businessmen in a city auditorium, I was on the stage greeting people when a man approached me and with a peculiar intensity of manner asked, "May I talk with you about a matter of desperate importance to me?"

I asked him to remain until the others had gone, then we went backstage and sat down.

"I'm in this town to handle the most important business [1/2] deal of my life," he explained. "If I succeed, it means everything to me. If I fail, I'm done for."

I suggested that he relax a little, that nothing was quite that final. If he succeeded, that was fine. If he didn't, well, tomorrow was another day.

"I have a terrible disbelief in myself," he said dejectedly. "I have no confidence. I just don't believe I can put it over. I am very discouraged and depressed. In fact," he lamented, "I'm just about sunk. Here I am, forty years old. Why is it that all my life I have been tormented by inferiority feelings, by lack of confidence, by self-doubt? I listened to your speech tonight in which you talked about the power

From the book *The Power of Positive Thinking* by Norman Vincent Peale. © 1952 by Prentice-Hall, Inc., Englewood Cliffs, New Jersey.

of positive thinking, and I want to ask how I can get some faith in myself."

"There are two steps to take," I replied. "First, it is important to discover why you have these feelings of no power. That requires analysis and will take time. We must approach the maladies of our emotional life as a physician probes to find something wrong physically. This cannot be done immediately, certainly not in our brief interview tonight, and it may require treatment to reach a permanent solution. But to pull you through this immediate problem I shall give you a formula which will work if you use it.

"As you walk down the street tonight I suggest that you repeat certain words which I shall give you. Say them over several times after you get into bed. When you awaken tomorrow, repeat them three times before arising. On the way to your important appointment say them three additional times. Do this with an attitude of faith and you will receive sufficient strength and ability to deal with this problem. Later, if you wish, we can go into an analysis of your basic problem, but whatever we come up with following that study, the formula which I am now going to give you can be a large factor in the eventual cure." [2/3]

Following is the affirmation which I gave him—"I can do all things through Christ which strengtheneth me." (Philippians 4:13) He was unfamiliar with these words so I wrote them on a card and had him read them over three times aloud.

"Now, follow that prescription, and I am sure things will come out all right."

He pulled himself up, stood quietly for a moment, then said with considerable feeling, "O.K., Doctor. O.K."

I watched him square his shoulders and walk out into the night. He seemed a pathetic figure, and yet the way he carried himself as he disappeared showed that faith was already at work in his mind.

Subsequently he reported that this simple formula "did wonders" for him and added, "It seems incredible that a few words from the Bible could do so much for a person."

This man later had a study made of the reasons for his inferiority attitudes. They were cleared away by scientific counseling and by the application of religious faith. He was taught how to have faith; was given certain specific instructions to follow (these are given later in this chapter). Gradually he attained a strong, steady, reasonable confidence. He never ceases to express amazement at the way in which things now flow toward rather than away from him. His personality has taken on a positive, not negative, character so that he no longer repels success, but, on the contrary, draws it to him. He now has an authentic confidence in his own powers.... [3/10]

Lack of self-confidence apparently is one of the great problems besetting people today. In a university a survey was made of six hundred students in psychology courses. The students were asked to state their most difficult personal problem. Seventy-five per cent listed lack of confidence. It can safely be assumed that the same large proportion is true of the population generally. Everywhere you encounter people who are inwardly afraid, who shrink from life, who suffer from a deep sense of inadequacy and insecurity, who doubt their own powers. Deep within themselves they mistrust their ability to meet responsibilities or to grasp opportunities. Always they are beset by the vague and sinister fear that something is not going to be quite right. They do not believe that they have it in them to be what they want to be, and so they try to make themselves content with something less than that of which they are capable. Thousands upon thousands go crawling through life on their hands and knees, defeated and afraid. And in most cases such frustration of power is unnecessary.

The blows of life, the accumulation of difficulties, the multiplication of problems tend to sap energy and leave [10/11] you spent and discouraged. In such a condition the true status of your power is often obscured, and a person yields to a discouragement that is not justified by the facts. It is virtally essential to re-appraise your personality assets. When done in an attitude of reasonableness, this evaluation will convince you that you are less defeated than you think you are.

For example, a man fifty-two years of age consulted me. He was in great despondency. He revealed utter despair. He said he "was all through." He informed me that everything he had built up over his lifetime had been swept away.

"Everything?" I asked.

"Everything," he repeated. He was through, he reiterated. "I have nothing left at all. Everything is gone. There is no hope, and I am too old to start all over again. I have lost all faith."

Naturally I felt sympathetic toward him, but it was evident that his chief trouble was the fact that dark shadows of hopelessness had entered his mind and discolored his outlook, distorting it. Behind this twisted thinking his true powers had retreated, leaving him without force.

"So," I said, "suppose we take a piece of paper and write down the values you have left."

"There's no use," he sighed. "I haven't a single thing left. I thought I told you that."

I said, "Let's just see anyway." Then asked, "Is your wife still with you?"

"Why, yes, of course, and she is wonderful. We have been married for thirty years. She would never leave me no matter how bad things are."

"All right, let us put that down—your wife is still with you and she will never leave you no matter what happens. How about your children? Got any children?"

"Yes," he replied, "I have three and they are certainly [11/12] wonderful. I have been touched by the way they have come to me and said, 'Dad, we love you, and we'll stand by you.'"

"Well, then," I said, "That is number two—three children who love you and who will stand by you. Got any friends?" I asked.

"Yes," he said, "I really have some fine friends. I must admit they have been pretty decent. They have come around and said they would like to help me, but what can they do? They can't do anything."

"That is number three—you have some friends who would like to help you and who hold you in esteem. How about your integrity? Have you done anything wrong?"

"My integrity is all right," he replied. "I have always tried to do the right thing and my conscience is clear."

"All right," I said, "We will put that down as number four—integrity. How about your health?"

"My health is all right," he answered. "I have had very few sick days and I guess I am in pretty good shape physically."

"So let's put down as number five—good physical health. How about the United States? Do you think it's still doing business and is the land of opportunity?"

"Yes," he said. "It is the only country in the world I would want to live in."

"That is number six—you live in the United States, land of opportunity, and you are glad to be here." Then I asked, "How about your religious faith? Do you believe in God and that God will help you?"

"Yes," he said. "I do not think I could have gotten through this at all if I hadn't had some help from God."

"Now," I said, "let's list the assets we have figured out:

"1. A wonderful wife—married for thirty years.

"2. Three devoted children who will stand by you.

"3. Friends who will help you and who hold you in esteem. [12/13]

"4. Integrity—nothing to be ashamed of.

"5. Good physical health.

"6. Live in the United States, the greatest country in the world.

"7. Have religious faith."

I shoved it across the table at him. "Take a look at that. I guess you have quite a total of assets. I thought you told me everything had been swept away."

He grinned ashamedly. "I guess I didn't think of those things. I never thought of it that way. Perhaps things aren't so bad at that," he said pensively. "Maybe I can start all over again if I can just get some confidence, if I can get the feel of some power within me."

Well, he got it, and he did start all over again. But he did so only when he changed his viewpoint, his mental attitude. Faith swept away his doubts, and more than enough power to overcome all his difficulties emerged from within him.

This incident illustrates a profound truth which is expressed in a very important statement made by the famous psychiatrist, Dr. Karl Menninger. He said, "Attitudes are more important than facts." That is worth repeating until its truth grips you. Any fact facing us, however difficult, even seemingly hopeless, is not so important as our attitude toward that fact. How you think about a fact may defeat you before you ever do anything about it. You may permit a fact to overwhelm you mentally before you start to deal with it actually. On the other hand, a confident and optimistic thought pattern can modify or overcome the fact altogether.... [13/15]

Emerson declared a tremndous truth, "They conquer who believe they can." And he added, "Do the thing you fear and the death of fear is certain." Practice confidence and faith and your fears and insecurities will soon have no power over you.... [15/16]

To sum up—what can you do *now* to build up your self-confidence? Following are ten simple, workable rules for overcoming inadequacy attitudes and learning to practice faith. Thousands have used these rules, reporting successful results. Undertake this program and you, too, will build up confidence in your powers. You, too, will have a new feeling of power.

1. Formulate and stamp indelibly on your mind a mental picture of yourself as succeeding. Hold this picture tenaciously. Never permit it to fade. Your mind will seek to develop this picture. Never think of yourself as failing; never doubt the reality of the mental image. That is most dangerous, for the mind always tries to complete what it pictures. So *always* picture "success" no matter how badly things seem to be going at the moment.

2. Whenever a negative thought concerning your personal powers comes to mind, deliberately voice a positive thought to cancel it out.

3. Do not build up obstacles in your imagination. Depreciate every so-called obstacle. Minimize them. Difficulties must be studied and efficiently dealt with to be eliminated, but they must be seen for only what they are. They must not be inflated by fear thoughts.

4. Do not be awestruck by other people and try to copy them. Nobody can be you as efficiently as YOU can. Remember also that most people, despite their confident appearance and demeanor, are often as scared as you are and as doubtful of themselves.

5. Ten times a day repeat these dynamic words, "If God be *for* us, who can be *against* us?" (Romans 8:31) [16/17] (Stop reading and repeat them NOW slowly and confidently.)

6. Get a competent counselor to help you understand why you do what you do. Learn the origin of your inferiority and self-doubt feelings which often begin in childhood. Self-knowledge leads to a cure.

7. Ten times each day practice the following affirmation, repeat-

ing it out loud if possible. "I can do all things through Christ which strengtheneth me." (Philippians 4:13) Repeat those words NOW. That magic statement is the most powerful antidote on earth to inferiority thoughts.

8. Make a true estimate of your own ability, then raise it 10 per cent. Do not become egotistical, but develop a wholesome self-respect. Believe in your own God-released powers.

9. Put yourself in God's hands. To do that simply state, "I am in God's hands." Then believe you are NOW receiving all the power you need. "Feel" it flowing into you. Affirm that "the kingdom of God is within you" (Luke 17:21) in the form of adequate power to meet life's demands.

10. Remind yourself that God is with you and nothing can defeat you. Believe that you *now* RECEIVE power from Him. [17]

B. INDIVIDUALISM

The Short and Simple Annals of A. Lincoln

ABRAHAM LINCOLN

I WAS BORN FEBRUARY 12, 1809, IN HARDIN COUNTY, KENTUCKY. MY parents were both born in Virginia, of undistinguished families— second families, perhaps I should say. My mother, who died in my tenth year, was of a family of the name of Hanks, some of whom now reside in Adams, some others in Macon Counties, Illinois. My paternal grandfather, Abraham Lincoln, emigrated from Rockingham County, Virginia, to Kentucky, about 1781 or 2, where, a year or two later, he was killed by Indians, not in battle, but by stealth, when he was laboring to open a farm in the forest. His ancestors, who were Quakers, went to Virginia from Berks County, Pennsylvania. An effort to identify them with the New England family of the same name ended in nothing more, definitely, than a similarity of Christian names in both

Based on a photographic reproduction of the original manuscript in *Lincoln Sesquicentennial 1809–1959: Handbook of Information* (Washington, D.C.: The Lincoln Sesquicentennial Commission, [1958]), pp. 16–18. Originally written December 20, 1859.

families, such as Enoch, Levi, Mordecai, Solomon, Abraham, and the like.

My father, at the death of his father, was but six years of age; and he grew up literally without education. He removed from Kentucky to what is now Spencer County, Indiana, in my eighth year. We reached our new home about the time the State came into the Union. It was a wild region with many bears and other wild animals still in the woods. There I grew up. There were some schools, so called, but no qualification was ever required of a teacher, beyond *"readin, writin, and cipherin"* to the Rule of Three. If a straggler, supposed to understand Latin, happened to sojourn in [16/17] the neighborhood, he was looked upon as a wizard. There was absolutely nothing to excite ambition for education. Of course when I came of age I did not know much. Still somehow, I could read, write, and cipher to the Rule of Three, but that was all. I have not been to school since. The little advance I now have upon this store of education, I have picked up from time to time under the pressure of necessity.

I was raised to farm work, which I continued till I was twenty-two. At twenty-one I came to Illinois, and passed the first year in Macon County. Then I got to New Salem, at that time in Sangamon, now in Menard County, where I remained a year as a sort of clerk in a store. Then came the Black Hawk War, and I was elected a captain of volunteers—a success which gave me more pleasure than any I have had since. I went the campaign, was elated, ran for the Legislature the same year (1832), and was beaten—the only time I ever have been beaten by the people. The next, and three succeeding biennial elections, I was elected to the Legislature. I was not a candidate afterwards. During this Legislative period I had studied law, and removed to Springfield to practice it. In 1846 I was elected to the lower House of Congress. Was not a candidate for re-election. From 1849 to 1854, both [17/18] inclusive, practiced law more assiduously than ever before. Always a Whig in politics, and generally on the Whig electoral tickets, making active canvasses. I was losing interest in politics, when the repeal of the Missouri Compromise aroused me again. What I have done since then is pretty well known.

If any personal description of me is thought desirable, it may be said, I am, in height, six feet, four inches, nearly; lean in flesh, weighing, on an average, one hundred and eighty pounds; dark complexion, with coarse black hair, and grey eyes. No other marks or brands recollected. [18]

The Rise of a Rustic Boy

WILLIAM DEAN HOWELLS

WE NOW FIND ABRAHAM LINCOLN BEGINNING TO ASSUME AN ACTIVE PART in the political affairs of Illinois.

He is known to the Whigs throughout the State, and his general popularity is as great as the esteem and regard in which he is held by those personally acquainted with him.

The talented young Whig has founded his reputation upon qualities that make every man proud to say he is the friend of Lincoln.

No admirer, who speaks in his praise, must pause to conceal a stain upon his good name. No true man falters in his affection at the remembrance of any mean action or littleness in the life of Lincoln.

The purity of his reputation, the greatness and dignity of his ambition, ennoble every incident of his career, and give significance to all the events of his past.

It is true that simply to have mauled rails, and commanded a flatboat, is not to have performed splendid actions. But the fact that Lincoln has done these things, and has risen above them by his own force, confers a dignity upon them; and the rustic boy, who is to be President in 1900, may well be consoled and encouraged in his labors when he recalls these incidents in the [50/51] history of one whose future once wore no brighter aspect than his own wears now.

The emigrant, at the head of the slow oxen that drag his household gods toward the setting sun—toward some Illinois yet further west—will take heart and hope when he remembers that Lincoln made no prouder entrance into the State of which he is now the first citizen.

The young student, climbing unaided up the steep ascent—he who has begun the journey after the best hours of the morning are lost forever—shall not be without encouragement when he finds the footprints of another in the most toilsome windings of his path.

Lincoln's future success or unsuccess can affect nothing in the past. The grandeur of his triumph over all the obstacles of fortune, will

From W. D. Howells, *Life of Abraham Lincoln* (Columbus, Ohio: Follett, Foster & Co., 1860), as reprinted by the Abraham Lincoln Association (Springfield, Illinois, 1938), pp. 50–55.

remain the same. Office can not confer honors brighter than those he has already achieved; it is the Presidency, not a great man, that is elevated, if such be chosen chief magistrate.

We have seen that, in 1842, he declines re-election to the State Legislature, after eight years' service in that body. He has already been on the Harrison electoral ticket, and has distinguished himself in the famous canvass of 1840.

But it is not as a politician alone, that Lincoln is heard of at this time. After Stuart's election to Congress has dissolved their connection, Lincoln forms a partnership with Judge Logan, one of the first in his profession at Springfield, and continues the practice of the law, with rising repute. [51/52]

His characteristics as an advocate are an earnestness and sincerity of manner, and a directness, conciseness, and strength of style; he appeals, at other times, to the weapons of good-humored ridicule as ably as to the heavier arms of forensic combat. He is strongest in civil cases, but in a criminal cause that enlists his sympathy he is also great. It is then that the advocate's convictions, presented to the jury in terse and forcible, yet eloquent language, sometimes outweigh the charge of the judge. Juries listen to him, and concur in his arguments; for his known truth has preceded his arguments, and he triumphs. There may be law and evidence against him, but the belief that Lincoln is *right,* nothing can shake in the minds of those who know the man.

He prepares his cases with infinite care, when he has nothing but technical work before him. The smallest detail of the affair does not escape him. All the parts are perfectly fitted together, and the peculiar powers of his keen, analytic mind are brought into full play. He has not the quickness which characterizes Douglas, and which is so useful to the man who adventures in law or politics. But he is sufficiently alert, and recovers himself in time to achieve success.

Lincoln does not grow rich at the law, and has not grown rich to this day, though possessing a decent competence, and owing no man anything. Poor men, who have the misfortune to do with courts, come to Lincoln, who has never been known to exact an exorbitant fee, [52/53] and whose demands are always proportioned to their poverty. There is record of a case which he gained for a young mechanic, after carrying it through three courts, and of his refusal to receive more than a comparative trifle in return.

Meantime, in the year 1842, Lincoln married a woman worthy to be the companion of his progress toward honor and distinction. Miss Mary Todd, who became his wife, is the daughter of Robert Todd, of Lexington, Kentucky, a man well known in that State, and formerly the clerk of the lower House of Congress. At the time of her marriage, Miss Todd was the belle of Springfield society—accomplished and intellectual, and possessing all the social graces native in the women of Kentucky.

If, at this point of his career, Lincoln looked back over his past life with proud satisfaction, his feeling was one in which every reader, who has traced his history, must sympathize.

It was hardly more than a half-score of years since he had entered Illinois, driving an ox-wagon, laden with the "plunder" of a backwoods emigrant. He was utterly unknown, and without friends who could advance him in any way. He was uneducated, and almost unlettered.

In ten years he had reversed all the relations of his [53/54] life. No man had now more friends among all classes of people. No man among his neighbors had a wider intelligence, or more eager and comprehensive mind. No man of his age stood better in his profession, or in politics. No one was in a fairer road to happiness and success. And all this had been accomplished through his own exertion, and the favor which his many noble traits awakened in those around him.

He might well exult in view of all that had been, and all that was.

But, however this may have been, Lincoln did not pause to exult. He exulted in full career; for already the great battle of 1844 was approaching, and he was to take a prominent part in the contest. Many of the people of Illinois have distinct recollection of the brilliant debates which he conducted with Calhoun and Thomas, and these are loth to concede that they have ever been surpassed. The debaters met in all the principal cities and towns of that State, and afterward carried the war into Indiana.

It may be supposed that the fortunes of the war varied, but there are popular stories related of these encounters that give rather amusing results of one of Lincoln's frequent successes.

The contest turned upon the annexation of Texas, to which measure Lincoln was opposed, in proportion as he loved and honored Henry Clay. It has been said that no man ever had such friends as Clay possessed. It may be said that he never possessed a friend more [54/55] ardent, attached, and faithful than Abraham Lincoln. Throughout that disastrous campaign of 1844, Lincoln was a zealous and indefatigable soldier in the Whig cause. His name was on the electoral ticket of Illinois, and he shared the defeat of his gallant leader—a defeat which precipitated the Mexican war, with its attendant evils, and the long train of dissensions, discords, and pro-slavery aggressions which have followed.

In the lull which comes after a Presidential battle, Lincoln, while mingling in State politics, devoted himself more particularly to professional affairs, though he continued an enemy to the Mexican war, and his election to Congress in 1846, took place in full view of this enmity. It is worthy of note, in this connection, that he was the only Whig elected in Illinois at that time. [55]

A Self-Made Man

FLOYD DELL

WHETHER ANDREW MARCH WAS DESCENDED FROM SAXON KINGS IS FOR genealogists to decide. Andrew's own knowledge of his ancestry went back only to his father, a restless Scotch-Irish-English workingman, and to his mother, who had been a cook in a frontier boarding-house.

James March had immigrated from England, where he had been a miner. He had taken up land in Ohio, and left it to become a miner again. He had drifted west to Michigan Territory—the remoter part, which is now Wisconsin—and there he became a lead miner, one of those who gradually displaced the Indian miners from their immemorial occupation, crowded them out of their lands, and helped to bring on the [6/7] Black Hawk war. Like all these miners in the early days, James March wintered at first in a dug-out; and these miners, burrowing into the hills for shelter like hibernating animals, were nicknamed "badgers," and gave their nickname to the state growing up around them. But as the lead-mining industry developed, a few boarding-houses sprang up; and in one of these, James March found a girl whose folks had come from England, and who had a strain of Scotch and Irish in her blood that endeared her to him in spite of their differences in disposition. She was a good Presbyterian, and made him stop drinking. They married. Andrew was their only child.

Once more James March tried farming, taking up land a little further north and west; and when the territory beyond the Mississippi was opened for settlement, he moved there—and died, leaving his wife and ten year old son penniless. Mrs. March was invited to come and live with a married cousin in White Falls, then recently settled.

Young Andrew, though he was accustomed to making himself useful, soon felt himself to be an encumbrance to these relatives; and when another of his mother's relatives, a baker in Chicago, wrote offering to take the boy to learn the trade, he was eager to accept. But his mother refused to let him go.

From Floyd Dell, *Janet March* (New York: Alfred A. Knopf, 1923), pp. 6–16. Copyright 1923, 1927, 1959, by Floyd Dell. Reprinted with the kind permission of the author.

99

"No, Andrew," she said, "and I'll tell you why." Andrew remembered this speech all his life long. "You're too young to go out in the world, with none but a man to look after you, and he not the kind a good mother would trust her son to. No, I'm an ailing woman, and I shan't be long here, I expect; but while I can, I'll do my duty by you. I've taught you reading and writing and figuring—none too well, maybe, but it's all the education you're likely to get. When you grow up, Andrew, and have children of your own, I want you to give them a good schooling, the best that's to be had. That's one thing. But there's something else that you can learn better from me than elsewhere—an important thing for a young lad, just as much as reading and writing and figuring—and that's how to be a decent Christian man. [7/8] When I'm gone, you'll make your way in the world all the better for biding with your mother now."

Death came to her, as she had expected, within a few years. The night before she died, she talked to her son. "Andrew," she said, "you'll have to look after yourself now, but I trust you to do it. You've been a good son to me, and you'll be a good man. And you'll get along, I've no doubt; the town is growing, and you've made friends for yourself. You'll do well, I've no fear of that. But I want you to remember this, that of any money you've got for odd jobs and brought home to me, I've always put a tithe in the contribution bag on Sunday. Oh, you've said nothing, but I could see you were cross with me more than once, because of the many things we needed the money for, ourselves! I told you a tenth was little enough to give to God. You'll remember that, Andrew, and tithe for yourself as I've done for you."

Andrew's children had heard this story often—too often. And they knew his earnest reply:

"Yes, mother, and the rest I shall put in the bank."

"Well—you'll be somebody of importance, I expect. And have nothing to be ashamed of, either."

The day after her funeral, Andrew, aged thirteen, began seriously to build his life's career. He knew better, now, than to wish to learn a trade; he was on the lookout for a business opportunity. But White Falls offered little. He must wait for his chance. In the meantime he could support himself by odd jobs, and make new friends.

His first job under these new conditions was like many he had had before—a week's wood-cutting for a neighbour. But it had its epochal significance, for all that. As wages for this week's work he received a dollar. He paid fifty cents of it to his relative for board and lodging; he was a man now, and must pay his way. He put ten cents, a tithe of his week's earning, in the contribution bag at church. Ten cents more went to pay for having a patch put on his shoes. The remaining thirty cents he deposited in the town bank, thereby opening an account.

The old banker, R. H. Royce's father, used to delight in [8/9] telling about that historic event. "I thought it was a pretty good joke," he would say, "starting an account with thirty cents! But the boy was so solemn about it, I couldn't refuse him. I said to him, That's the right spirit, Andy, this thirty cents may be the nest-egg of a big fortune!— Yes, sir, that's what I said in jest, little knowing how true it was!"

When Andrew was fourteen, he got a job in Macdougall's livery-stable. Macdougall was also more or less Scotch, and liked the boy; perhaps respecting him for the very priggishness of which he made continual fun. "Mac," as he was called, was a sporting man, originally from Kentucky; possibly he had left there under a cloud, but frontier towns were easy-going places and no one inquired too closely into such past histories. He was a genial, lazy, spendthrift soul, and everybody liked him—even his wife, who might have had some reason to complain. He was not much interested in his livery-stable as a business; always he talked of going back to Kentucky; he had bred a trotting colt that he said would make him a mint of money down there. He drove about the town and its outskirts in fine weather behind this colt, in a little cart, picking up idle young men and foolish girls for a ride, and boasting to them of what the filly could do if she had a chance. He chummed with steamboat crews, listening with homesick fascination to their stories of gay life in the river-towns to the south. He drank and played cards, by way of enlivening his dreary exile in White Falls. It was not a puritanical place, and these things were not condemned except by a very small minority of pious folk. Even the shadier side of his life, as rumoured, was merely a subject for jocular masculine remark. There were a few men in the village whose business took them away from time to time—a small trader who dealt in furs and went about visiting trappers in remote spots; a pedler who journeyed from farm to farm selling handkerchiefs, looking-glasses and such trifles to the farmers' wives and daughters; Firewater Pete, who [9/10] sold bad whisky to the neighbouring Indians—and the wives of these wanderers, women who had no "reputation" to begin with, were supposed to entertain Mac in their husbands' absence. If any married man in White Falls had to go away from town for any reason for a day or two, some witty friend was sure to ask gravely, "Won't your wife be lonesome?" and then add, "Well, it's all right, Mac will come and cheer her up if you ask him to!" Women were not supposed to hear these coarse jokes. But girls were warned by their mothers not to accept Mac's invitations to ride behind his trotting mare, and told that the silly girls who were seen riding with him were no better than they should be. This, however, did not prevent Mac from finding silly girls to go driving with on summer evenings.

Mac was sufficiently notorious as a reprobate, and Andrew was so well known in the village as a pious lad, that it was a cause of mild astonishment when Andrew went to work for Mac.

Mac's wife wondered about it, too. One morning of the first week of Andrew's employment, Mac having gone to the stable and Andrew come for breakfast, she sat watching him eat his plate of pancakes and sausage, and presently said with a little embarrassment, "I hear you're quite the model youth, Andy." She looked at the tall black-haired boy across the table, and laughed tolerantly. "Not that I think that's anything against you. You've lots of time yet to grow up and learn what the world's like. But aren't you afeared of learning bad tricks from Mac? I suppose you think he's the devil's own, what with his card-playing and drinking and all?"

"It's not for me to say so, ma'am," Andrew replied. "But you needn't be afeared for me, Mrs. Macdougall."

"Oh, well," said Mac's wife, "anyway there's a lot worse things to learn than what Mac could teach you!"

Andrew wondered briefly what these things could be, and doubted if she were right.

"Sometimes," she said, "a man is liked all the better for a few faults. Look at Mac, there isn't a man would have the [10/11] heart to take advantage of his free and easy ways. You can't help liking him, can you?"

But it was not the genial personality of Mac, nor even the cooking of Mac's wife, that had attracted Andrew. No. He had found his business opportunity.

Andrew intended to own that livery-stable some day.

Mac had already begun to tease him about his virtue. "When you get your first wages this week," he said, "maybe you'd like me to show you the best way to spend them. I've made a study of the subject, and there's many a young fellow I've assisted that way in my time, some of 'em right here in White Falls. Small and limited as the town is, I should say that you could get all of two dollars and a half's worth of devilment between Saturday night and Sunday morning, especially if you have a little expert advice. How about it, son?"

"I'm much obliged for the offer," said Andrew civilly. "But I'm putting two dollars and a quarter in the bank this week."

Mac made the old, inevitable joke: "What're you doing with the other two bits? You don't mean to tell me you're keeping a woman, Andy?"

Andrew flushed. "I'm not saying what the other twenty-five cents is for—but it's nothing I'm ashamed of."

"Ah, well," said Mac, "I'm glad to hear about that bank-account. Some day I may need money, and I'll call on you for some." And he laughed genially.

Nine years later, when Andrew was just turned twenty-three, that joke, like the banker's, bore its fruit of dead earnest. Mac was in trouble, about a girl. It was, perhaps, blackmail. Andrew did not trouble to sift the rumours. But when some one told him that Mac, in desperation, had said he would sell a half-interest in his livery-stable for a thousand dollars, Andrew went to him with an offer of the money. [11/12]

Mac was incredulous; Andrew's wages had been raised, year by year, and he knew that Andrew saved his money; but he could not believe that Andrew had, out of nothing, accumulated such a sum. And so Andrew went to the bank and returned with a thousand dollars in cash, together with a bill-of-sale which he had had the town lawyer draw up for him. And Mac, relieved of his anxieties, and laughing hugely at the joke on himself, signed the document.

But it was something more than a joke. And Mac began to see the other side of it. He looked queerly at Andrew.

Andrew could not understand why.

He came to dinner at Mac's house a few days later, bringing Mac's wife a cheap brooch, purchased from the pedlar, for a birthday present. He had followed explicitly certain advice of his mother's, and always gave little presents to his relatives and friends on their birthdays and at Christmas—"so that no one can call you close, Andrew!"

Mac, who had had dinner and gone to the livery-stable before Andrew left, had not spoken to him. And Mac's wife gave him a furious look when he entered. She had just had the whole story out of her husband.

Andrew's present mollified her a little. "You've a good heart, Andrew," she said. And then her face grew dark with anger again. "I can't make you out," she said. "Oh, you needn't look so innocent! Mac's been telling me about the dirty trick you played on him. I heard something about it before, but I didn't believe it. I'd never have thought it of you!"

"But," Andrew exclaimed, sitting more stiffly upright in his chair, "what have I done?"

"It's the joke of the town!" she said. "Of course, he told it on himself. Mac would! But it was bound to come out, anyway."

Andrew was genuinely puzzled and confused. "You mean, about the—the girl? I don't see what I—" [12/13]

Mac's wife snapped her fingers scornfully. "The girl!" she said. "That for the girl! You don't suppose I care about that fool nonsense, do you? It wouldn't be the first time that's happened. I'm talking about the dirty deal *you* gave him!"

"What," Andrew demanded, "have I done, that's wrong?"

She stared at him. "You've taken away his self-respect, if you want to know," she said.

Andrew was bewildered.

"I'm not sure I know what you're talking about," he began cautiously. "The only thing I've done—"

"I know what you've done," said Mac's wife impatiently. "You caught him with his pants down. I suppose you think you're smart!"

Andrew blushed, as he always did at any vulgarity of speech. "Are you referring, ma'am," he asked, "to the business deal between myself and your husband?"

"Business deal! Yes, I suppose you *would* call it that. I say you're as bad as the blackmailing hussy that was hounding him!"

"I well know," said Andrew, "that a half-interest in the livery-stable is worth more than a thousand dollars, if that's what you mean. But it was your husband's own proposition, I assure you it was. I simply took him up."

"Oh, Mac's a fool," she said bitterly. "But why need you have exposed him to the whole town? A bill-of-sale made out by a lawyer! You might have left him his pride."

"His pride?" Andrew repeated incredulously.

"Yes," said Mac's wife fiercely, "his pride! It's all he has."

Andrew pondered that, vainly. He shook his head. "Mrs. Mac-dougall," he said, "would you mind telling me what you think I *ought* to have done, under the circumstances, with Mac needing the money and me having it to spare?"

"Anything but what you did! Couldn't you have made it a loan between yourselves, if you wanted to help him out of his trouble?" [13/14]

Andrew had been bewildered; now he was staggered. He sat with his mouth hanging open, incapable of thought, occupied wholly with the shock of an idea alien to his scheme of life. Then he spoke, disjointedly, in sheer amazement. "A loan? A loan—to Mac? A loan—to help Mac?—My thousand dollars!"

A picture came into his mind. It was the picture of a pail of water, frozen over the top with ice. Beside it lay a hatchet. It was the pail from which he poured the water to wash in, in dark winter mornings, in his little room in the stable loft, with the thermometer at fifteen below zero. The hatchet was to break the ice with—the hatchet with which he had to break the ice on cold winter mornings. Up at four o'clock, to feed the horses and clean the stalls, and wait for Mac to drift in at seven or eight o'clock, or some days not till noon, so that he could go and get breakfast. He heard Mac's voice, taunting him with his virtue, describing lickerishly the delights of vice. With a kind of angry wonder he realized that this money of his was to Mac and his wife like *any other money!* This thousand dollars, made sacred by toil and self-denial, dedicated to high purposes, was to them a mere piece of good-luck, like a coin found in the gutter. This thousand dollars, which was to make of him all that his mother expected him to be, was to them something to be handed over to an adulterer, out of friendship. Yes, out of friendship! To Mac! His thousand dollars! His hopes, his plans, his life, abandoned to a fool and a waster!

Unconsciously he spoke aloud.

"Friendship! To a drunkard that will die blaspheming in the poor-house! My thousand dollars!"

It was the only time in his whole life that his emotions mastered him so wholly as to leave him without self-control and discretion. And it was too late when he realized that he was uttering his thoughts aloud.

Mac's wife turned pale, and then flamed. She rose from her chair opposite him. "I wonder," she said, "that you have the face to sit at his table!"

Andrew rose, too. "I am sorry I said those things," he [14/15] apologized. "I had no right to say them. It is for God to judge." He started to go away.

"No—wait!" said Mac's wife. "I want to tell you this. It isn't the damned livery-stable Mac cares about. He liked you, and he was going to *give* you a half interest in it next year, on your birthday. Believe it or not, it's God's truth!"

"Mrs. Macdougall," said Andrew severely, "I think you are talking just plain foolishness. And I'm going, so as not to hear any more of it. Good-bye."

He never sat at Mac's table again.

And before another year was out, Mac sold him the other half-interest in the livery-stable. The bank lent Andrew the money.

Mac and his wife left town.

It was this livery-stable which later became Andrew March's feed-store, and still later the March warehouse for storing grain to sell on commission. On its site was built the March grain-elevator. Thirty odd years after that first transaction by which Andrew became part owner of a livery-stable, he was a director in one of America's great businesses —a stockholder in the bank in which he had deposited that first thirty cents—and a trustee of the church in which he had given that first tithe.

He had lived up to his mother's expectations. He was somebody of importance.

And Mac, it seems, returned many years later, after varied wan-derings, to fulfil literally Andrew's prophecy—to die, a drunkard, in the poorhouse. Mac's wife was with him, still loyal, when he died.

This was a story that came to light, or almost came to light, through the enterprise of a girl reporter, assigned to attend a poor-farm funeral and get a "sob-story." The reporter interviewed the old woman who followed the coffin to the potter's field; and what she learned was so interesting that it never was printed at all. Andrew's son, John, in conference [15/16] with the managing editor, decided that it would not do to let that story be printed.

But when John reported this discreet decision to his father, old

Andrew was very angry—more angry than John had ever known him to be; and angry at John.

"Let them print the story," he said. "I've nothing to be ashamed of! I said that God would judge—and God has judged!"

And he repeated defiantly:

"I've nothing to be ashamed of!" [16]

C. THE LAW OF NATURE

The Trees in the Garden

STEPHEN CRANE

The trees in the garden rained flowers.
Children ran there joyously.
They gathered the flowers
Each to himself.
Now there were some
Who gathered great heaps—
Having opportunity and skill—
Until, behold, only chance blossoms
Remained for the feeble.
Then a little spindling tutor
Ran importantly to the father, crying:
"Pray, come hither!
See this unjust thing in your garden!"
But when the father had surveyed,
He admonished the tutor:
"Not so, small sage!
This thing is just.
For, look you,
Are not they who possess the flowers
Stronger, bolder, shrewder
Than they who have none?
Why should the strong—
The beautiful strong— [136/137]
Why should they not have the flowers?"

Stephen Crane, "The trees in the garden rained flowers," in *The Works of Stephen Crane,* ed. Wilson Follett (New York: Alfred A. Knopf, [1926]), VI, 136–137. Originally published 1899.

Upon reflection, the tutor bowed to the ground,
"My lord," he said,
"The stars are displaced
By this towering wisdom." [137]

Evolution of a Financier

THEODORE DREISER

FROM THE VERY START OF HIS LIFE FRANK WANTED TO KNOW ABOUT ECO-
nomics and politics. He cared nothing for books. He was a clean,
stocky, shapely boy with a bright, clean-cut, incisive face; large, clear
gray eyes; a wide forehead; short, bristly, dark-brown hair. He had an
incisive, quick-motioned, self-sufficient manner, and was forever asking
questions with a keen desire for a brief and intelligent reply. He did
not know what sickness was, never had an ache or pain, ate his food
with gusto, and ruled his brothers with a rod of iron. "Come on, Joe!
Hurry, Ed! These commands were issued in no rough, but always a
sure way; and Joe and Ed came. They looked up to Frank from the
first as a master; and what he had to say, or what he saw or encountered, was listened to eagerly. He himself was pondering, pondering, pondering—one fact astonishing him quite as much as another, for
he could not figure out how this thing he had come into—this life—was
organized. How did all these people get into the world? What were
they doing here? Who started things, anyhow? His mother told him the
story of Adam and Eve; but he didn't believe it. There was a fish-
market not so very far from his own home; and there, when he went to
see his father at the bank, or when he took his brothers on after-school
expeditions for mail or errands for his father, he liked to look at a
certain tank in front of one store where they [10/11] kept odd
specimens of sea-life which the Delaware Bay fishermen would bring
in. He saw once there a sea-horse—just a queer little sea-animal that
looked somewhat like a horse—and another time he saw an electric eel
which Franklin's discovery had explained. One day he saw a jelly-fish

put in, and then a squid, and then a lobster. The lobster and the squid came well along in his fish experiences; he was witness of a familiar tragedy in connection with these two, which stayed with him all his life and cleared things up considerably intellectually. The squid, it appeared from the talk of the idle bystanders who were always loafing about this market, was considered the rightful prey of the lobster; and the latter had no other food offered him. The lobster lay at the bottom of the clear glass tank on the yellow sand, apparently seeing nothing— you could not tell in which way his beady, black buttons of eyes were looking—but apparently they were never off the body of the squid. The latter, pale and waxy in texture, looking very much like pork fat or jade, was moving about in torpedo fashion; but his movements were apparently never out of the eyes of his enemy, for by degrees small portions of his body began to disappear, snapped off by the relentless claws of his pursuer. The latter, as young Cowperwood was one day a witness, would leap like a catapult to where the squid was apparently idly dreaming, and the squid, very alert, would dart away, shooting out at the same time a cloud of ink, behind which it would disappear. It was not always completely successful, however. Some small portions of its body or its tail were frequently left in the claws of the monster below. Days passed, and, now fascinated by the drama, young Cowperwood came daily.

"Say, pa," he said to his father, one night, "did you ever see that tank in front of Joralemon's?"

"Yes, I know where it is," said his father.

"Did you ever see the squid and lobster they got in there?" [11/12]

"I don't know. Why?"

"Well, that lobster's going to eat that squid. I can see more and more of him gone every day."

"How's that?" asked his father, indifferently.

"Why, that old lobster he just lies down there on the bottom of the tank, and he keeps his eyes fixed on that squid; and every now and then he jumps up with a bang, and he almost gets him. Sometimes he does get him—a little; but the squid pulls away. He's nipped off almost half his tail by now. And you know that ink-bag he carries—that stuff he shoots out to make a cloud?"

"Yes."

"Well, that's almost empty now. He's shot out so much he ain't got any more, or hardly any more."

"He hasn't any more," corrected his father.

"Well," went on his son, ignoring the correction, "you see, he's getting tired. I can see it. I've been watching him every day now for a week, and he's getting weaker all the time. That lobster won't give him any rest. I can see him looking at him all the time. He's goin' to get him. That squid's a goner. He's goin' to get him, sure!"

He paused, his eye alight, his whole body keyed up. He was

interested—not pityingly so much as dramatically interested. His young face was keen and hungry for further information.

"Well, what of that?" asked his father, curiously.

"Oh, nothing. Only I'm going by there in the morning. I want to see whether he's got him."

In the morning he went, his young pantalooned legs squared out solidly in front of the tank. The squid was not gone, but a piece of him; and his ink-bag was emptier than ever. In the corner of the tank sat the lobster, poised apparently for action.

Young Cowperwood put his nose to the glass. He looked solemnly at the lobster. He stayed as long as he could, the bitter struggle fascinating him. He liked to [12/13] study the rough claw with which the lobster did his deadly work. He liked to stare at the squid and think how fateful was his doom. Now, maybe, or in an hour or a day, he might die, slain by the lobster, and the lobster would eat him. He looked again at the greenish-copperish engine of destruction in the corner and wondered when this would be. To-night, maybe. He would come back to-night.

He returned one night, and lo! to his grief and astonishment, his wish was granted. There was a little crowd around the tank. The lobster was in the corner. Before him was the squid cut in two and partially devoured.

"He got him at last," observed one bystander. "I was standing right here an hour ago, and up he leaped and grabbed him. The squid was too tired. He wasn't quick enough. He did back up, but that lobster he calculated on his doing that. He's been figuring on his movements for a long time now. He got him to-day."

"Well, I swan!" somebody observed.

Cowperwood Junior only stared. He had missed this. It was too bad. He wanted to see it. The least touch of sorrow came to him for the squid as he stared at it slain. Then he stared at the victor.

"That's the way it has to be, I guess," he commented to himself. "That squid wasn't quick enough. He didn't have anything to feed on." He figured it out. The squid couldn't kill the lobster—he had no weapon. The lobster could kill the squid—he was heavily armed. There was nothing for the squid to feed on; the lobster had the squid as prey. What was the result to be? What else could it be? "He didn't have a chance," he said, finally, tucking his books under his arm and trotting on.

It made a great impression on him. It answered in a rough way that riddle which had been annoying him so much in the past: "How is life organized?" Things lived on each other—that was it. Lobsters lived on squids [13/14] and other things. What lived on lobsters? Men, of course! Sure, that was it! And what lived on men? he asked himself. Was it other men? Wild animals lived on men. And there were Indians and cannibals. And some men were killed by storms and accidents. He wasn't so sure about men living on men yet; but men did kill each other. How about wars and street fights and mobs? He had seen a mob once. It attacked the *Public Ledger* building as he was coming home from school. His father had explained what for, too. There was great excitement. It was about the slaves. That was it! Sure, men lived on men. Look at the slaves. They were men. That's what all this excitement was about these days. Men killing other men—negroes.

He went on home quite pleased with himself at his solution.

"Say," he said to his mother, that night, "he got him, mother!"

"Got who? What got what? Go wash your hands."

"Why, that lobster got that squid I was telling you and pa about."

"Well, that's all right. It's too bad. What makes you take any interest in such things? Run, wash your hands."

"Well, it's interesting. You don't often see anything like that. I never did."

He went out in the back yard, where there was a hydrant and a post with a little table on it, and on that a cleanly tin-pan and a bucket of water. Here he washed his face and hands.

"Say, papa," he said to his father, later, "you know that squid?"

"Yes."

"Well, he's dead. The lobster got him."

The father stared at his paper. "Well, that's too bad," he said, indifferently.

For days and weeks Frank thought of this and of the life [14/15] he was tossed into, for he was already thinking of what he should be in this world, and how he should get along. From seeing his father count money, he was sure that he would like banking; and Third Street, where his father's office was, seemed to him the cleanest, brightest, most fascinating street in the world. [15]

The Titan and the Governor

THEODORE DREISER

A PUBLIC-SERVICE-COMMISSION LAW MIGHT, IPSO FACTO, HAVE BEEN quietly passed at this session, if the arbitrary franchise-extending proviso had not been introduced, and this on the thin excuse that so novel

From *The Titan* by Theodore Dreiser. Copyright 1914 by John Lane Company; Copyright 1925 by Horace Liveright, Inc.; Copyright 1942 by The World Publishing Company. Published by arrangement with The World Publishing Company, Cleveland and New York.

a change in the working scheme of the state government might bring about hardship to some. This redounded too obviously to the benefit of one particular corporation. The newspaper men—as thick as flies about the halls of the state capitol at Springfield, and essentially watchful and loyal to their papers—were quick to sense the true state of affairs. Never were there such hawks as newspaper men. These wretches (employed by sniveling, mud-snouting newspapers of the opposition) were not only in the councils of politicians, in the pay of rival corporations, in the confidence of the governor, in the secrets of the senators and local representatives, but were here and there in one another's confidence. A piece of news—a rumor, a dream, a fancy— whispered by Senator Smith to Senator Jones, or by Representative Smith to Representative Jones, and confided by him in turn to Charlie White, of the *Globe*, or Eddie Burns, of the *Democrat*, would in turn be communicated to Robert Hazlitt, of the *Press*, or Harry Emonds, of the *Transcript*.

All at once a disturbing announcement in one or other of the papers, no one knowing whence it came. Neither Senator Smith nor Senator Jones had told any one. No word of the confidence imposed in Charlie White or Eddie Burns had ever been breathed. But there you were—the thing was in the papers, the storm of inquiry, opinion, opposition was on. No one knew, no one was to [482/483] blame, but it was on, and the battle had henceforth to be fought in the open.

Consider also the governor who presided at this time in the executive chamber at Springfield. He was a strange, tall, dark, osseous man who, owing to the brooding, melancholy character of his own disposition, had a checkered and a somewhat sad career behind him. Born in Sweden, he had been brought to America as a child, and allowed or compelled to fight his own way upward under all the grinding aspects of poverty. Owing to an energetic and indomitable temperament, he had through years of law practice and public labors of various kinds built up for himself a following among Chicago Swedes which amounted to adoration. He had been city tax-collector, city surveyor, district attorney, and for six or eight years a state circuit judge. In all these capacities he had manifested a tendency to do the right as he saw it and play fair—qualities which endeared him to the idealistic. Honest, and with a hopeless brooding sympathy for the miseries of the poor, he had as circuit judge, and also as district attorney, rendered various decisions which had made him very unpopular with the rich and powerful—decisions in damage cases, fraud cases, railroad claim cases, where the city or the state was seeking to oust various powerful railway corporations from possession of property—yards, water-frontages, and the like, to which they had no just claim. At the same time the populace, reading the news items of his doings and hearing him speak on various and sundry occasions, conceived a great fancy for him. He was primarily soft-hearted, sweet-minded, fiery, a brilliant

orator, a dynamic presence. In addition he was woman-hungry—a
phase which homely, sex-starved intellectuals the world over will
understand, to the shame of a lying age, that because of quixotic
dogma belies its greatest desire, its greatest sorrow, its greatest joy. All
these factors turned an ultra-conservative element in the community
against him, and he was considered dangerous. At the same time he
had by careful economy and investment built up a fair-sized fortune.
Recently, however, owing to the craze for sky-scrapers, he had placed
much of his holdings in a somewhat poorly constructed and therefore
unprofitable office [483/484] building. Because of this error financial
wreck was threatening him. Even now he was knocking at the doors of
large bonding companies for assistance.

This man, in company with the antagonistic financial element and
the newspapers, constituted, as regards Cowperwood's public-service-
commission scheme, a triumvirate of difficulties not easy to overcome.
The newspapers, in due time, catching wind of the true purport of the
plan, ran screaming to their readers with the horrible intelligence. In
the offices of Schryhart, Arneel, Hand, and Merrill, as well as in other
centers of finance, there was considerable puzzling over the situation,
and then a shrewd, intelligent deduction was made.

"Do you see what he's up to, Hosmer?" inquired Schryhart of
Hand. "He sees that we have him scotched here in Chicago. As things
stand now he can't go into the city council and ask for a franchise for
more than twenty years under the state law, and he can't do that for
three or four years yet, anyhow. His franchises don't expire soon
enough. He knows that by the time they do expire we will have public
sentiment aroused to such a point that no council, however crooked it
may be, will dare to give him what he asks unless he is willing to make
a heavy return to the city. If he does that it will end his scheme of
selling any two hundred million dollars of Union Traction at six per
cent. The market won't back him up. He can't pay twenty per cent. to
the city and give universal transfers and pay six per cent. on two
hundred million dollars, and everybody knows it. He has a fine scheme
of making a cool hundred million out of this. Well, he can't do it. We
must get the newspapers to hammer this legislative scheme of his to
death. When he comes into the local council he must pay twenty or
thirty per cent. of the gross receipts of his roads to the city. He must
give free transfers from every one of his lines to every other one. Then
we have him. I dislike to see socialistic ideas fostered, but it can't be
helped. We have to do it. If we ever get him out of here we can hush
up the newspapers, and the public will forget about it; at least we can
hope so."

In the mean time the governor had heard the whisper of "boodle"
—a word of the day expressive of a corrupt [484/485] legislative fund.
Not at all a small-minded man, nor involved in the financial campaign
being waged against Cowperwood, nor inclined to be influenced

mentally or emotionally by superheated charges against the latter, he nevertheless speculated deeply. In a vague way he sensed the dreams of Cowperwood. The charge of seducing women so frequently made against the street-railway magnate, so shocking to the yoked conventionalists, did not disturb him at all. Back of the onward sweep of the generations he himself sensed the mystic Aphrodite and her magic. He realized that Cowperwood had traveled fast—that he was pressing to the utmost a great advantage in the face of great obstacles. At the same time he knew that the present street-car service of Chicago was by no means bad. Would he be proving unfaithful to the trust imposed on him by the great electorate of Illinois if he were to advantage Cowperwood's cause? Must he not rather in the sight of all men smoke out the animating causes here—greed, overweening ambition, colossal self-interest as opposed to the selflessness of a Christian ideal and of a democratic theory of government?

Life rises to a high plane of the dramatic, and hence of the artistic, whenever and wherever in the conflict regarding material possession there enters a conception of the ideal. It was this that lit forever the beacon fires of Troy, that thundered eternally in the horses' hoofs at Arbela and in the guns at Waterloo. Ideals were here at stake—the dreams of one man as opposed perhaps to the ultimate dreams of a city or state or nation—the grovelings and wallowings of a democracy slowly, blindly trying to stagger to its feet. In this conflict—taking place in an inland cottage-dotted state where men were clowns and churls, dancing fiddlers at country fairs—were opposed, as the governor saw it, the ideals of one man and the ideals of men.

Governor Swanson decided after mature deliberation to veto the bill. Cowperwood, debonair as ever, faithful as ever to his logic and his conception of individuality, was determined that no stone should be left unturned that would permit him to triumph, that would carry him finally to the gorgeous throne of his own construction. Having first engineered the matter through the legislature [485/486] by a tortuous process, fired upon at every step by the press, he next sent various individuals—state legislators, representatives of the C. W. & I., members of outside corporations to see the governor, but Swanson was adamant. He did not see how he could conscientiously sanction the bill. Finally, one day, as he was seated in his Chicago business office—a fateful chamber located in the troublesome building which was subsequently to wreck his fortune and which was the *raison d'être* of a present period of care and depression—enter the smug, comfortable presence of Judge Nahum Dickensheets, at present senior counsel of the North Chicago Street Railway. He was a very mountain of a man physically—smooth-faced, agreeably clothed, hard and yet ingratiating of eye, a thinker, a reasoner. Swanson knew much of him by reputation and otherwise, although personally they were no more than speaking acquaintances.

"How are you, Governor? I'm glad to see you again. I heard you were back in Chicago. I see by the morning papers that you have that Southack public-service bill up before you. I thought I would come over and have a few words with you about it if you have no objection. I've been trying to get down to Springfield for the last three weeks to have a little chat with you before you reached a conclusion one way or the other. Do you mind if I inquire whether you have decided to veto it?"

The ex-judge, faintly perfumed, clean and agreeable, carried in his hand a large-sized black hand-satchel which he down beside him on the floor.

"Yes, Judge," replied Swanson, "I've practically decided to veto it. I can see no practical reason for supporting it. As I look at it now, it's specious and special, not particularly called for or necessary at this time."

The governor talked with a slight Swedish accent, intellectual, individual.

A long, placid, philosophic discussion of all the pros and cons of the situation followed. The governor was tired, distrait, but ready to listen in a tolerant way to more argument along a line with which he was already fully familiar. He knew, of course, that Dickensheets was counsel for the North Chicago Street Railway Company.

"I'm very glad to have heard what you have to say, [486/487] Judge," finally commented the governor. "I don't want you to think I haven't given this matter serious thought—I have. I know most of the things that have been done down at Springfield. Mr. Cowperwood is an able man; I don't charge any more against him than I do against twenty other agencies that are operating down there at this very moment. I know what his difficulties are. I can hardly be accused of sympathizing with his enemies, for they certainly do not sympathize with me. I am not even listening to the newspapers. This is a matter of faith in democracy—a difference in ideals between myself and many other men. I haven't vetoed the bill yet. I don't say that something may not arise to make me sign it. My present intention, unless I hear something much more favorable in its behalf than I have already heard, is to veto it."

"Governor," said Dickensheets, rising, "let me thank you for your courtesy. I would be the last person in the world to wish to influence you outside the line of your private convictions and your personal sense of fair play. At the same time I have tried to make plain to you how essential it is, how only fair and right, that this local street-railway-franchise business should be removed out of the realm of sentiment, emotion, public passion, envy, buncombe, and all the other influences that are at work to frustrate and make difficult the work of Mr. Cowperwood. All envy, I tell you. His enemies are willing to sacrifice every principle of justice and fair play to see him eliminated. That sums it up."

"That may all be true," replied Swanson. "Just the same, there is another principle involved here which you do not seem to see or do not care to consider—the right of the people under the state constitution to a consideration, a revaluation, of their contracts at the time and in the manner agreed upon under the original franchise. What you propose is sumptuary legislation; it makes null and void an agreement between the people and the street-railway companies at a time when the people have a right to expect a full and free consideration of this matter aside from state legislative influence and control. To persuade the state legislature, by influence or by any other means, to step in at this time and interfere is unfair. The [487/488] propositions involved in those bills should be referred to the people at the next election for approval or not, just as they see fit. That is the way this matter should be arranged. It will not do to come into the legislature and influence or buy votes, and then expect me to write my signature under the whole matter as satisfactory."

Swanson was not heated or antipathetic. He was cool, firm, well-intentioned.

Dickensheets passed his hand over a wide, high temple. He seemed to be meditating something—some hitherto untried statement or course of action.

"Well, Governor," he repeated, "I want to thank you, anyhow. You have been exceedingly kind. By the way, I see you have a large, roomy safe here." He had picked up the bag he was carrying. "I wonder if I might leave this here for a day or two in your care? It contains some papers that I do not wish to carry into the country with me. Would you mind locking it up in your safe and letting me have it when I send for it?"

"With pleasure," replied the governor.

He took it, placed it in lower storage space, and closed and locked the door. The two men parted with a genial hand-shake. The governor returned to his meditations, the judge hurried to catch a car.

About eleven o'clock the next morning Swanson was still working in his office, worrying greatly over some method whereby he could raise one hundred thousand dollars to defray interest charges, repairs, and other payments, on a structure that was by no means meeting expenses and was hence a drain. At this juncture his office door opened, and his very youthful office-boy presented him the card of F. A. Cowperwood. The governor had never seen him before. Cowperwood entered brisk, fresh, forceful. He was as crisp as a new dollar bill—as clean, sharp, firmly limned.

"Governor Swanson, I believe?"

"Yes, sir."

The two were scrutinizing each other defensively.

"I am Mr. Cowperwood. I come to have a very few words with you. I will take very little of your time. I do not wish to go over any of the arguments that have [488/489] been gone over before. I am satisfied that you know all about them."

"Yes, I had a talk with Judge Dickensheets yesterday."

"Just so, Governor. Knowing all that you do, permit me to put one more matter before you. I know that you are, comparatively, a poor man—that every dollar you have is at present practically tied in this building. I know of two places where you have applied for a loan of one hundred thousand dollars and have been refused because you haven't sufficient security to offer outside of this building, which is mortgaged up to its limit as it stands. The men, as you must know, who are fighting you are fighting me. I am a scoundrel because I am selfish and ambitious—a materialist. You are not a scoundrel, but a dangerous person because you are an idealist. Whether you veto this bill or not, you will never again be elected Governor of Illinois if the people who are fighting me succeed, as they will succeed, in fighting you."

Swanson's dark eyes burned illuminatively. He nodded his head in assent.

"Governor, I have come here this morning to bribe you, if I can. I do not agree with your ideals; in the last analysis I do not believe that they will work. I am sure I do not believe in most of the things that you believe in. Life is different at bottom perhaps from what either you or I may think. Just the same, as compared with other men, I sympathize with you. I will loan you that one hundred thousand dollars and two or three or four hundred thousand dollars more besides if you wish. You need never pay me a dollar—or you can if you wish. Suit yourself. In that black bag which Judge Dickensheets brought here yesterday, and which is in your safe, is three hundred thousand dollars in cash. He did not have the courage to mention it. Sign the bill and let me beat the men who are trying to beat me. I will support you in the future with any amount of money or influence that I can bring to bear in any political contest you may choose to enter, state or national."

Cowperwood's eyes glowed like a large, genial collie's. There was a suggestion of sympathetic appeal in them, rich and deep, and, even more than that, a philosophic [489/490] perception of ineffable things. Swanson arose. "You really don't mean to say that you are trying to bribe me openly, do you?" he inquired. In spite of a conventional impulse to burst forth in moralistic denunciation, solemnly phrased, he was compelled for the moment to see the other man's viewpoint. They were working in different directions, going different ways, to what ultimate end?

"Mr. Cowperwood," continued the governor, his face a physiognomy out of Goya, his eye alight with a kind of understanding sympathy, "I suppose I ought to resent this, but I can't. I see your point of view. I'm sorry, but I can't help you nor myself. My political belief, my ideals, compel me to veto this bill; when I forsake these I am done politically with myself. I may not be elected governor again, but that does not matter, either. I could use your money, but I won't. I shall have to bid you good morning."

He moved toward the safe, slowly, opened it, took out the bag and brought it over.

"You must take that with you," he added.

The two men looked at each other a moment curiously, sadly—the one with a burden of financial, political, and moral worry on his spirit, the other with an unconquerable determination not to be worsted even in defeat.

"Governor," concluded Cowperwood, in the most genial, contented, undisturbed voice, "you will live to see another legislature pass and another governor sign some such bill. It will not be done this session, apparently, but it will be done. I am not through, because my case is right and fair. Just the same, after you have vetoed the bill, come and see me, and I will loan you that one hundred thousand if you want it."

Cowperwood went out. Swanson vetoed the bill. It is on record that subsequently he borrowed one hundred thousand dollars from Cowperwood to stay him from ruin. [490]

D. THE ROLE OF SOCIETY

Main Chance, 1919

JOHN DOS PASSOS

DICK AND NED FELT PRETTY ROCKY THE MORNING THEY SIGHTED FIRE Island lightship. Dick wasn't looking forward to landing in God's Country with no money and the draft board to face, and he was worried about how his mother was going to make out. [397/398] All Ned was complaining about was wartime prohibition. They were both a little jumpy from all the cognac they'd drunk on the trip over. They were already in the slategreen shallow seas off Long Island;

From John Dos Passos, *Nineteen Nineteen* (Boston: Houghton Mifflin Company, 1946), pp. 397–408. From *U.S.A.* by John Dos Passos, copyright by John Dos Passos. Reprinted with the kind permission of the author. Originally published 1932.

no help for it now. The heavy haze to the west and then the low boxlike houses that looked as if they were drowned in the water and then the white strip of beach of the Rockaways; the scenic railways of Coney Island; the full green summer trees and the gray frame houses with their white trim on Staten Island; it was all heartbreakingly like home. When the immigration tug came alongside, Dick was surprised to see Hiram Halsey Cooper, in khaki uniform and puttees, clambering up the steps. Dick lit a cigarette and tried to look sober.

'My boy, it's a great relief to see you. . . . Your mother and I have been . . . er . . .' Dick interrupted to introduce him to Ned.

Mr. Cooper, who was in the uniform of a major, took him by the sleeve and drew him up the deck. 'Better put on your uniform to land.'

'All right, sir, I thought it looked rather shabby.'

'All the better. . . . Well, I suppose it's hell over there . . . and no chance for courting the muse, eh? . . . You're coming up to Washington with me tonight. We've been very uneasy about you, but that's all over now . . . made me realize what a lonely old man I am. Look here, my boy, your mother was the daugher of Major General Ellsworth, isn't that so?' Dick nodded. 'Of course she must have been because my dear wife was his niece. . . . Well, hurry and put your uniform on and remember . . . leave all the talking to me.'

While he was changing into the old Norton-Harjes uniform, Dick was thinking how suddenly Mr. Cooper had aged and wondering just how he could ask him to lend him fifteen dollars to pay the bill he'd run up at the bar.

New York had a funny lonely empty look in the summer afternoon sunlight; well, here he was home. At the Pennsylvania [398/399] Station there were policemen and plainclothes men at all the entrances demanding the registration cards of all the young men who were not in uniform. As he and Mr. Cooper ran for the train, he caught sight of a dejectedlooking group of men herded together in a corner hemmed by a cordon of sweating cops.

When they got in their seats in the parlorcar on the Congressional, Mr. Cooper mopped his face with a handkerchief. 'You understand why I said to put your uniform on. Well, I suppose it was hell?'

'Some of it was pretty bad,' said Dick casually. 'I hated to come back, though.'

'I know you did, my boy. . . . You didn't expect to find your old mentor in the uniform of a major . . . well, we must all put our shoulders to the wheel. I'm in the purchasing department of Ordnance. You see the chief of our bureau of personnel is General Sykes; he turns out to have served with your grandfather. I've told him about you, your experience on two fronts, your knowledge of languages and . . . well . . . naturally he's very much interested. . . . I think we can get you a commission right away.'

'Mr. Cooper, it's . . .' stammered Dick, 'it's extraordinarily decent . . . damn kind of you to interest yourself in me this way.'

'My boy, I didn't realize how I missed you . . . our chats about the muse and the ancients . . . until you had gone.' Mr. Cooper's voice was drowned out by the roar of the train. Well, here I am home, something inside Dick's head kept saying to him.

When the train stopped at the West Philadelphia Station the only sound was the quiet droning of the electric fans; Mr. Cooper leaned over and tapped Dick's knee, 'Only one thing you must promise . . . no more peace talk till we win the war. When the peace comes, we can put some in our poems. . . . Then'll be the time for us all to work for a lasting peace. . . . As for that little incident in Italy . . . it's nothing . . . forget it . . . nobody ever heard of it.' Dick nodded; it made him sore to feel that he was [339/400] blushing. They neither of them said anything until the waiter came through calling, 'Dinner now being served in the diningcar forward.'

In Washington (now you are home, something kept saying in Dick's head) Mr. Cooper had a room in the Willard where he put Dick up on the couch as the hotel was full and it was impossible to get another room anywhere. After he'd rolled up in the sheet, Dick heard Mr. Cooper tiptoe over and stand beside the couch breathing hard. He opened his eyes and grinned.

'Well, my boy,' said Mr. Cooper, 'it's nice to have you home . . . sleep well,' and he went back to bed.

Next morning he was introduced to General Sykes: 'This is the young man who wants to serve his country,' said Mr. Cooper with a flourish, 'as his grandfather served it. . . . In fact, he was so impatient that he went to war before his country did, and enlisted in the Volunteer Ambulance Service with the French and afterwards with the Italians.'

General Sykes was a little old man with bright eyes and a hawk nose and extremely deaf. "Yes, Ellsworth was a great fellow; we campaigned against Hieronimo together . . . Ah, the Old West . . . I was only fourteen at Gettysburg and damme I don't think he was there at all. We went through West Point in the same class after the war, poor old Ellsworth. . . . So you've smelled powder have you, my boy?' Dick colored and nodded.

'You see, General,' shouted Mr. Cooper, 'he feels he wants some more . . . er . . . responsible work than was possible in the Ambulance Service.'

'Yessiree, no place for a highspirited young fellow. . . . You know Andrews, Major . . .' The General was scribbling on a pad. 'Take him to see Colonel Andrews with this memorandum and he'll fix him up, has to decide on qualifications, etc. . . . You understand . . . good luck, my boy.'

Dick managed a passable salute and they were out in the corridor;

[400/401] Mr. Cooper was smiling broadly. 'Well, that's done. I must
be getting back to my office. You go and fill out the forms and take
your medical examination ... or perhaps that'll be at the camp ...
Anyway come and lunch with me at the Willard at one. Come up to
the room.' Dick saluted, smiling.

He spent the rest of the morning filling out blanks. After lunch he
went down to Atlantic City to see his mother. She looked just the same.
She was staying in a boardinghouse at the Chelsea end and was very
much exercised about spies. Henry had enlisted as a private in the
infantry and was somewhere in France. Mother said it made her blood
boil to think of the grandson of General Ellsworth being a mere
private, but that she felt confident he'd soon rise from the ranks. Dick
hadn't heard her speak of her father since she used to talk about him
when he was a child, and asked her about him. He had died when she
was quite a little girl leaving the family not too well off considering
their station in life. All she remembered was a tall man in blue with a
floppy felt hat caught up on one side and a white goatee; when she'd
first seen a cartoon of Uncle Sam she'd thought it was her father. He
always had hoarhound drops in a little silver bonbonnière in his pocket,
she'd been so excited about the military funeral and nice kind army
officer giving her his handkerchief. She'd kept the bonbonnière for
many years, but it had had to go with everything else when your poor
father ... er ... failed.

A week later Dick received a War Department envelope addressed to Savage, Richard Ellsworth, 2nd Lieut. Ord. Dept., enclosing
his commission and ordering him to proceed to Camp Merritt, N.J.,
within twenty-four hours. Dick found himself in charge of a casuals
company at Camp Merritt and wouldn't have known what on earth to
do if it hadn't been for the sergeant. Once they were on the transport it
was better; he had what had been a firstclass cabin with two other
second lieutenants and a major; Dick had the drop on them all because
he'd been at the [401/402] front. The transport was the *Leviathan;*
Dick began to feel himself again when he saw the last of Sandy Hook;
he wrote Ned a long letter in doggerel that began:

> His father was a jailbird and his mother had no kale
> He was much too fond of cognac and he drank it by the pail
> But now he's a Second Lieut and supported by the State
> Sports a handsome uniform and a military gait
> And this is the most terrific fate that ever can befall
> A boy whose grandpa was a Major-General.

The other two shavetails in the cabin were nondescript youngsters
from Leland Stanford, but Major Thompson was a West Pointer and
stiff as a ramrod. He was a middleaged man with a yellow round face,
thin lips and noseglasses. Dick thawed him out a little by getting him

a pint of whiskey through his sergeant who'd gotten chummy with the stewards, when he got seasick two days out, and discovered that he was a passionate admirer of Kipling and had heard Copeland read *Danny Deever* and been very much impressed. Furthermore, he was an expert on mules and horseflesh and the author of a monograph: 'The Spanish Horse.' Dick admitted that he'd studied with Copeland and somehow it came out that he was the grandson of the late General Ellsworth. Major Thompson began to take an interest in him and to ask him questions about the donkeys the French used to carry ammunition in the trenches, Italian cavalry horses, and the works of Rudyard Kipling. The night before they [402/403] reached Brest when everybody was flustered and the decks were all dark and silent for the zone, Dick went into a toilet and reread the long kidding letter he'd written Ned first day out. He tore it up into small bits, dropped them in the can and then flushed it carefully: no more letters.

In Brest, Dick took three majors downtown and ordered them a meal and good wine at the hotel; during the evening Major Thompson told stories about the Philippines and the Spanish War; after the fourth bottle Dick taught them all to sing *Mademoiselle from Armentières*. A few days later he was detached from his casuals company and sent to Tours; Major Thompson, who felt he needed somebody to speak French for him and to talk about Kipling with, had gotten him transferred to his office. It was a relief to see the last of Brest, where everybody was in a continual grouch from the drizzle and the mud and the discipline and the saluting and the formations and the fear of getting in wrong with the brasshats.

Tours was full of lovely creamystone buildings buried in dense masses of bluegreen late summer foliage. Dick was on commutation of rations and boarded with an agreeable old woman who brought him up his café au lait in bed every morning. He got to know a fellow in the Personnel Department through whom he began to work to get Henry transferred out of the infantry. He and Major Thompson and old Colonel Edgecombe and several other officers dined together very often; they got so they couldn't do without Dick who knew how to order a meal comme il faut, and the proper vintages of wines and could parleyvoo with the French girls and make up limericks and was the grandson of the late General Ellsworth.

When the Post Dispatch Service was organized as a separate outfit, Colonel Edgecombe, who headed it, got him away from Major Thompson and his horsedealers; Dick became one of his assistants with the rank of Captain. Immediately he managed to get Henry transferred from the officers' school to Tours. It [403/404] was too late, though, to get him more than a first lieutenancy.

When Lieutenant Savage reported to Captain Savage in his office, he looked brown and skinny and sore. That evening they drank a bottle of white wine together in Dick's room. The first thing Henry said when the door closed behind them was. 'Well, of all the goddam lousy grafts ... I don't know whether to be proud of the little kid brother or to sock him in the eye.'

Dick poured him a drink. 'It must have been Mother's doing,' he said. 'Honestly, I'd forgotten that Grandpa was a general.'

'If you knew what us guys at the front used to say about the S.O.S.'

'But somebody's got to handle the supplies and the ordnance and ...'

'And the mademosels and the vin blanc,' broke in Henry.

'Sure, but I've been very virtuous.... Your little brother's minding his *p*'s and *q*'s, and honestly I've been working like a nigger.'

'Writing loveletters for ordnance majors, I bet.... Hell, you can't beat it. He lands with his nose in the butter every time.... Anyway, I'm glad there's one successful member of the family to carry on the name of the late General Ellsworth.'

'Have a disagreeable time in the Argonne?'

'Lousy ... until they sent me back to officers' school.'

'We had a swell time there in the Ambulance Service in '17.'

'Oh, you would.'

Henry drank some more wine and mellowed up a little. Every now and then he'd look around the big room with its lace curtains and its scrubbed tile floor and its big fourposter bed and make a popping sound with his lips and mutter: 'Pretty soft.' Dick took him out and set him up to a fine dinner at his favorite bistro and then went around and fixed him up with Minette, who was the bestlooking girl at Madame Patou's.

After Henry had gone upstairs, Dick sat in the parlor a few minutes with a girl they called Dirty Gertie who had hair dyed [404/405] red and a big floppy painted mouth, drinking the bad cognac and feeling blue. 'Vous triste?' she said, and put her clammy hand on his forehead. He nodded. 'Fièvre ... trop penser ... penser no good ... moi aussi.' Then she said she'd kill herself, but she was afraid, not that she believed in God, but that she was afraid of how quiet it would be after she was dead. Dick cheered her up, 'Bientot guerre finée. Tout le monde content go back home.' The girl burst out crying and Madame Patou came running in screaming and clawing like a seagull. She was a heavy woman with an ugly jaw. She grabbed the girl by the hair and began shaking her. Dick was flustered. He managed to make the woman let the girl go back to her room, left some money and walked out. He felt terrible. When he got home he felt like writing some verse. He tried to recapture the sweet and heavy [405/406] pulsing of feelings he used to have when he sat down to write a poem. But all he could do was just feel miserable so he went to bed. All night half-thinking half-dreaming he couldn't get Dirty Gertie's face out of his head. Then he began remembering the times he used to have with

Hilda at Bay Head and had a long conversation with himself about love: Everything's so hellishly sordid ... I'm sick of whores and chastity, I want to have love affairs. He began planning what he'd do after the war, probably go home and get a political job in Jersey; a pretty sordid prospect.

He was lying on his back staring at the ceiling that was livid with dawn when he heard Henry's voice calling his name down in the street outside; he tiptoed down the cold tiled stairs and let him in.

'Why the hell did you let me go with that girl, Dick? I feel like a louse ... Oh Christ ... mind if I have half this bed, Dick? I'll get me a room in the morning.'

Dick found him a pair of pajamas and made himself small on his side of the bed. 'The trouble with you, Henry,' he said, yawning, 'is that you're just an old Puritan ... you ought to be more Continental.'

'I notice you didn't go with any of those bitches yourself.'

'I haven't got any morals, but I'm finicky, my dear, Epicurus' owne sonne,' Dick drawled sleepily.

'S—t, I feel like a dirty dishrag,' whispered Henry.

Dick closed his eyes and went to sleep.

Early in October, Dick was sent to Brest with a dispatch case that the Colonel said was too important to entrust to an enlisted man. At Rennes he had to wait two hours for the train, and was sitting eating in the restaurant when a doughboy with his arm in a sling came up to him saying, 'Hello, Dick, for crying out loud.' It was Skinny Murray.

'By gosh, Skinny, I'm glad to see you ... it must be five or six years ... Gee, we're getting old. Look, sit down ... no, I can't do that.'
[406/407]

'I suppose I ought to have saluted, sir,' said Skinny stiffly.

'Can that, Skinny ... but we've got to find a place to talk ... got any time before your train? You see it's me the M.P.'s would arrest if they saw me eating and drinking with an enlisted man.... Wait around till I've finished my lunch and we'll find a ginmill across from the station. I'll risk it.'

'I've got an hour ... I'm going to the Grenoble leave area.'

'Lucky bastard ... were you badly wounded, Skinny?'

'Piece of shrapnel in the wing, Captain,' said Skinny, coming to attention as a sergeant of M.P.'s stalked stiffly through the station restaurant. 'Those birds gimme the willies.'

Dick hurried through his lunch, paid, and walked across the square outside the station. One of the cafés had a back room that looked dark and quiet. They were just settling down to chat over two beers when Dick remembered the dispatch case. He'd left it at the table. Whispering breathlessly that he'd be back he ran across the square and into the station restaurant. Three French officers were at the table. 'Pardon, messieurs.' It was still where he'd left it under the table. 'If I'd lost that I'd have had to shoot myself,' he told Skinny.

They chatted about Trenton and Philadelphia and Bay Head and Doctor Atwood. Skinny was married and had a good job in a Philadelphia bank. He had volunteered for the tanks and was winged by a bit of shrapnel before the attack started, damn lucky for him, because his gang had been wiped out by a black maria. He was just out of hospital today and felt pretty weak on his pins. Dick took down his service data and said he'd get him transferred to Tours; just the kind of fellow they needed for a courier. Then Skinny had to run for his train, and Dick, with the dispatch case tightly wedged under his arm, went out to stroll around the town daintily colored and faintly gay under the autumn drizzle.

The rumor of the fake armistice set Tours humming like a swarm of bees; there was a lot of drinking and backslapping and officers and enlisted men danced snakedances in and out of the [407/408] office-buildings. When it turned out to be a false alarm Dick felt almost relieved. The days that followed everybody round the headquarters of the Dispatch Service wore a mysterious expression of knowing more than they were willing to tell. The night of the real armistice Dick ate supper a little deliriously with Colonel Edgecombe and some other officers. After dinner Dick happened to meet the Colonel in the courtyard out back. The Colonel's face was red and his mustache bristled.

'Well, Savage, it's a great day for the race,' he said, and laughed a great deal.

'What race?' said Dick shyly.

'The human race,' roared the Colonel.

Then he drew Dick aside: 'How would you like to go to Paris, my boy? It seems that there's to be a Peace Conference in Paris and that President Wilson is going to attend it in person . . . seems incredible . . . and I've been ordered to put this outfit at the disposal of the American delegation that's coming soon to dictate the peace, so we'll be Peace Conference couriers. Of course, I suppose if you feel you have to go home it could be arranged.'

'Oh, no, sir,' broke in Dick hurriedly. 'I was just beginning to worry about having to go home and look for a job. . . . The Peace Conference will be a circus and any chance to travel around Europe suits me.'

The Colonel looked at him with narrowed eyes. 'I wouldn't put it just that way . . . service should be our first thought . . . naturally what I said is strictly confidential.'

'Oh, strictly,' said Dick, but he couldn't help wearing a grin on his face when he went back to join the others at the table. [408]

The Big Money

JOHN DOS PASSOS

AT TWELVE-THIRTY HE WAS WAITING FOR J. W. IN THE LOBBY OF THE
Plaza chewing sensen to take the smell of the three whiskies he'd
swallowed at Tony's on the way up off his breath. At twelve-fortyfive
he saw coming from the checkroom J. W.'s large pear-shaped figure
with the paleblue eyes and the sleek strawgray hair, and beside him a
tall gaunt man with untidy white hair curling into ducktails over his
ears. The minute they stepped into the lobby, Dick began to hear a
rasping opinionated boom from the tall man.

'. . . never one of those who could hold my peace while injustice
ruled in the marketplace. It has been a long struggle and one which
from the vantage of those threescore and ten years that the prophets of
old promised to man upon this earth I can admit to have been largely
crowned with material and spiritual success. Perhaps it was my early
training for the pulpit, but I have always felt, and that feeling, Mr.
Moorehouse, is not rare among the prominent businessmen in this
country, that material success is not the only thing . . . there is the
attainment of the spirit of service. That is why I say to you frankly that
I have been grieved and wounded by this dark conspiracy. Who steals
my purse steals trash, but who would . . . what is it? . . . my [574/
575] memory's not what it was . . . my good name . . . Ah, yes, how
do you do, Mr. Savage?'

Dick was surprised by the wrench the handshake gave his arm. He
found himself standing in front of a gaunt loosejointed old man with a
shock of white hair and a big prognathous skull from which the
sunburned skin hung in folds like the jowls of a birddog. J. W. seemed
small and meek beside him.

'I'm very glad to meet you, sir,' E. R. Bingham said. 'I have often
said to my girls that had I grown up in your generation I would have

found happy and useful work in the field of public-relations. But alas, in my day the path was harder for a young man entering life with nothing but the excellent tradition of moral fervor and natural religion I absorbed if I may say so with my mother's milk. We had to put our shoulders to the wheel in those days and it was the wheel of an old muddy wagon drawn by mules, not the wheel of a luxurious motorcar.'

E. R. Bingham boomed his way into the diningroom. A covey of palefaced waiters gathered round, pulling out chairs, setting the table, bringing menucards.

'Boy, it is no use handing me the bill of fare,' E. R. Bingham addressed the headwaiter. 'I live by Nature's law. I eat only a few nuts and vegetables and drink raw milk.... Bring me some cooked spinach, a plate of grated carrots and a glass of unpasteurized milk. ...As a result, gentlemen, when I went a few days ago to a great physician at the request of one of the great lifeinsurance companies in this city he was dumbfounded when he examined me. He could hardly believe that I was not telling a whopper when I told him I was seventyone. "Mr. Bingham," he said, "you have the magnificent physique of a healthy athlete of fortyfive"... Feel that, young man.' E. R. Bingham flexed his arm under Dick's nose.

Dick gave the muscle a prod with two fingers. 'A sledgehammer,' Dick said, nodding his head.

E. R. Bingham was already talking again: 'You see I practice [575/576] what I preach, Mr. Moorehouse... and I expect others to do the same.... I may add that in the entire list of remedies and proprietary medicines controlled by Bingham Products and the Rugged Health Corporation, there is not a single one that contains a mineral, a drug, or any other harmful ingredient. I have sacrificed time and time again hundreds of thousands of dollars to strike from my list a concoction deemed injurious or habit-forming by Doctor Gorman and the rest of the splendid men and women who make up our research department. Our medicines and our systems of diet and cure are Nature's remedies, herbs and simples culled in the wilderness in the four corners of the globe according to the tradition of wise men and the findings of sound medical science.' [576]

'Would you have coffee now, Mr. Bingham, or later?'

'Coffee, sir, is a deadly poison, as are alcohol, tea, and tobacco. If the shorthaired women and the longhaired men and the wild-eyed cranks from the medical schools, who are trying to restrict the liberties of the American people to seek health and wellbeing, would restrict their activities to the elimination of these dangerous poisons that are sapping the virility of our young men and the fertility of our lovely American womanhood, I would have no quarrel with them. In fact, I would do everything I could to aid and abet them. Someday I shall put my entire fortune at the disposal of such a campaign. I know that the plain people of this country feel as I do because I'm one of them, born and raised on the farm of plain Godfearing farming folk. The American people need to be protected from cranks.'

'That, Mr. Bingham,' said J. W., 'will be the keynote of the campaign we have been outlining.' The fingerbowls had arrived. 'Well, Mr. Bingham,' said J. W., getting to his feet, 'this has been indeed a pleasure. I unfortunately shall have to leave you to go downtown to a rather important directors' meeting, but Mr. Savage here has everything right at his fingertips and can, I know, answer any further questions. I believe we are meeting with your sales department at five.'

As soon as they were alone, E. R. Bingham leaned over the table to Dick and said: 'Young man, I very much need a little relaxation this afternoon. Perhaps you could come to some entertainment as my guest.... All work and no play ... you know the adage. Chicago has always been my headquarters and whenever I've been in New York I've been too busy to get around.... Perhaps you could suggest some sort of show or musical extravaganza. I belong to the plain people, let's go where the plain people go.'

Dick nodded understandingly. 'Let's see, Monday afternoon ... I'll have to call up the office.... There ought to be vaudeville.... I can't think of anything but a burlesque show.' [577/578]

'That's the sort of thing, music and young women.... I have high regard for the human body. My daughters, thank God, are magnificent physical specimens.... The sight of beautiful female bodies is relaxing and soothing. Come along, you are my guest. It will help me to make up my mind about this matter.... Between you and me Mr. Moorehouse is a very extraordinary man. I think he can lend the necessary dignity.... But we must not forget that we are talking to the plain people.'

'But the plain people aren't so plain as they were, Mr. Bingham. They like things a little ritzy now,' said Dick, following E. R. Bingham's rapid stride to the checkroom.

'I never wear hat or coat, only that muffler, young lady,' E. R. Bingham was booming.

'Have you any children of your own, Mr. Savage?' asked E. R. Bingham when they were settled in the taxicab.

'No, I'm not married at the moment,' said Dick shakily, and lit himself a cigarette.

'Will you forgive a man old enough to be your father for pointing something out to you?' E. R. Bingham took Dick's cigarette between two long knobbed fingers and dropped it out of the window of the cab. 'My friend, you are poisoning yourself with narcotics and destroying your virility. When I was around forty years old, I was in the midst of a severe economic struggle. All my great organization was still in its infancy. I was a physical wreck. I was a slave to alcohol and tobacco. I had parted with my first wife and had I had a wife I wouldn't have been able to ... behave with her as a man should. Well, one day I said to myself: "Doc Bingham"—my friends called me Doc in those days—"like Christian of old you are bound for the City of Destruction, and when you're gone, you'll have neither chick nor child to drop a tear for you." I began to interest myself in the proper culture of the body ... my spirit, I may say, was already developed by familiarity with the classics in my youth and a memory that many have called prodigious.... The result has been success [578/579] in every line of endeavor.... Someday you shall meet my family and see what sweetness and beauty there can be in a healthy American home.'

E. R. Bingham was still talking when they went down the aisle to seats beside the gangplank at a burlesque show. Before he could say Jack Robinson, Dick found himself looking up a series of bare jiggling female legs spotted from an occasional vaccination. The band crashed and blared, the girls wiggled and sang and stripped in a smell of dust and armpits and powder and grease-paint in the glare of the moving spot that kept lighting up E. R. Bingham's white head. E. R. Bingham was particularly delighted when one of the girls stooped and cooed, 'Why, look at Grandpa,' and sang into his face and wiggled her geestring at him. E. R. Bingham nudged Dick and whispered, 'Get her telephone number.' After she'd moved on he kept exclaiming, 'I feel like a boy again.'

In the intermission Dick managed to call Miss Williams at the office and to tell her to suggest to people not to smoke at the conference. 'Tell J. W. the old buzzard thinks cigarettes are coffinnails,' he said.

'Oh, Mr. Savage,' said Miss Williams reprovingly.

At five Dick tried to get him out, but he insisted on staying till the end of the show. 'They'll wait for me, don't worry,' he said.

When they were back in a taxi on the way to the office, E. R. Bingham chuckled. 'By gad, I always enjoy a good legshow, the human form divine.... Perhaps we might, my friend, keep the story of our afternoon under our hats.' He gave Dick's knee a tremendous slap. 'It's great to play hookey.'

At the conference Bingham Products signed on the dotted line. Mr. Bingham agreed to anything and paid no attention to what went on. Halfway through, he said he was tired and was going home to bed and left yawning, leaving Mr. Goldmark and a representative of the J. Winthrop Hudson Company that did the advertising for Bingham Products to go over the details of the [579/580] project. Dick couldn't help admiring the quiet domineering way J. W. had with them. After the conference Dick got drunk and tried to make a girl he knew in a taxicab, but nothing came of it, and he went home to the empty apartment feeling frightful.

The next morning Dick overslept. The telephone woke him. It was Miss Williams calling from the office. Would Mr. Savage get himself a bag packed and have it sent down to the station so as to be ready to accompany Mr. Moorehouse to Washington on the Congressional. 'And, Mr. Savage,' she added, 'excuse me for saying so, but we all feel at the office that you were responsible for nailing the Bingham account. Mr. Moorehouse was saying you must have hypnotized them.'

'That's very nice of you, Miss Williams,' said Dick in his sweetest voice. [580]

A Promotion

JOHN P. MARQUAND

IT WAS GOOD BUSINESS TO LEARN UNOBTRUSIVELY ALL ONE COULD ABOUT one's superiors and through his years at the Stuyvesant Bank Charles had collected a considerable amount of information about Mr. Anthony Burton and his background. He had picked this up gradually, a little here and there from occasional remarks that Mr. Burton had made when there was general conversation, and more from Arthur Slade. In the course of time, Charles had been able to sift fact from gossip and to make his own evaluations, until now, if necessary, he could have written from memory a biographical character sketch of Tony Burton, and he could have filled in any gaps from his own firsthand observations of Tony Burton's habits. He knew that Tony Burton was both typical and exceptional—a rich man's son with inherited ability and with ambition that had somehow not been dulled by his having always been presented with what he had wanted. Though Charles knew that he would always observe Tony Burton from a distance, it was fascinating to speculate upon his drives and problems.

His life and Tony Burton's were actually two complete and separate circles, touching at just one point, and they were circles that would never coincide. Though they each could make certain ideas

From John P. Marquand, *Point of No Return* (Boston: Little, Brown and Company, 1949), pp. 542–559. Copyright 1947, 1948, 1949, by John P. Marquand. By permission of Little, Brown and Co.

comprehensible to the other, the very words they used had different meanings for each of them. Security, work, worry, future, position, and society, capital and government, all had diverging meanings. Charles could understand the Burton meanings and could interpret them efficiently and accurately, but only in an objective, not in an emotional, way, in the same manner he might have interpreted the [542/543] meanings of a Russian commissar or a Chinese mandarin. He could admire aspects of Tony Burton, he could even like him, but they could only understand each other theoretically.

When Tony Burton said, for instance, as he was recently fond of saying, that the neighborhood where he lived on Roger's Point was running down, it was not what Charles would have meant if he had made the statement. Tony Burton did not mean that any place on Roger's Point was growing shabby or that crude parvenus had pushed in on Roger's Point. He only meant that several places during the war had changed hands rather suddenly—nothing along the shore, of course, but in back. He did not mean that the new owners of these places were financially unstable or made noises when they ate their food. He only meant that one of the owners was the president of an advertising agency and that another controlled the stock of a depilatory preparation. Though these people were agreeable and wanted to do better, their having been allowed to buy into Roger's Point indicated that the general morale was running low. It would not have happened, for instance, when Mr. Burton, Senior, was alive. That was all he meant.

This did not sound serious to Charles, but it was to Tony Burton and Charles could understand it, intellectually. What was more, Tony Burton must have known he understood it, for he discussed the situation quite frankly with Charles, just as though Charles owned property on Roger's Point—not on the inside but on the water side. Yet they both obviously knew that Charles could never afford to live there. A backlog of inherited wealth was required to live there, unless one made a killing on the stock market or invented a laxative or a depilatory. There was no way of telling what might happen to Roger's Point. Anyone might live there in time, and Tony Burton could laugh ironically about it, and Charles, too, could laugh, sympathetically and intellectually, without ever fully savoring the suffering behind Tony Burton's mirth.

Tony Burton's father, Sanford Burton, had bought all of Roger's Point in 1886, when there were no houses there, and he had built the Burton house in 1888. He had already formed the brokerage firm of Burton and Fall, and the Point had been a profitable real [543/544] estate investment. It had not been difficult to sell off parts of it around the turn of the century to the proper sort of person. Simpkins, a director of U.S. Steel, had bought the cove, and the Marshalls, the Erie Railroad Marshalls, had bought the place next, and the Crawfords, the

Appellate Justice Crawfords, were there also. Charles could remember most of the owners' names. It was good business to know them as many of them had accounts at the Stuyvesant Bank. In fact Charles knew the names as well as did the watchman at the beginning of the private road:

"I'm going to Mr. Anthony Burton's," he said, and he could even employ the proper tone, intellectually. "Mr. Burton is expecting me for dinner."

"You needn't have told him all the family history," Nancy said. "Why didn't you tell him you're forty-three years old and show him our wedding certificate?" She was telling him indirectly that she was feeling better, that she was all right now.

"Oh, my God," she said, "here it is, and they've put on the lights."

She was referring to lights in the trees along the drive, a recent innovation of Tony Burton's, inspired by a winter's visit at the place of a friend of his in Fort Lauderdale, Florida. If they could have lights in coconut palms, Tony Burton said, there was no reason for not having them in the copper beeches at Roger's Point, but those new lights did not go so well with the house. Lampposts and gas-light would have fitted the whole scene better. The building had been designed by Richardson, the Romanesque architect—another fact that Charles had learned and filed away. It was too dark to see the detail of the slate roof, the brick walls and the arched doors and windows trimmed with old red sandstone, but its vague outline still looked indestructible. The light beneath the brick and sandstone porte cochere shone on the iron and glass front door and on the potted hothouse azaleas in rows beside the steps.

The doors had swung open already and Jeffreys, the Burton butler, had stepped outside—but not as far down as the lower step—and was saying good evening.

"You go in, Nancy," Charles said. "I'd better put the car somewhere." [544/545]

"There's no need to move it, Mr. Gray," Tony Burton's butler said. He was wearing a dinner coat with a stiff shirt. "There's no one else this evening."

"Oh," Charles said, "if you're sure it's all right." He had never been able to speak even an intellectual language with Tony Burton's butler. "It's a beautiful evening, isn't it?"

"Yes, sir," Tony Burton's butler said. "It's balmy for this time of year," and then Charles saw that a maid was behind him, relieving Nancy of her cloak.

It was impossible to forget Tony Burton's house once you had been inside it. In summer or winter the air in the hall was balmy like the evening and fragrant with the scent of hothouse flowers. It was a huge oak-paneled hall, with a double staircase and a gallery and a Romanesque fireplace. For a second he and Nancy stood in the shaded light of the hall almost indecisively. There was an especial feeling of timidity when one went there, a furtive sense of not belonging. Yet in another way he was perfectly at ease for at those semiannual dinners Tony Burton had always made them feel most welcome. Besides, each summer there was always that all-day party for everyone at the bank, with three-legged races and potato races and pingpong and bridge for the wives. Mrs. Burton, too, always made the bank wives feel comfortable. The bright light from the open parlor door shone across the dusky hall and Tony Burton was already in the oblong of light, a white carnation in the lapel of his dinner coat, holding out both hands, one for Nancy and one for him.

"Home is the sailor, home from sea," Tony Burton said, "and the hunter home from the hill. I wish you wouldn't always surprise me, Nancy my dear. Why are you more beautiful every time I see you, or do I just forget?"

"It might be that you just forget, mightn't it?" Nancy asked.

Tony Burton laughed. He had a delightful laugh.

"We've really got to do something about seeing each other more often," he said. "It's been too long, much too long. Why don't you come to work some morning instead of Charley? I'm getting pretty sick of seeing Charles around." He laughed again and slapped [545/546] Charles on the back and they walked behind Nancy into the drawing room.

Charles knew all about Tony Burton's drawing room, too, both from Tony Burton and from Arthur Slade. Mrs. Burton and the girls, before the girls had been married, had made Tony Burton do it entirely over. The enormous Persian carpet had come from the Anderson Gallery and so had the two Waterford chandeliers. Charles remembered them very well because Tony Burton had sent him to the auction to bid them in on one of the first occasions that Tony had ever paid any attention to him, and this did not seem so long ago. He also remembered the huge canvas of a mass of square-rigged ships—the British fleet at anchor. Mrs. Burton was always buying new things for the living room and besides Tony always loved boats. The cup he had won in one of the Bermuda races was standing on the concert grand piano. You could roll up the carpet and clear out all the furniture. It had been a great place for dancing before the girls had married.

"Althea," Tony Burton said, "I told you Nancy Gray would be wearing a long dress."

"Oh, my dear," Mrs. Burton said, "I should have called you up. Tony's getting so absent-minded lately. He spoke of it as supper. There should be set rules for short and long. Now just the other evening at the Drexels' the same thing happened to me. I thought it was dinner and it was supper. But the men thought this up. We didn't, did we?"

"Charles should have told me," Nancy said. "Why didn't you tell me it was supper, Charley?"

"It's always some man's fault, isn't it, Charley?" Tony Burton said.

"That's one of the truest things you ever said, sweetheart," Mrs. Burton said. "Everything that happens to a woman is always some man's fault."

"Jeffreys can bring us almost anything," Tony Burton said, "from sherry and a biscuit to Scotch on the rocks, but Charley and I will stick to dry Martinis, won't we, Charley? What will you have, Nancy my dear?" [546/547]

"A Martini," Nancy said, "and if I don't like it I can blame it on the men."

"But not on Tony," Mrs. Burton said. "Blame it on Jeffreys. Tony mixes terrible Martinis. Don't you think so, Mr. Gray, or have you ever tried one of his Martinis?"

It was characteristic of that relationship and perfectly suitable that Mrs. Burton should call him Mr. Gray. It meant that he was a business friend of Tony Burton's, or associate might have been a better word, who had come to supper on business with his little wife. She knew how to put Tony's business friends and associates at their ease, but there were certain limits and certain degrees of rank. They were not on a first-name basis yet and he was just as glad of it. It would have embarrassed him acutely, it would have seemed like a breach of etiquette, if he were to call Mrs. Burton Althea. He knew his place and they could meet on common ground by his calling Mr. Burton Tony and by Mrs. Burton's referring to Nancy as "my dear."

"I'm not in a position to say what I think of Tony's cocktails," Charles said, "except that Tony is always right."

"You all lick his boots so," Mrs. Burton said. "That's why he's so impossible when he comes home. Sherry, please, Jeffreys. Is Mr. Gray impossible when he comes home, my dear?"

"Usually," Nancy said. "Normally impossible."

"I wonder what they do at the bank," Mrs. Burton said. "I have a few vague ideas. That blond secretary of Tony's ... we can compare notes after dinner." The oil of small talk soothed the troubled waters, if there were troubled waters. Mrs. Tony Burton was putting Nancy at her ease. It was necessary business entertaining, household duty, and one of these suppers that must have helped in some vague way.

Everything moved so smoothly that when Charles tried to discover anything revealing in Mrs. Burton's voice or attitude, he could hit upon absolutely nothing. He could discover no new flicker of interest or no new warmth. She was simply being as nice as she could possibly be to one of the younger men whom Tony had to have around sometimes and to the little thing the younger man [547/548] had married. She had even dressed thoughtfully for the occasion in an oldish gown, with no jewelry except a simple strand of pearls, yet you could not say that she was dressing down to Nancy. Charles remembered Arthur Slade's saying that she was a good ten years younger than Tony, that she was one of the Philadelphia Brines, and Charles knew from the size of the Brine estate, which the bank was handling, that, like Tony Burton, she had always been free from want. He could tell it from the tilt of her head, from her confident happy mouth, and even from the tint of her hair. There was a single lock of gray in it and perhaps all of it should have been gray but he could not be quite sure.

"I love that little house of yours, my dear," she was saying, and he could see Nancy smiling at her with elaborate enthusiasm. "That whitewashed brick, and everything so compactly arranged. It must be a comfort to live in it instead of in a great barn, but Tony insists on the ancestral mansion."

"The only good thing about a small house," Nancy said, "is when the maid leaves."

"We've been marvelously lucky," Mrs. Burton said. "Ours keep staying on with us, I'm sure I don't know why."

Jeffreys, the butler, was passing round pieces of toast with cream cheese and recumbent anchovies on them, and a maid followed Jeffreys carrying an icy bowl of celery, raw carrots and olives.

"I hear that raw carrots are good for the eyesight," Charles said to Tony Burton.

"That's one of those new ideas," Tony said. He looked bright and alert as he always did before dinner. "It's on a par with the one about alcohol being good for hardening of the arteries. Have you heard the new one about Truman?"

Tony Burton always enjoyed those stories. Formerly it had been Franklin D. Roosevelt, though Tony was hardly what you would call a Roosevelt-hater, and now it was Truman.

"I don't know," Charles said. "I've heard a good many new ones lately." He had almost called Tony Burton sir but he had checked himself in time.

"I know just what you mean, my dear," he heard Mrs. Burton [548/549] saying. "These country day schools are never quite right. Now when the girls were growing up—"

"Always remember it might have been Wallace," he said to Tony Burton. Everything considered, Tony was surprisingly tolerant about politics and politicians. To him politics was like the weather. You could make occasional forecasts but you could not control it.

"I'd like to know what those playboys are going to try next," he said. "And that's a good name for them, playboys. Did you ever read the Van Bibber stories by Richard Harding Davis?"

"The Van Bibber stories?" Charles repeated. "I'm afraid I must have missed them."

"Well," Tony Burton said, "they belonged to my flight more than your flight, Charley." This must once have been a shooting term, Charles thought, used when one foregathered in a gunroom after a hard day on the moors. "They typified a certain era—the period when I was a playboy myself. There used to be a fashionable character, believe it or not—the gay blade about town, the white tie, the silk hat, we won't get home until morning. He's an extinct type now, of course, a product of a different social scene. Dick Davis hit him off rather well in the Van Bibber stories. Dick Davis was quite a playboy himself. I used to try to model my conduct after his, in a small way. Here comes Jeffreys. How about another cocktail?"

"Oh, no, I don't think so, thanks," Charles said. He did not want to refuse too quickly or too eagerly, and of course Tony Burton must have known that when urged he would take another.

"It won't hurt you to relax and tomorrow's Saturday and I'm going to have another."

"Well, thanks," Charles said, "if you are. They're very good cocktails."

He wished that he could relax as Tony Burton suggested, instead of trying to read a meaning into every simple action. Tony Burton would never have taken a second Martini if they were going to talk of anything seriously after dinner. It meant that everything was settled in one way or another.

"Now, Henry Wallace," Tony Burton was saying, "and all the rest of the New Deal crowd are the playboy type. They have the [549/550] same power and the same privileges expressed in different terms. They're all Van Bibbers."

Tony smiled at him triumphantly but it was hard for Charles to discuss the subject intelligently, not being familiar with the works of Richard Harding Davis.

"It's an interesting thought," he said, "but it might be that you're oversimplifying."

Tony Burton looked at him in a fixed, cool way that made Charles think that perhaps he had said too much. It was necessary not to forget just who he was and what he was. It was necessary to assume a convivial attitude and yet not too convivial, to be familiar and yet not overfamiliar.

"Sometimes you have a cryptic quality, Charley," Tony Burton said. "I never seem to know lately whether you're laughing at me or not. Sometimes you're an enigma."

"Well," Charles answered, "sometimes you're an enigma to me."

When he heard Tony Burton laugh he knew that he had been familiar but not too familiar.

"Oh, Jeffreys," Tony Burton said. "How about another one, Charley?"

"No, thanks," Charles said.

"Definitely not?"

"Definitely," Charles said. "You might start talking about books and authors again and I want to understand everything you say tonight."

It might have been too familiar but at least he had made a point. He waited smiling, watching Tony Burton, and he put his glass back on Tony Burton's butler's tray. He was thinking of what he had said to young Mrs. Whitaker in the apartment on Park Avenue when she had offered him a drink. He had told her that he did not think she would take one if she were in his place and she had said they were both very good for what they were. He watched Tony Burton and smiled an innocent friendly smile. He and Tony Burton were both very good for what they were. They had both been trained in the Stuyvesant Bank and they had the same veneer and discipline. He had come a long way from Clyde. [550/551]

"Tony," Mrs. Burton called, "if you can stop talking business with poor Mr. Gray we might all go in to dinner."

"Now, Althea," Tony Burton said, "Charley and I have a lot of other things to talk about. I wish you would get it out of your head that I always talk business with the boys."

The dining room with its heavy oak chairs, and an English leather screen placed before the pantry door, and its ornate Tiffany silver upon the massive sideboard, was also a long way from Clyde. The table, set for four, beneath another Waterford chandelier, looked too small for the room but imposingly beautiful with its Venetian tablecloth, its water and wine glasses and its bowl of tulips. He was glad there were only four of them because the conversation would be general and he would not have to talk to Mrs. Burton. He saw Nancy glance at him quickly as he sat down and he smiled at her. It was better to let the Burtons start the conversation. It was better not to say what a beautiful tablecloth it was or to speak about the tulips. It was better to make no remark about the surroundings that would show how little one was used to them, but there was no reason to worry, because Mrs. Burton was already speaking.

It was so nice, she was saying, to have them drop in like this instead of coming to a large dinner. Eight was the limit for general conversation and four was better than eight, and she was thinking, just the other day, about the first time she had ever heard about Mr. Gray—from poor Arthur Slade. She did not think she had seen Mr. Gray since that accident. It was tragic and so unnecessary. They had both been so fond of poor Arthur, but then she knew that Mr. Gray knew all about flying. The conversation was moving very pleasantly. It was not necessary to think carefully of what he was saying, now that they all were talking. Tony Burton was asking Nancy about the children, as though he knew them very well, and while they talked the plates were changing. There were soup and guinea hen and then a salad and then dessert. He was glad that it was not a long or complicated dinner. There was no obvious sense of strain but all the while he felt that Tony Burton was watching him.

"I wish," Tony Burton said, "there weren't so many words, or it

[551/552] may be because I'm getting old that they confuse me more than they used to. Somehow they keep having more shades of meaning. Now even with Charles and me it's difficult. I say a word and he says a word and we can look it up in the dictionary, but it doesn't mean the same thing to either of us and it would mean something a little different to Nancy and it would be a little different even to Althea. I don't suppose this is a very new thought of mine, but it's a thought."

"I can't imagine what you're talking about, Tony," Mrs. Burton said.

"But Charley knows," Tony Burton said, "don't you, Charley? We all may be worrying about the same thing but we worry about it in different ways."

It was startling to find that Tony Burton was thinking during dinner exactly what he had been thinking earlier.

"Yes," he said, "I know just what you mean."

He saw that Nancy looked startled too and he saw Tony Burton glance at her and then look back at him triumphantly.

"I wish we could all get together," Tony Burton said, "and we might do something with the world, but of course we never can get together. That's the exasperating thing about it."

"Really," Mrs. Burton said, "I don't know what you're talking about, Tony."

Charles himself could not gather what this was leading up to, but as he watched Tony Burton he could see that Tony's face was set in the expression he always wore when he was about to say a few graceful words before a group of people.

"Perhaps I'm being cryptic now," he said, "but all I'm saying is that I wish we might all be friends. I really hope we can be, in spite of anything that may happen in the future, and the future isn't as clear as it used to be. That's all I'm trying to say. And now if you girls will excuse us, I'm going to take Charley into the library. Charley and I want to have a little talk tonight but we'll be back as soon as we can."

Mrs. Burton stood up and as Charles rose he felt a slight wave of nausea. He could only put one interpretation on that hope for friendship. He guessed the final answer to their little talk already. [552/553] He felt the back of his chair biting into the palm of his hand but he still had to say the right thing.

"Why, of course," he said, "we'll always be friends, Tony." He said it automatically but he knew that they never had been and they never would be friends. They might wish it but it would never work for either of them, no matter what might happen.

"Don't stay too long and get too interested," Mrs. Burton said. "I don't see why Tony can't ever get through his business in New York."

Charles was no longer thinking clearly as he walked with Tony Burton from the dining room. What he desired most was to behave in such a way that no one would have the satisfaction of seeing how deeply he was hurt. That desire was partly discipline and partly human instinct for concealment. His own reaction was what shocked him most because he had believed that he was prepared for bad news and that he would not consider bad news as complete a disaster as was indicated by the sinking feeling in the pit of his stomach. Yet after that first moment the shock was giving way to relief. He suddenly felt free and a weight was lifted from him. There was no reason for him to try any longer, not the slightest reason. He did not know what he would say or do in that final interview but there was nothing more that he could expect from Tony Burton. He would never have to be obsequious and careful again. He would never have to go through anything like that dinner. If Tony wished that they could still be friends, this meant at least that Tony liked him personally, but that was inconsequential. There was no room for personal likes in a corporation.

It was not far from the dining room to the smaller room where men customarily gathered. They both walked across that gloomy hall without speaking and space had lost its significance. He was actually walking also over the road of his career, a feeble little human track like the progress of a sea creature in sand. It stretched all the way from the day on the stage at the City Hall to the accounting department in Wright-Sherwin, to Johnson Street, to Rush & Company, to the day his father died, to New York, to the day he met Nancy downtown, and now the track was ending in that walk [553/554] across the hall. There would never be the same hay in the bundle again. The ass would never have to walk after it so assiduously. He might still be useful, but in a business way his career was as good as over. He had gone as far as he would go.

It was amazing that his thoughts could move so far afield in such a short space of time. He was like a defeated general withdrawing to a prepared position. He could sell the house at Sycamore Park. Suburban real estate was still high. They could move to a smaller place. There would be funds enough to educate Bill, and there was that trust fund of his mother's which would revert to him eventually. He would never have his present reputation but he would have the commercial value of an educated wheel horse, if he knew his place. He would never have to try so hard again.

"It's over," he said to himself as he walked across the hall. "Thank God, it's over." It was the first time he had felt really free since the moment he had met Jessica at the firemen's muster.

Tony Burton's room had always reminded him of the corner of a men's club. It was filled with the mementos of the travels of Tony Burton, gathered on that trip to Bagdad and on two world cruises. There was a gilded Chinese Buddha on the mantel above the arched fireplace, and a Chinese ancestral portrait and other things, but Charles was no longer obliged to be interested in them. He seated himself in a comfortable armchair without waiting to see if it was Mr. Burton's chair or not. He no longer had to bother.

"Sugar and cream, sir?" Mr. Burton's butler asked.

"Just coffee, thank you," Charles said.

"And brandy, sir?"

"No, thanks," Charles said. "No brandy."

"Try it, Charley," Tony Burton said. "It's some of my father's brandy. There isn't much like it left."

Tony Burton was still standing up. He should have waited until Tony sat down but he no longer had to try so hard.

"Nancy always says I shouldn't drink after dinner," he said, "but all right if you're going to have some, Tony."

"Why not break down all the way and have a cigar?" Tony Burton said. [554/555]

"Why, thanks," he answered. "I'd like one."

"Now that I think of it, I've never seen you smoke a cigar, Charley."

"I don't often," Charles said, "but I'd rather like one tonight."

Tony Burton was still standing and again he wore the look he customarily assumed when he prepared to say a few graceful yet pointed words.

"Close the door, please, Jeffreys, when you go out," Tony Burton said.

It was like a meeting in the bank directors' room when someone who came in with papers was told to close the door when he left. Charles leaned back comfortably in his chair. It was up to Tony Burton and he did not have to try. He was thinking of other talks in other libraries, the Judge's library at Gow Street and that hypocritical library of Mr. Lovell's and his own library at Sycamore Park. Thank God, it was all over, but he still had a detached, academic sort of curiosity. He was waiting to see how Tony would handle the situation. Tony was sometimes slow and fumbling with decisions but when he made up his mind he carried them through cleanly.

"This friendship in business—" Tony Burton said. "It's always bothered me. They shouldn't be mixed together." He must still have been thinking of that speech in the dining room.

"They don't mix together," Charles said. "Don't try to make them, Tony." It was the first time he had ever spoken to Tony Burton exactly as an equal and it was a great relief. He flicked off the ash of his cigar and picked up his brandy glass and waited.

"And yet they must mix," Tony Burton said. "None of us can help it, Charley. If you see somebody every day, if you have any human instincts at all, you get interested in him. You're bound to like him, or things about him. I like everybody at the bank. They're like members of my family. Now take Blakesley. What do you think of Blakesley, Charley?"

It was not a fair question and there was no reason to give a fair answer and besides it did not matter what he thought of Roger Blakesley. [555/556]

"What do you want me to think?" he asked, and he was glad to see that Tony did not like the answer.

"It isn't what I want." Tony Burton gave his head an exasperated shake. "You and I are alone here, and you don't have to be so damned careful. There's no necessity for it any more. I want your opinion of him. Do you like him or don't you?"

"All right," Charles said, "as long as it doesn't matter any more, Tony. He's conscientious, energetic, and well-trained, but I don't like him much. Why should I?"

"I rather like him," Tony Burton said. "He's been on my conscience lately. He's been so damned anxious, so damned much on his toes. He's always in there trying."

"I don't know what else you could expect," Charles said, and he was almost amused, now that there was nothing to gain or lose. "I've been trying pretty hard myself."

He had never realized that it could be such a delightful moment, to sit sipping Tony Burton's brandy, entirely free, entirely without thought control.

"Not in the same way, Charley." Tony Burton shook his head again. "You're subtler. You've developed, you've matured. You don't fidget mentally—not in the same way, Charley."

"Thanks," Charles said, "but I wouldn't say that I've been very subtle, Tony."

Tony Burton shook his head impatiently as though he were being diverted from his train of thought.

"Of course I'm out of touch with things, being where I am," he said, "but I've been getting an idea lately . . . and maybe I'm entirely wrong. I wish you'd tell me, Charley. You're more in touch with the office than I am and you're in a position to know Blakesley. . . . It seems to me that he has some idea that we're considering him for Arthur Slade's place. Do you know anything about this, Charley?"

"My God," Charles said. "My God"; and he had a hysterical desire to laugh and then he found that he was laughing. "What did you think that Roger was considering?"

"I didn't give it much thought until about ten days ago," Tony [556/557] Burton said. "I'm glad if it amuses you. It doesn't amuse me. When anyone gets ideas like that it's a problem what to do with him later. You never thought that any of us were considering Blakesley seriously, did you? He was useful while you were away but he is not the right material. Of course, there had to be a decent interval after Arthur died but it never occurred to me that you'd have any doubts about it. Your name's coming up before the directors on Monday. Now what do you think we'd better do about Blakesley?"

Suddenly Charles felt dull and very tired.

"You'd better tell him something, Tony," he said, "instead of teasing him to death."

"I suppose I'll have to on Monday. I don't suppose I can put it off on anyone else," Tony Burton said. "I should have discouraged him long ago. I'm sorry about the whole thing but perhaps he had better resign."

It was like the time at Dartmouth when he had won the half mile at freshman track. He felt dull and very tired.

"That was all I meant in the dining room." Tony Burton shook his head again. "Now that we'll be working together more closely, Charley, I hope that we'll always be friends."

Tony's voice seemed to come from a long way off. There was a weight on Charles again, the same old weight, and it was heavier after that brief moment of freedom. In spite of all those years, in spite of all his striving, it was remarkable how little pleasure he took in final fulfillment. He was a vice-president of the Stuyvesant Bank. It was what he had dreamed of long ago and yet it was not the true texture of early dreams. The whole thing was contrived, as he had said to Nancy, an inevitable result, a strangely hollow climax. It had obviously been written in the stars, bound to happen, and he could not have changed a line of it, being what he was, and Nancy would be pleased, but it was not what he had dreamed.

"Well, Tony," he said, "I guess that means I can send Junior to Exeter," and Tony Burton was asking why Exeter? He would not send any boy of his to Exeter.

They were on a different basis already, now that he was a vice-president. Automatically, his thoughts were running along new [557/558] lines, well-trained, mechanically perfect thoughts, estimating a new situation. There would be no trouble with the directors. There were only five vice-presidents at the Stuyvesant, all of the others older than he, most of them close to the retirement age, like Tony Burton himself. For a moment he thought of Mr. Laurence Lovell on Johnson Street but Mr. Lovell would not have understood, or Jessica either, how far he had gone or what it meant to be a vice-president of the Stuyvesant Bank. Nancy would understand. Nancy had more ambition for him than he had for himelf. Nancy would be very proud. They would sell the house at Sycamore Park and get a larger place. They would resign from the Oak Knoll Club. And then there was the sailboat. It had its compensations but it was not what he had dreamed.

"A week from Saturday there'll be a little dinner. It's customary," Tony Burton said. "You'd better be ready to make a few remarks."

"All right," Charles said, "if it's customary."

"And now we'd better go back and see what the girls are doing, unless you have something else on your mind."

"Oh, no, Tony," he answered, "I don't think there's anything else."

They would have to turn in the old Buick as soon as he could get a new one. There were a great many things to think about but they could wait till morning.

Nancy and Mrs. Burton were sitting together on a sofa in the living room and he thought they both looked relieved to see the men come back.

"Well," Mrs. Burton said, "I hope you two have settled the affairs of the world. You look as though you have, and poor Mr. Gray looks tired."

He saw Nancy look at him and Nancy looked tired too. He wanted very much to tell her the news but it would have sounded blatant. Then Tony Burton must have noticed that there was a sense of strain.

"I don't see why you keep on calling Charley Mr. Gray," he said, "when Charley's in the family—or at least he will be on Monday," and then he must have felt that he should explain the situation [558/559] further because he turned to Nancy. "I don't suppose this comes as any great surprise. Why should it? It's hardly talking out of school. Charley's name is going before the directors on Monday, but I've spoken to them already. There won't be any trouble."

If it meant more to Nancy than it did to him, it made everything all the better, and he was very much impressed at the way she took it. She looked as though she had known all the time that he would be the new vice-president, that nothing else could possibly have happened. She was fitting into her new position more than adequately.

"I can't say I'm surprised," she said, "but it's nice to know definitely . . . Tony."

A minute before she would never have dreamed of calling him Tony, but it sounded very well.

"As long as we're all in the family," Tony Burton went on, "I was just telling Charley that I've been worried about Blakesley lately. Do you suppose he really may have thought that he was being considered?"

"Now that you mention it," Nancy said, "I think perhaps he did—a little." [559]

4. DISSIDENT VOICES

THE PURITAN COMPROMISE WITH WEALTH, EVEN THOUGH AT TIMES AN uneasy one in the consciences of a few of the more unworldly, was nevertheless effectively adopted. The work of the world went on under the blessing of the church; and only a few lonely voices, such as that of the great eighteenth-century Calvinist theologian Jonathan Edwards, were heard reminding the faithful to look more toward God than toward worldly concerns. Certainly few prominent leaders, even religious ones, followed the example of the Quaker John Woolman, who deliberately restricted his profitable tailoring trade in the fear that wealth was a source of corruption to the life of the spirit.

In general, religious objections to the pursuit of wealth, even the few that were raised, lost their effectiveness by the time of the Revolution. Objections to the money culture of the early nineteenth century came from other sources. After the Revolution the breakdown of political and social barriers opened new avenues for success and placed men, all men at least in theory, in a position where success was attainable. And to most people success meant wealth. The simple desire for money, or land, or other tangible possessions, was therefore recognized as a national passion, accepted as legitimate by most, by others condemned as a national vice.

Among the voices raised in objection to the new commercial values—perhaps the most influential voices in the early days of the nineteenth century—were those of the self-styled aristocrats in the new society. James Fenimore Cooper, for instance, himself a large landholder, was sharply critical of the vulgar behavior of the ambitious lawyers and merchants who were seeking the "main chance," aspiring in effect to the position that Cooper himself held. Cooper seemed to object to their manner of behavior, but his objections in addition touched ethical and moral questions. For instance, he was prepared to lose vast sums of money in lawsuits to protect certain principles—the inviolability of a man's reputation, for one. If Cooper can be accepted as a reasonable example of an aristocrat, it can be asserted that this aristocrat valued certain gentlemanly and chivalric codes of behavior—codes which the simple ambition for money often seemed to cheapen and violate.

Perhaps the most serious nineteenth-century criticism of success and money culture appeared in the writings of the New England transcendentalists. Ralph Waldo Emerson and Henry David Thoreau, to name the two most prominent of the transcendentalists, and their fellow poet, Walt Whitman, objected to their neighbors' rapt search for money and possessions not because they felt that the search was vulgar or that it violated valid ethical codes but because they felt the search resulted in a severe displacement of energies. By the diversions of a man's energies into channels of money making, self-fulfillment can only be restricted. The true activity of man was the development of his moral and spiritual nature, his inner self. Nathaniel Hawthorne, normally not considered in the transcendentalist school, nevertheless reveals his kinship to them in the conclusion to his story "The Great Stone Face." His hero emerges as the human equivalent of the "face" which through the years he has modestly and humbly worshiped. The interior achievement of man is his proper goal, according to these writers, not the money and prestige façade which appeared to them to be America's public goals.

In the period following the Civil War and even into the early twentieth century, there were several major critical reactions to the American money culture. Humorists and satirists such as Mark Twain and Sinclair Lewis chose to reveal its true nature by means of ridicule. Criticisms leveled in the name of humanitarianism appear in the writings of the leftist writers Edward Bellamy and John Dos Passos, who charged that a capitalist society appeals to the selfish natures of men and that man in his selfishness victimizes his fellow man. The examples included in this section are only a few of the illustrations in the literature of social protest. Another group of writers dealt with the failures—with those who were acutely conscious of the aspiration toward success but who failed to reach its promised rewards. The psychological, social, and economic implications in the stories of the failures are perhaps the most serious indictments of America's success culture.

Failures can be divided into several groups: those who are simple victims of an economic condition or specifically of another man's greed (for example, the toilers of Edward Bellamy's coach metaphor in *Looking Backward*); those who are victims of their own ambitions or their own presumptions (Mr. X— in Theodore Dreiser's "'Vanity, Vanity,' Saith the Preacher"); the ones who cynically pursue money with no awareness of the spiritual desert their pursuit is creating (Richard Savage in *U. S. A.* by John Dos Passos); the complacent ones who cannot realize a cure to their unhappiness because they fail to recognize that they have a disease (Sinclair Lewis's Babbitt); the unhappy ones caught in the pitiless routine of an indifferent commercialized culture (many of Sherwood Anderson's characters, such as the father in "The Egg"), inventing their own local hopes for quick money because they have lost the perspective of alternatives to the commercial culture.

Finally, there are the dreamers—the Clyde Griffiths, the Gatsbys; the victims of the glamorous illusions that have been exploited so successfully by producers of the mass media. The American dream of success has been a public dream. Those who accepted the dream innocently and literally looked as if in a public mirror for confidence and reassurance. The wise and resourceful perhaps realized the distortions, but many were not wise and not resourceful. The moment of recognition for the victim is poignant not so much because he suffers from poverty or from his shame in the fact of failure as because he has lost an ideal and a faith. No longer can he rest in the security of his belief. From a distance he sees progress moving swiftly by him; he stands alone in his failure and faces the sense of his isolation. Of all the voices of dissent in the history of America's success culture, probably the most effective are those critics who described sympathetically the ones whom this culture had left behind.

But from whatever the source, from the religionist, the moralist, the socialist, or the humanitarian, the critical target was the same: money worship is a national vice, vulgar in its demonstrations and destructive in its effects. The philosopher William James has recognized America's "exclusive worship of the bitch-goddess SUCCESS. That—with the squalid interpretation put on the word success—is our national disease."

A. MORAL AND SOCIAL CRITICISM

A Plea for the Poor

JOHN WOOLMAN

I

WEALTH DESIRED FOR ITS' OWN SAKE OBSTRUCTS THE INCREASE OF VIRTUE, and large possessions in the hands of selfish men have a bad tendency, for by their means too small a number of people are employed in useful things, and some of them are necessitated to labour too hard, while others would want business to earn their bread, were not employments invented which, having no real usefulness, serve only to please the vain mind.

Rents on lands are often so high that persons of but small substance are straitened in taking farms, and while tenants are healthy and prosperous in business, they often find occasion to labour harder than was intended by our gracious Creator. Oxen and horses are often seen at work when, through heat and too much labour, their eyes and the motions of their bodies manifest that they are oppressed. Their loads in wagons are frequently so heavy that when weary with hauling them far, their drivers find occasion in going up hills, or through mire, to get them forward by whipping. Many poor people are so thronged in their business that it is difficult for them to provide shelter for their cattle against the storms. These things are common when in health, but through sickness and inability to labour, through loss of cattle, and miscarriage in business, many are so straitened that much of their increase goes to pay rent, and they have not wherewith to buy what they require.

Hence one poor woman, in providing for her family and attending the sick, does as much business as would for the [243/244] time be suitable employment for two or three; and honest persons are often straitened to give their children suitable learning. The money which the wealthy receive from the poor, who do more than a proper share of

From John Woolman, *A Plea for the Poor; or, A Word of Remembrance and Caution to the Rich*, in *The Journal and Other Writings* (London: J. M. Dent & Sons; New York: E. P. Dutton & Co., Everyman's Library, 1910), pp. 243–246. Originally published 1793; written in 1763. Reprinted by permission of E. P. Dutton & Co., Inc.

business in raising it, is frequently paid to other poor people for doing business which is foreign to the true use of things. Men who have large estates and live in the spirit of charity; who carefully inspect the circumstances of those who occupy their estates, and, regardless of the customs of the times, regulate their demands agreeably to universal love, being righteous on principle, do good to the poor without placing it to an act of bounty. Their example in avoiding superfluities tends to excite moderation in others; their uprightness in not exacting what the laws and customs would support them in tends to open the channel to moderate labour in useful affairs, and to discourage those branches of business which have not their foundation in true wisdom.

To be busied in that which is but vanity and serves only to please the insatiable mind, tends to an alliance with those who promote that vanity, and is a snare in which many poor tradesmen are entangled. To be employed in things connected with virtue is most agreeable with the character and inclinations of an honest man. While industrious, frugal people are borne down with poverty, and oppressed with too much labour in useful things, the way to apply money without promoting pride and vanity remains open to such as truly sympathize with them in their various difficulties.

II

The Creator of the earth is the owner of it. He gave us being thereon, and our nature requires nourishment from the produce of it. He is kind and merciful to his creatures; and while they live answerably to the design of their creation, they are so far entitled to convenient subsistence that we may not justly deprive them of it. By the agreements and contracts of our predecessors, and by [244/245] our own doings, some enjoy a much greater share of this world than others; and while those possessions are faithfully improved for the good of the whole, it agrees with equity; but he who, with a view to self-exaltation, causeth some to labour immoderately, and with the profits arising therefrom employs others in the luxuries of life, acts contrary to the gracious designs of Him who is the owner of the earth; nor can any possessions, either acquired or derived from ancestors, justify such conduct. Goodness remains to be goodness, and the direction of pure wisdom is obligatory on all reasonable creatures.

Though the poor occupy our estates by a bargain, to which they in their poor circumstances agree, and we may ask even less than a punctual fulfilling of their agreement, yet if our views are to lay up riches, or to live in conformity, to customs which have not their foundations in the truth, and our demands are such as require from them greater toil or application to business than is consistent with pure love, we invade their rights as inhabitants of a world of which a good and gracious God is the proprietor, and under whom we are tenants.

Were all superfluities and the desire of outward greatness laid aside, and the right use of things universally attended to, such a number of people might be employed in things useful as that moderate labour with the blessing of Heaven would answer all good purposes, and a sufficient number would have time to attend to the proper affairs of civil society.

III

While our spirits are lively, we go cheerfully through business; either too much or too little action is tiresome, but a right portion is healthful to the body and agreeable to an honest mind.

Men who have great estates stand in a place of trust; and to have it in their power to live without difficulty in that manner which occasions much labour, and at the same time to confine themselves to that use of things [245/246] prescribed by our Redeemer, and confirmed by his example and the examples of many who lived in the early age of the Christian church, that they may more extensively relieve objects of charity, requires close attention to Divine love.

Our gracious Creator cares and provides for all his creatures. His tender mercies are over all his works, and so far as true love influences our minds, so far we become interested in his workmanship and feel a desire to make use of every opportunity to lessen the distresses of the afflicted and to increase the happiness of the creation. Here we have a prospect of one common interest from which our own is inseparable, so that to turn all we possess into the channel of universal love becomes the business of our lives.

Men of large estates, whose hearts are thus enlarged, are like fathers to the poor; and in looking over their brethren in distressed circumstances, and considering their own more easy condition, they find a field for humble meditation, and feel the strength of the obligations they are under to be kind and tender-hearted towards them. Poor men, eased of their burdens and released from too close an application to business, are enabled to hire assistance, to provide well for their cattle, and to find time to perform those duties among their neighbours which belong to a well-guided social life. When the latter reflect on the opportunity such had to oppress them, and consider the goodness of their conduct, they behold it lovely and consistent with brotherhood; and as the man whose mind is conformed to universal love hath his truth settled in God and finds a firm foundation in any changes or revolutions that happen among men, so also the goodness his conduct tends to spread a kind, benevolent disposition in the world. [246]

The Opportunist

JAMES FENIMORE COOPER

THE SERVICE AT MR. EFFINGHAM'S TABLE WAS MADE IN THE QUIET BUT thorough manner that distinguishes a French dinner. Every dish was removed, carved by the domestics, and handed in turn to each guest. But there were a delay and a finish in this arrangement that suited neither Aristabulus' go-ahead-ism, nor his organ of acquisitiveness. Instead of waiting, therefore, for the more graduated movements of the domestics, he began to take care of himself, an office that he performed with a certain dexterity that he had acquired by frequenting ordinaries—a school, by the way, in which he had obtained most of his notions of the proprieties of the table. One or two slices were obtained in the usual manner, or by means of the regular service; and then, like one who had laid the foundation of a fortune by some lucky windfall in the commencement of his career, he began to make accessions, right and left, as opportunity offered. Sundry *entremets,* or light dishes that had a peculiarly tempting appearance, came first under his grasp. Of these he soon accumulated all within his reach, by taxing his neighbors, when he ventured to send his plate here and there, or wherever he saw a dish that promised to reward his trouble. By such means, which were resorted to, however, with a quiet and unobtrusive assiduity that escaped much observation, Mr. Bragg contrived to make his own plate a sample epitome of the first course. It contained in the centre, fish, beef, and ham; and around these staple articles he had arranged croquettes, rognons, râgouts, vegetables, and other light things, until not only was the plate completely covered, but it was actually covered in double and triple layers; mustard, cold butter, salt, and even pepper garnishing its edges. These different accumulations were the work of time and address, and most of the company had repeatedly changed their plates before Aristabulus had eaten a mouthful, the soup excepted. The happy moment when his ingenuity was to be rewarded had now arrived, and the land agent was about to commence the

From James Fenimore Cooper, *Home as Found* (New York: G. P. Putnam's Sons, n.d.), pp. 18–25. Originally published 1838.

process of mastication, [18/19] or of deglutition rather, for he troubled himself very little with the first operation, when the report of a cork drew his attention towards the champagne. To Aristabulus this wine never came amiss, for, relishing its piquancy, he had never gone far enough into the science of the table to learn which were the proper moments for using it. As respected all the others at table, this moment had in truth arrived, though, as respected himself, he was no nearer to it, according to a regulated taste, than when he first took his seat. Perceiving that Pierre was serving it, however, he offered his own glass, and enjoyed a delicious instant as he swallowed a beverage that much surpassed anything he had ever known to issue out of the waxed and leaded nozzles that, pointed like so many enemies' batteries loaded with headaches and disordered stomachs, garnished sundry village bars of his acquaintance.

Aristabulus finished. his glass at a draught, and when he took breath he fairly smacked his lips. That was an unlucky instant; his plate, burdened with all its treasures, being removed at this unguarded moment; the man who performed this unkind office fancying that a dislike to the dishes could alone have given rise to such an *omnium-gatherum.*

It was necessary to commence *de novo,* but this could no longer be done with the first course, which was removed, and Aristabulus set to with zeal forthwith on the game. Necessity compelled him to eat, as the different dishes were offered; and such was his ordinary assiduity with the knife and fork, that, at the end of the second remove, he had actually disposed of more food than any other person at table. He now began to converse, and we shall open the conversation at the precise point in the dinner when it was in the power of Aristabulus to make one of the interlocutors.

Unlike Mr. Dodge, he had betrayed no peculiar interest in the baronet, being a man too shrewd and worldly to set his heart on trifles of any sort; and Mr. Bragg no more hesitated about replying to Sir George Templemore or Mr. Effingham, than he would have hesitated about answering one [19/20] of his own nearest associates. With him age and experience formed no particular claims to be heard, and, as to rank, it is true he had some vague ideas about there being such a thing in the militia, but as it was unsalaried rank, he attached no great importance to it. Sir George Templemore was inquiring concerning the recording of deeds, a regulation that had recently attracted attention in England; and one of Mr. Effingham's replies contained some immaterial inaccuracy, which Aristabulus took occasion to correct, as his first appearance in the general discourse.

"I ask pardon, sir," he concluded his explanations by saying, "but I ought to know these little niceties, having served a short part of a term as a county clerk, to fill a vacancy occasioned by a death."

"You mean, Mr. Bragg, that you were employed to write in a

county clerk's office," observed John Effingham, who so much disliked untruth, that he did not hesitate much about refuting it, or what he now fancied to be an untruth.

"As county clerk, sir. Major Pippin died a year before his time was out, and I got the appointment. As regular a county clerk, sir, as there is in the fifty-six counties of New York."

"When I had the honor to engage you as Mr. Effingham's agent, sir," returned the other, a little sternly, for he felt his own character for veracity involved in that of the subject of his selection, "I believed, indeed, that you were writing in the office, but I did not understand it was as the clerk."

"Very true, Mr. John," returned Aristabulus, without discovering the least concern, "I was then engaged by my successor as a clerk; but a few months earlier, I filled the office myself."

"Had you gone on, in the regular line of promotion, my dear sir," pithily inquired Captain Truck, "to what preferment would you have risen by this time?"

"I believe I understand you, gentlemen," returned the unmoved Aristabulus, who perceived a general smile. "I know that some people are particular about keeping pretty [20/21] much on the same level, as to office: but I hold to no such doctrine. If one good thing cannot be had, I do not see that it is a reason for rejecting another. I ran that year for sheriff, and finding I was not strong enough to carry the county, I accepted my successor's offer to write in the office, until something better might turn up."

"You practised all this time, I believe, Mr. Bragg?" observed John Effingham.

"I did a little in that way, too, sir; or as much as I could. Law is flat with us of late, and many of the attorneys are turning their attention to other callings."

"And pray, sir," asked Sir George, "what is the favorite pursuit with most of them just now?"

"Some, our way, have gone into the horse line; but much the greater portion are just now dealing in Western cities."

"In Western cities!" exclaimed the baronet, looking as if he distrusted a mystification.

"In such articles, and in mill-seats, and railroad lines, and other expectations."

"Mr. Bragg means that they are buying and selling lands on which it is hoped all these conveniences may exist, a century hence," explained John Effingham.

"The hope is for next year, or next week even, Mr. John," returned Aristabulus with a sly look, "though you may be very right as to the reality. Great fortunes have been made on a capital of hopes, lately, in this country."

"And have you been able yourself to resist these temptations?"

asked Mr. Effingham. "I feel doubly indebted to you, sir, that you should have continued to devote your time to my interests, while so many better things were offering."

"It was my duty, sir," said Aristabulus, bowing so much the lower, from the consciousness that he had actually deserted his post for some months, to embark in the Western speculations that were then so active in the country, "not to say my pleasure. There are many profitable occupations in this country, Sir George, that have been overlooked in the eagerness to embark in the town-trade–" [21/22]

"Mr. Bragg does not mean trade in town, but trade in towns," explained John Effingham.

"Yes, sir, the traffic in cities. I never come this way without casting an eye about me, in order to see if there is anything to be done that is useful; and I confess that several available opportunities have offered, if one had capital. Milk is a good business."

"*Le lait!*" exclaimed Mademoiselle Viefville, involuntarily.

"Yes, ma'am, for ladies as well as gentlemen. Sweet potatoes I have heard well spoken of, and peaches are really making some rich men's fortunes."

"All of which are honester and better occupations than the traffic in cities, that you have mentioned," quietly observed Mr. Effingham.

Aristabulus looked up in a little surprise, for with him everything was eligible that returned a good profit, and all things honest that the law did not actually punish. Perceiving, however, that the company was disposed to listen, and having by this time recovered the lost ground, in the way of food, he cheerfully resumed his theme.

"Many families have left Otsego, this and the last summer, Mr. Effingham, as emigrants for the West. The fever has spread far and wide."

"The fever! Is old Otsego," for so its inhabitants loved to call a county of half a century's existence, it being venerable by comparison, "is old Otsego losing its well-established character for salubrity?"

"I do not allude to an animal fever, but to the Western fever."

"*Ce pays de l'ouest, est-il bien malsain?*" whispered Mademoiselle Viefville.

"*Apparemment, Mademoiselle, sur plusieurs rapports.*"

"The Western fever has seized old and young, and it has carried off many active families from our part of the world," continued Aristabulus, who did not understand the little aside just mentioned, and who, of course, did not heed it; "most of the counties adjoining our own have lost a considerable portion of their population." [22/23]

"And they who have gone, do they belong to the permanent families, or are they merely the floating inhabitants?" inquired Mr. Effingham.

"Most of them belong to the regular movers."

"Movers!" again exclaimed Sir George; "is there any material part of your population who actually deserve this name?"

"As much so as the man who shoes a horse ought to be called a smith, or a man who frames a house a carpenter," answered John Effingham.

"To be sure," continued Mr. Bragg, "we have a pretty considerable leaven of them in our political dough, as well as in our active business. I believe, Sir George, that in England men are tolerably stationary."

"We love to continue for generations on the same spot. We love the tree that our forefathers planted, the roof that they built, the fireside by which they sat, the sods that cover their remains."

"Very poetical, and I dare say there are situations in life in which such feelings come in without much effort. It must be a great check to business operations, however, in your part of the world, sir!"

"Business operations! what is business, as you term it, sir, to the affections, to the recollections of ancestry, and to the solemn feelings connected with history and tradition?"

"Why, sir, in the way of history, one meets with but few incumbrances in this country, but he may do very much as interest dictates, so far as that is concerned, at least. A nation is much to be pitied that is weighed down by the past, in this manner, since its industry and enterprise are constantly impeded by obstacles that grow out of its recollections. America may, indeed, be termed a happy and a free country, Mr. John Effingham, in this, as well as in all other things!"

Sir George Templemore was too well-bred to utter all he felt at that moment, as it would unavoidably wound the feelings of his hosts, but he was rewarded for his forbearance by intelligent smiles from Eve and Grace, the latter [23/24] of whom the young baronet fancied, just at that moment, was quite as beautiful as her cousin, and if less finished in manners, she had the most interesting *naiveté*.

"I have been told that most old nations have to struggle with difficulties that we escape," returned John Effingham, "though I confess this is a superiority on our part that never before presented itself to my mind."

"The political economists, and even the geographers, have overlooked it, but practical men see and feel its advantages every hour in the day. I have been told, Sir George Templemore, that in England, there are difficulties in running highways and streets through homesteads and dwellings; and that even a railroad or a canal is obliged to make a curve to avoid a churchyard or a tombstone?"

"I confess to the sin, sir."

"Our friend Mr. Bragg," put in John Effingham, "considers life as all means and no end."

"An end cannot be got at without the means, Mr. John Effingham, as I trust you will yourself admit. I am for the end of the road at least, and must say that I rejoice in being a native of a country in which as few impediments as possible exist to onward impulses. The man who should resist an improvement in our part of the country, on account of his forefathers, would fare badly among his contemporaries."

"Will you permit me to ask, Mr. Bragg, if you feel no local attachments yourself," inquired the baronet, throwing as much delicacy into the tones of his voice, as a question that he felt ought to be an insult to a man's heart would allow, "if one tree is not more pleasant than another; the house you were born in more beautiful than a house into which you never entered; or the altar at which you have long worshipped, more sacred than another at which you never knelt?"

"Nothing gives me greater satisfaction than to answer the questions of gentlemen that travel through our country," returned Aristabulus, "for I think, in making nations acquainted with each other, we encourage trade and render business more secure. To reply to your inquiry, a [24/25] human being is not a cat, to love a locality rather than its own interests. I have found some trees much pleasanter than others, and the pleasantest tree I can remember was one of my own, out of which the sawyers made a thousand feet of clear stuff, to say nothing of middlings. The house I was born in was pulled down shortly after my birth, as indeed has been its successor, so I can tell you nothing on that head; and as for altars, there are none in my persuasion."

"The church of Mr. Bragg has stripped itself as naked as he would strip everything else, if he could," said John Effingham. "I much question if he ever knelt even; much less before an altar."

"We are of the standing order, certainly," returned Aristabulus, glancing towards the ladies to discover how they took his wit, "and Mr. John Effingham is as near right as a man need be, in a matter of faith. In the way of houses, Mr. Effingham, I believe it is the general opinion you might have done better with your own, than to have repaired it. Had the materials been disposed of, they would have sold well, and by running a street through the property, a pretty sum might have been realized."

"In which case I should have been without a home, Mr. Bragg."

"It would have been no great matter to get another on cheaper land. The old residence would have made a good factory, or an inn."

"Sir, I am a cat, and like the places I have long frequented."

Aristabulus, though not easily daunted, was awed by Mr. Effingham's manner, and Eve saw that her father's fine face had flushed. This interruption, therefore, suddenly changed the discourse, which has been related at some length, as likely to give the reader a better insight into a character that will fill some space in our narrative, than a more labored description.[25]

The Great Stone Face

NATHANIEL HAWTHORNE

ONE AFTERNOON, WHEN THE SUN WAS GOING DOWN, A MOTHER AND HER little boy sat at the door of their cottage, talking about the Great Stone Face. They had but to lift their eyes, and there it was plainly to be seen, though miles away, with the sunshine brightening all its features.

And what was the Great Stone Face?

Embosomed amongst a family of lofty mountains, there was a valley so spacious that it contained many thousand inhabitants. Some of these good people dwelt in log-huts, with the black forest all around them, on the steep and difficult hill-sides. Others had their homes in comfortable farm-houses, and cultivated the rich soil on the gentle slopes or level surfaces of the valley. Others, again, were congregated into populous villages, where some wild, highland rivulet, tumbling down from its birthplace in the upper mountain region, had been caught and tamed by human cunning, and compelled to turn the machinery of cotton-factories. The inhabitants of this valley, in short, were numerous, and of many modes of life. But all of them, grown people and children, had a kind of familiarity with the Great Stone Face, although some possessed the gift of distinguishing this grand natural phenomenon more perfectly than many of their neighbors.

The Great Stone Face, then, was a work of Nature in her mood of majestic playfulness, formed on the [413/414] perpendicular side of a mountain by some immense rocks, which had been thrown together in such a position as, when viewed at a proper distance, precisely to resemble the features of the human countenance. It seemed as if an enormous giant, or a Titan, had sculptured his own likeness on the precipice. There was the broad arch of the forehead, a hundred feet in height; the nose, with its long bridge; and the vast lips, which, if they could have spoken, would have rolled their thunder accents from one

Nathaniel Hawthorne, "The Great Stone Face," *The Works of Nathaniel Hawthorne,* ed. George Parsons Lathrop (Boston and New York: Houghton, Mifflin and Company, 1883), III, 413–438. Included in *The Snow-Image and Other Twice-Told Tales* (1851).

end of the valley to the other. True it is, that if the spectator approached too near, he lost the outline of the gigantic visage, and could discern only a heap of ponderous and gigantic rocks, piled in chaotic ruin one upon another. Retracing his steps, however, the wondrous features would again be seen; and the farther he withdrew from them, the more like a human face, with all its original divinity intact, did they appear; until, as it grew dim in the distance, with the clouds and glorified vapor of the mountains clustering about it, the Great Stone Face seemed positively to be alive.

It was a happy lot for children to grow up to manhood or womanhood with the Great Stone Face before their eyes, for all the features were noble, and the expression was at once grand and sweet, as if it were the glow of a vast, warm heart, that embraced all mankind in its affections, and had room for more. It was an education only to look at it. According to the belief of many people, the valley owed much of its fertility to this benign aspect that was continually beaming over it, illuminating the clouds, and infusing its tenderness into the sunshine.

As we began with saying, a mother and her little boy sat at their cottage-door, gazing at the Great Stone [414/415] Face, and talking about it. The child's name was Ernest.

"Mother," said he, while the Titanic visage smiled on him, "I wish that it could speak, for it looks so very kindly that its voice must needs be pleasant. If I were to see a man with such a face, I should love him dearly."

"If an old prophecy should come to pass," answered his mother, "we may see a man, some time or other, with exactly such a face as that."

"What prophecy do you mean, dear mother?" eagerly inquired Ernest. "Pray tell me about it!"

So his mother told him a story that her own mother had told to her, when she herself was younger than little Ernest; a story, not of things that were past, but of what was yet to come; a story, nevertheless, so very old, that even the Indians, who formerly inhabited this valley, had heard it from their forefathers, to whom, as they affirmed, it had been murmured by the mountain streams, and whispered by the wind among the tree-tops. The purport was, that, at some future day, a child should be born hereabouts, who was destined to become the greatest and noblest personage of his time, and whose countenance, in manhood, should bear an exact resemblance to the Great Stone Face. Not a few old-fashioned people, and young ones likewise, in the ardor of their hopes, still cherished an enduring faith in this old prophecy. But others, who had seen more of the world, had watched and waited till they were weary, and had beheld no man with such a face, nor any man that proved to be much greater or nobler than his neighbors, concluded it to be nothing but an idle tale. At all events, the great man of the prophecy had not yet appeared. [415/416]

"O mother, dear mother!" cried Ernest, clapping his hands above his head, "I do hope that I shall live to see him!"

His mother was an affectionate and thoughtful woman, and felt that it was wisest not to discourage the generous hopes of her little boy. So she only said to him, "Perhaps you may."

And Ernest never forgot the story that his mother told him. It was always in his mind, whenever he looked upon the Great Stone Face. He spent his childhood in the log-cottage where he was born, and was dutiful to his mother, and helpful to her in many things, assisting her much with his little hands, and more with his loving heart. In this manner, from a happy yet often pensive child, he grew up to be a mild, quiet, unobtrusive boy, and sun-browned with labor in the fields, but with more intelligence brightening his aspect than is seen in many lads who have been taught at famous schools. Yet Ernest had had no teacher, save only that the Great Stone Face became one to him. When the toil of the day was over, he would gaze at it for hours, until he began to imagine that those vast features recognized him, and gave him a smile of kindness and encouragement, responsive to his own look of veneration. We must not take upon us to affirm that this was a mistake, although the Face may have looked no more kindly at Ernest than at all the world besides. But the secret was that the boy's tender and confiding simplicity discerned what other people could not see; and thus the love, which was meant for all, became his peculiar portion.

About this time there went a rumor throughout the valley, that the great man, foretold from ages long [416/417] ago, who was to bear a resemblance to the Great Stone Face, had appeared at last. It seems that, many years before, a young man had migrated from the valley and settled at a distant seaport, where, after getting together a little money, he had set up as a shopkeeper. His name—but I could never learn whether it was his real one, or a nickname that had grown out of his habits and success in life—was Gathergold. Being shrewd and active, and endowed by Providence with that inscrutable faculty which develops itself in what the world calls luck, he became an exceedingly rich merchant, and owner of a whole fleet of bulky-bottomed ships. All of the countries of the globe appeared to join hands for the mere purpose of adding heap after heap to the mountainous accumulation of this one man's wealth. The cold regions of the north, almost within the gloom and shadow of the Arctic Circle, sent him their tribute in the shape of furs; hot Africa sifted for him the golden sands of her rivers, and gathered up the ivory tusks of her great elephants out of the forest; the East came bringing him the rich shawls, and spices, and teas, and the effulgence of diamonds, and the gleaming purity of large pearls. The ocean, not to be behindhand with the earth, yielded up her mighty whales, that Mr. Gathergold might sell their oil, and make a profit of it. Be the original commodity what it might, it was gold within his grasp. It might be said of him, as of Midas in the fable, that whatever he touched with his finger immediately glistened, and grew yellow, and was changed at once into sterling metal, or, which suited him still better, into piles of coin. And, when Mr. Gathergold had become so very rich that it would have taken him a hundred years only to count his wealth, he bethought [417/418] himself of his native valley, and resolved to go back thither, and end his days where he was born. With this purpose in view, he sent a skilful architect to build him such a palace as should be fit for a man of his vast wealth to live in.

As I have said above, it had already been rumored in the valley that Mr. Gathergold had turned out to be the prophetic personage so long and vainly looked for, and that his visage was the perfect and undeniable similitude of the Great Stone Face. People were the more ready to believe that this must needs be the fact, when they beheld the splendid edifice that rose, as if by enchantment, on the site of his father's old weatherbeaten farm-house. The exterior was of marble, so dazzlingly white that it seemed as though the whole structure might melt away in the sunshine, like those humbler ones which Mr. Gathergold, in his young play-days, before his fingers were gifted with the touch of transmutation, had been accustomed to build of snow. It had a richly ornamented portico, supported by tall pillars, beneath which was a lofty door, studded with silver knobs, and made of a kind of variegated wood that had been brought from beyond the sea. The windows, from the floor to the ceiling of each stately apartment, were composed, respectively, of but one enormous pane of glass, so transparently pure that it was said to be a finer medium than even the vacant atmosphere. Hardly anybody had been permitted to see the interior of this palace; but it was reported, and with good semblance of truth, to be far more gorgeous than the outside, insomuch that whatever was iron or brass in other houses was silver or gold in this; and Mr. Gathergold's bedchamber, especially, made such a glittering appearance that no ordinary [418/419] man would have been able to close his eyes there. But, on the other hand, Mr. Gathergold was now so inured to wealth, that perhaps he could not have closed his eyes unless where the gleam of it was certain to find its way beneath his eyelids.

In due time, the mansion was finished; next came the upholsterers, with magnificent furniture; then, a whole troop of black and white servants, the harbingers of Mr. Gathergold, who, in his own majestic person, was expected to arrive at sunset. Our friend Ernest, meanwhile, had been deeply stirred by the idea that the great man, the noble man, the man of prophecy, after so many ages of delay, was at length to be made manifest to his native valley. He knew, boy as he was, that there were a thousand ways in which Mr. Gathergold, with his vast wealth,

might transform himself into an angel of beneficence, and assume a
control over human affairs as wide and benignant as the smile of the
Great Stone Face. Full of faith and hope, Ernest doubted not that
what the people said was true, and that now he was to behold the
living likeness of those wondrous features on the mountain-side. While
the boy was still gazing up the valley, and fancying, as he always did,
that the Great Stone Face returned his gaze and looked kindly at him,
the rumbling of wheels was heard, approaching swiftly along the
winding road.

"Here he comes!" cried a group of people who were assembled to
witness the arrival. "Here comes the great Mr. Gathergold!"

A carriage, drawn by four horses, dashed round the turn of the
road. Within it, thrust partly out of the window, appeared the physiognomy of the old man, with a skin as yellow as if his own Midas-hand
had [419/420] transmuted it. He had a low forehead, small, sharp
eyes, puckered about with innumerable wrinkles, and very thin lips,
which he made still thinner by pressing them forcibly together.

"The very image of the Great Stone Face!" shouted the people.
"Sure enough, the old prophecy is true; and here we have the great
man come, at last!"

And, what greatly perplexed Ernest, they seemed actually to
believe that here was the likeness which they spoke of. By the roadside
there chanced to be an old beggar-woman and two little beggar-
children, stragglers from some far-off region, who, as the carriage rolled
onward, held out their hands and lifted up their doleful voices, most
piteously beseeching charity. A yellow claw—the very same that had
clawed together so much wealth—poked itself out of the coach-
window, and dropt some copper coins upon the ground; so that,
though the great man's name seems to have been Gathergold, he
might just as suitably have been nicknamed Scattercopper. Still, nevertheless, with an earnest shout, and evidently with as much good faith
as ever, the people bellowed,—

"He is the very image of the Great Stone Face!"

But Ernest turned sadly from the wrinkled shrewdness of that
sordid visage, and gazed up the valley, where, amid a gathering mist,
gilded by the last sunbeams, he could still distinguish those glorious
features which had impressed themselves into his soul. Their aspect
cheered him. What did the benign lips seem to say?

"He will come! Fear not, Ernest; the man will come!"

The years went on, and Ernest ceased to be a boy. [420/421] He
had grown to be a young man now. He attracted little notice from the
other inhabitants of the valley; for they saw nothing remarkable in his
way of life, save that, when the labor of the day was over, he still loved
to go apart and gaze and meditate upon the Great Stone Face. According to their idea of the matter, it was a folly, indeed, but pardonable,
inasmuch as Ernest was industrious, kind, and neighborly, and neg-

lected no duty for the sake of indulging this idle habit. They knew not that the Great Stone Face had become a teacher to him, and that the sentiment which was expressed in it would enlarge the young man's heart, and fill it with wider and deeper sympathies than other hearts. They knew not that thence would come a better wisdom than could be learned from books, and a better life than could be moulded on the defaced example of other human lives. Neither did Ernest know that the thoughts and affections which came to him so naturally, in the fields and at the fireside, and wherever he communed with himself, were of a higher tone than those which all men shared with him. A simple soul,— simple as when his mother first taught him the old prophecy,— he beheld the marvellous features beaming adown the valley, and still wondered that their human counterpart was so long in making his appearance.

By this time poor Mr. Gathergold was dead and buried; and the oddest part of the matter was, that his wealth, which was the body and spirit of his existence, had disappeared before his death, leaving nothing of him but a living skeleton, covered over with a wrinkled yellow skin. Since the melting away of his gold, it had been very generally conceded that there was no such striking resemblance, after all, [421/422] betwixt the ignoble features of the ruined merchant and that majestic face upon the mountain-side. So the people ceased to honor him during his lifetime, and quietly consigned him to forgetfulness after his decease. Once in a while, it is true, his memory was brought up in connection with the magnificent palace which he had built, and which had long ago been turned into a hotel for the accommodation of strangers, multitudes of whom came, every summer, to visit that famous natural curiosity, the Great Stone Face. Thus, Mr. Gathergold being discredited and thrown into the shade, the man of prophecy was yet to come.

It so happened that a native-born son of the valley, many years before, had enlisted as a soldier, and, after a great deal of hard fighting, had now become an illustrious commander. Whatever he may be called in history, he was known in camps and on the battle-field under the nickname of Old Blood-and-Thunder. This war-worn veteran being now infirm with age and wounds, and weary of the turmoil of a military life, and the roll of the drum and the clangor of the trumpet, that had so long been ringing in his ears, had lately signified a purpose of returning to his native valley, hoping to find repose where he remembered to have left it. The inhabitants, his old neighbors and their grown-up children, were resolved to welcome the renowned warrior with a salute of cannon and a public dinner; and all the more enthusiastically, it being affirmed that now, at last, the likeness of the Great Stone Face had actually appeared. An aide-de-camp of Old Blood-and-Thunder, travelling through the valley, was said to have been struck with the resemblance. Moreover the schoolmates and early acquaintances of the general were ready to testify, on [422/423] oath, that, to the best of their recollection, the aforesaid general had been exceedingly like the majestic image, even when a boy, only the idea had never occurred to them at that period. Great, therefore, was the excitement throughout the valley; and many people, who had never once thought of glancing at the Great Stone Face for years before, now spent their time in gazing at it, for the sake of knowing exactly how General Blood-and-Thunder looked.

On the day of the great festival, Ernest, with all the other people of the valley, left their work, and proceeded to the spot where the sylvan banquet was prepared. As he approached, the loud voice of the Rev. Dr. Battleblast was heard, beseeching a blessing on the good things set before them, and on the distinguished friend of peace in whose honor they were assembled. The tables were arranged in a cleared space of the woods, shut in by the surrounding trees, except where a vista opened eastward, and afforded a distant view of the Great Stone Face. Over the general's chair, which was a relic from the home of Washington, there was an arch of verdant boughs, with the laurel profusely intermixed, and surmounted by his country's banner, beneath which he had won his victories. Our friend Ernest raised himself on his tiptoes, in hopes to get a glimpse of the celebrated guest; but there was a mighty crowd about the tables anxious to hear the toasts and speeches, and to catch any word that might fall from the general in reply; and a volunteer company, doing duty as a guard, pricked ruthlessly with their bayonets at any particularly quiet person among the throng. So Ernest, being of an unobtrusive character, was thrust quite into the background, where he could see no more of Old Blood- [423/424] and-Thunder's physiognomy than if it had been still blazing on the battle-field. To console himself, he turned towards the Great Stone Face, which, like a faithful and long-remembered friend, looked back and smiled upon him through the vista of the forest. Meantime, however, he could overhear the remarks of various individuals, who were comparing the features of the hero with the face on the distant mountain-side.

" 'Tis the same face, to a hair!" cried one man, cutting a caper for joy.

"Wonderfully like, that's a fact!" responded another.

"Like! why, I call it Old Blood-and-Thunder himself, in a monstrous looking-glass!" cried a third. "And why not? He's the greatest man of this or any other age, beyond a doubt."

And then all three of the speakers gave a great shout, which communicated electricity to the crowd, and called forth a roar from a thousand voices, that went reverberating for miles among the mountains, until you might have supposed that the Great Stone Face had poured its thunder-breath into the cry. All these comments, and this vast enthusiasm, served the more to interest our friend; nor did he think of questioning that now, at length, the mountain-visage had found its human counterpart. It is true, Ernest had imagined that this long-looked-for personage would appear in the character of a man of peace, uttering wisdom, and doing good, and making people happy. But, taking an habitual breadth of view, with all his simplicity, he contended that Providence should choose its own method of blessing mankind, and could conceive that this great end might be effected even by a warrior and a bloody sword, should inscrutable wisdom see fit to order matters so. [424/425]

"The general! the general!" was now the cry. "Hush! silence! Old Blood-and-Thunder's going to make a speech."

Even so; for, the cloth being removed, the general's health had been drunk, amid shouts of applause, and he now stood upon his feet to thank the company. Ernest saw him. There he was, over the shoulders of the crowd, from the two glittering epaulets and embroidered collar upward, beneath the arch of green boughs with intertwined laurel, and the banner drooping as if to shade his brow! And there, too, visible in the same glance, through the vista of the forest, appeared the Great Stone Face! And was there, indeed, such a resemblance as the crowd had testified? Alas, Ernest could not recognize it! He beheld a war-worn and weather-beaten countenance, full of energy, and expressive of an iron will; but the gentle wisdom, the deep, broad, tender sympathies, were altogether wanting in Old Blood-and-Thunder's visage; and even if the Great Stone Face had assumed his look of stern command, the milder traits would still have tempered it.

"This is not the man of prophecy," sighed Ernest to himself, as he made his way out of the throng. "And must the world wait longer yet?"

The mists had congregated about the distant mountain-side, and there were seen the grand and awful features of the Great Stone Face, awful but benignant, as if a mighty angel were sitting among the hills, and enrobing himself in a cloud-vesture of gold and purple. As he looked, Ernest could hardly believe but that a smile beamed over the whole visage, with a radiance still brightening, although without motion of the lips. It was probably the effect of the western [425/426] sunshine, melting through the thinly diffused vapors that had swept between him and the object that he gazed at. But—as it always did—the aspect of his marvellous friend made Ernest as hopeful as if he had never hoped in vain.

"Fear not, Ernest," said his heart, even as if the Great Face were whispering to him,—fear not, Ernest; he will come."

More years sped swiftly and tranquilly away. Ernest still dwelt in his native valley, and was now a man of middle age. By imperceptible degrees, he had become known among the people. Now, as heretofore, he labored for his bread, and was the same simple-hearted man that he had always been. But he had thought and felt so much, he had given so many of the best hours of his life to unworldly hopes for some great good to mankind, that it seemed as though he had been talking with the angels, and had imbibed a portion of their wisdom unawares. It was visible in the calm and well-considered beneficence of his daily life, the quiet stream of which had made a wide green margin all along its course. Not a day passed by, that the world was not the better because this man, humble as he was, had lived. He never stepped aside from his own path, yet would always reach a blessing to his neighbor. Almost involuntarily, too, he had become a preacher. The pure and high simplicity of his thought, which, as one of its manifestations, took shape in the good deeds that dropped silently from his hand, flowed also forth in speech. He uttered truths that wrought upon and moulded the lives of those who heard him. His auditors, it may be, never suspected that Ernest, their own neighbor and familiar friend, was more than an ordinary man; least of all did Ernest [426/427] himself suspect it; but, inevitably as the murmur of a rivulet, came thoughts out of his mouth that no other human lips had spoken.

When the people's minds had had a little time to cool, they were ready enough to acknowledge their mistake in imagining a similarity between General Blood-and-Thunder's truculent physiognomy and the benign visage on the mountain-side. But now, again, there were reports and many paragraphs in the newspapers, affirming that the likeness of the Great Stone Face had appeared upon the broad shoulders of a certain eminent statesman. He, like Mr. Gathergold and Old Blood-and-Thunder, was a native of the valley, but had left it in his early days, and taken up the trades of law and politics. Instead of the rich man's wealth and the warrior's sword, he had but a tongue, and it was mightier than both together. So wonderfully eloquent was he, that whatever he might choose to say, his auditors had no choice but to believe him; wrong looked like right, and right like wrong; for when it pleased him, he could make a kind of illuminated fog with his mere breath, and obscure the natural daylight with it. His tongue, indeed, was a magic instrument: sometime it rumbled like the thunder; sometimes it warbled like the sweetest music. It was the blast of war, the song of peace; and it seemed to have a heart in it, when there was no such matter. In good truth, he was a wondrous man; and when his tongue had acquired him all other imaginable success,—when it had been heard in halls of state, and in the courts of princes and potentates,—after it had made him known all over the world, even as a voice crying from shore to shore,—it finally persuaded his countrymen to select him for the Presidency. [427/428] Before this time,—indeed, as soon as he began to grow celebrated,—his admirers had found out the resemblance between him and the Great Stone Face; and so much were they struck by it, that throughout the country this distinguished gentleman was known by the name of Old Stony Phiz. The phrase was considered as giving a highly favorable aspect to his political prospects; for, as is likewise the case with the Popedom, nobody ever becomes President without taking a name other than his own.

While his friends were doing their best to make him President, Old Stony Phiz, as he was called, set out on a visit to the valley where he was born. Of course, he had no other object than to shake hands with his fellow-citizens and neither thought nor cared about any effect which his progress through the country might have upon the election. Magnificent preparations were made to receive the illustrious statesman; a cavalcade of horsemen set forth to meet him at the boundary line of the State, and all the people left their business and gathered along the wayside to see him pass. Among these was Ernest. Though more than once disappointed, as we have seen, he had such a hopeful and confiding nature, that he was always ready to believe in whatever seemed beautiful and good. He kept his heart continually open, and thus was sure to catch the blessing from on high when it should come. So now again, as buoyantly as ever, he went forth to behold the likeness of the Great Stone Face.

The cavalcade came prancing along the road, with a great clattering of hoofs and a mighty cloud of dust, which rose up so dense and high that the visage of the mountain-side was completely hidden from Ernest's [428/429] eyes. All the great men of the neighborhood were there on horseback; militia officers, in uniform; the member of Congress; the sheriff of the county; the editors of newspapers; and many a farmer, too, had mounted his patient steed, with his Sunday coat upon his back. It really was a very brilliant spectacle, especially as there were numerous banners flaunting over the cavalcade, on some of which were gorgeous portraits of the illustrious statesman and the Great Stone Face, smiling familiarly at one another, like two brothers. If the pictures were to be trusted, the mutual resemblance, it must be confessed, was marvellous. We must not forget to mention that there was a band of music, which made the echoes of the mountains ring and reverberate with the loud triumph of its strains; so that airy and soul-thrilling melodies broke out among all the heights and hollows, as if every nook of his native valley had found a voice, to welcome the distinguished guest. But the grandest effect was when the far-off mountain precipice flung back the music; for then the Great Stone Face itself seemed to be swelling the triumphant chorus, in acknowledgment that, at length, the man of prophecy was come.

All this while the people were throwing up their hats and shouting, with enthusiasm so contagious that the heart of Ernest kindled up, and he likewise threw up his hat, and shouted, as loudly as the loudest, "Huzza for the great man! Huzza for Old Stony Phiz!" But as yet he had not seen him.

"Here he is, now!" cried those who stood near Ernest. "There!

There! Look at Old Stony Phiz and then at the Old Man of the Mountain, and see if they are not as like as two twin-brothers!"

In the midst of all this gallant array came an open [429/430] barouche, drawn by four white horses; and in the barouche, with his massive head uncovered, sat the illustrious statesman, Old Stony Phiz himself.

"Confess it," said one of Ernest's neighbors to him, "the Great Stone Face has met its match at last!"

Now, it must be owned that, at his first glimpse of the countenance which was bowing and smiling from the barouche, Ernest did fancy that there was a resemblance between it and the old familiar face upon the mountain-side. The brow, with its massive depth and loftiness, and all the other features, indeed, were boldly and strongly hewn, as if in emulation of a more than heroic, of a Titanic model. But the sublimity and stateliness, the grand expression of a divine sympathy, that illuminated the mountain visage and etherealized its ponderous granite substance into spirit, might here be sought in vain. Something had been originally left out, or had departed. And therefore the marvellously gifted statesman had always a weary gloom in the deep caverns of his eyes, as of a child that has outgrown its playthings or a man of mighty faculties and little aims, whose life, with all its high performances, was vague and empty, because no high purpose had endowed it with reality.

Still, Ernest's neighbor was thrusting his elbow into his side, and pressing him for an answer.

"Confess! confess! Is not he the very picture of your Old Man of the Mountain?"

"No!" said Ernest bluntly, "I see little or no likeness."

"Then so much the worse for the Great Stone Face!" answered his neighbor; and again he set up a shout for Old Stony Phiz.

But Ernest turned away, melancholy, and almost [430/431] despondent: for this was the saddest of his disappointments, to behold a man who might have fulfilled the prophecy, and had not willed to do so. Meantime, the cavalcade, the banners, the music, and the barouches swept past him, with the vociferous crowd in the rear, leaving the dust to settle down, and the Great Stone Face to be revealed again, with the grandeur that it had worn for untold centuries.

"Lo, here I am, Ernest!" the benign lips seemed to say. "I have waited longer than thou, and am not yet weary. Fear not; the man will come."

The years hurried onward, treading in their haste on one another's heels. And now they began to bring white hairs, and scatter them over the head of Ernest; they made reverend wrinkles across his forehead, and furrows in his cheeks. He was an aged man. But not in vain had he grown old: more than the white hairs on his head were the sage thoughts in his mind; his wrinkles and furrows were inscriptions that

Time had graved, and in which he had written legends of wisdom that
had been tested by the tenor of a life. And Ernest had ceased to be
obscure. Unsought for, undesired, had come the fame which so many
seek, and made him known in the great world, beyond the limits of the
valley in which he had dwelt so quietly. College professors, and even
the active men of cities, came from far to see and converse with Ernest;
for the report had gone abroad that this simple husbandman had ideas
unlike those of other men, not gained from books, but of a higher
tone,—a tranquil and familiar majesty, as if he had been talking with
the angels as his daily friends. Whether it were sage, statesman, or
philanthropist, Ernest received these visitors with the gentle sincerity
that had characterized him from [431/432] boyhood, and spoke freely
with them of whatever came uppermost, or lay deepest in his heart or
their own. While they talked together, his face would kindle, unawares,
and shine upon them, as with a mild evening light. Pensive with the
fulness of such discourse, his guests took leave and went their way; and
passing up the valley, paused to look at the Great Stone Face,
imagining that they had seen its likeness in a human countenance, but
could not remember where.

While Ernest had been growing up and growing old, a bountiful
Providence had granted a new poet to this earth. He likewise, was a
native of the valley, but had spent the greater part of his life at a
distance from that romantic region, pouring out his sweet music amid
the bustle and din of cities. Often, however, did the mountains which
had been familiar to him in his childhood lift their snowy peaks into
the clear atmosphere of his poetry. Neither was the Great Stone Face
forgotten, for the poet had celebrated it in an ode, which was grand
enough to have been uttered by its own majestic lips. This man of
genius, we may say, had come down from heaven with wonderful
endowments. If he sang of a mountain, the eyes of all mankind beheld
a mightier grandeur reposing on its breast, or soaring to its summit,
than had before been seen there. If his theme were a lovely lake, a
celestial smile had now been thrown over it, to gleam forever on its
surface. If it were the vast old sea, even the deep immensity of its dead
bosom seemed to swell the higher, as if moved by the emotions of the
song. Thus the world assumed another and a better aspect from the
hour that the poet blessed it with his happy eyes. The Creator had
bestowed him, as the last best touch to his own handiwork. [432/433]
Creation was not finished till the poet came to interpret, and so
complete it.

The effect was no less high and beautiful, when his human
brethren were the subject of his verse. The man or woman, sordid with
the common dust of life, who crossed his daily path, and the little child
who played in it, were glorified if he beheld them in his mood of poetic
faith. He showed the golden links of the great chain that intertwined
them with an angelic kindred; he brought out the hidden traits of a

celestial birth that made them worthy of such kin. Some, indeed, there were, who thought to show the soundness of their judgment by affirming that all the beauty and dignity of the natural world existed only in the poet's fancy. Let such men speak for themselves, who undoubtedly appear to have been spawned forth by Nature with a contemptuous bitterness; she having plastered them up out of her refuse stuff, after all the swine were made. As respects all things else, the poet's ideal was the truest truth.

The songs of this poet found their way to Ernest. He read them after his customary toil, seated on the bench before his cottage-door, where for such a length of time he had filled his repose with thought, by gazing at the Great Stone Face. And now as he read stanzas that caused the soul to thrill within him, he lifted his eyes to the vast countenance beaming on him so benignantly.

"O majestic friend," he murmured, addressing the Great Stone Face, "is not this man worthy to resemble thee?"

The Face seemed to smile, but answered not a word.

Now it happened that the poet, though he dwelt so far away, had not only heard of Ernest, but had [433/434] meditated much upon his character, until he deemed nothing so desirable as to meet this man, whose untaught wisdom walked hand in hand with the noble simplicity of his life. One summer morning, therefore, he took passage by the railroad, and, in the decline of the afternoon, alighted from the cars at no great distance from Ernest's cottage. The great hotel, which had formerly been the palace of Mr. Gathergold, was close at hand, but the poet, with his carpet-bag on his arm, inquired at once where Ernest dwelt, and was resolved to be accepted as his guest.

Approaching the door, he there found the good old man, holding a volume in his hand, which alternately he read, and then, with a finger between the leaves, looked lovingly at the Great Stone Face.

"Good evening," said the poet. "Can you give a traveller a night's lodging?"

"Willingly," answered Ernest; and then he added, smiling, "Methinks I never saw the Great Stone Face look so hospitably at a stranger."

The poet sat down on the bench beside him, and he and Ernest talked together. Often had the poet held intercourse with the wittiest and the wisest, but never before with a man like Ernest, whose thoughts and feelings gushed up with such a natural freedom, and who made great truths so familiar by his simple utterance of them. Angels, as had been so often said, seemed to have wrought with him at his labor in the fields; angels seemed to have sat with him by the fireside; and, dwelling with angels as friend with friends, he had imbibed the sublimity of their ideas, and imbued it with the sweet and lowly charm of household words. So thought the poet. And Ernest, on the other hand, was moved and agitated by the living images which [434/435] the poet flung out of his mind, and which peopled all the air about the cottage-door with shapes of beauty, both gay and pensive. The sympathies of these two men instructed them with a profounder sense than either could have attained alone. Their minds accorded into one strain, and made delightful music which neither of them could have claimed as all his own, nor distinguished his own share from the other's. They led one another, as it were, into a high pavilion of their thoughts, so remote, and hitherto so dim, that they had never entered it before, and so beautiful that they desired to be there always.

As Ernest listened to the poet, he imagined that the Great Stone Face was bending forward to listen too. He gazed earnestly into the poet's glowing eyes.

"Who are you, my strangely gifted guest?" he said.

The poet laid his finger on the volume that Ernest had been reading.

"You have read these poems," said he. "You know me, then,—for I wrote them."

Again, and still more earnestly than before, Ernest examined the poet's features; then turned towards the Great Stone Face; then back, with an uncertain aspect, to his guest. But his countenance fell; he shook his head, and sighed.

"Wherefore are you sad?" inquired the poet.

"Because," replied Ernest, "all through life I have awaited the fulfilment of a prophecy; and, when I read these poems, I hoped that it might be fulfilled in you."

"You hoped," answered the poet, faintly smiling, "to find in me the likeness of the Great Stone Face. And you are disappointed, as formerly with Mr. Gathergold, [435/436] and Old Blood-and-Thunder, and Old Stony Phiz. Yes, Ernest, it is my doom. You must add my name to the illustrious three, and record another failure of your hopes. For—in shame and sadness do I speak it, Ernest—I am not worthy to be typified by yonder benign and majestic image."

"And why?" asked Ernest. He pointed to the volume. "Are not those thoughts divine?"

"They have a strain of the Divinity," replied the poet. "You can hear in them the far-off echo of a heavenly song. But my life, dear Ernest, has not corresponded with my thought. I have had grand dreams, but they have been only dreams, because I have lived—and that, too, by my own choice—among poor and mean realities. Sometimes even—shall I dare to say it?—I lack faith in the grandeur, the beauty, and the goodness, which my own words are said to have made more evident in nature and in human life. Why, then, pure seeker of the good and true, shouldst thou hope to find me, in yonder image of the divine?"

The poet spoke sadly, and his eyes were dim with tears. So, likewise, were those of Ernest.

At the hour of sunset, as had long been his frequent custom, Ernest was to discourse to an assemblage of the neighboring inhabitants in the open air. He and the poet, arm in arm, still talking together as they went along, proceeded to the spot. It was a small nook among the hills, with a gray precipice behind, the stern front of which was relieved by the pleasant foliage of many creeping plants that made a tapestry for the naked rock, by hanging their festoons from all its rugged angles. At a small elevation above the ground, set in a rich framework of verdure, there appeared a niche, spacious enough to admit a human [436/437] figure, with freedom for such gestures as spontaneously accompany earnest thought and genuine emotion. Into this natural pulpit Ernest ascended, and threw a look of familiar kindness around upon his audience. They stood, or sat, or reclined upon the grass, as seemed good to each, with the departing sunshine falling obliquely over them, and mingling its subdued cheerfulness with the solemnity of a grove of ancient trees, beneath and amid the boughs of which the golden rays were constrained to pass. In another direction was seen the Great Stone Face, with the same cheer, combined with the same solemnity, in its benignant aspect.

Ernest began to speak, giving to the people of what was in his heart and mind. His words had power, because they accorded with his thoughts; and his thoughts had reality and depth, because they harmonized with the life which he had always lived. It was not mere breath that this preacher uttered; they were the words of life, because a life of good deeds and holy love was melted into them. Pearls, pure and rich, had been dissolved into this precious draught. The poet, as he listened, felt that the being and character of Ernest were a nobler strain of poetry than he had ever written. His eyes glistening with tears, he gazed reverentially at the venerable man, and said within himself that never was there an aspect so worthy of a prophet and a sage as that mild, sweet, thoughtful countenance, with the glory of white hair diffused about it. At a distance, but distinctly to be seen, high up in the golden light of the setting sun, appeared the Great Stone Face, with hoary mists around it, like the white hairs around the brow of Ernest. Its look of grand beneficence seemed to embrace the world. [437/438]

At that moment, in sympathy with a thought which he was about to utter, the face of Ernest assumed a grandeur of expression, so imbued with benevolence, that the poet, by an irresistible impulse, threw his arms aloft and shouted,—

"Behold! Behold! Ernest is himself the likeness of the Great Stone Face!"

Then all the people looked, and saw that what the deep-sighted poet said was true. The prophecy was fulfilled. But Ernest, having finished what he had to say, took the poet's arm, and walked slowly homeward still hoping that some wiser and better man than himself would by and by appear, bearing a resemblance to the GREAT STONE FACE. [438]

Success

RALPH WALDO EMERSON

OUR AMERICAN PEOPLE CANNOT BE TAXED WITH SLOWNESS IN PERFORM-ance or in praising their performance. The earth is shaken by our engineries. We are feeling our youth and nerve and bone. We have the power of territory and of seacoast, and know the use of these. We count our census, we read our growing valuations, we survey our map, which becomes old in a year or two. Our eyes run approvingly along the lengthened lines of railroad and telegraph. We have gone nearest to the Pole. We have discovered the Antarctic continent. We interfere in Central and South America, at Canton and in Japan; we are adding to an already enormous territory. Our political constitution is the hope of the world, and we value ourselves on all these feats.

'T is the way of the world; 't is the law of youth, and of unfolding strength. Men are made each with some triumphant superiority, which, through some adaptation of fingers or ear or eye or ciphering or pugilistic or musical or literary craft, enriches the community with a new art; and not only we, but all men of European [283/284] stock, value these certificates. Giotto could draw a perfect circle: Erwin of Steinbach could build a minster; Olaf, king of Norway, could run round his galley on the blades of the oars of the rowers when the ship was in motion; Ojeda could run out swiftly on a plank projected from the top of a tower, turn round swiftly and come back; Evelyn writes from Rome: "Bernini, the Florentine sculptor, architect, painter and poet, a little before my coming to Rome, gave a public opera, wherein

Ralph Waldo Emerson, "Success," in *The Complete Works of Ralph Waldo Emerson,* ed. Edward Waldo Emerson (Boston and New York: Houghton Mifflin Company, 1903–1904), VII, 283–312. Included in *Society and Solitude* (1870). The footnotes have been omitted.

he painted the scenes, cut the statues, invented the engines, composed the music, writ the comedy and built the theatre."

"There is nothing in war," said Napoleon, "which I cannot do by my own hands. If there is nobody to make gunpowder, I can manufacture it. The gun-carriages I know how to construct. If it is necessary to make cannons at the forge, I can make them. The details of working them in battle, if it is necessary to teach, I shall teach them. In administration, it is I alone who have arranged the finances, as you know."

It is recorded of Linnæus, among many proofs of his beneficent skill, that when the timber in the shipyards of Sweden was ruined by rot, Linnæus was desired by the government to find a remedy. [284/285] He studied the insects that infested the timber, and found that they laid their eggs in the logs within certain days in April, and he directed that during ten days at that season the logs should be immersed under water in the docks; which being done, the timber was found to be uninjured.

Columbus at Veragua found plenty of gold; but leaving the coast, the ship full of one hundred and fifty skilful seamen,—some of them old pilots, and with too much experience of their craft and treachery to him,—the wise admiral kept his private record of his homeward path. And when he reached Spain he told the King and Queen that "they may ask all the pilots who came with him where is Veragua. Let them answer and say if they know where Veragua lies. I assert that they can give no other account than that they went to lands where there was abundance of gold, but they do not know the way to return thither, but would be obliged to go on a voyage of discovery as much as if they had never been there before. There is a mode of reckoning," he proudly adds, "derived from astronomy, which is sure and safe to any one who understands it."

Hippocrates in Greece knew how to stay the [285/286] devouring plague which ravaged Athens in his time, and his skill died with him. Dr. Benjamin Rush, in Philadelphia, carried that city heroically through the yellow fever of the year 1793. Leverrier carried the Copernican system in his head, and knew where to look for the new planet. We have seen an American woman write a novel of which a million copies were sold, in all languages, and which had one merit, of speaking to the universal heart, and was read with equal interest to three audiences, namely, in the parlor, in the kitchen and in the nursery of every house. We have seen women who could institute hospitals and schools in armies. We have seen a woman who by pure song could melt the souls of whole populations. And there is no limit to these varieties of talent.

These are arts to be thankful for,—each one as it is a new direction of human power. We cannot choose but respect them. Our civilization is made up of a million contributions of this kind. For success, to

be sure we esteem it a test in other people, since we do first in ourselves. We respect ourselves more if we have succeeded. Neither do we
grudge to each of these benefactors the praise or the profit which
accrues from his industry. [286/287]

Here are already quite different degrees of moral merit in these
examples. I don't know but we and our race elsewhere set a higher
value on wealth, victory and coarse superiority of all kinds, than other
men,—have less tranquillity of mind, are less easily contented. The
Saxon is taught from his infancy to wish to be first. The Norseman was
a restless rider, fighter, free-booter. The ancient Norse ballads describe
him as afflicted with this inextinguishable thirst of victory. The mother
says to her son:—

> "Success shall be in thy courser tall,
> Success in thyself, which is best of all,
> Success in thy hand, success in thy foot,
> In struggle with man, in battle with brute:—
> The holy God and Saint Drothin dear
> Shall never shut eyes on thy career;
>   Look out, look out, Svend Vonved!"

These feats that we extol do not signify so much as we say. These
boasted arts are of very recent origin. They are local conveniences, but
do not really add to our stature. The greatest men of the world have
managed not to want them. Newton was a great man, without telegraph, or gas, or steam-coach, or rubber shoes, or lucifer-matches, or
ether for his pain; so was Shakspeare and Alfred and Scipio and
Socrates. [287/288] These are local conveniences, but how easy to go
now to parts of the world where not only all these arts are wanting, but
where they are despised. The Arabian sheiks, the most dignified people
in the planet, do not want them; yet have as much self-respect as the
English, and are easily able to impress the Frenchman or the American
who visits them with the respect due to a brave and sufficient man.

These feats have to be sure great difference of merit, and some of
them involve power of a high kind. But the public values the invention
more than the inventor does. The inventor knows there is much more
and better where this came from. The public sees in it a lucrative
secret. Men see the reward which the inventor enjoys, and they think,
'How shall we win that?' Cause and effect are a little tedious; how to
leap to the result by short or by false means? We are not scrupulous.
What we ask is victory, without regard to the cause; after the Rob Roy
rule, after the Napoleon rule, to be the strongest to-day,—the way of
the Talleyrands, prudent people, whose watches go faster than their
neighbors', and who detect the first moment of decline and throw
themselves on the instant on the winning side. I have heard that
Nelson used to say, [288/289] "Never mind the justice or the impu-
dence, only let me succeed." Lord Brougham's single duty of counsel is,

"to get the prisoner clear." Fuller says 'tis a maxim of lawyers that "a crown once worn cleareth all defects of the wearer thereof." *Rien ne réussit mieux que le succès*. And we Americans are tainted with this insanity, as our bankruptcies and our reckless politics may show. We are great by exclusion, grasping and egotism. Our success takes from all what it gives to one. 'T is a haggard, malignant, careworn running for luck.

Egotism is a kind of buckram that gives momentary strength and concentration to men, and seems to be much used in Nature for fabrics in which local and spasmodic energy is required. I could point to men in this country, of indispensable importance to the carrying on of American life, of this humor, whom we could ill spare; any one of them would be a national loss. But it spoils conversation. They will not try conclusions with you. They are ever thrusting this pampered self between you and them. It is plain they have a long education to undergo to reach simplicity and plain-dealing, which are what a wise man mainly cares for in his companion. Nature knows how to convert evil to [289/290] good; Nature utilizes misers, fanatics, show-men, egotists, to accomplish her ends; but we must not think better of the foible for that. The passion for sudden success is rude and puerile, just as war, cannons and executions are used to clear the ground of bad, lumpish, irreclaimable savages, but always to the damage of the conquerors.

I hate this shallow Americanism which hopes to get rich by credit, to get knowledge by raps on midnight tables, to learn the economy of the mind by phrenology, or skill without study, or mastery without apprenticeship, or the sale of goods through pretending that they sell, or power through making believe you are powerful, or through a packed jury or caucus, bribery and "repeating" votes, or wealth by fraud. They think they have got it, but they have got something else,—a crime which calls for another crime, and another devil behind that; these are steps to suicide, infamy and the harming of mankind. We countenance each other in this life of show, puffing, advertisement and manufacture of public opinion; and excellence is lost sight of in the hunger for sudden performance and praise.

There was a wise man, an Italian artist, Michel [290/291] Angelo, who writes thus of himself: "Meanwhile the Cardinal Ippolito, in whom all my best hopes were placed, being dead, I began to understand that the promises of this world are for the most part vain phantoms, and that to confide in one's self, and become something of worth and value, is the best and safest course." Now, though I am by no means sure that the reader will assent to all my propositions, yet I think we shall agree in my first rule for success,—that we shall drop the brag and the advertisement, and take Michel Angelo's course, "to confide in one's self, and be something of worth and value."

Each man has an aptitude born with him. Do your work. I have to say this often, but Nature says it oftener. 'T is clownish to insist on doing all with one's own hands, as if every man should build his own clumsy house, forge his hammer, and bake his dough; but he is to dare to do what he can do best; not help others as they would direct him, but as he knows his helpful power to be. To do otherwise is to neutralize all those extraordinary special talents distributed among men. Yet whilst this self-truth is essential to the exhibition of the world and to the growth and glory of each mind, it is rare to find a [291/292] man who believes his own thought or who speaks that which he was created to say. As nothing astonishes men so much as common sense and plain dealing, so nothing is more rare in any man than an act of his own. Any work looks wonderful to him, except that which he can do. We do not believe our own thought; we must serve somebody; we must quote somebody; we dote on the old and the distant; we are tickled by great names; we import the religion of other nations; we quote their opinions; we cite their laws. The gravest and learnedest courts in this country shudder to face a new question, and will wait months and years for a case to occur that can be tortured into a precedent, and thus throw on a bolder party the *onus* of an initiative. Thus we do not carry a counsel in our breasts, or do not know it; and because we cannot shake off from our shoes this dust of Europe and Asia, the world seems to be born old, society is under a spell, every man is a borrower and a mimic, life is theatrical and literature a quotation; and hence that depression of spirits, that furrow of care, said to mark every American brow.

Self-trust is the first secret of success, the belief that if you are here the authorities of the universe put you here, and for cause, or with [292/293] some task strictly appointed you in your constitution, and so long as you work at that you are well and successful. It by no means consists in rushing prematurely to a showy feat that shall catch the eye and satisfy spectators. It is enough if you work in the right direction. So far from the performance being the real success, it is clear that the success was much earlier than that, namely, when all the feats that make our civility were the thoughts of good heads. The fame of each discovery rightly attaches to the mind that made the formula which contains all the details, and not to the manufacturers who now make their gain by it; although the mob uniformly cheers the publisher, and not the inventor. It is the dulness of the multitude that they cannot see the house in the ground-plan; the working, in the model of the projector. Whilst it is a thought, though it were a new fuel, or a new food, or the creation of agriculture, it is cried down, it is a chimera; but when it is a fact, and comes in the shape of eight per cent., ten per cent., a hundred per cent., they cry, 'It is the voice of God.' Horatio Greenough the sculptor said to me of Robert Fulton's visit to Paris: "Fulton knocked at the door of Napoleon with steam, and was rejected; and Napoleon [293/294] lived long enough to know that he had excluded a greater power than his own."

Is there no loving of knowledge, and of art, and of our design, for itself alone? Cannot we please ourselves with performing our work, or gaining truth and power, without being praised for it? I gain my point, I gain all points, if I can reach my companion with any statement which teaches him his own worth. The sum of wisdom is, that the time is never lost that is devoted to work. The good workman never says, 'There, that will do;' but, 'There, that is it: try it, and come again, it will last always.' If the artist, in whatever art, is well at work on his own design, it signifies little that he does not yet find orders or customers. I pronounce that young man happy who is content with having acquired the skill which he had aimed at, and waits willingly when the occasion of making it appreciated shall arrive, knowing well that it will not loiter. The time your rival spends in dressing up his work for effect, hastily, and for the market, you spend in study and experiments towards real knowledge and efficiency. He has thereby sold his picture or machine, or won the prize, or got the appointment; but you have raised yourself into a higher school of [294/295] art, and a few years will show the advantage of the real master over the short popularity of the showman. I know it is a nice point to discriminate this self-trust, which is the pledge of all mental vigor and performance, from the disease to which it is allied,—the exaggeration of the part which we can play;—yet they are two things. But it is sanity to know that, over my talent or knack, and a million times better than any talent, is the central intelligence which subordinates and uses all talents; and it is only as a door into this, that any talent or the knowledge it gives is of value. He only who comes into this central intelligence, in which no egotism or exaggeration can be, comes into self-possession.

My next point is that in the scale of powers it is not talent but sensibility which is best: talent confines, but the central life puts us in relation to all. How often it seems the chief good to be born with a cheerful temper and well adjusted to the tone of the human race. Such a man feels himself in harmony, and conscious by his receptivity of an infinite strength. Like Alfred, "good fortune accompanies him like a gift of God." Feel yourself, and be not daunted by things. 'T is the fulness of man that runs over into objects, [295/296] and makes his Bibles and Shakspeares and Homers so great. The joyful reader borrows of his own ideas to fill their faulty outline, and knows not that he borrows and gives.

There is something of poverty in our criticism. We assume that there are few great men, all the rest are little; that there is but one Homer, but one Shakspeare, one Newton, one Socrates. But the soul in her beaming hour does not acknowledge these usurpations. We should know how to praise Socrates, or Plato, or Saint John, without impoverishing us. In good hours we do not find Shakspeare or Homer over-great, only to have been translators of the happy present, and every man and woman divine possibilities. 'T is the good reader that makes the good book; a good head cannot read amiss, in every book he finds passages which seem confidences or asides hidden from all else and unmistakably meant for his ear.

The light by which we see in this world comes out from the soul of the observer. Wherever any noble sentiment dwelt, it made the faces and houses around to shine. Nay, the powers of this busy brain are miraculous and illimitable. Therein are the rules and formulas by which the whole empire of matter is worked. There is [296/297] no prosperity, trade, art, city, or great material wealth of any kind, but if you trace it home, you will find it rooted in a thought of some individual man. [297/307] . . .

One more trait of true success. The good mind chooses what is positive, what is advancing,—embraces the affirmative. Our system is one of poverty. 'T is presumed, as I said, there is but one Shakspeare, one Homer, one Jesus,—not that all are or shall be inspired. But we must begin by affirming. Truth and goodness subsist forevermore. It is true there is evil and good, night and day: but these are not equal. The day is great and final. The night is for the day, but the day is not for the night. What is this immortal demand for more, which belongs to our constitution? this enormous ideal? There is no such critic and beggar as this terrible Soul. No historical person begins to content us. We know the satisfactoriness of justice, the sufficiency of truth. We know the answer that leaves nothing to ask. We know the Spirit by its victorious tone. The searching tests to apply to every new pretender are amount [307/308] and quality,—what does he add? and what is the state of mind he leaves me in? Your theory is unimportant; but what new stock you can add to humanity, or how high you can carry life? A man is a man only as he makes life and nature happier to us.

I fear the popular notion of success stands in direct opposition in all points to the real and wholesome success. One adores public opinion, the other private opinion; one fame, the other desert; one feats, the other humility; one lucre, the other love; one monopoly, and the other hospitality of mind.

We may apply this affirmative law to letters, to manners, to art, to the decorations of our houses, etc. I do not find executions or tortures or lazar-houses, or grisly photographs of the field on the day after the battle, fit subjects for cabinet pictures. I think that some so-called "sacred subjects" must be treated with more genius than I have seen in the masters of Italian or Spanish art to be right pictures for houses and churches. Nature does not invite such exhibition. Nature lays the ground-plan of each creature accurately, sternly fit for all his functions; then veils it scrupulously. See how carefully she covers up the skeleton. The eye shall not see [308/309] it; the sun shall not shine on it. She weaves her tissues and integuments of flesh and skin and hair and beautiful colors of the day over it, and forces death down underground, and makes haste to cover it up with leaves and vines, and wipes carefully out every trace by new creation. Who and what are you that would lay the ghastly anatomy bare?

Don't hang a dismal picture on the wall, and do not daub with sables and glooms in your conversation. Don't be a cynic and disconsolate preacher. Don't bewail and bemoan. Omit the negative propositions. Nerve us with incessant affirmatives. Don't waste yourself in rejection, nor bark against the bad, but chant the beauty of the good. When that is spoken which has a right to be spoken, the chatter and the criticism will stop. Set down nothing that will not help somebody;—

> "For every gift of noble origin
> Is breathed upon by Hope's perpetual breath."

The affirmative of affirmatives is love. As much love, so much perception. As caloric to matter, so is love to mind; so it enlarges, and so it empowers it. Good will makes insight, as one finds his way to the sea by embarking on a river. I have seen scores of people who can [309/310] silence me, but I seek one who shall make me forget or overcome the frigidities and imbecilities into which I fall. The painter Giotto, Vasari tells us, renewed art because he put more goodness into his heads. To awake in man and to raise the sense of worth, to educate his feeling and judgment so that he shall scorn himself for a bad action, that is the only aim.

'Tis cheap and easy to destroy. There is not a joyful boy or an innocent girl buoyant with fine purposes of duty, in all the street full of eager and rosy faces, but a cynic can chill and dishearten with a single word. Despondency comes readily enough to the most sanguine. The cynic has only to follow their hint with his bitter confirmation, and they check that eager courageous pace and go home with heavier step and premature age. They will themselves quickly enough give the hint he wants to the cold wretch. Which of them has not failed to please where they most wished it? or blundered where they were most ambitious of success? or found themselves awkward or tedious or incapable of study, thought or heroism, and only hoped by good sense and fidelity to do what they could and pass unblamed? And this witty malefactor makes their little hope less with satire and skepticism, [310/311] and slackens the springs of endeavor. Yes, this is easy; but to help the young soul, add energy, inspire hope and blow the coals into a useful flame, to redeem defeat by new thought, by firm action, that is not easy, that is the work of divine men.

We live on different planes or platforms. There is an external life, which is educated at school, taught to read, write, cipher and trade; taught to grasp all the boy can get, urging him to put himself forward, to make himself useful and agreeable in the world, to ride, run, argue and contend, unfold his talents, shine, conquer and possess.

But the inner life sits at home, and does not learn to do things, nor value these feats at all. 'T is a quiet, wise perception. It loves truth, because it is itself real; it loves right, it knows nothing else; but it makes no progress; was as wise in our first memory of it as now; is just the same now in maturity and hereafter in age, it was in youth. We have grown to manhood and womanhood; we have powers, connection, children, reputations, professions: this makes no account of them all. It lives in the great present; it makes the present great. This tranquil, well-founded, wide-seeing soul is no express-rider, no [311/ 312] attorney, no magistrate: it lies in the sun and broods on the world. A person of this temper once said to a man of much activity, "I will pardon you that you do so much, and you me that I do nothing." And Euripides says that "Zeus hates busybodies and those who do too much." [312]

Days

RALPH WALDO EMERSON

Daughters of Time, the hypocritic Days,
Muffled and dumb like barefoot dervishes,
And marching single in an endless file,
Bring diadems and fagots in their hands.
To each they offer gifts after his will,
Bread, kingdoms, stars, and sky that holds them all.
I, in my pleached garden, watched the pomp,
Forgot my morning wishes, hastily
Took a few herbs and apples, and the Day
Turned and departed silent. I, too late,
Under her solemn fillet saw the scorn. [228]

Ralph Waldo Emerson, "Days," in *The Complete Works of Ralph Waldo Emerson,* ed. Edward Waldo Emerson (Boston and New York: Houghton Mifflin Company, 1903–1904), IX, 228. Written 1851.

Life without Principle

HENRY DAVID THOREAU

AT A LYCEUM, NOT LONG SINCE, I FELT THAT THE LECTURER HAD CHOSEN A
theme too foreign to himself, and so failed to interest me as much as he
might have done. He described things not in or near to his heart, but
toward his extremities and superficies. There was, in this sense, no truly
central or centralizing thought in the lecture. I would have had him
deal with his privatest experience, as the poet does. The greatest
compliment that was ever paid me was when one asked me what *I
thought*, and attended to my answer. I am surprised, as well as
delighted, when this happens, it is such a rare use he would make of
me, as if he were acquainted with the tool. Commonly, if men want
anything of me, it is only to know how many acres I make of their
land,—since I am a surveyor,—or, at most, what trivial news I have
burdened myself with. They never will go to law for my meat; they
prefer the shell. A man once came a considerable distance to ask me to
lecture on Slavery; but on conversing with him, I found that he and his
clique expected seven [253/254] eighths of the lecture to be theirs, and
only one eighth mine; so I declined. I take it for granted, when I am
invited to lecture anywhere,—for I have had a little experience in that
business,—that there is a desire to hear what *I think* on some subject,
though I may be the greatest fool in the country,—and not that I
should say pleasant things merely, or such as the audience will assent
to; and I resolve, accordingly, that I will give them a strong dose of
myself. They have sent for me, and engaged to pay for me, and I am
determined that they shall have me, though I bore them beyond all
precedent.

So now I would say something similar to you, my readers. Since
you are my readers, and I have not been much of a traveler, I will not
talk about people a thousand miles off, but come as near home as I can.

From Henry David Thoreau, "Life Without Principle," in *The Writings of
Henry David Thoreau* (Boston and New York: Houghton, Mifflin and Company,
1896), X, 253–261. Originally published 1863.

As the time is short, I will leave out all the flattery, and retain all the criticism.

Let us consider the way in which we spend our lives.

This world is a place of business. What an infinite bustle! I am awaked almost every night by the panting of the locomotive. It interrupts my dreams. There is no sabbath. It would be glorious to see mankind at leisure for once. It is nothing but work, work, work. I cannot easily buy a blank-book to write [254/255] thoughts in; they are commonly ruled for dollars and cents. An Irishman, seeing me making a minute in the fields, took it for granted that I was calculating my wages. If a man was tossed out of a window when an infant, and so made a cripple for life, or scared out of his wits by the Indians, it is regretted chiefly because he was thus incapacitated for—business! I think that there is nothing, not even crime, more opposed to poetry, to philosophy, ay, to life itself, than this incessant business.

There is a coarse and boisterous money-making fellow in the outskirts of our town, who is going to build a bank-wall under the hill along the edge of his meadow. The powers have put this into his head to keep him out of mischief, and he wishes me to spend three weeks digging there with him. The result will be that he will perhaps get some more money to hoard, and leave for his heirs to spend foolishly. If I do this, most will commend me as an industrious and hard-working man; but if I choose to devote myself to certain labors which yield more real profit, though but little money, they may be inclined to look on me as an idler. Nevertheless, as I do not need the police of meaning-less labor to regulate me, and do not see anything absolutely praise-worthy in this fellow's undertaking any more than in many [255/256] an enterprise of our own or foreign governments, however amusing it may be to him or them, I prefer to finish my education at a different school.

If a man walk in the woods for love of them half of each day, he is in danger of being regarded as a loafer; but if he spends his whole day as a speculator, shearing off those woods and making earth bald before her time, he is esteemed an industrious and enterprising citizen. As if a town had no interest in its forests but to cut them down!

Most men would feel insulted if it were proposed to employ them in throwing stones over a wall, and then in throwing them back, merely that they might earn their wages. But many are no more worthily employed now. For instance: just after sunrise, one summer morning, I noticed one of my neighbors walking beside his team, which was slowly drawing a heavy hewn stone swung under the axle, surrounded by an atmosphere of industry,—his day's work begun,—his brow commenced to sweat,—a reproach to all sluggards and idlers,—pausing abreast the shoulders of his oxen, and half turning round with a flourish of his merciful whip, while they gained their length on him. And I thought, Such is the labor which the American Congress exists to

protect,—honest, manly toil, [256/257]—honest as the day is long,—
that makes his bread taste sweet, and keeps society sweet,—which all
men respect and have consecrated; one of the sacred band, doing the
needful but irksome drudgery. Indeed, I felt a slight reproach, because
I observed this from a window, and was not abroad and stirring about
a similar business. The day went by, and at evening I passed the yard
of another neighbor, who keeps many servants, and spends much
money foolishly, while he adds nothing to the common stock, and there
I saw the stone of the morning lying beside a whimsical structure
intended to adorn this Lord Timothy Dexter's premises, and the
dignity forthwith departed from the teamster's labor, in my eyes. In my
opinion, the sun was made to light worthier toil than this. I may add
that his employer has since run off, in debt to a good part of the town,
and, after passing through Chancery, has settled somewhere else, there
to become once more a patron of the arts.

The ways by which you may get money almost without exception
lead downward. To have done anything by which you earned money
merely is to have been truly idle or worse. If the laborer gets no more
than the wages which his employer pays him, he is cheated, he cheats
himself. If you would get money as a writer [257/258] or lecturer, you
must be popular, which is to go down perpendicularly. Those services
which the community will most readily pay for, it is most disagreeable
to render. You are paid for being something less than a man. The State
does not commonly reward a genius any more wisely. Even the poet-
laureate would rather not have to celebrate the accidents of royalty.
He must be bribed with a pipe of wine; and perhaps another poet is
called away from his muse to gauge that very pipe. As for my own
business, even that kind of surveying which I could do with most
satisfaction my employers do not want. They would prefer that I
should do my work coarsely and not too well, ay, not well enough.
When I observe that there are different ways of surveying, my employer commonly asks which will give him the most land, not which is
most correct. I once invented a rule for measuring cord-wood, and
tried to introduce it in Boston; but the measurer there told me that the
sellers did not wish to have their wood measured correctly,—that he
was already too accurate for them, and therefore they commonly got
their wood measured in Charlestown before crossing the bridge.

The aim of the laborer should be, not to get his living, to get
"a good job," but to perform [258/259] well a certain work; and, even
in a pecuniary sense, it would be economy for a town to pay its
laborers so well that they would not feel that they were working for
low ends, as for a livelihood merely, but for scientific, or even moral
ends. Do not hire a man who does your work for money, but him who
does it for love of it.

It is remarkable that there are few men so well employed, so much
to their minds, but that a little money or fame would commonly buy

them off from their present pursuit. I see advertisements for *active* young men, as if activity were the whole of a young man's capital. Yet I have been surprised when one has with confidence proposed to me, a grown man, to embark in some enterprise of his, as if I had absolutely nothing to do, my life having been a complete failure hitherto. What a doubtful compliment this to pay me! As if he had met me halfway across the ocean beating up against the wind, but bound nowhere, and proposed to me to go along with him! If I did, what do you think the underwriters would say? No, no! I am not without employment at this stage of the voyage. To tell the truth, I saw an advertisement for able-bodied seamen, when I was a boy, sauntering in my native port, and as soon as I came of age I embarked.

The community has no bribe that will tempt [259/260] a wise man. You may raise money enough to tunnel a mountain, but you cannot raise money enough to hire a man who is minding *his own* business. An efficient and valuable man does what he can, whether the community pay him for it or not. The inefficient offer their inefficiency to the highest bidder, and are forever expecting to be put into office. One would suppose that they were rarely disappointed.

Perhaps I am more than usually jealous with respect to my freedom. I feel that my connection with and obligation to society are still very slight and transient. Those slight labors which afford me a livelihood, and by which it is allowed that I am to some extent serviceable to my contemporaries, are as yet commonly a pleasure to me, and I am not often reminded that they are a necessity. So far I am successful. But I foresee that if my wants should be much increased, the labor required to supply them would become a drudgery. If I should sell both my forenoons and afternoons to society, as most appear to do, I am sure that for me there would be nothing left worth living for. I trust that I shall never thus sell my birthright for a mess of pottage. I wish to suggest that a man may be very industrious, and yet not spend his time well. There is no more fatal blunderer than he who consumes the greater part of his [260/261] life getting his living. All great enterprises are self-supporting. The poet, for instance, must sustain his body by his poetry, as a steam planing-mill feeds its boilers with the shavings it makes. You must get your living by loving. But as it is said of the merchants that ninety-seven in a hundred fail, so the life of men generally, tried by this standard, is a failure, and bankruptcy may be surely prophesied. . . . [261]

Four Poems

WALT WHITMAN

When I Peruse the Conquer'd Fame

When I peruse the conquer'd fame of heroes and the victories of
    mighty generals, I do not envy the generals,
Nor the President in his Presidency, nor the rich in his great house,
But when I hear of the brotherhood of lovers, how it was with them,
How together through life, through dangers, odium, unchanging, long
    and long,
Through youth and through middle and old age, how unfaltering, how
    affectionate and faithful they were,
Then I am pensive—I hastily walk away fill'd with the bitterest envy.
[I, 155]

No Labor-Saving Machine

No labor-saving machine,
Nor discovery have I made,
Nor will I be able to leave behind me any wealthy bequest to found a
    hospital or library,
Nor reminiscence of any deed of courage for America,
Nor literary success nor intellect, nor book for the book-shelf,
But a few carols vibrating through the air I leave,
For comrades and lovers. [I, 157]

My Legacy

The business man the acquirer vast,
After assiduous years surveying results, preparing for departure,

From *The Complete Writings of Walt Whitman*, ed. Richard Maurice
Bucke, Thomas B. Harned, and Horace L. Traubel (New York and London:
G. P. Putnam's Sons, 1902), I, 155, 157; II, 281, 38. The first two poems were
originally published in 1860; the others, in order, appeared in 1872 and 1881.

Devises houses and lands to his children, bequeaths stocks, goods,
    funds for a school or hospital,
Leaves money to certain companions to buy tokens, souvenirs of gems
    and gold.

But I, my life surveying, closing,
With nothing to show to devise from its idle years,
Nor houses nor lands, nor tokens of gems or gold for my friends,
Yet certain remembrances of the war for you, and after you,
And little souvenirs of camps and soldiers, with my love,
I bind together and bequeath in this bundle of songs. [II, 281]

Hast Never Come to Thee an Hour

Has never come to thee an hour,
A sudden gleam divine, precipitating, bursting all these bubbles,
    fashions, wealth?
These eager business aims—books, politics, art, amours,
To utter nothingness? [II, 38]

Story of the Bad Little Boy

MARK TWAIN

ONCE THERE WAS A BAD LITTLE BOY WHOSE NAME WAS JIM—THOUGH, IF
you will notice, you will find that bad little boys are nearly always
called James in your Sunday-school books. It was strange, but still it
was true that this one was called Jim.

He didn't have any sick mother either—a sick mother who was
pious and had the consumption, and would be glad to lie down in the
grave and be at rest but for the strong love she bore her boy, and the
anxiety she felt that the world might be harsh and cold towards him
when she was gone. Most bad boys in the Sunday-books are named
James, and have sick mothers, [51/52] who teach them to say, "Now, I
lay me down," etc., and sing them to sleep with sweet, plaintive voices,

Mark Twain, "Story of the Bad Little Boy," in *Mark Twain's Sketches, New
and Old* (Hartford, Conn., and Chicago, Ill.: The American Publishing Company,
1875), pp. 51–55. Originally published 1865.

and then kiss them good-night, and kneel down by the bedside and weep. But it was different with this fellow. He was named Jim, and there wasn't anything the matter with his mother—no consumption, nor anything of that kind. She was rather stout than otherwise, and she was not pious; moreover, she was not anxious on Jim's account. She said if he were to break his neck it wouldn't be much loss. She always spanked Jim to sleep, and she never kissed him good-night; on the contrary, she boxed his ears when she was ready to leave him.

Once this little bad boy stole the key of the pantry, and slipped in there and helped himself to some jam, and filled up the vessel with tar, so that his mother would never know the difference; but all at once a terrible feeling didn't come over him, and something didn't seem to whisper to him, "Is it right to disobey my mother? Isn't it sinful to do this? Where do bad little boys go who gobble up their good kind mother's jam?" and then he didn't kneel down all alone and promise never to be wicked any more, and rise up with a light, happy heart, and go and tell his mother all about it, and beg her forgiveness, and be blessed by her with tears of pride and thankfulness in her eyes. No; that is the way with all other bad boys in the books; but it happened otherwise with this Jim, strangely enough. He ate that jam, and said it was bully, in his sinful, vulgar way; and he put in the tar, and said that was bully also, and laughed, and observed "that the old woman would get up and snort" when she found it out; and when she did find it out, he denied knowing anything about it, and she whipped him severely, and he did the crying himself. [52/53] Everything about this boy was curious— everything turned out differently with him from the way it does to the bad Jameses in the books.

Once he climbed up in Farmer Acorn's apple-tree to steal apples, and the limb didn't break, and he didn't fall and break his arm, and get torn by the farmer's great dog, and then languish on a sick bed for weeks, and repent and become good. Oh! no; he stole as many apples as he wanted and came down all right; and he was all ready for the dog too, and knocked him endways with a brick when he came to tear him. It was very strange—nothing like it ever happened in those mild little books with marbled backs, and with pictures in them of men with swallow-tailed coats and bell-crowned hats, and pantaloons that are short in the legs, and women with the waists of their dresses under their arms, and no hoops on. Nothing like it in any of the Sunday-school books.

Once he stole the teacher's pen-knife, and, when he was afraid it would be found out and he would get whipped, he slipped it into George Wilson's cap—poor Widow Wilson's son, the moral boy, the good little boy of the village, who always obeyed his mother, and never told an untruth, and was fond of his lessons, and infatuated with Sunday-school. And when the knife dropped from the cap, and poor George hung his head and blushed, as if in conscious guilt, and the

grieved teacher charged the theft upon him, and was just in the very
act of bringing the switch down upon his trembling shoulders, a white-
haired, improbable justice of the peace did not suddenly appear in
their midst, and strike an attitude and say, "Spare this noble boy—
there stands the cowering culprit! I was passing the school-door at
recess, and unseen myself, I saw the theft committed!" And then Jim
didn't get whaled, and the venerable justice didn't read the tearful
school a homily, and take George by the hand and say such a boy
deserved to be exalted, and then tell him to come and make his home
with him, and sweep out the office, and make fires, and run errands,
and chop wood, and study law, and help his wife do household labors,
and have all the balance of the time to play, and get forty cents a
month, and be happy. No; it would have happened that way in the
books, but it didn't happen that way to Jim. No meddling old clam of a
justice dropped in to make trouble, and so the model boy George got
thrashed, and Jim was glad of it because, you know, Jim hated [53/
54] moral boys. Jim said he was "down on them milksops." Such was
the coarse language of this bad, neglected boy.

But the strangest thing that ever happened to Jim was the time he
went boating on Sunday, and didn't get drowned, and that other time
that he got caught out in the storm when he was fishing on Sunday,
and didn't get struck by lightning. Why, you might look, and look, all
through the Sunday-school books from now till next Christmas, and
you would never come across anything like this. Oh no; you would find
that all the bad boys who go boating on Sunday invariably got
drowned; and all the bad boys who get caught out in storms when they
are fishing on Sunday infallibly get struck by lightning. Boats with bad
boys in them always upset on Sunday, and it always storms when bad
boys go fishing on the Sabbath. How this Jim ever escaped is a mystery
to me.

This Jim bore a charmed life—that must have been the way of it.
Nothing could hurt him. He even gave the elephant in the menagerie a
plug of tobacco, and the elephant didn't knock the top of his head off
with his trunk. He browsed around the cupboard after essence of
peppermint, and didn't make a mistake and drink *aqua fortis*. He stole
his father's gun and went hunting on the Sabbath, and didn't shoot
three or four of his fingers off. He struck his little sister on the temple
with his fist when he was angry, and she didn't linger in pain through
long summer days, and die with sweet words of forgiveness upon her
lips that redoubled the anguish of his breaking heart. No; she got over
it. He ran off and went to sea at last, and didn't come back and find
himself sad and alone in the world, his loved ones sleeping in the quiet
churchyard, and the vine-embowered [54/55] home of his boyhood
tumbled down and gone to decay. Ah! no; he came home as drunk as a
piper, and got into the station-house the first thing.

And he grew up and married, and raised a large family, and

brained them all with an axe one night, and got wealthy by all manner of cheating and rascality; and now he is the infernalest wickedest scoundrel in his native village, and is universally respected, and belongs to the Legislature.

So you see there never was a bad James in the Sunday-school books that had such a streak of luck as this sinful Jim with the charmed life. [55]

The Coach of Capitalism

EDWARD BELLAMY

BY WAY OF ATTEMPTING TO GIVE THE READER SOME GENERAL IMPRESSION of the way people lived together in those days, and especially of the relations of the rich and poor to one another, perhaps I cannot do better than to compare society as it then was to a prodigious coach which the masses of humanity were harnessed to and dragged toilsomely along a very hilly and sandy road. The driver was hunger, and permitted no lagging, though the pace was necessarily very slow. Despite the difficulty of drawing the coach at all along so hard a road, the top was covered with passengers who never got down, even at the steepest ascents. These seats on top were very breezy and comfortable. Well up out of the dust, their occupants could enjoy the scenery at their leisure, or critically discuss the merits of the straining team. Naturally such places were in great demand and the competition for them was keen, every one seeking as the first end of life to secure a seat on the coach for himself and to leave it to his child after him. By the rule of the coach a man could leave his seat to whom he [3/4] wished, but on the other hand there were many accidents by which it might at any time be wholly lost. For all that there were so easy, the seats were very insecure, and at every sudden jolt of the coach persons were slipping out of them and falling to the ground, where they were instantly compelled to take hold of the rope and help to drag the coach on which they had before ridden so pleasantly. It was naturally

From Edward Bellamy, *Looking Backward 2000–1887* (New York: The Modern Library, n.d.), pp. 3–6. Originally published 1888.

regarded as a terrible misfortune to lose one's seat, and the apprehension that this might happen to them or their friends was a constant cloud upon the happiness of those who rode.

But did they think only of themselves? you ask. Was not their very luxury rendered intolerable to them by comparison with the lot of their brothers and sisters in the harness, and the knowledge that their own weight added to their toil? Had they no compassion for fellow beings from whom fortune only distinguished them? Oh, yes; commiseration was frequently expressed by those who rode for those who had to pull the coach, especially when the vehicle came to a bad place in the road, as it was constantly doing, or to a particularly steep hill. At such times, the desperate straining of the team, their agonized leaping and plunging under the pitiless lashing of hunger, the many who fainted at the rope and were trampled in the mire, made a very distressing spectacle, which often called forth highly creditable displays of feeling on the top of the coach. At such times the passengers would call down encouragingly to the toilers of the rope, exhorting them to patience, and holding out hopes of possible compensation in another world for the hardness of their lot, while others contributed to buy salves and liniments for the crippled and injured. It was agreed [4/5] that it was a great pity that the coach should be so hard to pull, and there was a sense of general relief when the specially bad piece of road was gotten over. This relief was not, indeed, wholly on account of the team, for there was always some danger at these bad places of a general overturn in which all would lose their seats.

It must in truth be admitted that the main effect of the spectacle of the misery of the toilers at the rope was to enhance the passengers' sense of the value of their seats upon the coach, and to cause them to hold on to them more desperately than before. If the passengers could only have felt assured that neither they nor their friends would ever fall from the top, it is probable that, beyond contributing to the funds for liniments and bandages, they would have troubled themselves extremely little about those who dragged the coach.

I am well aware that this will appear to the men and women of the twentieth century an incredible inhumanity, but there are two facts, both very curious, which partly explain it. In the first place, it was firmly and sincerely believed that there was no other way in which Society could get along, except the many pulled at the rope and the few rode, and not only this, but that no very radical improvement even was possible, either in the harness, the coach, the roadway, or the distribution of the toil. It had always been as it was, and it always would be so. It was a pity, but it could not be helped, and philosophy forbade wasting compassion on what was beyond remedy.

The other fact is yet more curious, consisting in a singular hallucination which those on the top of the coach generally shared, that they were not exactly like their brothers and sisters who pulled at the rope,

but of finer clay, in [5/6] some way belonging to a higher order of
beings who might justly expect to be drawn. This seems unaccountable, but, as I once rode on this very coach and shared that very
hallucination, I ought to be believed. The strangest thing about the
hallucination was that those who had but just climbed up from the
ground, before they had outgrown the marks of the rope upon their
hands, began to fall under its influence. As for those whose parents and
grand-parents before them had been so fortunate as to keep their seats
on the top, the conviction they cherished of the essential difference
between their sort of humanity and the common article was absolute.
The effect of such a delusion in moderating fellow feeling for the
sufferings of the mass of men into a distant and philosophical compassion is obvious. To it I refer as the only extenuation I can offer for
the indifference which, at the period I write of, marked my own
attitude toward the misery of my brothers. [6]

A Servant of Society

SINCLAIR LEWIS

HIS MORNING WAS NOT SHARPLY MARKED INTO DIVISIONS. INTERWOVEN
with correspondence and advertisement-writing were a thousand nervous details: calls from clerks who were incessantly and hopefully
seeking five furnished rooms and bath at sixty dollars a month; advice
to Mat Penniman on getting money out of tenants who had no money.

Babbitt's virtues as a real-estate broker—as the servant of society
in the department of finding homes for families and shops for distrib-
utors of food—were steadiness and diligence. He was conventionally
honest, he kept his records of buyers and sellers complete, he had
experience with leases and titles and an excellent memory for prices.
His shoulders were broad enough, his voice deep enough, his relish of
hearty humor strong enough, to establish him as one of the ruling caste
of Good Fellows. Yet his eventual importance to mankind was perhaps
lessened by his large and complacent ignorance of all architecture save

the types of houses turned out by speculative builders; all landscape gardening save the use of curving roads, grass, and six ordinary shrubs; and all the commonest axioms of economics. He serenely believed that the one purpose of the real-estate business was to make money for George F. Babbitt. True, it was a good advertisement at Boosters' Club lunches, and all the varieties of Annual Banquets to which Good Fellows were invited, to speak sonorously of Unselfish Public Service, the Broker's Obligation to Keep Inviolate the Trust of His Clients, and a thing called Ethics, whose nature was confusing but if you had it you were a High-class Realtor and if you hadn't you were a shyster, a piker, and a fly-by-night. These virtues awakened Confidence, and enabled you to handle Bigger Propositions. But they didn't imply that [42/43] you were to be impractical and refuse to take twice the value of a house if a buyer was such an idiot that he didn't jew you down on the asking-price.

Babbitt spoke well—and often—at these orgies of commercial righteousness about the "realtor's function as a seer of the future development of the community, and as a prophetic engineer clearing the pathway for inevitable changes"—which meant that a real-estate broker could make money by guessing which way the town would grow. This guessing he called Vision.

In an address at the Boosters' Club he had admitted, "It is at once the duty and the privilege of the realtor to know everything about his own city and its environs. Where a surgeon is a specialist on every vein and mysterious cell of the human body, and the engineer upon electricity in all its phases, or every bolt of some great bridge majestically arching o'er a mighty flood, the realtor must know his city, inch by inch, and all its faults and virtues."

Though he did know the market-price, inch by inch, of certain districts of Zenith, he did not know whether the police force was too large or too small, or whether it was in alliance with gambling and prostitution. He knew the means of fire-proofing buildings and the relation of insurance-rates to fire-proofing, but he did not know how many firemen there were in the city, how they were trained and paid, or how complete their apparatus. He sang eloquently the advantages of proximity of school-buildings to rentable homes, but he did not know—he did not know that it was worth while to know—whether the city schoolrooms were properly heated, lighted, ventilated, furnished; he did not know how the teachers were chosen; and though he chanted "One of the boasts of Zenith is that we pay our teachers adequately," that was because he had read the statement in the *Advocate-Times*. Himself, he could not have given the average salary of teachers in Zenith or anywhere else. [43/44]

He had heard it said that "conditions" in the County Jail and the Zenith City Prison were not very "scientific"; he had, with indignation at the criticism of Zenith, skimmed through a report in which the notorious pessimist Seneca Doane, the radical lawyer, asserted that to throw boys and young girls into a bull-pen crammed with men suffering from syphilis, delirium tremens, and insanity was not the perfect way of educating them. He had controverted the report by growling, "Folks that think a jail ought to be a bloomin' Hotel Thornleigh make me sick. If people don't like a jail, let 'em behave 'emselves and keep out of it. Besides, these reform cranks always exaggerate." That was the beginning and quite completely the end of his investigations into Zenith's charities and corrections; and as to the "vice districts" he brightly expressed it, "Those are things that no decent man monkeys with. Besides, smatter fact, I'll tell you confidentially: it's a protection to our daughters and to decent women to have a district where tough nuts can raise Cain. Keeps 'em away from our own homes."

As to industrial conditions, however, Babbitt had thought a great deal, and his opinions may be coördinated as follows:

"A good labor union is of value because it keeps out radical unions, which would destroy property. No one ought to be forced to belong to a union, however. All labor agitators who try to force men to join a union should be hanged. In fact, just between ourselves, there oughtn't to be any unions allowed at all; and as it's the best way of fighting the unions, every business man ought to belong to an employers'-association and to the Chamber of Commerce. In union there is strength. So any selfish hog who doesn't join the Chamber of Commerce ought to be forced to."

In nothing—as the expert on whose advice families moved to new neighborhoods to live there for a generation—was Babbitt more splendidly innocent than in the science of sanitation. He did not know a malaria-bearing mosquito from a bat; he knew nothing about tests of drinking water; and in the [44/45] matters of plumbing and sewage he was as unlearned as he was voluble. He often referred to the excellence of the bathrooms in the houses he sold. He was fond of explaining why it was that no European ever bathed. Some one had told him, when he was twenty-two, that all cesspools were unhealthy, and he still denounced them. If a client impertinently wanted him to sell a house which had a cesspool, Babbitt always spoke about it— before accepting the house and selling it.

When he laid out the Glen Oriole acreage development, when he ironed woodland and dipping meadow into a glenless, orioleless, sunburnt flat prickly with small boards displaying the names of imaginary streets, he righteously put in a complete sewage-system. It made him feel superior; it enabled him to sneer privily at the Martin Lumsen development, Avonlea, which had a cesspool; and it provided a chorus for the full-page advertisements in which he announced the beauty, convenience, cheapness, and supererogatory healthfulness of Glen Oriole. The only flaw was that the Glen Oriole sewers had insufficient outlet, so that waste remained in them, not very agreeably, while the Avonlea cesspool was a Waring septic tank.

The whole of the Glen Oriole project was a suggestion that Babbitt, though he really did hate men recognized as swindlers, was not too unreasonably honest. Operators and buyers prefer that brokers should not be in competition with them as operators and buyers themselves, but attend to their clients' interests only. It was supposed that the Babbitt-Thompson Company were merely agents for Glen Oriole, serving the real owner, Jake Offutt, but the fact was that Babbitt and Thompson owned sixty-two per cent. of the Glen, the president and purchasing agent of the Zenith Street Traction Company owned twenty-eight per cent., and Jake Offutt (a gang-politician, a small manufacturer, a tobacco-chewing old farceur who enjoyed dirty politics, business diplomacy, and cheating at poker) had only ten per cent., which Babbitt and the Traction officials [45/46] had given to him for "fixing" health inspectors and fire inspectors and a member of the State Transportation Commission.

But Babbitt was virtuous. He advocated, though he did not practise, the prohibition of alcohol; he praised, though he did not obey, the laws against motor-speeding; he paid his debts; he contributed to the church, the Red Cross, and the Y. M. C. A.; he followed the custom of his clan and cheated only as it was sanctified by precedent; and he never descended to trickery—though, as he explained to Paul Riesling:

"Course I don't mean to say that every ad I write is literally true or that I always believe everything I say when I give some buyer a good strong selling-spiel. You see—you see it's like this: In the first place, maybe the owner of the property exaggerated when he put it into my hands, and it certainly isn't my place to go proving my principal a liar! And then most folks are so darn crooked themselves that they expect a fellow to do a little lying, so if I was fool enough to never whoop the ante I'd get the credit for lying anyway! In self-defense I got to toot my own horn, like a lawyer defending a client—his bounden duty, ain't it, to bring out the poor dub's good points? Why, the Judge himself would bawl out a lawyer that didn't, even if they both knew the guy was guilty! But even so, I don't pad out the truth like Cecil Rountree or Thayer or the rest of these realtors. Fact, I think a fellow that's willing to deliberately up and profit by lying ought to be shot!"

Babbitt's value to his clients was rarely better shown than this morning, in the conference at eleven-thirty between himself, Conrad Lyte, and Archibald Purdy.

Conrad Lyte was a real-estate speculator. He was a nervous speculator. Before he gambled he consulted bankers, lawyers, architects, contracting builders, and all of their clerks and [46/47] stenographers who were willing to be cornered and give him advice. He was a bold entrepreneur, and he desired nothing more than complete safety in his investments, freedom from attention to details, and the thirty or forty per cent. profit which, according to all authorities, a pioneer deserves for his risks and foresight. He was a stubby man with a cap-like mass of short gray curls and clothes which, no matter how well cut, seemed shaggy. Below his eyes were semicircular hollows, as though silver dollars had been pressed against them and had left an imprint.

Particularly and always Lyte consulted Babbitt, and trusted in his slow cautiousness.

Six months ago Babbitt had learned that one Archibald Purdy, a grocer in the indecisive residential district known as Linton, was talking of opening a butcher shop beside his grocery. Looking up the ownership of adjoining parcels of land, Babbitt found that Purdy owned his present shop but did not own the one available lot adjoining. He advised Conrad Lyte to purchase this lot, for eleven thousand dollars, though an appraisal on a basis of rents did not indicate its value as above nine thousand. The rents, declared Babbitt, were too low; and by waiting they could make Purdy come to their price. (This was Vision.) He had to bully Lyte into buying. His first act as agent for Lyte was to increase the rent of the battered store-building on the lot. The tenant said a number of rude things, but he paid.

Now, Purdy seemed ready to buy, and his delay was going to cost him ten thousand extra dollars—the reward paid by the community to Mr. Conrad Lyte for the virtue of employing a broker who had Vision and who understood Talking Points, Strategic Values, Key Situations, Underappraisals, and the Psychology of Salesmanship.

Lyte came to the conference exultantly. He was fond of Babbitt, this morning, and called him "old hoss." Purdy, the grocer, a long-nosed man and solemn, seemed to care less for [47/48] Babbitt and for Vision, but Babbitt met him at the street door of the office and guided him toward the private room with affectionate little cries of "This way, Brother Purdy!" He took from the correspondence-file the entire box of cigars and forced them on his guests. He pushed their chairs two inches forward and three inches back, which gave an hospitable note, then leaned back in his desk-chair and looked plump and jolly. But he spoke to the weakling grocer with firmness.

"Well, Brother Purdy, we been having some pretty tempting offers from butchers and a slew of other folks for that lot next to your store, but I persuaded Brother Lyte that we ought to give you a shot at the property first. I said to Lyte, 'It'd be a rotten shame,' I said, 'if some-body went and opened a combination grocery and meat market right next door and ruined Purdy's nice little business.' Especially—" Babbitt leaned forward, and his voice was harsh, "—it would be hard luck if one of these cash-and-carry chain-stores got in there and started cutting prices below cost till they got rid of competition and forced you to the wall!"

Purdy snatched his thin hands from his pockets, pulled up his trousers, thrust his hands back into his pockets, tilted in the heavy oak chair, and tried to look amused, as he struggled:

"Yes, they're bad competition. But I guess you don't realize the Pulling Power that Personality has in a neighborhood business."

The great Babbitt smiled. "That's so. Just as you feel, old man. We thought we'd give you first chance. All right then—"

"Now look here!" Purdy wailed. "I know f'r a fact that a piece of property 'bout same size, right near, sold for less 'n eighty-five hundred, 'twa'nt two years ago, and here you fellows are asking me twenty-four thousand dollars! Why, I'd have to mortgage— I wouldn't mind so much paying twelve thousand but— Why good God, Mr. Babbitt, you're asking [48/49] more 'n twice its value! And threatening to ruin me if I don't take it!"

"Purdy, I don't like your way of talking! I don't like it one little bit! Supposing Lyte and I were stinking enough to want to ruin any fellow human, don't you suppose we know it's to our own selfish interest to have everybody in Zenith prosperous? But all this is beside the point. Tell you what we'll do: We'll come down to twenty-three thousand—five thousand down and the rest on mortgage—and if you want to wreck the old shack and rebuild, I guess I can get Lyte here to loosen up for a building-mortgage on good liberal terms. Heavens, man, we'd be glad to oblige you! We don't like these foreign grocery trusts any better 'n you do! But it isn't reasonable to expect us to sacrifice eleven thousand or more just for neighborliness, *is* it! How about it, Lyte? You willing to come down?"

By warmly taking Purdy's part, Babbitt persuaded the benevolent Mr. Lyte to reduce his price to twenty-one thousand dollars. At the right moment Babbitt snatched from a drawer the agreement he had had Miss McGoun type out a week ago and thrust it into Purdy's hands. He genially shook his fountain pen to make certain that it was flowing, handed it to Purdy, and approvingly watched him sign.

The work of the world was being done. Lyte had made something over nine thousand dollars, Babbitt had made a four-hundred-and-fifty dollar commission, Purdy had, by the sensitive mechanism of modern finance, been provided with a business-building, and soon the happy inhabitants of Linton would have meat lavished upon them at prices only a little higher than those down-town.

It had been a manly battle, but after it Babbitt drooped. This was the only really amusing contest he had been planning. There was nothing ahead save details of leases, appraisals, mortgages.

He muttered, "Makes me sick to think of Lyte carrying off [49/ 50] most of the profit when I did all the work, the old skinflint! And— What else have I got to do to-day? ... Like to take a good long vacation. Motor trip. Something." ... [50]

Emperor of the Caribbean

JOHN DOS PASSOS

WHEN MINOR C. KEITH DIED ALL THE NEWSPAPERS CARRIED HIS PICTURE, a brighteyed man with a hawknose and a respectable bay window, and an uneasy look under the eyes.

Minor C. Keith was a rich man's son, born in a family that liked the smell of money, they could smell money halfway round the globe in that family.

His Uncle was Henry Meiggs, the Don Enrique of the West Coast. His father had a big lumber business and handled realestate in Brooklyn;

young Keith was a chip of the old block

(Back in fortynine Don Enrique had been drawn to San Francisco by the gold rush. He didn't go prospecting in the hills, he didn't die of thirst sifting alkalidust in Death Valley. He sold outfits to the other guys. He stayed in San Francisco and played politics and high finance until he got in too deep and had to get aboard ship in a hurry.

The vessel took him to Chile. He could smell money in Chile. [283/284]

He was the capitalista yanqui. He'd build the railroad from Santiago to Valparaiso. There were guano deposits on the Chincha Islands. Meiggs could smell money in guano. He dug himself a fortune out of guano, became a power on the West Coast, juggled figures, railroads, armies, the politics of the local caciques and politicos; they were all chips in a huge pokergame. Behind a big hand he heaped up the dollars.

He financed the unbelievable Andean railroads.

When Tomas Guardia got to be dictator of Costa Rica he wrote to Don Enrique to build him a railroad;

From John Dos Passos, *The 42nd Parallel* (Boston: Houghton Mifflin Company, 1946), pp. 283–286. From *U.S.A.* by John Dos Passos, copyright by John Dos Passos. Reprinted with the kind permission of the author. Originally published 1930.

Meiggs was busy in the Andes, a $75,000 dollar contract was hardly worth his while,
so he sent for his nephew Minor Keith.

They didn't let grass grow under their feet in that family:
at sixteen Minor Keith had been on his own, selling collars and ties in a clothingstore.
After that he was a lumber surveyor and ran a lumber business.
When his father bought Padre Island off Corpus Christi, Texas, he sent Minor down to make money out of it.
Minor Keith started raising cattle on Padre Island and seining for fish,
but cattle and fish didn't turn over money fast enough
so he bought hogs and chopped up the steers and boiled the meat and fed it to the hogs and chopped up the fish and fed it to the hogs,
but hogs didn't turn over money fast enough,
so he was glad to be off to Limon.

Limon was one of the worst pestholes on the Caribbean, even the Indians died there of malaria, yellowjack, dysentery.
Keith went back up to New Orleans on the steamer *John G.* [284/285] *Meiggs* to hire workers to build the railroad. He offered a dollar a day and grub and hired seven hundred men. Some of them had been down before in the filibustering days of William Walker.
Of that bunch about twentyfive came out alive.
The rest left their whiskey-scalded carcasses to rot in the swamps.
On another load he shipped down fifteen hundred; they all died to prove that only Jamaica Negroes could live in Limon.

Minor Keith didn't die.

In 1882 there were twenty miles of railroad built and Keith was a million dollars in the hole;
the railroad had nothing to haul.
Keith made them plant bananas so that the railroad might have something to haul, to market the bananas he had to go into the shipping business;
this was the beginning of the Caribbean fruittrade.
All the while the workers died of whiskey, malaria, yellowjack, dysentery.
Minor Keith's three brothers died.
Minor Keith didn't die.
He built railroads, opened retail stores up and down the coast in Bluefields, Belize, Limon, bought and sold rubber, vanilla, tortoise-shell, sarsaparilla, anything he could buy cheap he bought, anything he could sell dear he sold.
In 1898 in co-operation with the Boston Fruit Company he formed

the United Fruit Company that has since become one of the most
powerful industrial units in the world.

In 1912 he incorporated the International Railroads of Central
America;

all of it built out of bananas;

in Europe and the United States people had started to eat
bananas, [285/286]

so they cut down the jungles through Central America to plant
bananas,

and built railroads to haul the bananas,

and every year more steamboats of the Great White Fleet
steamed north loaded with bananas,

and that is the history of the American empire in the Caribbean,

and the Panama Canal and the future Nicaragua Canal and the
marines and the battleships and the bayonets.

Why that uneasy look under the eyes, in the picture of Minor C.
Keith the pioneer of the fruit trade, the railroad-builder, in all the
pictures the newspapers carried of him when he died? [286]

B. PORTRAITS OF FAILURE

Millions and Millions

MARK TWAIN

THE SUPPER AT COL. SELLERS'S WAS NOT SUMPTUOUS, IN THE BEGINNING,
but it improved on acquaintance. That is to say, that what Washington
regarded at first sight as mere lowly potatoes, presently became awe-
inspiring agricultural productions that had been reared in some ducal
garden beyond the sea, under the sacred eye of the duke himself, who
had sent them to Sellers; the bread was from corn which could be
grown in only one favored locality in the earth and only a favored few
could get it; the Rio coffee, which at first seemed execrable to the taste,
took to itself an improved flavor when [92/93] Washington was told
to drink it slowly and not hurry what should be a lingering luxury in
order to be fully appreciated—it was from the private stores of a

From Mark Twain and Charles Dudley Warner, *The Gilded Age* (New
York and London: Harper & Brothers Publishers, 1901), I, 92–103. Originally
published 1873.

Brazilian nobleman with an unrememberable name. The Colonel's tongue was a magician's wand that turned dried apples into figs and water into wine as easily as it could change a hovel into a palace and present poverty into imminent future riches.

Washington slept in a cold bed in a carpetless room and woke up in a palace in the morning; at least the palace lingered during the moment that he was rubbing his eyes and getting his bearings—and then it disappeared and he recognized that the Colonel's inspiring talk had been influencing his dreams. Fatigue had made him sleep late; when he entered the sitting-room he noticed that the old haircloth sofa was absent; when he sat down to breakfast the Colonel tossed six or seven dollars in bills on the table, counted them over, said he was a little short and must call upon his banker; then returned the bills to his wallet with the indifferent air of a man who is used to money. The breakfast was not an improvement upon the supper, but the Colonel talked it up and transformed it into an oriental feast. By and by, he said:

"I intend to look out for you, Washington, my boy. I hunted up a place for you yesterday, but I am not referring to that, now—that is a mere livelihood—mere bread and butter; but when I say I mean to look out for you I mean something very [93/94] different. I mean to put things in your way that will make a mere livelihood a trifling thing. I'll put you in a way to make more money than you'll ever know what to do with. You'll be right here where I can put my hand on you when anything turns up. I've got some prodigious operations on foot; but I'm keeping quiet; mum's the word; your old hand don't go around pow-wowing and letting everybody see his k'yards and find out his little game. But all in good time, Washington, all in good time. You'll see. Now, there's an operation in corn that looks well. Some New York men are trying to get me to go into it—buy up all the growing crops and just boss the market when they mature—ah, I tell you it's a great thing. And it only costs a trifle; two millions or two and a half will do it. I haven't exactly promised yet—there's no hurry—the more indifferent I seem, you know, the more anxious those fellows will get. And then there is the hog speculation—that's bigger still. We've got quiet men at work," [he was very impressive here,] "mousing around, to get propositions out of all the farmers in the whole West and Northwest for the hog crop, and other agents quietly getting propositions and terms out of all the manufactories—and don't you see, if we can get all the hogs and all the slaughter-houses into our hands on the dead quiet—whew! it would take three ships to carry the money. I've looked into the thing—calculated all the chances for and all the chances against, and though I shake my head [94/95] and hesitate and keep on thinking, apparently, I've got my mind made up that if the thing can be done on a capital of six millions, that's the horse to put up money on! Why, Washington—but what's the use of talking about it—any man can see that there's whole Atlantic oceans of cash in it, gulfs and bays thrown in. But there's a bigger thing than that, yet—a bigger——"

"Why, Colonel, you can't want anything bigger!" said Washington, his eyes blazing. "Oh, I wish I could go into either of those specula-tions—I only wish I had money—I wish I wasn't cramped and kept down and fettered with poverty, and such prodigious chances lying right here in sight! Oh, it is a fearful thing to be poor. But don't throw away those things—they are so splendid and I can see how sure they are. Don't throw them away for something still better and maybe fail in it! I wouldn't, Colonel. I would stick to these. I wish father were here and were his old self again. Oh, he never in his life had such chances as these are. Colonel, you *can't* improve on these—no man can improve on them!"

A sweet, compassionate smile played about the Colonel's features, and he leaned over the table with the air of a man who is "going to show you" and do it without the least trouble:

"Why Washington, my boy, these things are nothing. They *look* large—of course they look large to a novice, but to a man who has been all his life [95/96] accustomed to large operations—shaw! They're well enough to while away an idle hour with, or furnish a bit of employ-ment that will give a trifle of idle capital a chance to earn its bread while it is waiting for something to *do*, but—now just listen a moment —just let me give you an idea of what we old veterans of commerce call 'business.' Here's the Rothschilds' proposition—this is between you and me, you understand——"

Washington nodded three or four times impatiently, and his glowing eyes said, "Yes, yes—hurry—I understand——"

"——for I wouldn't have it get out for a fortune. They want me to go in with them on the sly—agent was here two weeks ago about it—go in on the sly" [voice down to an impressive whisper, now] "and buy up a hundred and thirteen wildcat banks in Ohio, Indiana, Kentucky, Illinois, and Missouri—notes of these banks are at all sorts of discount now—average discount of the hundred and thirteen is forty-four per cent.—buy them all up, you see, and then all of a sudden let the cat out of the bag! Whiz! the stock of every one of those wildcats would spin up to a tremendous premium before you could turn a handspring—profit on the speculation not a dollar less than forty millions!" [An eloquent pause, while the marvelous vision settled into W.'s focus.] "Where's your hogs now! Why, my dear innocent boy, we would just sit [96/97] down on the front doorsteps and peddle banks like lucifer matches!"

Washington finally got his breath and said:

"Oh, it is perfectly wonderful! Why couldn't these things have happened in my father's day? And I—it's of no use—they simply lie before my face and mock me. There is nothing for me but to stand helpless and see other people reap the astonishing harvest."

"Never mind, Washington, don't you worry. I'll fix you. There's plenty of chances. How much money have you got?"

In the presence of so many millions, Washington could not keep from blushing when he had to confess that he had but eighteen dollars in the world.

"Well, all right—don't despair. Other people have been obliged to begin with less. I have a small idea that may develop into something for us both, all in good time. Keep your money close and add to it. I'll make it breed. I've been experimenting (to pass away the time) on a little preparation for curing sore eyes—a kind of decoction nine-tenths water and the other tenth drugs that don't cost more than a dollar a barrel; I'm still experimenting; there's one ingredient wanted yet to perfect the thing, and somehow I can't just manage to hit upon the thing that's necessary, and I don't dare talk with a chemist, of course. But I'm progressing, and before many weeks I wager the country will ring with the fame of Beriah Sellers' [97/98] Infallible Imperial Oriental Optic Liniment and Salvation for Sore Eyes—the Medical Wonder of the Age! Small bottles fifty cents, large ones a dollar. Average cost, five and seven cents for the two sizes. The first year sell, say, ten thousand bottles in Missouri, seven thousand in Iowa, three thousand in Arkansas, four thousand in Kentucky, six thousand in Illinois, and say twenty-five thousand in the rest of the country. Total, fifty-five thousand bottles; profit clear of all expenses, twenty thousand dollars at the very lowest calculation. All the capital needed is to manufacture the first two thousand bottles—say a hundred and fifty dollars—then the money would begin to flow in. The second year, sales would reach 200,000 bottles—clear profit, say, $75,000—and in the meantime the great factory would be building in St. Louis, to cost, say, $100,000. The third year we could easily sell 1,000,000 bottles in the United States and——"

"O, splendid!" said Washington. "Let's commence right away— let's——"

"——1,000,000 bottles in the United States—profit at least $350,-000—and *then* it would begin to be time to turn our attention toward the *real* idea of the business."

"The *real* idea of it! Ain't $350,000 year a pretty real"——

"Stuff! Why, what an infant you are, Washington—what a guile-less, short-sighted, easily-contented [98/99] innocent you are, my poor little country-bred know-nothing! Would I go to all that trouble and bother for the poor crumbs a body might pick up in *this* country? Now do I look like a man who—does my history suggest that I am a man who deals in trifles, contents himself with the narrow horizon that hems in the common herd, sees no further than the end of his nose? Now, *you* know that that is not me—couldn't *be* me. You ought to know that if I throw my time and abilities into a patent medicine, it's a patent medicine whose field of operations is the solid earth! its clients the swarming nations that inhabit it! Why what is the republic of America for an eye-water country? Lord bless you, it is nothing but a barren highway that you've got to cross to get *to* the true eye-water market! Why, Washington, in the Oriental countries people swarm like the sands of the desert; every square mile of ground upholds its thousands upon thousands of struggling human creatures—and every separate and individual devil of them's got the ophthalmia! It's as natural to them as noses are—and sin. It's born with them, it stays with them, it's all that some of them have left when they die. Three years of introductory trade in the Orient and what will be the result? Why, our headquarters would be in Constantinople and our hindquarters in Further India! Factories and warehouses in Cairo, Ispahan, Bagdad, Damascus, Jerusalem, Yedo, Peking, Bangkok, Delhi, Bombay, and Calcutta! Annual income—[99/100] well, God only knows how many millions and millions apiece!"

Washington was so dazed, so bewildered—his heart and his eyes had wandered so far away among the strange lands beyond the seas, and such avalanches of coin and currency had fluttered and jingled confusedly down before him, that he was now as one who has been whirling round and round for a time, and, stopping all at once, finds his surroundings still whirling and all objects a dancing chaos. However, little by little the Sellers family cooled down and crystallized into shape, and the poor room lost its glitter and resumed its poverty. Then the youth found his voice and begged Sellers to drop everything and hurry up the eye-water; and he got his eighteen dollars and tried to force it upon the Colonel—pleaded with him to take it—implored him to do it. But the Colonel would not; said he would not need the capital (in his native magnificent way he called that eighteen dollars capital) till the eye-water was an accomplished fact. He made Washington easy in his mind, though, by promising that he would call for it just as soon as the invention was finished, and he added the glad tidings that nobody but just they two should be admitted to a share in the speculation.

When Washington left the breakfast table he could have worshiped that man. Washington was one of that kind of people whose hopes are in the very clouds one day, and in the gutter the next. He [100/101] walked on air, now. The Colonel was ready to take him around and introduce him to the employment he had found for him, but Washington begged for a few moments in which to write home; with his kind of people, to ride to-day's new interest to death and put off yesterday's till another time, is nature itself. He ran upstairs and wrote glowingly, enthusiastically, to his mother about the hogs and the corn, the banks and the eye-water—and added a few inconsequential millions to each project. And he said that people little dreamed what a man Col. Sellers was, and that the world would open its eyes when it found out. And he closed his letter thus:

"So make yourself perfectly easy, mother—in a little while you shall have everything you want, and more. I am not likely to stint *you* in anything, I fancy. This money will not be for me, alone, but for all of us. I want all to share alike; and there is going to be far more for each than one person can spend. Break it to father cautiously—you understand the need of that—break it to him cautiously, for he has had such cruel hard fortune, and is so stricken by it that great good news might prostrate him more surely than even bad, for he is used to the bad but is grown sadly unaccustomed to the other. Tell Laura—tell all the children. And write to Clay about it if he is not with you yet. You may tell Clay that whatever I get he can freely share in—freely. He knows that that is true—there will be no need that I should swear to that to make him believe it. Good-bye—and mind what I say: Rest perfectly easy, one and all of you, for our troubles are nearly at an end."

Poor lad, he could not know that his mother would cry some loving, compassionate tears over his letter and put off the family with a synopsis of its contents which conveyed a deal of love to them but not much idea of his prospects or projects. [101/102] And he never dreamed that such a joyful letter could sadden her and fill her night with sighs, and troubled thoughts, and bodings of the future, instead of filling it with peace and blessing it with restful sleep.

When the letter was done, Washington and the Colonel sallied forth, and as they walked along Washington learned what he was to be. He was to be a clerk in a real estate office. Instantly the fickle youth's dreams forsook the magic eye-water and flew back to the Tennessee Land. And the gorgeous possibilities of that great domain straightway began to occupy his imagination to such a degree that he could scarcely manage to keep even enough of his attention upon the Colonel's talk to retain the general run of what he was saying. He was glad it was a real estate office—he was a made man now, sure.

The Colonel said that General Boswell was a rich man and had a good and growing business; and that Washington's work would be light and he would get forty dollars a month and be boarded and lodged in the General's family—which was as good as ten dollars more; and even better, for he could not live as well even at the "City Hotel" as he would there, and yet the hotel charged fifteen dollars a month where a man had a good room.

General Boswell was in his office; a comfortable looking place, with plenty of outline maps hanging about the walls and in the windows, and a spectacled man was marking out another one on a long table. [102/103] The office was in the principal street. The General received Washington with a kindly but reserved politeness. Washington rather liked his looks. He was about fifty years old, dignified, well preserved, and well dressed. After the Colonel took his leave, the General talked a while with Washington—his talk consisting chiefly of instructions about the clerical duties of the place. He seemed satisfied as to Washington's ability to take care of the books, he was evidently a pretty fair theoretical bookkeeper, and experience would soon harden theory into practice. By and by dinner-time came, and the two walked to the General's house; and now Washington noticed an instinct in himself that moved him to keep not in the General's rear, exactly, but yet not at his side—somehow the old gentleman's dignity and reserve did not inspire familiarity. [103]

Richard Cory

EDWIN ARLINGTON ROBINSON

Whenever Richard Cory went down town,
We people on the pavement looked at him:
He was a gentleman from sole to crown,
Clean favored, and imperially slim.

And he was always quietly arrayed,
And he was always human when he talked;
But still he fluttered pulses when he said,
"Good-morning," and he glittered when he walked.

And he was rich—yes, richer than a king—
And admirably schooled in every grace:
In fine, we thought that he was every thing
To make us wish that we were in his place.

So on we worked, and waited for the light,
And went without the meat, and cursed the bread;
And Richard Cory, one calm summer night,
Went home and put a bullet through his head. [82]

Reprinted with the permission of Charles Scribner's Sons from *The Children of the Night* by Edwin Arlington Robinson (1897). Selection taken from *Collected Poems* (New York: The Macmillan Company, 1939), p. 82.

"Vanity, Vanity," Saith the Preacher

THEODORE DREISER

SOMETIMES A SINGLE LIFE WILL CLEARLY AND EFFECTIVELY ILLUSTRATE A period. Hence, to me, the importance of this one.

I first met X—— at a time when American financial methods and American finances were at their apex of daring and splendor, and when the world was in a more or less tolerant mood toward their grandiose manners and achievements. It was the golden day of Mr. Morgan, Senior, Mr. Belmont, Mr. Harriman, Mr. Sage, Mr. Gates, Mr. Brady, and many, many others who were still extant and ruling distinctly and drastically, as was proved by the panic of 1907. In opposition to them and yet imitating their methods, now an old story to those who have read "Frenzied Finance," "Lawless Wealth," and other such exposures of the methods which produced our enormous American fortunes, were such younger men as Charles W. Morse (the victim of the 1907 panic), F. Augustus Heinze (another if less conspicuous victim of the same "panic"), E. R. Thomas, an ambitious young millionaire, himself born to money, David A. Sullivan, and X——. I refuse to mention his name because he is still alive although no longer conspicuous, and anxious perhaps to avoid the uncomfortable glare of publicity when all the honors and comforts which made it endurable in the first place are absent. [263/267] . . .

On my first visit [to X——'s studio], as I was leaving, I was introduced to the host just within his picture gallery, hung with many fine examples of the Dutch and Spanish schools. I found him to be as described: picturesque and handsome, even though somewhat plump, phlegmatic and lethargic—yet active enough. He was above the average in height, well built, florid, with a huge, round handsome head, curly black hair, keen black eyes, heavy overhanging eyebrows, full red

From *Twelve Men* by Theodore Dreiser. Copyright 1919 by Boni & Liveright, Inc.; Copyright 1946 by Helen Dreiser. Published by arrangement with The World Publishing Company, Cleveland, and New York.

lips, a marked chin ornamented by a goatee. In any costume ball he
would have made an excellent Bacchus or Pan. He appeared to have
the free, easy and gracious manner of those who have known much of
life and have achieved, in part at least, their desires. He smiled, wished
to know if I had met all the guests, hoped that the sideboard had not
escaped me, that I had enjoyed the [267/268] singing. Would I come
some evening when there was no crowd—or, better yet, dine with him
and my friend de Shay, whose personality appeared to be about as
agreeable to him as his own. He was sorry he could not give me more
attention now.

Interestingly enough, and from the first, I was impressed with this
man; not because of his wealth (I knew richer men) but because of a
something about him which suggested dreams, romance, a kind of
sense or love of splendor and grandeur which one does not often
encounter among the really wealthy. Those cracked shoes were in my
mind, I suppose. He seemed to live among great things, but in no
niggardly, parsimonious or care-taking way. Here was ease, largess, a
kind of lavishness which was not ostentation but which seemed rather
to say, "What are the minute expenses of living and pleasuring as
contrasted with the profits of skill in the world outside?" He suggested
the huge and Aladdin-like adventures with which so many of the great
financiers of the day, the true tigers of Wall Street, were connected. [268/276]

During this fall and winter I was engaged in work which kept me
very much to myself. During the period I read much of X——, banks
he was combining, new ventures he was undertaking. Yet all at once
one winter's day, and out of a clear sky, the papers were full of an
enormous financial crash of which he was the center. According to the
newspapers, the first and foremost of a chain of banks of which he was
the head, to say nothing of a bonding and realty company and some
street railway project on Long Island, were all involved in the crash.
Curiously, although no derogatory mention had previously been made
of him, the articles and editorials were now most vituperative. Their
venom was especially noticeable. He was a get-rich-quick villain of the
vilest stripe; he had been juggling a bank, a trust company, an
insurance company and a land and street railway speculative scheme
as one would [276/277] glass balls. The money wherewith he gambled
was not his. He had robbed the poor, deceived them. Yet among all
this and in the huge articles which appeared the very first day, I noted
one paragraph which stuck in my mind, for I was naturally interested
in all this and in him. It read:

"Wall Street heard yesterday that Superintendent H—— got his first
information concerning the state in which X——'s affairs were from quarters
where resentment may have been cherished because of his activity in the
Long Island Traction field. This is one of the Street's 'clover patches' and

the success which the newcomer seemed to be meeting did not provoke great pleasure."

Another item read:

"A hitch in a deal that was to have transferred the South Shore to the New York and Queens County System, owned by the Long Island Railroad, at a profit of almost $2,000,000 to X——, was the cause of all the trouble. Very active displeasure on the part of certain powers in Wall Street blocked, it is said, the closing of the deal for the railroad. They did not want him in this field, and were powerful enough to prevent it. At the same time pressure from other directions was brought to bear on him. The clearing-house refused to clear for his banks. X—— was in need of cash, but still insisting on a high rate of remuneration for the road which he had developed to an important point. Their sinister influences entered and blocked the transfer until it was no longer possible for him to hold out."

Along with these two items was a vast mass of data, really pages, showing how, when, where he had done thus and so, "juggled accounts" between one bank and another, all of which he controlled however and most of which he owned, [277/278] drew out large sums and put in their place mortages on or securities in, new companies which he was organizing—tricks which were the ordinary routine of Wall Street and hence rather ridiculous as the sub-stone of so vast a hue and cry.

I was puzzled and, more than that, moved by the drama of the man's sudden end, for I understood a little of finance and its ways, also of what place and power had plainly come to mean to him. It must be dreadful. Yet how could it be, I asked myself, if he really owned fifty-one per cent or more in so many companies that he could be such a dark villain? After all, ownership is ownership, and control, control. On the face of the reports themselves his schemes did not look so black. I read everything in connection with him with care.

As the days passed various other things happened. For one thing, he tried to commit suicide by jumping out of a window of his studio in New York; for another, he tried to take poison. Now of a sudden a bachelor sister, of whom I had never heard in all the time I had known him, put in an appearance as his nearest of kin—a woman whose name was not his own but a variation of it, an "-ovitch" having suddenly been tacked onto it. She took him to a sanitarium, from which he was eventually turned out as a criminal, then to a hospital, until finally he surrendered himself to the police. The names of great lawyers and other bankers began to enter the case. Alienists of repute, those fine chameleons of the legal world, were employed who swore first that he was insane, then that he was not. His sister, who was a physician and scientist of repute, asked the transfer of all his property to her on the ground that he was incompetent and that she was his next of kin. To this she swore, giving as her reasons for believing him insane that he had "illusions of grandeur" and that he believed himself "persecuted by eminent financiers," things which smacked more of sanity than anything else to [278/279] me. At the same time he and she, as time rather indicated, had arranged this in part in the hope of saving something out of the great wreck. There were other curious features: Certain eminent men in politics and finance who from revelations made by the books of the various banks were in close financial if not personal relations with X—— denied this completely. Curiously, the great cry on the part of these was that he was insane, must be, and that he was all alone in his schemes. His life on Broadway, on Long Island, in his studio in New York, were ransacked for details. Enough could not be made of his gay, shameful, spendthrift life. No one else, of course, had ever been either gay or shameful before—especially not the eminent and hounding financiers.

Then from somewhere appeared a new element. In a staggeringly low tenement region in Brooklyn was discovered somehow or other a very old man and woman, most unsatisfactory as relatives of such imposing people, who insisted that they were his parents, that years before because he and his sister were exceedingly restless and ambitious, they had left them and had only returned occasionally to borrow money, finally ceasing to come at all. In proof of this, letters, witnesses, old photos, were produced. It really did appear as if he and his sister, although they had long vigorously denied it, really were the son and daughter of the two who had been petty bakers in Brooklyn, laying up a little competence of their own. I never knew who "dug" them up, but the reason why was plain enough. The sister was laying claim to the property as the next of kin. If this could be offset, even though X—— were insane, the property would at once be thrown into the hands of the various creditors and sold under a forced sale, of course—in other words, for a song—for their benefit. Naturally it was of interest to those who wished to have his affairs wound up to have the old people produced. But the great financier had been spreading the report all [279/280] along that he was from Russia, that his parents, or pseudo-parents, were still there, but that really he was the illegitimate son of the Czar of Russia, boarded out originally with a poor family. Now, however, the old people were brought from Brooklyn and compelled to confront him. It was never really proved that he and his sister had neglected them utterly or had done anything to seriously injure them, but rather that as they had grown in place and station they had become more or less estranged and so ignored them, having changed their names and soared in a world little dreamed of by their parents. Also a perjury charge was made against the sister which effectually prevented her from controlling his estate, a lease long enough to give the financiers time for their work. Naturally there was a great hue and cry over her, the scandal, the shame, that they should thus publicly refuse to recognize their parents as they did or had when confronted by them. Horrible! There were most heavily illustrated and tearful Sunday articles, all blazoned forth with pictures of his house and studio, his banks, cars, yacht, groups of guests, while the motives of those who produced the parents were overlooked. The pictures of the parents confronting X—— and his sister portrayed very old and feeble people, and were rather moving. They insisted that they were his parents and wept brokenly in their hands. But why? And he denying it! His sister, who resented all this bitterly and who stood by him valiantly, repudiated, for his sake of course, his and her so-called parents and friends.

I never saw such a running to cover of "friends" in all my life. Of all those I had seen about his place and in his company, scores on scores of people reasonably well known in the arts, the stage, the worlds of finance and music, all eating his dinners, riding in his cars, drinking his wines, there was scarcely any one now who knew him anything more that "casually" or "slightly"—oh, so slightly! When rumors as [280/281] to the midnight suppers, the Bacchic dancing, the automobile parties to his great country place and the spirited frolics which occurred there began to get abroad, there was no one whom I knew who had ever been there or knew anything about him or them. For instance, of all the people who had been close or closest and might therefore have been expected to be friendly and deeply concerned was de Shay, his fidus Achates and literally his pensioner—yet de Shay was almost the loudest in his denunciation or at least deprecation of X——, his habits and methods! Although it was he who had told me of Mme.—— and her relation to X——, who urged me to come here, there and the other place, expecially where X—— was the host, always assuring me that it would be so wonderful and that X—— was really such a great man, so generous, so worth-while, he was now really the loudest or at least the most stand-offish in his comments, pretending never to have been very close to X——, and lifting his eyebrows in astonishment as though he had not even guessed what he had actually engineered. His "Did-you-hears," "Did-you-knows" and "Wouldn't-have-dreamed" would have done credit to a tea-party. He was so shocked, especially at X——'s robbing poor children and orphans, although in so far as my reading of the papers went I could find nothing that went to prove that he had any intention of robbing anybody—that is, directly. In the usual Wall Street high finance style he was robbing Peter to pay Paul, that is, he was using the monies of one corporation which he controlled to bolster up any of the others which he controlled, and was "washing one hand with the other," a proceeding so common in finance that to really radically and truly oppose it, or do away with it, would mean to bring down the whole fabric of finance in one grand crash.

Be that as it may. In swift succession there now followed the so-called "legal" seizure and confiscation of all his properties. [281/282] In the first place, by alienists representing the District Attorney and the State banking department, he was declared sane and placed on trial for embezzlement. Secondly, his sister's plea that his property be put into her hands as trustee or administrator was thrown out of court and she herself arrested and confined for perjury on the ground that she had perjured herself in swearing that she was his next of kin when in reality his real parents, or so they swore, were alive and in America. Next, his banks, trust companies and various concerns, including his great country estate, were swiftly thrown into the hands of receivers (what an appropriate name!) and wound up "for the benefit of creditors." All the while X—— was in prison, protesting that he was really not guilty, that he was solvent, or had been until he was attacked by the State bank examiner or the department back of him, and that he was the victim of a cold-blooded conspiracy which was using the State banking department and other means to drive him out of financial life, and that solely because of his desire to grow and because by chance he had been impinging upon one of the choicest and most closely guarded fields of the ultra-rich of Wall Street—the street railway area in New York and Brooklyn.

One day, so he publicly swore to the grand jury, by which he was being examined, as he was sitting in his great offices, in one of the great sky-scrapers of New York, which occupied an entire floor and commanded vast panoramas in every direction (another evidence of the man's insane "delusion of grandeur," I presume), he was called to answer the telephone. One Mr. Y——, so his assistant said, one of the eminent financiers of Wall Street and America, was on the wire. Without any preliminary and merely asking was this Mr. X—— on the wire, the latter proceeded, "This is Mr. Y——. Listen closely to what I am going to say. I want you to get out of the street railway business in New York or something is going [282/283] to happen to you. I am giving you a reasonable warning. Take it." Then the phone clicked most savagely and ominously and superiorly at the other end.

"I knew at the time," went on X——, addressing the grand jury, "that I was really listening to the man who was most powerful in such affairs in New York and elsewhere and that he meant what he said. At the same time I was in no position to get out without closing up the one deal which stood to net me two million dollars clear if I closed it. At the same time I wanted to enter this field and didn't see why I shouldn't. If I didn't it spelled not ruin by any means but a considerable loss, a very great loss, to me, in more ways than one. Oddly enough, just at this time I was being pressed by those with whom I was associated to wind up this particular venture and turn my attention to other things. I have often wondered, in the light of their subsequent actions, why they should have become so pressing just at this time. At the same time, perhaps I was a little vain and self-sufficient. I had once got the better of some agents of another great financier in a Western Power deal, and I felt that I could put this thing through too. Hence I refused to heed the warning. However, I found that all those who were previously interested to buy or at least develop the property were now suddenly grown cold, and a little later when, having entered on several other matters, I needed considerable cash, the State banking department descended on me and, crying fraud and insolvency, closed all my banks.

"You know how it is when they do this to you. Cry 'Fire!' and you can nearly wreck a perfectly good theater building. Depositors withdraw, securities tumble, investigation and legal expenses begin, your financial associates get frightened or ashamed and desert you. Nothing is so squeamish or so retiring and nervous as money. Time will show that I was not insolvent at the time. The books will show a few technically [283/284] illegal things, but so would the books or the affairs of any great bank, especially at this time, if quickly examined. I was doing no more than all were doing, but they wanted to get me out—and they did."

Regardless of proceedings of various kinds—legal, technical and the like—X—— was finally sent to the penitentiary, and spent some time there. At the same time his confession finally wrecked about nine other eminent men, financiers all. A dispassionate examination of all the evidence eight years later caused me to conclude without hesitation that the man had been a victim of a cold-blooded conspiracy, the object of which was to oust him from opportunities and to forestall him in methods which would certainly have led to enormous wealth. He was apparently in a position and with the brains to do many of the things which the ablest and coldest financiers of his day had been and were doing, and they did not want to be bothered with, would not brook, in short, his approaching rivalry. Like the various usurpers of regal powers in ancient days, they thought it best to kill a possible claimant to the throne in his infancy.

But that youth of his! The long and devious path by which he had come! Among the papers relating to the case and to a time when he could not have been more than eighteen, and when he was beginning his career as a book agent, was a letter written to his mother (August, 1892), which read:

"MY DEAR PARENTS: Please answer me at once if I can have anything of you, or something of you or nothing. Remember this is the first and the last time in my life that I beg of you anything. You have given to the other child not $15 but hundreds, and now when I, the very youngest, ask of you, my parents, $15, are you going to be so hard-hearted as to refuse me? Without these $15 it is left to me to be without income for two or three weeks. [284/285]

"For God's sake, remember what I ask of you, and send me at once so that I should cease thinking of it. Leon, as I have told you, will give me $10, $15 he has already paid for the contract, and your $15 will make $25. Out of this I need $10 for a ticket and $15 for two or three weeks' board and lodging.

"Please answer at once. Don't wait for a minute, and send me the money or write me one word 'not.' Remember this only that if you refuse me I will have nothing in common with you.

"Your son,

"_____"

There was another bit of testimony on the part of one Henry Dom, a baker, who for some strange reason came forward to identify him as some one he had known years before in Williamsburgh, which read:

"I easily recognize them" (X—— and his sister) "from their pictures in the newspapers. I worked for X——'s father, who was a baker in Williamsburgh, and frequently addressed letters that were written by X—— Senior and his wife to Dr. Louise X—— who was then studying medicine in Philadelphia. X—— was then a boy going to school, but working in his father's bakery mornings and evenings. He did not want to do that, moaned a great deal, and his parents humored him in his attitude. He was very vain, liked to appear intellectual. They kept saying to their friends that he should have a fine future. Five years later, after I had left them once, I met the mother and she told me that X—— was studying banking and getting along fine."

Some seven years after the failure and trial by which he had so summarily been disposed of and after he had been released from prison, I was standing at a certain unimportant [285/286] street corner in New York waiting for a car when I saw him. He was passing in the opposite direction, not very briskly, and, as I saw, plainly meditatively. He was not so well dressed. The clothes he wore while good were somehow different, lacking in that exquisite something which had characterized him years before. His hat—well, it was a hat, not a Romanoff shako nor a handsome panama such as he had affected in the old days. He looked tired, a little worn and dusty, I thought.

My first impulse was of course to hail him, my second not, since he had not seen me. It might have been embarrassing, and at any rate he might not have even remembered me. But as he walked I thought of the great house by the sea, the studio, the cars, the 40,000 roses, the crowds at his summer place, the receptions in town and out, Madame of the earrings (afterward married to a French nobleman), and then of the letter to his mother as a boy, the broken shoes in the winter time, his denial of his parents, the telephone message from the financial tiger. "Vanity, vanity," saith the preacher. The shores of our social seas are strewn with pathetic wrecks, the whitening bone of half-sand-buried ships.

At the next corner he paused, a little uncertain apparently as to which way to go, then turned to the left and was lost. I have never seen nor heard of him since. [286]

The Egg

SHERWOOD ANDERSON

MY FATHER WAS, I AM SURE, INTENDED BY NATURE TO BE A CHEERFUL, kindly man. Until he was thirty-four years old he worked as a farm-hand for a man named Thomas Butterworth whose place lay near the town of Bidwell, Ohio. He had then a horse of his own and on Saturday evenings drove into town to spend a few hours in social intercourse with other farm-hands. In town he drank several glasses of beer and stood about in Ben Head's saloon—crowded on Saturday evenings with visiting farm-hands. Songs were sung and glasses thumped on the bar. At ten o'clock father drove home along a lonely country road, made his horse comfortable for the night and himself went to bed, quite happy in his position in life. He had at that time no notion of trying to rise in the world.

It was in the spring of his thirty-fifth year that father married my mother, then a country school-teacher, and in the following spring I came wriggling and crying into the world. Something happened to the two people. They became ambitious. The American passion for getting up in the world took possession of them. [46/47]

It may have been that mother was responsible. Being a school-teacher she had no doubt read books and magazines. She had, I presume, read of how Garfield, Lincoln, and other Americans rose from poverty to fame and greatness and as I lay beside her—in the days of her lying-in—she may have dreamed that I would some day rule men and cities. At any rate she induced father to give up his place as a farm-hand, sell his horse and embark on an independent enterprise of his own. She was a tall silent woman with a long nose and troubled grey eyes. For herself she wanted nothing. For father and myself she was incurably ambitious.

The first venture into which the two people went turned out badly. They rented ten acres of poor stony land on Griggs's Road, eight miles from Bidwell, and launched into chicken raising. I grew into boyhood on the place and got my first impressions of life there. From the beginning they were impressions of disaster and if, in my turn, I am a gloomy man inclined to see the darker side of life, I attribute it to the fact that what should have been for me the happy joyous days of childhood were spent on a chicken farm.

One unversed in such matters can have no notion of the many and tragic things that can happen to a chicken. It is born out of an egg, lives for a few weeks as a tiny fluffy thing such as you will see pictured on Easter cards, then becomes hideously naked, eats quantities [47/ 48] of corn and meal bought by the sweat of your father's brow, gets diseases called pip, cholera, and other names, stands looking with stupid eyes at the sun, becomes sick and dies. A few hens and now and then a rooster, intended to serve God's mysterious ends, struggle through to maturity. The hens lay eggs out of which come other chickens and the dreadful cycle is thus made complete. It is all unbelievably complex. Most philosophers must have been raised on chicken farms. One hopes for so much from a chicken and is so dreadfully disillusioned. Small chickens, just setting out on the journey of life, look so bright and alert and they are in fact so dreadfully stupid. They are so much like people they mix one up in one's judgments of life. If disease does not kill them they wait until your expectations are thoroughly aroused and then walk under the wheels of a wagon—to go squashed and dead back to their maker. Vermin infest their youth, and fortunes must be spent for curative powders. In later life I have seen how a literature has been built up on the subject of fortunes to be made out of the raising of chickens. It is intended to be read by the gods who have just eaten of the tree of the knowledge of good and evil. It is a hopeful literature and declares that much may be done by simple ambitious people who own a few hens. Do not be led astray by it. It was not written for you. Go hunt for gold on the frozen hills of Alaska, put your faith in [48/49] the honesty of a politician, believe if you will that the world is daily growing better and that good will triumph over evil, but do not read and believe the literature that is written concerning the hen. It was not written for you.

I, however, digress. My tale does not primarily concern itself with the hen. If correctly told it will centre on the egg. For ten years my father and mother struggled to make our chicken farm pay and then they gave up that struggle and began another. They moved into the town of Bidwell, Ohio and embarked in the restaurant business. After ten years of worry with incubators that did not hatch, and with tiny—and in their own way lovely—balls of fluff that passed on into

semi-naked pullethood and from that into dead hen-hood, we threw all
aside and packing our belongings on a wagon drove down Griggs's
Road toward Bidwell, a tiny caravan of hope looking for a new place
from which to start on our upward journey through life.

We must have been a sad looking lot, not, I fancy, unlike refugees
fleeing from a battlefield. Mother and I walked in the road. The wagon
that contained our goods had been borrowed for the day from Mr.
Albert Griggs, a neighbor. Out of its sides stuck the legs of cheap
chairs and at the back of the pile of beds, tables, and boxes filled with
kitchen utensils was a crate of live chickens, and on top of that the baby
carriage in [49/50] which I had been wheeled about in my infancy.
Why we stuck to the baby carriage I don't know. It was unlikely other
children would be born and the wheels were broken. People who have
few possessions cling tightly to those they have. That is one of the facts
that make life so discouraging.

Father rode on top of the wagon. He was then a bald-headed man
of forty-five, a little fat and from long association with mother and the
chickens he had become habitually silent and discouraged. All during
our ten years on the chicken farm he had worked as a laborer on
neighboring farms and most of the money he had earned had been
spent for remedies to cure chicken diseases, on Wilmer's White Wonder Cholera Cure or Professor Bidlow's Egg Producer or some other
preparations that mother found advertised in the poultry papers. There
were two little patches of hair on father's head just above his ears. I
remember that as a child I used to sit looking at him when he had gone
to sleep in a chair before the stove on Sunday afternoons in the winter.
I had at that time already begun to read books and have notions of my
own and the bald path that led over the top of his head was, I fancied,
something like a broad road, such a road as Caesar might have made
on which to lead his legions out of Rome and into the wonders of an
unknown world. The tufts of hair that grew above father's ears were, I
thought, like forests. I fell into a half-sleeping, [50/51] half-waking
state and dreamed I was a tiny thing going along the road into a far
beautiful place where there were no chicken farms and where life was
a happy eggless affair.

One might write a book concerning our flight from the chicken
farm into town. Mother and I walked the entire eight miles—she to be
sure that nothing fell from the wagon and I to see the wonders of the
world. On the seat of the wagon beside father was his greatest
treasure. I will tell you of that.

On a chicken farm where hundreds and even thousands of
chickens come out of eggs surprising things sometimes happen. Grotesques are born out of eggs as out of people. The accident does not
often occur—perhaps once in a thousand births. A chicken is, you see,
born that has four legs, two pairs of wings, two heads or what not. The
things do not live. They go quickly back to the hand of their maker

that has for a moment trembled. The fact that the poor little things could not live was one of the tragedies of life to father. He had some sort of notion that if he could but bring into henhood or roosterhood a five-legged hen or a two-headed rooster his fortune would be made. He dreamed of taking the wonder about to county fairs and of growing rich by exhibiting it to other farm-hands.

At any rate he saved all the little monstrous things that had been born on our chicken farm. They were [51/52] preserved in alcohol and put each in its own glass bottle. These he had carefully put into a box and on our journey into town it was carried on the wagon seat beside him. He drove the horses with one hand and with the other clung to the box. When we got to our destination the box was taken down at once and the bottles removed. All during our days as keepers of a restaurant in the town of Bidwell, Ohio, the grotesques in their little glass bottles sat on a shelf back of the counter. Mother sometimes protested but father was a rock on the subject of his treasure. The grotesques were, he declared, valuable. People, he said, liked to look at strange and wonderful things.

Did I say that we embarked in the restaurant business in the town of Bidwell, Ohio? I exaggerated a little. The town itself lay at the foot of a low hill and on the shore of a small river. The railroad did not run through the town and the station was a mile away to the north at a place called Pickleville. There had been a cider mill and pickle factory at the station, but before the time of our coming they had both gone out of business. In the morning and in the evening busses came down to the station along a road called Turner's Pike from the hotel on the main street of Bidwell. Our going to the out of the way place to embark in the restaurant business was mother's idea. She talked of it for a year and then one day went off and rented an empty store building opposite the railroad [52/53] station. It was her idea that the restaurant would be profitable. Travelling men, she said, would be always waiting around to take trains out of town and town people would come to the station to await incoming trains. They would come to the restaurant to buy pieces of pie and drink coffee. Now that I am older I know that she had another motive in going. She was ambitious for me. She wanted me to rise in the world, to get into a town school and become a man of the towns.

At Pickleville father and mother worked hard as they always had done. At first there was the necessity of putting our place into shape to be a restaurant. That took a month. Father built a shelf on which he put tins of vegetables. He painted a sign on which he put his name in large red letters. Below his name was the sharp command—"EAT HERE"—that was so seldom obeyed. A show case was bought and filled with cigars and tobacco. Mother scrubbed the floor and the walls of the room. I went to school in the town and was glad to be away from the farm and from the presence of the discouraged, sad-looking chickens. Still I was not very joyous. In the evening I walked home from school along Turner's Pike and remembered the children I had seen playing in the town school yard. A troop of little girls had gone hopping about and singing. I tried that. Down along the frozen road I went hopping solemnly on one leg. "Hippity [53/54] Hop To The Barber Shop," I sang shrilly. Then I stopped and looked doubtfully about. I was afraid of being seen in my gay mood. It must have seemed to me that I was doing a thing that should not be done by one who, like myself, had been raised on a chicken farm where death was a daily visitor.

Mother decided that our restaurant should remain open at night. At ten in the evening a passenger train went north past our door followed by a local freight. The freight crew had switching to do in Pickleville and when the work was done they came to our restaurant for hot coffee and food. Sometimes one of them ordered a fried egg. In the morning at four they returned north-bound and again visited us. A little trade began to grow up. Mother slept at night and during the day tended the restaurant and fed our boarders while father slept. He slept in the same bed mother had occupied during the night and I went off to the town of Bidwell and to school. During the long nights, while mother and I slept, father cooked meats that were to go into sandwiches for the lunch baskets of our boarders. Then an idea in regard to getting up in the world came into his head. The American spirit took hold of him. He also became ambitious.

In the long nights when there was little to do father had time to think. That was his undoing. He decided that he had in the past been an unsuccessful man [54/55] because he had not been cheerful enough and that in the future he would adopt a cheerful outlook on life. In the early morning he came upstairs and got into bed with mother. She woke and the two talked. From my bed in the corner I listened.

It was father's idea that both he and mother should try to entertain the people who came to eat at our restaurant. I cannot now remember his words, but he gave the impression of one about to become in some obscure way a kind of public entertainer. When people, particularly young people from the town of Bidwell, came into our place, as on very rare occasions they did, bright entertaining conversation was to be made. From father's words I gathered that something of the jolly inn-keeper effect was to be sought. Mother must have been doubtful from the first, but she said nothing discouraging. It was father's notion that a passion for the company of himself and mother would spring up in the breasts of the younger people of the town of Bidwell. In the evening bright happy groups would come singing down Turner's Pike. They would troop shouting with joy and laughter into our place. There would be song and festivity. I do not mean to give the impression that father spoke so elaborately of the matter. He was as I have said an uncommunicative man. "They want some place to go. I tell you they want some place to go," he said over and over. That was as far as he [55/56] got. My own imagination has filled in the blanks.

For two or three weeks this notion of father's invaded our house. We did not talk much, but in our daily lives tried earnestly to make smiles take the place of glum looks. Mother smiled at the boarders and I, catching the infection, smiled at our cat. Father became a little feverish in his anxiety to please. There was no doubt, lurking somewhere in him, a touch of the spirit of the showman. He did not waste much of his ammunition on the railroad men he served at night but seemed to be waiting for a young man or woman from Bidwell to come in to show what he could do. On the counter in the restaurant there was a wire basket kept always filled with eggs, and it must have been before his eyes when the idea of being entertaining was born in his brain. There was something pre-natal about the way eggs kept themselves connected with the development of his idea. At any rate an egg ruined his new impulse in life. Late one night I was awakened by a roar of anger coming from father's throat. Both mother and I sat upright in our beds. With trembling hands she lighted a lamp that stood on a table by her head. Downstairs the front door of our restaurant went shut with a bang and in a few minutes father tramped up the stairs. He held an egg in his hand and his hand trembled as though he were having a chill. There was a half insane light in his eyes. As he stood glaring at us I was sure he [56/57] intended throwing the egg at either mother or me. Then he laid it gently on the table beside the lamp and dropped on his knees beside mother's bed. He began to cry like a boy and I, carried away by his grief, cried with him. The two of us filled the little upstairs room with our wailing voices. It is ridiculous, but of the picture we made I can remember only the fact that mother's hand continually stroked the bald path that ran across the top of his head. I have forgotten what mother said to him and how she induced him to tell her of what had happened down-stairs. His explanation also has gone out of my mind. I remember only my own grief and fright and the shiny path over father's head glowing in the lamp light as he knelt by the bed.

As to what happened downstairs. For some unexplainable reason I know the story as well as though I had been a witness to my father's discomfiture. One in time gets to know many unexplainable things. On that evening young Joe Kane, son of a merchant of Bidwell, came to Pickleville to meet his father, who was expected on the ten o'clock evening train from the South. The train was three hours late and Joe came into our place to loaf about and to wait for its arrival. The local freight train came in and the freight crew were fed. Joe was left alone in the restaurant with father.

From the moment he came into our place the Bidwell [57/58]

young man must have been puzzled by my father's actions. It was his notion that father was angry at him for hanging around. He noticed that the restaurant keeper was apparently disturbed by his presence and he thought of going out. However, it began to rain and he did not fancy the long walk to town and back. He bought a five-cent cigar and ordered a cup of coffee. He had a newspaper in his pocket and took it out and began to read. "I'm waiting for the evening train. It's late," he said apologetically.

For a long time father, whom Joe Kane had never seen before, remained silently gazing at his visitor. He was no doubt suffering from an attack of stage fright. As so often happens in life he had thought so much and so often of the situation that now confronted him that he was somewhat nervous in its presence.

For one thing, he did not know what to do with his hands. He thrust one of them nervously over the counter and shook hands with Joe Kane. "How-de-do," he said. Joe Kane put his newspaper down and stared at him. Father's eye lighted on the basket of eggs that sat on the counter and he began to talk. "Well," he began hesitatingly, "well, you have heard of Christopher Columbus, eh?" He seemed to be angry. "That Christopher Columbus was a cheat," he declared emphatically. "He talked of making an egg stand on its end. He talked, he did, and then he went and broke the end of the egg." [58/59]

My father seemed to his visitor to be beside himself at the duplicity of Christopher Columbus. He muttered and swore. He declared it was wrong to teach children that Christopher Columbus was a great man when, after all, he cheated at the critical moment. He had declared he would make an egg stand on end and then when his bluff had been called he had done a trick. Still grumbling at Columbus, father took an egg from the basket on the counter and began to walk up and down. He rolled the egg between the palms of his hands. He smiled genially. He began to mumble words regarding the effect to be produced on an egg by the electricity that comes out of the human body. He declared that without breaking its shell and by virtue of rolling it back and forth in his hands he could stand the egg on its end. He explained that the warmth of his hands and the gentle rolling movement he gave the egg created a new centre of gravity, and Joe Kane was mildly interested. "I have handled thousands of eggs," father said. "No one knows more about eggs than I do."

He stood the egg on the counter and it fell on its side. He tried the trick again and again, each time rolling the egg between the palms of his hands and saying the words regarding the wonders of electricity and the laws of gravity. When after a half hour's effort he did succeed in making the egg stand for a moment he looked up to find that his visitor was no [59/60] longer watching. By the time he had succeeded in calling Joe Kane's attention to the success of his effort the egg had again rolled over and lay on its side.

Afire with the showman's passion and at the same time a good deal disconcerted by the failure of his first effort, father now took the bottles containing the poultry monstrosities down from their place on the shelf and began to show them to his visitor. "How would you like to have seven legs and two heads like this fellow?" he asked, exhibiting the most remarkable of his treasures. A cheerful smile played over his face. He reached over the counter and tried to slap Joe Kane on the shoulder as he had seen men do in Ben Head's saloon when he was a young farm-hand and drove to town on Saturday evenings. His visitor was made a little ill by the sight of the body of the terribly deformed bird floating in the alcohol in the bottle and got up to go. Coming from behind the counter father took hold of the young man's arm and led him back to his seat. He grew a little angry and for a moment had to turn his face away and force himself to smile. Then he put the bottles back on the shelf. In an outburst of generosity he fairly compelled Joe Kane to have a fresh cup of coffee and another cigar at his expense. Then he took a pan and filling it with vinegar, taken from a jug that sat beneath the counter, he declared himself about to do a new trick. "I will heat this egg in this pan of vinegar," he [60/61] said. "Then I will put it through the neck of a bottle without breaking the shell. When the egg is inside the bottle it will resume its normal shape and the shell will become hard again. Then I will give the bottle with the egg in it to you. You can take it about with you wherever you go. People will want to know how you got the egg in the bottle. Don't tell them. Keep them guessing. That is the way to have fun with this trick."

Father grinned and winked at his visitor. Joe Kane decided that the man who confronted him was mildly insane but harmless. He drank the cup of coffee that had been given him and began to read his paper again. When the egg had been heated in vinegar father carried it on a spoon to the counter and going into a back room got an empty bottle. He was angry because his visitor did not watch him as he began to do his trick, but nevertheless went cheerfully to work. For a long time he struggled, trying to get the egg to go through the neck of the bottle. He put the pan of vinegar back on the stove, intending to reheat the egg, then picked it up and burned his fingers. After a second bath in the hot vinegar the shell of the egg had been softened a little but not enough for his purpose. He worked and worked and a spirit of desperate determination took possession of him. When he thought that at last the trick was about to be consummated the delayed train came in at the station [61/62] and Joe Kane started to go nonchalantly out at the door. Father made a last desperate effort to conquer the egg and make it do the thing that would establish his reputation as one who knew how to entertain guests who came into his restaurant. He worried the egg. He attempted to be somewhat rough with it. He swore and the sweat stood out on his forehead. The egg broke under his hand.

When the contents spurted over his clothes, Joe Kane, who had stopped at the door, turned and laughed.

A roar of anger rose from my father's throat. He danced and shouted a string of inarticulate words. Grabbing another egg from the basket on the counter, he threw it, just missing the head of the young man as he dodged through the door and escaped.

Father came upstairs to mother and me with an egg in his hand. I do not know what he intended to do. I imagine he had some idea of destroying it, of destroying all eggs, and that he intended to let mother and me see him begin. When, however, he got into the presence of mother something happened to him. He laid the egg gently on the table and dropped on his knees by the bed as I have already explained. He later decided to close the restaurant for the night and to come upstairs and get into bed. When he did so he blew out the light and after much muttered conversation both he and mother went to sleep. I suppose I went to sleep also, but my sleep was troubled. [62/63] I awoke at dawn and for a long time looked at the egg that lay on the table. I wondered why eggs had to be and why from the egg came the hen who again laid the egg. The question got into my blood. It has stayed there, I imagine, because I am the son of my father. At any rate, the problem remains unsolved in my mind. And that, I conclude, is but another evidence of the complete and final triumph of the egg—at least as far as my family is concerned. [63]

The Crack-Up

F. SCOTT FITZGERALD

Handle with Care

March, 1936

IN A PREVIOUS ARTICLE THIS WRITER TOLD ABOUT HIS REALIZATION THAT what he had before him was not the dish that he had ordered for his forties. In fact—since he and the dish were one, he described himself as a cracked plate, the kind that one wonders whether it is worth preserving. Your editor thought that the article suggested too many aspects without regarding them closely, and probably many readers felt the same way—and there are always those to whom all self-revelation is contemptible, unless it ends with a noble thanks to the gods for the Unconquerable Soul.

But I had been thanking the gods too long, and thanking them for nothing. I wanted to put a lament into my record, without even the background of the Euganean Hills to give it color. There weren't any Euganean hills that I could see.

Sometimes, though, the cracked plate has to be retained in the pantry, has to be kept in service as a household necessity. It can never again be warmed on the stove nor shuffled with the other plates in the dishpan; it will not be brought out for company, but it will do to hold crackers late at night or to go into the ice box under left-overs . . .

Hence this sequel—a cracked plate's further history.

Now the standard cure for one who is sunk is to consider those in actual destitution or physical suffering—this is an all-weather beatitude for gloom in general and fairly salutory day-time advice for everyone. But at three o'clock in the morning, a forgotten package has the same tragic importance as a death sentence, and the cure doesn't work—and in a real dark night of the soul it is always three o'clock in the morning, day after day. At that hour the tendency is to refuse to face things as long as possible by retiring into an infantile dream—but one is continually startled out of this by various contacts with the world. One meets these occasions as quickly and carelessly as possible and retires once more back into the dream, hoping that things will adjust themselves by some great material or spiritual bonanza. [75/76] But as the withdrawal persists there is less and less chance of the bonanza—one is not waiting for the fade-out of a single sorrow, but rather being an unwilling witness of an execution, the disintegration of one's own personality . . .

Unless madness or drugs or drink come into it, this phase comes to a dead-end, eventually, and is succeeded by a vacuous quiet. In this you can try to estimate what has been sheared away and what is left. Only when this quiet came to me, did I realize that I had gone through two parallel experiences.

The first time was twenty years ago, when I left Princeton in junior year with a complaint diagnosed as malaria. It transpired, through an X-ray taken a dozen years later, that it had been tuberculosis—a mild case, and after a few months of rest I went back to college. But I had lost certain offices, the chief one was the presidency of the Triangle Club, a musical comedy idea, and also I dropped back a class. To me college would never be the same. There were to be no badges of pride, no medals, after all. It seemed on one March afternoon that I had lost every single thing I wanted—and that night was the first time that I hunted down the spectre of womanhood that, for a little while, makes everything else seem unimportant.

Years later I realized that my failure as a big shot in college was all right—instead of serving on committees, I took a beating on English poetry; when I got the idea of what it was all about, I set about learning how to write. On Shaw's principle that "If you don't get what you like, you better like what you get," it was a lucky break—at the moment it was a harsh and bitter business to know that my career as a leader of men was over.

Since that day I have not been able to fire a bad servant, and I am astonished and impressed by people who can. Some old desire for personal dominance was broken and gone. Life around me was a solemn dream, and I lived on the letters I wrote to a girl in another city. A man does not recover from such jolts—he becomes a different person and, eventually, the new person finds new things to care about.

The other episode parallel to my current situation took [76/77] place after the war, when I had again over-extended my flank. It was one of those tragic loves doomed for lack of money, and one day the girl closed it out on the basis of common sense. During a long summer of despair I wrote a novel instead of letters, so it came out all right, but it came out all right for a different person. The man with the jingle of money in his pocket who married the girl a year later would always cherish an abiding distrust, an animosity, toward the leisure class—not the conviction of a revolutionist but the smouldering hatred of a peasant. In the years since then I have never been able to stop wondering where my friends' money came from, nor to stop thinking that at one time a sort of *droit de seigneur* might have been exercised to give one of them my girl.

For sixteen years I lived pretty much as this latter person, distrusting the rich, yet working for money with which to share their mobility and the grace that some of them brought into their lives. During this time I had plenty of the usual horses shot from under me—I remember some of their names—*Punctured Pride, Thwarted Expectation, Faithless, Show-off, Hard Hit, Never Again.* And after awhile I wasn't twenty-five, then not even thirty-five, and nothing was quite as good. But in all these years I don't remember a moment of discouragement. I saw honest men through moods of suicidal gloom—some of them gave up and died; others adjusted themselves and went on to larger success than mine; but my morale never sank below the level of self-disgust when I had put on some unsightly personal show. Trouble has no necessary connection with discouragement—discouragement has a germ of its own, as different from trouble as arthritis is different from a stiff joint.

When a new sky cut off the sun last spring, I didn't at first relate it to what had happened fifteen or twenty years ago. Only gradually did a certain family resemblance come through—an over-extension of the flank, a burning of the candle at both ends; a call upon physical resources that I did not command, like a man over-drawing at his bank. In its impact this blow was more violent than the other two but it was the same in kind—a feeling that I was standing [77/78] at twilight on a deserted range, with an empty rifle in my hands and the targets down. No problem set—simply a silence with only the sound of my own breathing.

In this silence there was a vast irresponsibility toward every obligation, a deflation of all my values. A passionate belief in order, a disregard of motives or consequences in favor of guess work and prophecy, a feeling that craft and industry would have a place in any world—one by one, these and other convictions were swept away. I saw that the novel, which at my maturity was the strongest and supplest medium for conveying thought and emotion from one human being to another, was becoming subordinated to a mechanical and communal art that, whether in the hands of Hollywood merchants or Russian idealists, was capable of reflecting only the tritest thought, the most obvious emotion. It was an art in which words were subordinate to images, where personality was worn down to the inevitable low gear of collaboration. As long past as 1930, I had a hunch that the talkies would make even the best selling novelist as archaic as silent pictures. People still read, if only Professor Canby's book of the month—curious children nosed at the slime of Mr. Tiffany Thayer in the drugstore libraries—but there was a rankling indignity, that to me had become almost an obsession, in seeing the power of the written word subordinated to another power, a more glittering, a grosser power . . .

I set that down as an example of what haunted me during the long night—this was something I could neither accept nor struggle against, something which tended to make my efforts obsolescent, as the chain stores have crippled the small merchant, an exterior force, unbeatable—

(I have the sense of lecturing now, looking at a watch on the desk before me and seeing how many more minutes—).

Well, when I had reached this period of silence, I was forced into a measure that no one ever adopts voluntarily: I was impelled to think. God, was it difficult! The moving about of great secret trunks. In the first exhausted halt, I wondered whether I had ever thought. After a long time I came to these conclusions, just as I write them here: [78/79]

(1) That I had done very little thinking, save within the problems of my craft. For twenty years a certain man had been my intellectual conscience. That was Edmund Wilson.

(2) That another man represented my sense of the "good life," though I saw him once in a decade, and since then he might have been hung. He is in the fur business in the Northwest and wouldn't like his

name set down here. But in difficult situations I had tried to think what *he* would have thought, how *he* would have acted.

(3) That a third contemporary had been an artistic conscience to me—I had not imitated his infectious style, because my own style, such as it is, was formed before he published anything, but there was an awful pull toward him when I was on a spot.

(4) That a fourth man had come to dictate my relations with other people when these relations were successful: how to do, what to say. How to make people at least momentarily happy (in opposition to Mrs. Post's theories of how to make everyone thoroughly uncomfortable with a sort of systematized vulgarity). This always confused me and made me want to go out and get drunk, but this man had seen the game, analyzed it and beaten it, and his word was good enough for me.

(5) That my political conscience had scarcely existed for ten years save as an element of irony in my stuff. When I became again concerned with the system I should function under, it was a man much younger than myself who brought it to me, with a mixture of passion and fresh air.

So there was not an "I" any more—not a basis on which I could organize my self-respect—save my limitless capacity for toil that it seemed I possessed no more. It was strange to have no self—to be like a little boy left alone in a big house, who knew that now he could do anything he wanted to do, but found that there was nothing that he wanted to do—

(The watch is past the hour and I have barely reached my thesis. I have some doubts as to whether this is of general interest, but if anyone wants more, there is plenty left, and your editor will tell me. If you've had enough, say so—but not too loud, because I have the feeling that someone, I'm [79/80] not sure who, is sound asleep—someone who could have helped me to keep my shop open. It wasn't Lenin, and it wasn't God.)

Pasting It Together

April, 1936

I have spoken in these pages of how an exceptionally optimistic young man experienced a crack-up of all values, a crack-up that he scarcely knew of until long after it occurred. I told of the succeeding period of desolation and of the necessity of going on, but without benefit of Henley's familiar heroics, "my head is bloody but unbowed." For a check-up of my spiritual liabilities indicated that I had no particular head to be bowed or unbowed. Once I had had a heart but that was about all I was sure of.

This was at least a starting place out of the morass in which I floundered: "I felt—therefore I was." At one time or another there had been many people who had leaned on me, come to me in difficulties or written me from afar, believed implicitly in my advice and my attitude toward life. The dullest platitude monger or the most unscrupulous Rasputin who can influence the destinies of many people must have some individuality, so the question became one of finding why and where I had changed, where was the leak through which, unknown to myself, my enthusiasm and my vitality had been steadily and prematurely trickling away.

One harassed and despairing night I packed a brief case and went off a thousand miles to think it over. I took a dollar room in a drab little town where I knew no one and sunk all the money I had with me in a stock of potted meat, crackers and apples. But don't let me suggest that the change from a rather overstuffed world to a comparative asceticism was any Research Magnificent—I only wanted absolute quiet to think out why I had developed a sad attitude toward sadness, a melancholy attitude toward melancholy and a [80/81] tragic attitude toward tragedy—*why I had become indentified with the objects of my horror or compassion.*

Does this seem a fine distinction? It isn't: identification such as this spells the death of accomplishment. It is something like this that keeps insane people from working. Lenin did not willingly endure the sufferings of his proletariat, nor Washington of his troops, nor Dickens of his London poor. And when Tolstoy tried some such merging of himself with the objects of his attention, it was a fake and a failure. I mention these because they are the men best known to us all.

It was dangerous mist. When Wordsworth decided that "there had passed away a glory from the earth," he felt no compulsion to pass away with it, and the Fiery Particle Keats never ceased his struggle against t. b. nor in his last moments relinquished his hope of being among the English poets.

My self-immolation was something sodden-dark. It was very distinctly not modern—yet I saw it in others, saw it in a dozen men of honor and industry since the war. (I heard you, but that's too easy—there were Marxians among these men.) I had stood by while one famous contemporary of mine played with the idea of the Big Out for half a year; I had watched when another, equally eminent, spent months in an asylum unable to endure any contact with his fellow men. And of those who had given up and passed on I could list a score.

This led me to the idea that the ones who had survived had made some sort of clean break. This is a big word and is no parallel to a jailbreak when one is probably headed for a new jail or will be forced back to the old one. The famous "Escape" or "run away from it all" is an excursion in a trap even if the trap includes the south seas, which are only for those who want to paint them or sail them. A clean break is something you cannot come back from; that is irretrievable because it makes the past cease to exist. So, since I could no longer fulfill the obligations that life had set for me or that I had set for myself, why not slay the empty shell who had been posturing at it for four years? I [81/82] must continue to be a writer because that was my only way of life, but I would cease any attempts to be a person—to be kind, just or generous. There were plenty of counterfeit coins around that would pass instead of these and I knew where I could get them at a nickel on the dollar. In thirty-nine years an observant eye has learned to detect where the milk is watered and the sugar is sanded, the rhinestone passed for diamond and the stucco for stone. There was to be no more giving of myself—all giving was to be outlawed henceforth under a new name, and that name was Waste.

The decision made me rather exuberant, like anything that is both real and new. As a sort of beginning there was a whole shaft of letters to be tipped into the waste basket when I went home, letters that wanted something for nothing—to read this man's manuscript, market this man's poem, speak free on the radio, indite notes of introduction, give this interview, help with the plot of this play, with this domestic situation, perform this act of thoughtfulness or charity.

The conjuror's hat was empty. To draw things out of it had long been a sort of sleight of hand, and now, to change the metaphor, I was off the dispensing end of the relief roll forever.

The heady villanous feeling continued.

I felt like the beady-eyed men I used to see on the commuting train from Great Neck fifteen years back—men who didn't care whether the world tumbled into chaos tomorrow if it spared their houses. I was one with them now, one with the smooth articles who said:

"I'm sorry but business is business." Or:

"You ought to have thought of that before you got into this trouble." Or:

"I'm not the person to see about that."

And a smile—ah, I would get me a smile. I'm still working on that smile. It is to combine the best qualities of a hotel manager, an experienced old social weasel, a head-master on visitors' day, a colored elevator man, a pansy pulling a profile, a producer getting stuff at half its market value, a trained nurse coming on a new job, a body-vender [82/83] in her first rotogravure, a hopeful extra swept near the camera, a ballet dancer with an infected toe, and of course the great beam of loving kindness common to all those from Washington to Beverly Hills who must exist by virtue of the contorted pan.

The voice too—I am working with a teacher on the voice. When I have perfected it the larynx will show no ring of conviction except the conviction of the person I am talking to. Since it will be largely called upon for the elicitation of the word "Yes," my teacher (a lawyer) and I are concentrating on that, but in extra hours. I am learning to bring into it that polite acerbity that makes people feel that far from being welcome they are not even tolerated and are under continual and scathing analysis at every moment. These times will of course not coincide with the smile. This will be reserved exclusively for those from whom I have nothing to gain, old worn-out people or young struggling people. They won't mind—what the hell, they get it most of the time anyhow.

But enough. It is not a matter of levity. If you are young and you should write asking to see me and learn how to be a sombre literary man writing pieces upon the state of emotional exhaustion that often overtakes writers in their prime—if you should be so young and so fatuous as to do this, I would not do so much as acknowledge your letter, unless you were related to someone very rich and important indeed. And if you were dying of starvation outside my window, I would go out quickly and give you the smile and the voice (if no longer the hand) and stick around till somebody raised a nickel to phone for the ambulance, that is if I thought there would be any copy in it for me.

I have now at last become a writer only. The man I had persistently tried to be became such a burden that I have "cut him loose" with as little compunction as a Negro lady cuts loose a rival on Saturday night. Let the good people function as such—let the overworked doctors die in harness, with one week's "vacation" a year that they can devote to straightening out their family affairs, and let the underworked doctors scramble for cases at one dollar a throw; let [83/84] the soldiers be killed and enter immediately into the Valhalla of their profession. That is their contract with the gods. A writer need have no such ideals unless he makes them for himself, and this one has quit. The old dream of being an entire man in the Goethe-Byron-Shaw tradition, with an opulent American touch, a sort of combination of J. P. Morgan, Topham Beauclerk and St. Francis of Assisi, has been relegated to the junk heap of the shoulder pads worn for one day on the Princeton freshman football field and the overseas cap never worn overseas.

So what? This is what I think now: that the natural state of the sentient adult is a qualified unhappiness. I think also that in an adult the desire to be finer in grain than you are, "a constant striving" (as those people say who gain their bread by saying it) only adds to this unhappiness in the end—that end that comes to our youth and hope. My own happiness in the past often approached such an ecstasy that I could not share it even with the person dearest to me but had to walk it away in quiet streets and lanes with only fragments of it to distil into little lines in books—and I think that my happiness, or talent for self-delusion or what you will, was an exception. It was not the natural thing but the unnatural—unnatural as the Boom; and my recent experience parallels the wave of despair that swept the nation when the Boom was over.

I shall manage to live with the new dispensation, though it has

taken some months to be certain of the fact. And just as the laughing
stoicism which has enabled the American Negro to endure the intolerable conditions of his existence has cost him his sense of the truth—so
in my case there is a price to pay. I do not any longer like the postman,
nor the grocer, nor the editor, nor the cousin's husband, and he in turn
will come to dislike me, so that life will never be very pleasant again,
and the sign *Cave Canem* is hung permanently just above my door. I
will try to be a correct animal though, and if you throw me a bone with
enough meat on it I may even lick your hand. [84]

The Pot of Gold

JOHN CHEEVER

YOU COULD NOT SAY FAIRLY OF RALPH AND LAURA WHITTEMORE THAT
they had the failings and the characteristics of incorrigible treasure
hunters, but you could say truthfully of them that the shimmer and the
smell, the peculiar force of money, the promise of it, had an untoward
influence on their lives. They were always at the threshold of fortune;
they always seemed to have something on the fire. Ralph was a fair
young man with a tireless commercial imagination and an evangelical
credence in the romance and sorcery of business success, and although
he held an obscure job with a clothing manufacturer, this never
seemed to him anything more than a point of departure.

The Whittemores were not importunate or overbearing people,
and they had an uncompromising loyalty to the gentle manners of the
middle class. Laura was a pleasant girl of no particular beauty who
had come to New York from Wisconsin at about the same time that
Ralph had reached the city from Illinois, but it had taken two years of
comings and goings before they had been brought together, late one
afternoon, in the lobby of a lower Fifth Avenue office building. So true
was Ralph's heart, so well did it serve him then, that the moment he

John Cheever, "The Pot of Gold," in *The Enormous Radio and Other
Stories* (New York: Funk & Wagnalls Company, 1953), pp. 28–46. Reprinted
from *The Enormous Radio and Other Stories* by John Cheever. By permission of
the publishers, Funk & Wagnalls, New York.

saw Laura's light hair and her pretty and sullen face he was enraptured. He followed her out of the lobby, pushing his way through the crowd, and since she had dropped nothing, since [28/29] there was no legitimate excuse to speak to her, he shouted after her, "*Louise! Louise! Louise!*," and the urgency in his voice made her stop. He said he'd made a mistake. He said he was sorry. He said she looked just like a girl named Louise Hatcher. It was a January night and the dark air tasted of smoke, and because she was a sensible and a lonely girl, she let him buy her a drink.

This was in the thirties, and their courtship was hasty. They were married three months later. Laura moved her belongings into a walkup on Madison Avenue, above a pants presser's and a florist's, where Ralph was living. She worked as a secretary, and her salary, added to what he brought home from the clothing business, was little more than enough to keep them going, but they never seemed touched by the monotony of a saving and gainless life. They ate dinners in drugstores. She hung a reproduction of van Gogh's "Sunflowers" above the sofa she had bought with some of the small sum of money her parents had left her. When their aunts and uncles came to town—their parents were dead—they had dinner at the Ritz and went to the theatre. She sewed curtains and shined his shoes, and on Sundays they stayed in bed until noon. They seemed to be standing at the threshold of plenty; and Laura often told people that she was terribly excited because of this wonderful job that Ralph had lined up.

In the first year of their marriage, Ralph worked nights on a plan that promised him a well-paying job in Texas, but through no fault of his own this promise was never realized. There was an opening in Syracuse a year later, but an older man was decided upon. There were many other profitable but elusive openings and projects between these two. In the third year of their marriage, a firm that was almost identical in size and character with the firm Ralph worked for underwent a change of ownership, and Ralph was approached and asked if he would be interested in joining the overhauled firm. His own job promised only meagre security after a series of slow promotions and he was glad of the chance to escape. He met the new [29/30] owners, and their enthusiasm for him seemed intense. They were prepared to put him in charge of a department and pay him twice what he was getting then. The arrangement was to remain tacit for a month or two, until the new owners had secured their position, but they shook hands warmly and had a drink on the deal, and that night Ralph took Laura out to dinner at an expensive restaurant.

They decided, across the table, to look for a larger apartment, to have a child, and to buy a second-hand car. They faced their good fortune with perfect calm, for it was what they had expected all along. The city seemed to them a generous place, where people were rewarded either by a sudden and deserved development like this or by the capricious bounty of lawsuits, eccentric and peripheral business ventures, unexpected legacies, and other windfalls. After dinner, they walked in Central Park in the moonlight while Ralph smoked a cigar. Later, when Laura had fallen asleep, he sat in the open bedroom window in his pajamas.

The peculiar excitement with which the air of the city seems charged after midnight, when its life falls into the hands of watchmen and drunks, had always pleased him. He knew intimately the sounds of the night street: the bus brakes, the remote sirens, and the sound of water turning high in the air—the sound of water turning a mill wheel—the sum, he supposed, of many echoes, although, often as he had heard the sound, he had never decided on its source. Now he heard all this more keenly because the night seemed to him portentous.

He was twenty-eight years old; poverty and youth were inseparable in his experience, and one was ending with the other. The life they were about to leave had not been hard, and he thought with sentiment of the soiled tablecloth in the Italian restaurant where they usually went for their celebrations, and the high spirits with which Laura on a wet night ran from the subway to the bus stop. But they were drawing away from all this. Shirt sales in department-store basements, lines at meat counters, weak drinks, the roses he brought her up from the [30/31] subway in the spring, when roses were cheap—these were all unmistakably the souvenirs of the poor, and while they seemed to him good and gentle, he was glad that they would soon be memories.

Laura resigned from her job when she got pregnant. The reorganization and Ralph's new position hung fire, but the Whittemores talked about it freely when they were with friends. "We're *terribly* pleased with the way things are going," Laura would say. "All we need is patience." There were many delays and postponements, and they waited with the patience of people expecting justice. The time came when they both needed clothes, and one evening Ralph suggested that they spend some of the money they had put aside. Laura refused. When he brought up the subject, she didn't answer him and seemed not to hear him. He raised his voice and lost his temper. He shouted. She cried. He thought of all the other girls he could have married—the dark blonde, the worshipful Cuban, the rich and pretty one with a cast in her right eye. All his desires seemed to lie outside the small apartment Laura had arranged. They were still not speaking in the morning, and in order to strengthen his position he telephoned his potential employers. Their secretary told him they were both out. This made him apprehensive. He called several times from the telephone booth in the lobby of the building he worked in and was told that they were busy, they were out, they were in conference with lawyers, or they were talking long distance. This variety of excuses frightened him. He said nothing to Laura that evening and tried to call them the next day. Late in the afternoon, after many tries, one of them came to the phone. "We gave the job to somebody else, sonny," he said. Like a saddened father, he spoke to Ralph in a hoarse and gentle voice. "Don't try and get us on the telephone any more. We've got other things to do besides answer the telephone. This other fellow seemed better suited, sonny. That's all I can tell you, and don't try to get me on the telephone any more."

Ralph walked the miles from his office to his apartment that night, hoping to free himself in this way from some of the [31/32] weight of his disappointment. He was so unprepared for the shock that it affected him like vertigo, and he walked with an odd, high step, as if the paving were quicksand. He stood downstairs in front of the building he lived in, trying to decide how to describe the disaster to Laura, but when he went in, he told her bluntly. "Oh, I'm sorry, darling," she said softly and kissed him. "I'm terribly sorry." She wandered away from him and began to straighten the sofa cushions. His frustration was so ardent, he was such a prisoner of his schemes and expectations, that he was astonished at the serenity with which she regarded the failure. There was nothing to worry about, she said. She still had a few hundred dollars in the bank, from the money her parents had left her. There was nothing to worry about.

When the child, a girl, was born, they named her Rachel, and a week after the delivery Laura returned to the Madison Avenue walkup. She took all the care of the baby and continued to do the cooking and the housework.

Ralph's imagination remained resilient and fertile, but he couldn't seem to hit on a scheme that would fit into his lack of time and capital. He and Laura, like the hosts of the poor everywhere, lived a simple life. They still went to the theatre with visiting relatives and occasionally they went to parties, but Laura's only continuous contact with the bright lights that surrounded them was vicarious and came to her through a friend she made in Central Park.

She spent many afternoons on a park bench during the first years of Rachel's life. It was a tyranny and a pleasure. She resented her enchainment but enjoyed the open sky and the air. One winter afternoon, she recognized a woman she had met at a party, and a little before dark, as Laura and the other mothers were gathering their stuffed animals and preparing their children for the cold journey home, the woman came across the playground and spoke to her. She was Alice Holinshed, she said. They had met at the Galvins'. She was pretty and friendly, and walked with Laura to the edge of the Park. She had a boy of [32/33] about Rachel's age. The two women met again the following day. They became friends.

Mrs. Holinshed was older than Laura, but she had a more youthful and precise beauty. Her hair and her eyes were black, her pale and perfectly oval face was delicately colored, and her voice was pure. She lighted her cigarettes with Stork Club matches and spoke of the inconvenience of living with a child in a hotel. If Laura had any regrets about her life, they were expressed in her friendship for this pretty woman, who moved so freely through expensive stores and restaurants.

It was a friendship circumscribed, with the exception of the Galvins', by the sorry and touching countryside of Central Park. The women talked principally about their husbands, and this was a game that Laura could play with an empty purse. Vaguely, boastfully, the two women discussed the irons their men had in the fire. They sat together with their children through the sooty twilights, when the city to the south burns like a Bessemer furnace, and the air smells of coal, and the wet boulders shine like slag, and the Park itself seems like a strip of woods on the edge of a coal town. Then Mrs. Holinshed would remember that she was late—she was always late for something mysterious and splendid—and the two women would walk together to the edge of the woods. This vicarious contact with comfort pleased Laura, and the pleasure would stay with her as she pushed the baby carriage over to Madison Avenue and then began to cook supper, hearing the thump of the steam iron and smelling the cleaning fluid from the pants presser's below.

One night, when Rachel was about two years old, the frustration of Ralph's search for the goat track that would let him lead his family to a realm of reasonable contentment kept him awake. He needed sleep urgently, and when this blessing eluded him, he got out of bed and sat in the dark. The charm and excitement of the street after midnight escaped him. The explosive brakes of a Madison Avenue bus made him jump. He shut the window, but the noise of traffic continued to pass through it. [33/34] It seemed to him that the penetrating voice of the city had a mortal effect on the precious lives of the city's inhabitants and that it should be muffled.

He thought of a Venetian blind whose outer surfaces would be treated with a substance that would deflect or absorb sound waves. With such a blind, friends paying a call on a spring evening would not have to shout to be heard above the noise of trucks in the street below. Bedrooms could be silenced that way—bedrooms, above all, for it seemed to him then that sleep was what everyone in the city sought and only half captured. All the harried faces on the streets at dusk, when even the pretty girls talk to themselves, were looking for sleep. Night-club singers and their amiable customers, the people waiting for taxis in front of the Waldorf on a wet night, policemen, cashiers, window washers—sleep eluded them all.

He talked over this Venetian blind with Laura the following night, and the idea seemed sensible to her. He bought a blind that would fit their bedroom window, and experimented with various paint mixtures. At last he stumbled on one that dried to the consistency of felt and was porous. The paint had a sickening smell, which filled their apartment during the four days it took him to coat and recoat the outer surface of the slats. When the paint had dried, he hung the blind, and they opened the window for a test. Silence—a relative silence—charmed their ears. He wrote down his formula, and took it during his lunch hour to a patent attorney. It took the lawyer several weeks to discover that a similar formula had been patented some years earlier. The patent owner—a man named Fellows—had a New York address, and the lawyer suggested that Ralph get in touch with him and try to reach some agreement.

The search for Mr. Fellows began one evening when Ralph had finished work, and took him first to the attic of a Hudson Street rooming house, where the landlady showed Ralph a pair of socks that Mr. Fellows had left behind when he moved out. Ralph went south from there to another rooming house and [34/35] then west to the neighborhood of ship chandlers and marine boarding houses. The nocturnal search went on for a week. He followed the thread of Mr. Fellows' goings south to the Bowery and then to the upper West Side. He climbed stairs past the open doors of rooms where lessons in Spanish dancing were going on, past whores, past women practicing the "Emperor" Concerto, and one evening he found Mr. Fellows sitting on the edge of his bed in an attic room, rubbing the spots out of his necktie with a rag soaked in gasoline.

Mr. Fellows was greedy. He wanted a hundred dollars in cash and fifty per cent of the royalties. Ralph got him to agree to twenty per cent of the royalties, but he could not get him to reduce the initial payment. The lawyer drew up a paper defining Ralph's and Mr. Fellows' interests, and a few nights later Ralph went over to Brooklyn and got to a Venetian-blind factory after its doors had closed but while the lights of the office were still burning. The manager agreed to manufacture some blinds to Ralph's specifications, but he would not take an order of less than a hundred dollars. Ralph agreed to this and to furnish the compound for the outer surface of the slats. These expenditures had taken more than three-fourths of the Whittemores' capital, and now the problem of money was joined by the element of time. They put a small advertisement in the paper for a housewares salesman, and for a week Ralph interviewed candidates in the living room after supper. He chose a young man who was leaving at the end of the week for the Midwest. He wanted a fifty-dollar advance, and pointed out to them that Pittsburgh and Chicago were just as noisy as New York. A department-store collection agency was threatening to bring them into the small-claims court at this time, and they had come to a place where any illness, any fall, any damage to themselves or to the few clothes they owned would be critical. Their salesman promised to write them from Chicago at the end of the week, and they counted on good news, but there was no news from Chicago at all. Ralph wired the salesman twice, and the wires must have been forwarded, for he replied [35/36] to them from Pittsburgh: "Can't merchandise blinds. Returning samples express." They put another advertisement for a salesman in the paper and took the first one who rang their bell, an old gentleman with a cornflower in his buttonhole. He had a number of other lines—mirror wastebaskets, orange-juicers—and he said that he knew all the Manhattan housewares buyers intimately. He was garrulous, and when he was unable to sell the blinds, he came to the Whittemores' apartment and discussed their product at length, and with a blend of criticism and charity that we usually reserve for human beings.

Ralph tried to borrow money, but neither his salary nor his patent was considered adequate collateral for a loan at anything but ruinous rates, and one day, at his office, he was served a summons by the department-store collection agency. He went out to Brooklyn and offered to sell the Venetian blinds back to the manufacturer. The man gave him sixty dollars for what had cost a hundred, and Ralph was able to pay the collection agency. They hung the samples in their windows and tried to put the venture out of their minds.

Now they were poorer than ever, and they ate lentils for dinner every Monday and sometimes again on Tuesday. Laura washed the dishes after dinner while Ralph read to Rachel. When the girl had fallen asleep, he would go to his desk in the living room and work on one of his projects. There was always something coming. There was a job in Dallas and a job in Peru. There were the plastic arch preserver, the automatic closing device for ice-box doors, and the scheme to pirate marine specifications and undersell Jane's. For a month, he was going to buy some fallow acreage in upstate New York and plant Christmas trees on it, and then, with one of his friends, he projected a luxury mail-order business, for which they could never get backing. When the Whittemores met Uncle George and Aunt Helen at the Ritz, they seemed delighted with the way things were going. They were terribly excited, Laura said, about a sales agency in Paris that had been offered to Ralph but that they had decided against, because of the threat of war. [36/37]

The Whittemores were apart for two years during the war. Laura took a job. She walked Rachel to school in the morning and met her at the end of the day. Working and saving, Laura was able to buy herself and Rachel some clothes. When Ralph returned at the end of the war, their affairs were in good order. The experience seemed to have refreshed him, and while he took up his old job as an anchor to windward, as an ace in the hole, there had never been more talk about jobs—jobs in Venezuela and jobs in Iran. They resumed all their old habits and economies. They remained poor.

Laura gave up her job and returned to the afternoons with Rachel in Central Park. Alice Holinshed was there. The talk was the same. The

Holinsheds were living in a hotel. Mr. Holinshed was vice-president of a new firm manufacturing a soft drink, but the dress that Mrs. Holinshed wore day after day was one that Laura recognized from before the war. Her son was thin and bad-tempered. He was dressed in serge, like an English schoolboy, but his serge, like his mother's dress, looked worn and outgrown. One afternoon when Mrs. Holinshed and her son came into the Park, the boy was crying. "I've done a dreadful thing," Mrs. Holinshed told Laura. "We've been to the doctor's and I forgot to bring any money, and I wonder if you could lend me a few dollars, so I can take a taxi back to the hotel." Laura said she would be glad to. She had only a five-dollar bill with her, and she gave Mrs. Holinshed this. The boy continued to cry, and his mother dragged him off toward Fifth Avenue. Laura never saw them in the Park again.

Ralph's life was, as it had always been, dominated by anticipation. In the years directly after the war, the city appeared to be immensely rich. There seemed to be money everywhere, and the Whittemores, who slept under their worn overcoats in the winter to keep themselves warm, seemed separated from their enjoyment of this prosperity by only a little patience, resourcefulness, and luck. On Sunday, when the weather was fine, they walked with the prosperous crowds on upper Fifth [37/38] Avenue. It seemed to Ralph that it might only be another month, at the most another year, before he found the key to the prosperity they deserved. They would walk on Fifth Avenue until the afternoon was ended and then go home and eat a can of beans for dinner and, in order to balance the meal, an apple for dessert.

They were returning from such a walk one Sunday when, as they climbed the stairs to their apartment, the telephone began to ring. Ralph went on ahead and answered it.

He heard the voice of his Uncle George, a man of the generation that remains conscious of distance, who spoke into the telephone as if he were calling from shore to a passing boat. "This is Uncle George, Ralphie!" he shouted, and Ralph supposed that he and Aunt Helen were paying a surprise visit to the city, until he realized that his uncle was calling from Illinois. "Can you hear me?" Uncle George shouted. "Can you hear me, Ralphie? . . . I'm calling you about a job, Ralphie. Just in case you're looking for a job. Paul Hadaam came through—can you hear me, Ralphie?—Paul Hadaam came through here on his way East last week and he stopped off to pay me a visit. He's got a lot of money, Ralphie—he's rich—and he's starting this business out in the West to manufacture synthetic wool. Can you hear me, Ralphie? . . . I told him about you, and he's staying at the Waldorf, so you go and see him. I saved his life once. I pulled him out of Lake Erie. You go and see him tomorrow at the Waldorf, Ralphie. You know where that is? The Waldorf Hotel. . . . Wait a minute, here's Aunt Helen. She wants to talk with you."

Now the voice was a woman's, and it came to him faintly. All his cousins had been there for dinner, she told him. They had had a turkey for dinner. All the grandchildren were there and they behaved very well. George took them all for a walk after dinner. It was hot, but they sat on the porch, so they didn't feel the heat. She was interrupted in her account of Sunday by her husband, who must have seized the instrument from her to continue his refrain about going to see Mr. Hadaam at [38/39] the Waldorf. "You go see him tomorrow, Ralphie —the nineteenth—at the Waldorf. He's expecting you. Can you hear me? . . . The Waldorf Hotel. He's a millionaire. I'll say goodbye now."

Mr. Hadaam had a parlor and a bedroom in the Waldorf Towers, and when Ralph went to 'see him, late the next afternoon, on his way home from work, Mr. Hadaam was alone. He seemed to Ralph a very old man, but an obdurate one, and in the way he shook hands, pulled at his ear lobes, stretched himself, and padded around the parlor on his bandy legs Ralph recognized a spirit that was unimpaired, independent, and canine. He poured Ralph a strong drink and himself a weak one. He was undertaking the manufacture of synthetic wool on the West Coast, he explained, and had come East to find men who were experienced in merchandising wool. George had given him Ralph's name, and he wanted a man with Ralph's experience. He would find the Whittemores a suitable house, arrange for their transportation, and begin Ralph at a salary of fifteen thousand. It was the size of the salary that made Ralph realize that the proposition was an oblique attempt to repay his uncle for having saved Mr. Hadaam's life, and the old man seemed to sense what he was feeling. "This hasn't got anything to do with your uncle's saving my life," he said roughly. "I'm grateful to him—who wouldn't be?—but this hasn't got anything to do with your uncle, if that's what you're thinking. When you get to be as old and as rich as I am, it's hard to meet people. All my old friends are dead—all of them but George. I'm surrounded by a cordon of associates and relatives that's damned near impenetrable, and if it wasn't for George giving me a name now and then, I'd never get to see a new face. Last year, I got into an automobile accident. It was my fault. I'm a terrible driver. I hit this young fellow's car and I got right out and went over to him and introduced myself. We had to wait about twenty minutes for the wreckers and we got to talking. Well, he's working for me today and he's one of the best friends [39/40] I've got, and if I hadn't run into him, I'd never have met him. When you get to be as old as me, that's the only way you can meet people—automobile accidents, fires, things like that."

He straightened up against the back of his chair and tasted his drink. His rooms were well above the noise of traffic and it was quiet there. Mr. Hadaam's breath was loud and steady, and it sounded, in a pause, like the heavy breath of someone sleeping. "Well, I don't want to rush you into this," he said. "I'm going back to the Coast the day after tomorrow. You think it over and I'll telephone you." He took out an engagement book and wrote down Ralph's name and telephone number. "I'll call you on Tuesday evening, the twenty-seventh, about nine o'clock—nine o'clock your time. George tells me you've got a nice wife, but I haven't got time to meet her now. I'll see her on the Coast." He started talking about baseball and then brought the conversation back to Uncle George. "He saved my life. My damned boat capsized and then righted herself and sunk right from underneath me. I can still feel her going down under my feet. I couldn't swim. Can't swim today. Well, goodbye." They shook hands, and as soon as the door closed, Ralph heard Mr. Hadaam begin to cough. It was the profane, hammering cough of an old man, full of bitter complaints and distempers, and it hit him pitilessly for all the time that Ralph was waiting in the hallway for the elevator to take him down.

On the walk home, Ralph felt that this might be it, that this preposterous chain of contingencies that had begun with his uncle's pulling a friend out of Lake Erie might be the one that would save them. Nothing in his experience made it seem unlikely. He recognized that the proposition was the vagary of an old man and that it originated in the indebtedness Mr. Hadaam felt to his uncle—an indebtedness that age seemed to have deepened. He gave Laura the details of the interview when he came in, and his own views on Mr. Hadaam's conduct, and, to his mild surprise, Laura said that it looked to her like the bonanza. They were both remarkably calm, considering the change that confronted them. There was no talk of celebrating, [40/41] and he helped her wash the dishes. He looked up the site of Mr. Hadaam's factory in an atlas, and the Spanish place name on the coast north of San Francisco gave them a glimpse of a life of reasonable contentment.

Eight days lay between Ralph's interview and the telephone call, and he realized that nothing would be definite until Tuesday, and that there was a possibility that old Mr. Hadaam, while crossing the country, might, under the subtle influence of travel, suffer a change of heart. He might be poisoned by a fish sandwich and be taken off the train in Chicago, to die in a nursing home there. Among the people meeting him in San Francisco might be his lawyer, with the news that he was ruined or that his wife had run away. But eventually Ralph was unable to invent any new disasters or to believe in the ones he had invented.

This inability to persevere in doubting his luck showed some weakening of character. There had hardly been a day when he had not been made to feel the power of money, but he found that the force of money was most irresistible when it took the guise of a promise, and that years of resolute self-denial, instead of rewarding him with reserves of fortitude, had left him more than ordinarily susceptible to temptation. Since the change in their lives still depended upon a telephone call, he refrained from talking—from thinking, so far as possible—about the life they might have in California. He would go so far as to say that he would like some white shirts, but he would not go beyond this deliberately contrite wish, and here, where he thought he was exercising restraint and intelligence, he was, instead, beginning to respect the bulk of superstition that is supposed to attend good fortune, and when he wished for white shirts, it was not a genuinely modest wish so much as it was a memory—he could not have put it into words himself—that the gods of fortune are jealous and easily deceived by false modesty. He had never been a superstitious man, but on Tuesday he scooped the money off his coffee and was elated when he saw a ladybug on the bathroom window sill. He could not remember when he [41/42] had heard money and this insect associated, but neither could he have explained any of the other portents that he had begun to let govern his movements.

Laura watched this subtle change that anticipation worked on her husband, but there was nothing she could say. He did not mention Mr. Hadaam or California. He was quiet; he was gentle with Rachel; he actually grew pale. He had his hair cut on Wednesday. He wore his best suit. On Saturday, he had his hair cut again and his nails manicured. He took two baths a day, put on a fresh shirt for dinner, and frequently went into the bathroom to wash his hands, brush his teeth, and wet down his cowlick. The preternatural care he gave his body and his appearance reminded her of an adolescent surprised by early love.

The Whittemores were invited to a party for Monday night and Laura insisted that they go. The guests at the party were the survivors of a group that had coalesced ten years before, and if anyone had called the roll of the earliest parties in the same room, like the retreat ceremony of a breeched and decimated regiment, "Missing.... Missing.... Missing" would have been answered for the squad that had gone into Westchester; "Missing.... Missing.... Missing" would have been spoken for the platoon that divorce, drink, nervous disorders, and adversity had slain or wounded. Because Laura had gone to the party in indifferent spirits, she was conscious of the missing.

She had been at the party less than an hour when she heard some people coming in, and, looking over her shoulder, saw Alice Holinshed and her husband. The room was crowded and she put off speaking to Alice until later. Much later in the evening, Laura went into the toilet, and when she came out of it into the bedroom, she found Alice sitting on the bed. She seemed to be waiting for Laura. Laura sat down at the dressing table to straighten her hair. She looked at the image of her friend in the glass.

"I hear you're going to California," Alice said. [42/43]

"We hope to. We'll know tomorrow."

"Is it true that Ralph's uncle saved his life?"

"That's true."

"You're lucky."

"I suppose we are."

"You're lucky, all right." Alice got up from the bed and crossed the room and closed the door, and came back across the room again and sat on the bed. Laura watched her in the glass, but she was not watching Laura. She was stooped. She seemed nervous. "You're lucky," she said. "You're so lucky. Do you know how lucky you are? Let me tell you about this cake of soap," she said. "I have this cake of soap. I mean I had this cake of soap. Somebody gave it to me when I was married, fifteen years ago. I don't know who. Some maid, some music teacher—somebody like that. It was good soap, good English soap, the kind I like, and I decided to save it for the big day when Larry made a killing, when he took me to Bermuda. First, I was going to use it when he got the job in Bound Brook. Then I thought I could use it when we were going to Boston, and then Washington, and then when he got this new job, I thought maybe this is it, maybe *this* is the time when I get to take the boy out of that rotten school and pay the bills and move out of those bum hotels we've been living in. For fifteen years I've been planning to use this cake of soap. Well, last week I was looking through my bureau drawers and I saw this cake of soap. It was all cracked. I threw it out. I threw it out because I knew I was never going to have a chance to use it. Do you realize what that means? Do you know what that feels like? To live for fifteen years on promises and expectations and loans and credits in hotels that aren't fit to live in, never for a single day to be out of debt, and yet to pretend, to feel that every year, every winter, every job, every meeting is going to be the one. To live like this for fifteen years and then to realize that it's never going to end. Do you know what that feels like?" She got up and went over to the dressing table and stood in front of Laura. Tears had risen into her large eyes, and her voice [43/44] was harsh and loud. "I'm never going to get to Bermuda," she said. "I'm never even going to get to Florida. I'm never going to get out of hock, ever, ever, *ever*. I know that I'm never going to have a decent home and that everything I own that is worn and torn and no good is going to stay that way. I know that for the rest of my life, for the rest of my life, I'm going to wear ragged slips and torn nightgowns and torn underclothes and shoes that hurt me. I know that for the rest of my life nobody is going to come up to me and tell me that I've got on a pretty dress, because I'm not going to be able to afford that kind of a dress. I know that for the rest of my life every taxi-driver and doorman and headwaiter in this town is going to know in a minute that I haven't got five bucks in that black imitation-suède purse that I've been brushing and brushing and brushing and carrying around for ten years. How do you get it? How do you rate it? What's so wonderful about you that you get a break like this?" She ran her fingers down Laura's bare arm. The dress she was wearing smelled of benzine. "Can I rub it off you? Will that make me lucky? I swear to Jesus I'd murder somebody if I thought it would bring us in any money. I'd wring somebody's neck—yours, anybody's—I swear to Jesus I would—"

Someone began knocking on the door. Alice strode to the door, opened it, and went out. A woman came in, a stranger looking for the toilet. Laura lighted a cigarette and waited in the bedroom for about ten minutes before she went back to the party. The Holinsheds had gone. She got a drink and sat down and tried to talk, but she couldn't keep her mind on what she was saying.

The hunt, the search for money that had seemed to her natural, amiable, and fair when they first committed themselves to it, now seemed like a hazardous and piratical voyage. She had thought, earlier in the evening, of the missing. She thought now of the missing again. Adversity and failure accounted for more than half of them, as if beneath the amenities in the pretty room a keen race were in progress, in which the [44/45] loser's forfeits were extreme. Laura felt cold. She picked the ice out of her drink with her fingers and put it in a flower vase, but the whiskey didn't warm her. She asked Ralph to take her home.

After dinner on Tuesday, Laura washed the dishes and Ralph dried them. He read the paper and she took up some sewing. At a quarter after eight, the telephone, in the bedroom, rang, and he went to it calmly. It was someone with two theatre tickets for a show that was closing. The telephone didn't ring again, and at half past nine he told Laura that he was going to call California. It didn't take long for the connection to be made, and the fresh voice of a young woman spoke to him from Mr. Hadaam's number. "Oh, yes, Mr. Whittemore," she said. "We tried to get you earlier in the evening but your line was busy."

"Could I speak to Mr. Hadaam?"

"No, Mr. Whittemore. This is Mr. Hadaam's secretary. I know he meant to call you, because he had entered this in his engagement book. Mrs. Hadaam has asked me to disappoint as few people as possible, and I've tried to take care of all the calls and appointments in his engagement book. Mr. Hadaam had a stroke on Sunday. We don't expect him to recover. I imagine he made you some kind of promise, but I'm afraid he won't be able to keep it."

"I'm very sorry," Ralph said. He hung up.

Laura had come into the bedroom while the secretary was talking. "Oh, darling!" she said. She put her sewing basket on the bureau and went toward the closet. Then she went back and looked for something in the sewing basket and left the basket on her dressing table. Then she took off her shoes, treed them, slipped her dress over her head and hung it up neatly. Then she went to the bureau, looking for her sewing basket, found it on the dressing table, and took it into the closet, where she put it on a shelf. Then she took her brush and comb into the bathroom and began to run the water for a bath. [45/46]

The lash of frustration was laid on and the pain stunned Ralph. He sat by the telephone for he did not know how long. He heard Laura come out of the bathroom. He turned when he heard her speak.

"I feel dreadfully about old Mr. Hadaam," she said. "I wish there were something we could do." She was in her nightgown, and she sat down at the dressing table like a skillful and patient woman establishing herself in front of a loom, and she picked up and put down pins and bottles and combs and brushes with the thoughtless dexterity of an experienced weaver, as if the time she spent there were all part of a continuous operation. "It did look like the treasure . . ."

The word surprised him, and for a moment he saw the chimera, the pot of gold, the fleece, the treasure buried in the faint lights of a rainbow, and the primitivism of his hunt struck him. Armed with a sharp spade and a homemade divining rod, he had climbed over hill and dale, though droughts and rain squalls, digging wherever the maps he had drawn himself promised gold. Six paces east of the dead pine, five panels in from the library door, underneath the creaking step, in the roots of the pear tree, beneath the grape arbor lay the bean pot full of doubloons and bullion.

She turned on the stool and held her thin arms toward him, as she had done more than a thousand times. She was no longer young, and more wan, thinner than she might have been if he had found the doubloons to save her anxiety and unremitting work. Her smile, her naked shoulders had begun to trouble the indecipherable shapes and symbols that are the touchstones of desire, and the light from the lamp seemed to brighten and give off heat and shed that unaccountable complacency, that benevolence, that the spring sunlight brings to all kinds of fatigue and despair. Desire for her delighted and confused him. Here it was, here it all was, and the shine of the gold seemed to him then to be all around her arms. [46]

5. CROSS CURRENTS

THE SHORT STORY "THE WALLS OF ÁVILA" MAY FITTINGLY STAND ALONE as the concluding section of this volume. Although it is rich in its observations on friendship, childhood, early love, marriage, home, travel, and ambition, it is particularly valuable as a study of contemporary attitudes toward success. It reveals clearly that the views of earlier periods are still present, though in various states of preservation, and it suggests the paradoxes implicit in current attitudes toward these views. A careful analysis of the story will show that these attitudes are complex and ambiguous. The character who most closely adheres to Franklin's formula appears shallow and narrow; yet he is a leading and respected citizen. The major character, who has deliberately led an apparently aimless existence but who has attained the greatest measure of satisfaction, is a contemporary dissenting voice; yet he is himself aware that he will probably never succeed in his quest for the elusive "private god who guided him." Another character, who has held fast to the bright hope of some kind of success, is tragically conscious of the lure of both the "private god" and the public measure of success.

In the concluding chapter of *Walden*, Henry David Thoreau inquires, "Why should we be in such desperate haste to succeed, and in such desperate enterprises? If a man does not keep pace with his companions, perhaps it is because he hears a different drummer. Let him step to the music which he hears, however measured or far away." The major character obviously hears a different drummer, and his friend—the respectable citizen—labels him "a damn fool." The story suggests that his epithet might well be applied to himself. Although the characters in the story take widely divergent paths in their search for success and judge others on the basis of their personal definitions of success, the driving motive in the lives of all of them is the realization of its persistent—if indistinct—promise.

The Walls of Ávila

EVAN S. CONNELL, JR.

Thou shalt make castels in Spayne,
And dreme of joye, al but in vayne.

—ROMAUNT OF THE ROSE

ÁVILA LIES ONLY A FEW KILOMETERS WEST AND A LITTLE NORTH OF Madrid, and is surrounded by a grim stone wall that was old when Isabella was born. Life in this town has not changed very much from the days when the earth was flat; somehow it is as though news of the passing centuries has never arrived in Ávila. Up the cobbled street saunters a donkey with a wicker basket slung on each flank, and on the donkey's bony rump sits a boy nodding drowsily in the early morning sun. The boy's dark face looks medieval. He is delivering bread. At night the stars are metallic, with a bluish tint, and the Spaniards stroll gravely back and forth beside the high stone wall. There are not so many gypsies, or *gitanos*, in this town as there are in, say, Valencia or Seville. Ávila is northerly and was not impressed by these passionate Asiatic people, at least not the way Córdoba was, or Granada. [83/84]

These were things we learned about Avila when J. D. returned. He came home after living abroad for almost ten years. He was thinner and taller than any of us remembered, and his crew-cut hair had turned completely gray although he was just thirty-eight. It made him look very distinguished, even a little dramatic. His skin was now as brown as coffee, and there were wind wrinkles about his restless cerulean blue eyes, as though the light of strange beaches and exotic plazas had stamped him like a visa to prove he had been there. He smiled a good deal, perhaps because he did not feel at ease with his old friends any more. Ten years did not seem long to us, not really long, and we were disconcerted by the great change in him. Only his voice was familiar. At the bus station where three of us had gone to meet him only Dave Zobrowski recognized him.

Evan S. Connell, Jr., "The Walls of Ávila," in *The Anatomy Lesson and Other Stories* (New York: The Viking Press, 1957), pp. 83–112. Copyright 1957 by Evan S. Connell, Jr. Reprinted by permission of the Viking Press, Inc.

Apparently this town of Ávila meant a great deal to J. D., although he could not get across to us its significance. He said that one night he was surprised to hear music and laughter coming from outside the walls, so he hurried through the nearest gate, which was set between two gigantic watch towers, and followed the wall around until he came to a carnival. There were concessions where you could fire corks at cardboard boxes, each containing a chocolate bar, or dip for celluloid fishes with numbered bellies, and naturally there was a carousel, the same as in America. It rotated quite slowly, he said, with mirrors flashing from its peak while enameled stallions gracefully rose and descended on their gilded poles. But nothing was so well attended as a curious swing in which two people stood, facing each other, grasping a handle, and propelled themselves so high that at the summit they were nearly [84/85] upside down. The shadow of this swing raced up the wall and down again. "Like this!" J. D. exclaimed, gesturing, and he stared at each of us in turn to see if we understood. He said it was like the shadow of some grotesque instrument from the days of the Inquisition, and he insisted that if you gazed up into the darkness long enough you could make out, among the serrated ramparts of the ancient wall, the forms of helmeted men leaning on pikes and gazing somberly down while their black beards moved in the night wind.

He had tales of the Casbah in Tangiers and he had souvenirs from the ruins of Carthage. On his key chain was a fragment of polished stone, drilled through the center, that he had picked up from the hillside just beyond Tunis. And he spoke familarly of the beauty of Istanbul, and of Giotto's tower, and the Seine, and the golden doors of Ghiberti. He explained how the Portuguese are fuller through the cheeks than are the Spaniards, their eyes more indolent and mischievous, and how their songs—fados, he called them—were no more than lazy cousins of the fierce flamenco one heard throughout Andalusia.

When Zobrowski asked in what year the walls of Ávila were built J. D. thought for quite a while, his lean face sober while he gently rocked a tumbler of iced rum, but at last he said the fortifications were probably begun seven or eight hundred years ago. They had been repaired occasionally and were still impregnable to primitive force. It was queer, he added, to come upon such a place, indestructible when assaulted on its own terms, yet obsolete.

He had postal cards of things that had interested him. He had not carried a camera because he thought it bad manners. We did not completely understand what he [85/86] meant by this but we had no time to discuss it because he was running on, wanting to know if we were familiar with Giambologna, saying, as he displayed a card, "In a grotto of the Boboli Gardens not far from the Uffizi—" He stopped abruptly. It had occurred to him that he might be embarrassed. No one said anything. None of us had ever heard of the Boboli Gardens, or of the sculptor Giambologna, or of the Venus that J. D. had wanted to describe.

"Here's the Sistine Chapel, of course," he said, taking another card from his envelope. "That's the Libyan sybil."

"Yes," said Zobrowski. "I remember this. There was a print of it in one of our high-school textbooks. Good God, how time does pass."

"Those damn textbooks," J. D. answered. "They ruin everything. They've ruined Shakespeare and the Acropolis and half the things on earth that are really worth seeing. Just like the Lord's Prayer—I can't hear it. I don't know what it says. Why wasn't I left to discover it for myself? Or the Venus de Milo. I sat in front of it for an hour but I couldn't see it."

He brought out a postal card of a church tower. At the apex was a snail-like structure covered with what appeared to be huge tile baseballs.

"That's the *Sagrada Familia*," he explained. "It's not far from the bull ring in Barcelona."

The *Sagrada Familia* was unfinished; in fact it consisted of nothing but a façade with four tremendous towers rising far above the apartment buildings surrounding it. He said it was a landmark of Barcelona, that if you should get lost in the city you had only to get to a clearing and look around for this weird church. On the front of it was a cement Christmas tree, painted green and hung with cement [86/87] ornaments, while the tiled spires were purple and yellow. And down each spire ran vertical lettering that could be read a kilometer away. Zobrowski asked what was written on the towers.

"There's one word on each tower," said J. D. "The only one I recall is 'Ecstasy.'"

Dave Zobrowski listened with a patient, critical air, as though wondering how a man could spend ten years in such idle traveling. Russ Lyman, who had once been J. D.'s closest friend, listened in silence with his head bowed. When we were children together it had been Russ who intended to go around the world some day, but he had not, for a number of reasons. He seemed to hold a monopoly on bad luck. The girl he loved married somebody else, then his business failed, and so on and on through the years. Now he worked as a drugstore clerk and invested his pitiful savings in gold mines or wildcat oil wells. He had been thirty-two when the girl he loved told him good-by, tapping the ash from her cigarette onto his wrist to emphasize that she meant it; he promptly got drunk, because he could not imagine anything else to do, and a few days later he began going around with a stout, amiable girl named Eunice who had grown up on a nearby farm. One October day when the two of them were walking through an abandoned orchard they paused to rest in the shade of an old stone wall in which some ivy and small flowers were growing. Eunice was full of the delicate awkwardness of certain large girls, and while

Russell was looking at her a leaf came fluttering down to rest on her shoulder. He became aware of the sound of honeybees flickering through the noonday sun, and of the uncommonly sweet odor of apples moldering among the clover, and he was [87/88] seized with such passion that he immediately took the willing girl. She became pregnant, so they got married, although he did not want to, and before much longer he stopped talking about going around the world.

J. D., handing Russell a card of a little street in some North African town, remarked that on this particular street he had bought a tasseled red fez. And Russell nodded a bit sadly.

"Now, this is Lisbon," J. D. said. "Right over here on the far side of this rectangular plaza is where I lived. I used to walk down to the river that you see at the edge of the card, and on the way back I'd wander through some little shops where you can buy miniature galleons of filigreed gold."

"I suppose you bought one," said Zobrowski.

"I couldn't resist," said J. D. with a smile. "Here's a view of Barcelona at night, and right here by this statue of Columbus I liked to sit and watch the tide come sweeping in. An exact copy of the *Santa Maria* is tied up at the dock near the statue. And whenever the wind blew down from the hills I could hear the butter-pat clap of the gypsies dancing on the Ramblas." He looked at us anxiously to see if we were interested. It was clear that he loved Spain. He wanted us to love it, too.

"One time in Galicia," he said, "at some little town where the train stopped I bought a drink of water from a wrinkled old woman who was holding up an earthen jug and calling, '*Agua! Agua fria!*'" He drew a picture of the jug—it was called a *porrón*—and he demonstrated how it was to be held above your head while you drank. Your lips were never supposed to touch the spout. The Spaniards could drink without swallowing, simply letting the stream [88/89] of water pour down their throats, and after much dribbling and choking J. D. had learned the trick. But what he most wanted to describe was the old woman who sold him the water. She could have been sixty or ninety. She was toothless, barefoot, and with a rank odor, but somehow, in some way he could not get across to us, they had meant a great deal to each other. He tried to depict a quality of arrogance or ferocity about her, which in the days when she was young, must have caused old men to murmur and young men to fall silent whenever she passed by. He could not forget an instant when he reached out the train window to give her back the clay jug and met her deep, unwavering eyes.

"The train was leaving," he said, leaning forward. "It was leaving forever. And I heard her scream at me. I didn't know what she said, but there was a Spaniard in the same compartment who told me that this old Galician woman had screamed at me, 'Get off the train! Stay in my land!'" He paused, apparently remembering, and slowly shook his head.

It was in Spain, too, in a cheap water-front night club called *El Hidalgo*—and he answered Russell's question by saying that Don Quixote, for example, was an *hidalgo*—it was here that he fell in love for the only time in his life. The cabaret was in an alley of the Gothic quarter where tourists seldom ventured. J. D. often spent his evenings there, buying lottery tickets and brown paper cigarettes and drinking a yellowish wine called *manzanilla*. One night the flamenco dancers were in a furious mood—he said he could feel the tension gathering the way electricity will sometimes gather on a midwestern afternoon until it splits the air. An enormously fat gypsy woman was dancing [89/90] by herself, dancing the symbols of fertility that have survived a thousand generations. She was dressed in what he likened to a bedspread covered with orange polka dots. Raising and lowering her vast arms she snapped her fingers and angrily danced alone; then all at once a savage little man in high-heeled boots sprang out of the crowd and began leaping around her. The staccato of his boots made the floor tremble and caused the manzanilla to sway inside the bottles.

"Everybody was howling and clapping," said J. D., and he clapped once as the gypsies clap, not with the entire hand but with three fingers flat against the palm. It sounded like a pistol shot. "Somebody was looking at me," he went on. "I could feel someone's eyes on me. I looked into the shadows and saw her. She was about nineteen, very tall and imperial, with her hair in braids. She began walking toward me, and she was singing. She sang to me that her name was Paquita—"

"She was improvising a song," said Zobrowski.

J. D. nodded. "It had the sound of a lament. Those old tragedies you hear in Spain, they're paralyzing."

"Just what do you mean?" Zobrowski asked.

"I don't know," said J. D. "It's as if a dagger was still plunged to the hilt in her breast."

Zobrowski smiled. "Go on. No doubt this young woman was beautiful."

"Yes. And she never stopped looking at me. I don't remember what happened, but she must have walked across the room because I realized I was standing up and she was standing directly in front of me, touching my lips with one finger."

"I have had similar dreams," said Zobrowski. [90/91]

Russell was listening avidly. "I didn't think Spanish women could ever get away from their chaperons."

"*Dueña*, I believe, is the word," Zobrowski said.

"There was no *dueña* for that girl," answered J. D. He was silent for a little while and then concluded his story. "Later that night I saw her walking the streets."

"Well, that explains everything," Zobrowski smiled. "You simply mistook her professional interest in you for some sort of transcendental love."

J. D. looked at Dave Zobrowski for a long time, and finally said, "I didn't think I could make you understand." To Russell he said, "I find myself repeating her name. In the night I see her everywhere. In Paris, or in Rome, or even in this town, I see a girl turning away and my heart hesitates as it did that night in Barcelona."

"You should have married her," said Russell.

"I think he has done enough foolish things as it is," Zobrowski replied, and that seemed to end the matter. At least J. D. never referred to Paquita again. He spoke of the Andalusian gypsies, saying that they are a mixture of Arab and Indian, while the Catalonians are almost pure Sudra Indian. He gave this information as though it were important; he seemed to value knowledge for itself alone. But, looking into our faces, he saw that we could not greatly care about Spanish gypsies one way or another.

He had a pale gray cardboard folder with a drawing of St. George on the cover. Inside was a map of the geographical limits of the Catalan language, and this inscription: "With the best wishes for all the friends of the Catalan speaking countries once free in the past they will be free and whole again thanks to the will and strength of the Catalan people." [91/92]

This was a folder of the resistance movement; it had been given to him, at the risk of imprisonment and perhaps at the risk of life itself, by a charwoman of Valencia. Zobrowski inquired if these were the people who opposed Franco. J. D. said that was correct. In Algiers he had met a waiter who had fought against Franco and barely escaped the country; this waiter had been in Algiers since 1938 and had no hope of seeing his family again, though he believed, as the charwoman believed, that one day Spain would be free.

After inspecting the pathetic little folder Zobrowski suggested, "I can easily appreciate your concern for these people. However you might also spend some time considering your own situation. Frankly, time is getting on, while you elect to dawdle about the water fronts of the world."

J. D. shrugged.

"I've been meaning to ask," said Zobrowski. "Did you ever receive the letter I addressed to you in Vienna?"

"I don't remember it," said J. D.

"It concerned an executive position with the Pratt Hanover Company. They manufacture farm implements. I spoke to Donald Pratt about you and he was very much interested."

"No, I never got the letter," said J. D. and he grinned. "I was traveling quite a bit and I guess a lot of letters never caught up with me."

"Would you have come back if you had received the offer from Pratt?"

"No, I guess not," said J. D., rather apologetically.

"We've known each other a long time, haven't we?"

J. D. nodded. "Since we were kids, Dave." [92/93]

"Exactly. I would like to know how you manage to live."

"Oh, I work here and there. I had a job at the American embassy in Switzerland for a while, and to be honest about it, I've done some black marketing. I've learned how to get along, how to pull the levers that operate the world."

Then he began to describe Lucerne. It seemed far distant, in every dimension, from the days when we were children and used to bicycle down the river road to the hickory woods and hunt for squirrels. Each of us had a .22 rifle, except J. D., who went hunting with a lemonwood bow. He had made it himself, and he had braided and waxed the string, and sewn a quiver, and planed his arrows. He did not hit many squirrels with his equipment and we would often taunt him about losing the arrows among the high weeds and underbrush, but he never seemed to mind; he would go home to his father's tool chest in the basement and calmly set about planing another batch of sticks. We would watch him clip turkey feathers into crisp rhomboids and carefully glue them into place, bracing each feather with matchsticks until the glue hardened. We would sit on the wash tub, or on his father's work bench, and smoke pieces of grapevine while we studied the new arrows. When he fitted on the bronze tip and banded each arrow with hunter's green and white Russell would watch with an almost hypnotized expression. But Dave Zobrowski, even in those days, was puzzled and a trifle impatient with J. D.

Remembering such things as J. D.'s bow and arrow we could see that it was he, and not Russell, who was destined to go away. We thought he had left a good deal of value here in the midwest of America. Our town is not exotic, [93/94] but it is comprehensible and it is clean. This is partly due to Dave Zobrowski, who has always been vehement about cleanliness. That he grew up to become a physician and a member of the sanitary commission surprised no one. He likes to tell of disgusting conditions he has seen in other cities. While he was in Chicago at a medical convention he investigated a hotel charging the same price as the Pioneer House here in town, and he reported, all too graphically, how the ceiling was stained from leakage, how there was pencil writing on the walls, together with the husks of smashed roaches, and how he found a red hair embedded in the soap. Even the towel was rancid. Looking out the smoky window he saw wine bottles and decaying fruit in the gutter.

Visitors to this town often wonder how it is possible to exist without ballet, opera, and so forth, but it usually turns out that they themselves attend only once or twice each season, if at all. Then, too, if

you are not accustomed to a certain entertainment you do not miss it.
Russell, for example, grew up in a home devoid of music but cheerful
and harmonious all the same. To his parents music was pointless,
unless at Christmas time, when the phonograph would be wound up,
the needle replaced, and the carols dusted off; consequently Mozart
means nothing to him.

A Brooklyn police captain named Lehmbruck drove out here to
spend his vacation but went back east after a week, saying it was too
quiet to sleep. However he seemed to be interested in the sunset,
remarking that he had never seen the sun go down anywhere except
behind some buildings. And he had never eaten old ham—he studied
the white specks very dubiously, and with some embarrassment asked
if the ham was spoiled. The Chamber of Commerce [94/95] later
received a wistful little note from Captain Lehmbruck, hinting that he
might have another try at the prairie next summer.

Christmas here is still made instead of bought, even if we think no
more of Christ than anyone else. And during the summer months the
sidewalks are overhung with white or lavender spirea, and we can
watch the rain approaching, darkening the farmland. Life here is
reasonable and tradition not discounted, as evidenced by the new
public library which is a modified Parthenon of Tennessee marble.
There was a long and bitter argument about the inscription for its
façade. One group wanted the so-called living letter, while the majority
sought reassurance in the Doric past. At last we chiseled it with "Pvb-
lic," "Covnty," "Strvctvre," and so forth.

J. D. knew about all these things, but he must have wanted more,
and as he talked to us about his travels we could read in his restless
blue eyes that he was not through searching. We thought he would
come home when his father died, at least for a little while. Of course he
was six thousand miles away, but most men would have returned from
any distance. We did not know what he thought of us, the friends who
had been closest to him, and this was altogether strange because our
opinions about him were no secret—the fact that Russell envied him
and that Zobrowski thought his life was going to rot.

Russell, to be sure, envied everybody. For a time after the
marriage we believed Russell would collect himself, whatever it was
needed collecting, because he went around looking very pleased with
himself, although Eunice seemed a bit confused. He began to go
shooting in the hickory woods again, firing his old .22 more to exult in
its noise [95/96] than to kill a squirrel. Yet something within him had
been destroyed. Whether it could have been an insufferable jealousy of
J. D.—who was then in Finland—or love that was lost, or the hard core
of another sickness unknown to anyone on earth, no one could say, but
it was to be only a few years after J. D.'s visit that we would find
Russell lying in the garage with his head almost torn off and a black .45
service automatic in his hand.

"Here is where Dante first met Beatrice," said J. D. adding with a smile that several locations in Florence claimed this distinction, even as half the apartments in Toledo insist El Greco painted there. And he had a picture of Cala Ratjada where he had lived with a Danish girl named Vivian. We had forgotten, if indeed we had ever realized it, that in other countries people are not required to be so furtive about their affairs. We learned that Cala Ratjada was a fishing village on the eastern end of Majorca. Majorca we had heard of because the vacation magazines were publicizing it.

"I understand there's a splendid cathedral in the capital," Zobrowski said. "Palma, isn't it?"

J. D. agreed rather vaguely. It was plain he did not care much for cathedrals, unless there was something queer about them as there was about the *Sagrada Familia*. He preferred to tell about the windmills on Majorca, and about his bus ride across the island with a crate of chickens on the seat beside him. We had not known there was a bus across the island; the travel magazines always advised tourists to hire a car with an English-speaking driver. So we listened, because there is a subtle yet basic difference between one who travels and one who does not.

He had lived with this Danish girl all of one summer in [96/97] a boarding house—a *pension* he called it—and every afternoon they walked through some scrubby little trees to a white sandy beach and went swimming nude. They took along a leather bag full of heavy amber wine and drank this and did some fancy diving off the rocks. He said the Mediterranean there at Cala Ratjada was more translucent even than the harbor of Monte Carlo. When their wine was finished and the sand had become cool and the shadows of the trees were touching the water they walked back to the village. For a while they stopped on the embarcadero to watch the Balearic fishermen spreading their nets to dry. Then J. D. and the Danish girl returned to the *pension* for dinner. They ate such things as fried octopus, or baby squid, or a huge seafood casserole called a *paella*.

"Where is she now?" Russell asked.

"Vivian?" said J. D. "Oh, I don't know. She sent me a card from Frederikshavn a year or so ago. She'd been wanting to go to India, so maybe that's where she is now."

"Didn't she expect you to marry her?"

J. D. looked at Russell and then laughed out loud; it was the first time he had laughed all evening.

"Neither of us wanted to get married," he said. "We had a good summer. Why should we ruin it?"

This was a kind of reasoning we were aware of, via novels more impressive for poundage than content; otherwise it bore no relation to us. What bound them together was as elementary as a hyphen, and we suspected they could meet each other years later without embarrassment. They had loved without aim or sense, as young poets do. We could imagine this, to be sure, but we could not imagine it actually happening. There were women in our town, matrons now, with whom we had been intimate to [97/98] some degree a decade or so ago, but now when we met them, or were entertained in their homes, we were restrained by the memory of the delicate past. Each of us must carry, as it were, a balloon inked with names and dates.

So far as we knew, J. D. looked up only one of the women he used to know here in town. He called on Helen Louise Sawyer who used to win the local beauty contests. When we were young most of us were afraid of her, because there is something annihilating about too much beauty; only J. D. was not intimidated. Perhaps he could see then what we learned to see years later—that she was lonely, and that she did not want to be coveted for the perfection of her skin or for the truly magnificent explosion of her bosom. When Helen Louise and J. D. began going around together we were astonished and insulted because Russell, in those days, was much more handsome than J. D., and Dave Zobrowski was twice as smart. All the same she looked at no one else. Then he began leaving town on longer and longer expeditions. He would return wearing a southern California sport shirt, or with a stuffed grouper he had caught off Key West. Helen Louise eventually went into the real-estate business.

He telephoned her at the office and they went to dinner at the Wigwam, which is now the swank place to eat. It is decorated with buffalo skins and tomahawks and there are displays of flint arrowheads that have been picked up by farmers in neighboring counties. The only incongruities are the pink jade ashtrays that, by midnight, seem to have been planted with white, magenta-tipped stalks to remind the diners that a frontier has vanished. And well it has. The scouts are buried, the warriors mummified. Nothing but [98/99] trophies remain: a coup stick hung by the Wigwam's flagstone hearth, a pipe smoked by Satanta, a cavalry saber and a set of moldering blue gloves crossed on the mantel, a tan robe laced to the western wall, a dry Pawnee scalp behind the bar. The wind still sweeps east from the lofty Colorado plains, but carries with it now only the clank of machinery in the wheat fields. The Mandans have gone, like the minor chords of an Iowa death song, with Dull Knife and Little Wolf whose three hundred wretched squaws and starving men set out to fight their way a thousands miles to the fecund Powder River that had been their home.

There is a gratification to the feel of history behind the places one has known, and the Wigwam's historical display is extensive. In addition, the food is good. There is hot biscuit with clover honey, and the old ham so mistrusted by Captain Lehmbruck of Brooklyn. There are Missouri fried chicken, spare ribs, venison with mushrooms, catfish, beef you can cut with a fork, wild rice and duck buried under pineapple sauce, as well as various European dishes. That evening J. D.

asked for a certain Madeira wine and apparently was a little taken aback to find that the Wigwam had it. Travelers, real travelers, come to think of their homes as provincial and are often surprised.

Helen Louise had metamorphosed, as even we could see, and we knew J. D. was in for a shock. Through the years she had acquired that faintly resentful expression that comes from being stared at, and she seemed to be trying to compensate for her beauty. Although there was nothing wrong with her eyes she wore glasses; she had cropped her beautiful golden hair to a Lesbian style; and somehow she did not even walk the way she used to. The pleasing undulations had mysteriously given way to a militant stride. [99/100] Her concern in life was over such items as acreage and location. At the business she was quite good; every real-estate man in town hated her, no doubt thinking she should have become a housewife instead of the demon that she was. But apparently she had lost her desire to marry, or sublimated it. At the lunch hour she could be seen in an expensive suit, speaking in low tones to another businesswoman, and her conversation when overheard would be, "...referred the order to me...Mrs. Pabst's opinion... second mortgage...bought six apartments..."

We guessed that J. D.'s evening with Helen Louise might be an indication that he had grown tired of wandering around the earth, and that he wanted to come home for good. Helen Louise, if no longer as voluptuous as she had been at twenty or twenty-five, was still provocative, and if she married was it not possible she might come to look very much as she had looked ten years before? But J. D. had very little to say about his evening with her; and after he was gone Helen Louise never mentioned him.

"Did you know that in Cadiz," he said—because it was to him a fact worth noting, like that fact that in Lisbon he had lived on a certain plaza—"Did you know that in Cadiz you can buy a woman for three *pesetas?*" Whether or not he might have been referring to Helen Louise we did not know, nor did anyone ask.

"Once I talked with Manolete," he said, as though it were the first line of a poem.

"I've heard that name," Zobrowski answered. "He's a toreador, is he not?"

"I think 'toreador' was invented by Bizet," J. D. replied. "Manolete was a matador. But he's dead. It was in Linares that he was *cogido*. On the twenty-seventh of August in [100/101] nineteen-forty-seven. At five in the afternoon, as the saying goes." And he continued, telling us that the real name of this bullfighter had been Manuel Rodriguez, and that after he was gored in Linares the ambulance which was taking him to a hospital started off in the wrong direction, and there was a feeling of bitterness in Spain when the news was broadcast that he was dead of his wounds.

"What you are trying to express," Zobrowski suggested, "is that this fellow was a national hero."

"Yes," said J. D.

"Like Babe Ruth."

"No," said J. D. instantly and with a vexed expression. He gestured helplessly and then shrugged. He went on to say that he happened to be in Heidelberg when death came for Manolete in the town of Linares. He looked around at us as if this circumstance were very strange. As he spoke he gestured excitedly and often skipped from one topic to another because there was so little time and he had so much to tell us. In a way he created a landscape of chiaroscuro, illuminating first one of his adventures and now another, but leaving his canvas mostly in shadow.

"One morning in Basle," he said, "it began to snow while I was having breakfast. Snow was falling on the Rhine." He was sitting by a window in a tea shop overlooking the river. He described the sunless, blue-gray atmosphere with large white flakes of snow piling up on the window ledge, and the dark swath of the river. Several waitresses in immaculate uniforms served his breakfast from a heavy silver tray. There was coffee in a silver pitcher, warm breads wrapped in thick linen napkins, and several kinds of jam and preserves; all the while the snow kept mounting on the ledge just outside the window, and [101/102] the waitresses murmured in German. He returned to Basle on the same morning of the following year—all the way from Palermo—just to have his breakfast there.

Most of his ten years abroad had been spent on the borders of the Mediterranean, and he agreed with Zobrowski's comment that the countries in that area must be the dirtiest in Europe. He told about a servant girl in one of his *pensions* who always seemed to be on her knees scrubbing the floor, but who never bathed herself. She had such a pervasive odor that he could tell whenever she had recently been in a room.

He said that Pompeii was his biggest disappointment. He had expected to find the city practically buried under a cliff of lava. But there was no lava. Pompeii was like any city abandoned and overgrown with weeds. He had visited the Roman ruins of North Africa, but the names he mentioned did not mean anything to us. Carthage did, but if we had ever read about the others in school we had long since stored their names and dates back in the dusty bins alongside algebra and Beowulf. Capri was the only celebrated spot he visited that surpassed all pictures of it, and he liked Sorrento too, saying that he had returned to the mainland about sundown when the cliffs of Sorrento become red and porous like the cliffs of the Grand Canyon. And in a town called Amalfi he had been poisoned—he thought it was the eggs.

All this was delivered by a person we had known since childhood, yet it might as well have come from a foreign lecturer. J. D. was not trying to flaunt his adventures; he described them because we were his friends and he could not conceive of the fact that the ruins of Pompeii would mean less to us than gossip on the women's page. He [102/103] wanted to tell us about the ballet in Cannes, where the audience was so quiet that he had heard the squeak of the dancer's slippers. But none of us had ever been to a ballet, or especially wanted to go. There was to us something faintly absurd about men and women in tights. When Zobrowski suggested as much, J. D. looked at him curiously and seemed to be struggling to remember what it was like to live in our town.

A number of things he said did not agree with our concept. According to him the Swedish girls are not in the least as they appear on calendars, which invariably depict them driving some cows down a pea-green mountainside. J. D. said the Swedes were long and gaunt with cadaverous features and gloomy dispositions, and their suicide rate was among the highest on earth.

Snails, he said, though no one had inquired, have very little taste. You eat them with a tiny two-pronged fork and some tongs that resemble a surgeon's forceps. The garlic-butter sauce is excellent, good enough to drink, but snail meat tasted to him rubbery like squid.

About the taxi drivers of Paris: they were incredibly avaricious. If you were not careful they would give you a gilded two-franc piece instead of a genuine fifty-franc piece for change, and if you caught them at it they became furious. But he did say that the French were the most urbane people to be found.

He had traveled as far east as Teheran and as far north as Trondheim. He had been to Lithuania and to Poland, and to Egypt and to the edge of the Sahara, and from his gestures as well as the animation of his voice we could tell he was not through yet. While he was telling us about his plans as we sat comfortably in the cocktail lounge of the [103/104] Pioneer House, a bellboy came in and respectfully said to Dave, "Dr. Zobrowski, the hospital is calling."

Without a word Zobrowski stood up and followed the boy. A few minutes later he returned wearing his overcoat and carrying his gray Homburg. "I'm sorry, but it's an emergency," he said to us all, and then to J. D., "Since you are not to be in town much longer I suppose this is goodby."

J. D. uncrossed his long legs and casually stood up.

"No doubt you lead an entertaining life," Zobrowski observed, not bothering to conceal his disapproval. "But a man cannot wander the face of the earth forever."

"That's what everybody tells me," J. D. answered with a grin. "It doesn't bother me much any more."

Zobrowski pulled on his yellow pigskin gloves and with a severe expression he began to settle the fingers as carefully as though he had put on surgical gloves. "In my opinion," he said suddenly, and lifted his eyes, "you are a damn fool."

They stared at each other for perhaps a minute, not with hostility, nor exactly with surprise, but as though they had never quite seen each other until that instant. Yet these were the two men who, about thirty years previously, had chipped in equal shares to buy a dog, a squat little beast with peculiar teeth that made it look like a beaver.

"From birth we carry the final straw," said Zobrowski at last.

J. D. only smiled.

Zobrowski's normally hard features contracted until he looked cruel, and he inclined his head, saying by this gesture, "As you wish." He had always known how to use [104/105] silence with devastating force, yet J. D. was undismayed and did nothing but shrug like a Frenchman.

Zobrowski turned to Russell. "I had lunch with my broker the other day. He has some information on that Hudson's Bay mining stock of yours that makes me feel we should have a talk. Stop by my office tomorrow morning at eight-thirty. I have had my receptionist cancel an appointment because of this matter."

Russell's mouth slowly began to drop open as he gazed at Zobrowski. He never made reasonable investments and several times had been saved from worse ones only because he confided his financial plans, along with everything else, to anybody who would listen. Then, too, the making of money necessitates a callousness he had never possessed.

"That stock's all right," he said weakly. "I'm positive it's all right. Really it is, Dave. You should have bought some."

"Yes," Zobrowski said, looking down on him with disgust. And turning to J. D. he said, "Let us hear from you. Good-by." Then he went striding across the lounge.

"Oh, God!" mumbled Russell, taking another drink. He was ready to weep from humiliation and from anxiety over the investment. In the past few years he had become quite bald and flabby, and had taken to wearing suspenders because a belt disturbed his intestines. He rubbed his jowls and looked around with a vague, desperate air.

"Whatever happened to little Willie Grant?" J. D. asked, though Grant had never meant a thing to him.

"He's—he's in Denver," Russell said, gasping for breath.

"What about Martha Mathews?"

This was the girl who rejected Russell, but J. D. was [105/106] abroad when it happened and may never have heard. He looked astonished when Russell groaned. Economically speaking, she was a great deal better off than if she had married Russell. She had accepted a housing contractor with more ambition than conscience, and now spent most of her time playing cards on the terrace of the country club.

J. D. had been in love, moderately, in the abstract, with a long-legged sloe-eyed girl named Minnette whose voice should have been poured into a glass and drunk. Her mother owned a bakery. We usually saw Minnette's mother when we came trotting home from school at the noon hour; she would be standing at the door with arms rolled in her apron while she talked to the delivery man, or, in winter time, we would often see her as she bent over, pendulous, tranquil, somehow everlasting, to place chocolate éclairs in the bakery window while sleet bounced indignantly off the steaming glass. At such moments she looked the way we always wanted our own harried mothers to look. If the truth were known it might be that we found her more stimulating than her daughter, although this may have been because we were famished when we passed the bakery. In any event he inquired about Minnette, so we told him her eyes still had that look, and that she was married to the mortician, an extremely tall man named Knopf who liked to underline trenchant phrases in the little books on Success that you buy for a quarter.

Answering these somehow anachronistic questions stirred us the way an old snapshot will do when you come upon it while hunting for something else. Later on Russell was to say that when J. D. mentioned the yellow brick building where the four of us began our schooling he remembered [106/107] for the first time in possibly a decade how we used to sit around a midget table and wield those short, blunt, red-handled scissors. We had a paste pot and sheets of colored paper, and when our labors were done the kindergarten windows displayed pumpkins, Christmas trees, owls, eggs, rabbits, or whatever was appropriate to the season. J. D. could always draw better than anyone else. When visiting night for parents came around it would be his work they admired. David Zobrowski, of course, was the scholar; we were proud to be Dave's best friends. Russell managed to remain undistinguished in any way until time for the singing class. Here no one could match him. Not that anyone wanted to. He sang worse than anyone who ever attended our school. It was as if his voice operated by a pulley, and its tenor was remotely canine. The class consisted of bluebirds and robins, with the exception of Russ who was placed at a separate desk and given no designation at all. Usually he gazed out the window at the interminable fields, but when it came to him that he, too, could sing, and his jaw began to work and his throat to contract, he would be warned into silence by the waving baton. It hurt his feelings very much.

Going to and from the business district ordinarily meant passing this musty little building, which had long since been converted into headquarters for the Boy Scout troop, and which now related to us no more than the Wizard of Oz, but until J. D. spoke of it we had not realized that the swings and the slide were gone, and crab grass was growing between the bricks of the front walk.

When we were in high school J. D. occasionally returned to

wander through the corridors of the elementary school. The rest of us had been glad enough to move on [107/108] and we considered his visits a bit queer, but otherwise never paused to think about them.

These were the streets where we had lived, these the houses, during a period of time when today could not influence tomorrow, and we possessed the confidence to argue about things we did not understand. Though, of course, we still did that. On winter nights we dropped away to sleep while watching the snow come drifting by the street light, and in summer we could see the moths outside the screens fluttering desperately, as though to tell us something. Our childhood came and went before we were ready to grasp it. Things were different now. The winged seeds that gyrate down from the trees now mean nothing else but that we must sweep them from the automobile hood because stains on the finish lower the trade-in value. Now, in short, it was impractical to live as we used to live with the abandon of a mule rolling in the dust.

In those days our incipient manhood had seemed a unique power, and our single worry that some girl might become pregnant. We danced with our eyes closed and our noses thrust into the gardenias all the girls wore in their hair, meanwhile estimating our chances. And, upon discovering literature, thanks to the solemn pedantry of a sophomore English teacher, we affected bow ties and cigarette holders and were able to quote contemporary poets with a faintly cynical tone.

On a postcard of a Rotterdam chocolate factory, sent to Russell but addressed to us all, J. D. scribbled, "I see nothing but the noon dust a-blowing and the green grass a-growing." If not contemporary it was at least familiar, and caused Zobrowski to remark, with a certain unconscious measure, "As fond as I am of him I sometimes lose [108/109] patience. In a furrow he has found a feather of Pegasus and what should have been a blessing has become a curse."

Now J. D. was inquiring after one or two we had forgotten, or who had moved away, leaving no more trace than a cloud, and about a piano teacher who had died one sultry August afternoon on the streetcar. Yet his interest was superficial. He was being polite. He could not really care or he would not have gone away for ten years. He wondered whatever became of the bearded old man who used to stand on a street corner with a stack of Bibles and a placard promising a free copy of the New Testament to any Jew who would renounce the faith. We did not know what happened to the old man; somehow he had just vanished. Quite a few things were vanishing.

J. D. cared very little for the men who had once been our fraternity brothers, which was odd because in our hearts we still believed that those days and those men had been so extraordinary that people were still talking about them. Yet we could recall that he took no pride in being associated with them. The militant friendship of fraternity life made him surly. He refused to shake hands as often as he was expected to. We had been warned that, as pledges, we would be thrown into the river some night. This was part of learning to become a finer man. When the brothers came for us about three o'clock one morning, snatching away our blankets and singing the good fellowship song, we put up the traditional fight—all of us except J. D. He refused to struggle. He slumped in the arms of his captors as limp as an empty sack. This puzzled and annoyed the brothers, who held him aloft by his ankles and who bounced his head on the floor. He would not even open his eyes. They jabbed him stiffly in the ribs, they [109/110] twisted his arms behind his back, they kicked him in the pants, they called him names, and finally, very angry, they dragged him to the river and flung him in. But even when he went sailing over the bullrushes he was silent as a corpse. Strangely, he did not hit the water with a loud splash. Years later he told us that he twisted at the last moment and dove through the river scum, instead of landing flat on his back as Russell did. They vanished together, as roommates should, but Russell was again audible in a few seconds—thrashing back to shore, where the brothers helped him out and gave him a towel and a bathrobe and a drink of brandy.

J. D., however, did not reappear. Even before Russell had reached the shore we were beginning to worry about J. D. There was no moon that night and the river had an evil look. We stood in a row at the edge of the water. We heard the bullfrogs, and the dark bubbling and plopping of whatever calls the river home, but nothing more. And all at once the structure of the fraternity collapsed. The last vestige of unity disappeared. We were guilty individuals. Some people began lighting matches and peering into the river, while others called his name. But there was no answer, except in the form of rotten, half-submerged driftwood floating, by, revolving in the sluggish current, and, beyond the confused whispering, the brief, crying shadows of night birds dipping in wild alarm over the slimy rushes.

When we saw him again we asked what happened, but several years passed before he told anyone. Then he said—and only then was his revenge complete—"Oh, I just swam under water as far as I could. After that I let the river carry me out of sight." He swam ashore a mile or two downstream, and by a back road he returned to the fraternity [110/111] house. Nobody was there; everybody was at the river searching for his body. The fraternity was almost ruined because of J. D.

Now he had climbed the Matterhorn, and we were not surprised. He knew what it was like in Venice, or in Copenhagen, and as we reflected on his past we came to understand that his future was inevitable. We knew he would leave us again, perhaps forever.

Russell, tamping out a cheap cigar, said boldly, "Eunice and I have been thinking about a trip to the Bahamas next year, or year after." He considered the nicotine on his fingertips, and after a pause, because his boast was empty, and because he knew that we knew how empty it was, he added, "Though it depends." He began picking helplessly at his fingertips. He would never go anywhere.

"You'll like the Bahamas," J. D. said.

"We consider other places," Russell said unexpectedly, and there were tears in his eyes.

J. D. was watching him with a blank, pitiless gaze.

"I think I'll go to Byzantium," Russell said.

"That doesn't exist any more."

Russell took a deep breath to hush the panic that was on him, and at last he said, "Well, gentlemen, I guess I'd better get some shut-eye if I'm going to talk business with Dave in the morning."

"It's late," J. D. agreed.

Then we asked when he would be coming home for good, although it was a foolish question, and J. D. laughed at it. Later, in talking about him, we would recall his reason for not wanting to live here. He had explained that the difference between our town and these other places he had been was that when you go walking down a boulevard [111/112] in some strange land and you see a tree burgeoning you understand that this is beautiful, and there comes with the knowledge a moment of indescribable poignance in the realization that as this tree must die, so will you die. But when, in the home you have always known, you find a tree in bud you think only that spring has come again. Here he stopped. It did not make much sense to us, but for him it had meaning of some kind.

So we asked when he would be coming back for another visit. He said he didn't know. We asked what was next. He replied that as soon as he could scrape together a few more dollars he thought he might like to see the Orient.

"They say that in Malaya . . ." he began, with glowing eyes. But we did not listen closely. He was not speaking to us anyway, only to himself, to the matrix which had spawned him and to the private god who guided him. His voice reached us faintly, as if from beyond the walls of Ávila. [112]

QUESTIONS FOR STUDY, DISCUSSION, AND WRITING

Perspectives

Adams: *American Ideals*. What was the basis of the American claim in 1796 that Europe was a full century behind America? What, according to Adams, were the characteristics of the American society at that time? What goals spurred the ambitious man forward? What were the ideals of Jefferson that paralleled those of the nation? How did they appear to be illusory ideals? For what reason was "the charge that Americans were too fond of money to win the confidence of Europeans ... a curious inconsistency"? What purpose other than money getting did American inventions and technical improvements serve? In general, how did the ideals of America help to spur the American people toward success?

Weber: *The Spirit of Capitalism*. What is the basic difference between the view of life described by Franklin and that suggested by the remark of Jacob Fugger? What is the particular ethos of modern capitalism? In what way is Franklin's attitude "closely connected with certain religious ideas"? According to Weber, in what way does the spirit of modern capitalism affect the entire society, even its non-business aspects? By what means does the spirit of capitalism give a religious sanction to secular success?

Griswold: *Three Puritans on Prosperity*. What features of America have been important in encouraging the pursuit of material success? How does Cotton Mather, in his *Two Brief Discourses*, give religious sanction to man's quest for wealth and success in his occupation? Does Griswold believe that the social ethics of the Puritans were the result of their religion or of the frontier environment? What is Franklin's contribution to the Puritan attention to material prosperity? Does Griswold think he was sincere in his advice about morality? On what grounds other than the traditionally Puritan ones does Timothy Dwight justify the acquisition of money?

Lerner: *The Rise and Decline of the Titan*. How do the observations of De Tocqueville support the thesis expounded by Weber and Griswold? What answer does Adams ("American Ideals") have to the charge made by Charles Dickens? How do the remarks of James Parton reveal that the Puritan ethic was still popular in the 1870s? What were the attitudes of the muckrakers and the novelists toward the Titan? What are the characteristics of the two types of Titans that Lerner describes? What changes in the image of the Titan took place following World War I and during the Great Depression? What effect has the corporation had on the Titan? Why?

Mills: *The New Entrepreneur*. What are the three types of organization that combine to form the personnel of the bureaucratic business? What two types of managers most closely fit the bureaucratic stereotype? What are the principal characteristics of the New Entrepreneur? How does he differ from what Lerner describes as the Titan? What conditions in the business world have created the New Entrepreneur? What determines his success? How does his definition of success differ from that of the types Mills calls "the glum men" and "the old veterans"?

The Promise of Success

Crèvecoeur: *What Is an American?* What are the differences, according to Crèvecoeur, between life and society in America and in Europe? What are the characteristics of the American people? Compare Crèvecoeur's definition of the American with the one given by Adams. What is the role of government in providing a setting for the belief in the possibilities for success?

Greeley: *Advice to Young Men*. What are the principal requirements for success discussed by Greeley? How does Greeley reflect the earlier statements of Franklin and Crèvecoeur?

Conwell: *Acres of Diamonds*. What does Conwell mean by the phrase "acres of diamonds"? What arguments does Conwell use to support his statement that it is man's duty to get rich? Is he reflecting the Puritan attitude discussed by Griswold? How does Conwell relate religion and the acquisition of material wealth? What is Conwell's definition of a successful man?

Dreiser: *The City of My Dreams*. What does Dreiser see as the particular charm of New York? In what way is it a city not only of Dreiser's dreams but of American dreams? Why does Dreiser refer to the dream as an "illusion," a "hypnosis deep and moving"? Which remarks of Adams in "American Ideals" touch upon the subject of this essay?

Success in a Changing America

Franklin: *Arriving at Moral Perfection*. What was Franklin's purpose in his "bold and arduous project of arriving at moral perfection"? What do you infer to be Franklin's definition of morality? Which of his virtues have only utilitarian value? To which of the virtues did he attribute his success? Do Franklin's comments on the usefulness of his virtues agree with what Max Weber says of Franklin's virtues?

Alger: *First Lessons for Sam Barker*. What clear parallels in morality and didacticism exist between Alger and Franklin? How does Alger's formula for success parallel the advice in Andrew Carnegie's "The Road to Business Success"?

Carnegie: *The Road to Business Success*. What points of Carnegie's advice reflect his strong religious background? Are the virtues that he advocates based upon moral or upon utilitarian considerations? What does he say about the acquisition of wealth as an end in itself? What does he consider the proper use of wealth? Compare Carnegie's concept of the businessman with that implicit in Sinclair Lewis's description of George F. Babbitt.

Fitzgerald: *Gatsby's General Resolves*. What two standards of success are dramatized by this selection? Does Mr. Gatz have any understanding of what his son's life had meant? What comment does the selection make on the Franklin-Alger formula for success?

Peale: *Positive Thinking*. What vestiges of the American promise of success are evident in this selection? What definition of success is implicit in Dr. Peale's remarks? What applicability does the first point of Dr. Peale's formula have to the central characters of Mark Twain, Sherwood Anderson, and John Cheever (in the selections included under "Dissident Voices")? What changes in American society can be deduced by comparing Dr. Peale's formula with Franklin's? Does Dr. Peale in any way follow in the tradition of Cotton Mather (see Griswold's comments on Mather and his quotations from Mather)?

Lincoln: *The Short and Simple Annals of A. Lincoln*. Which of Lincoln's statements suggest that he was not eager to disguise his humble origins? What general features of the sketch are in keeping with Lincoln's reputation for humility? What do the circumstances of the grandfather's death suggest about the Lincoln family? Why would Lincoln include this information? Why should Lincoln's election as captain of volunteers have given him more pleasure than any other success he had up to the time of writing?

Howells: *The Rise of a Rustic Boy*. To what qualities does Howells attribute Lincoln's success? In discussing Lincoln's wealth, how does Howells relate money to success as well as to virtue in a way that would satisfy both Franklin and John Woolman? Which of the characteristics of Lincoln would account for the great admiration Walt

Whitman had for Lincoln, despite Whitman's comment on the Presidency in "When I Peruse the Conquer'd Fame"?

Dell: *A Self-Made Man*. What comment does Dell make on the Puritan ethic? How do his virtues differ from Lincoln's (as portrayed by Howells)? In what way is MacDougall successful? In what way is Andrew March a failure? Is he, despite his self-image of virtue and innocence, a hypocrite like Babbitt, willing to set aside moral convictions when they interfere with business opportunity? Is Dell's portrait of Andrew March ironic?

Crane: *The Trees in the Garden*. What do the flowers in the poem symbolize? What answers does Crane expect us to give to the father's two questions? Explain how the poem illustrates a Darwinian view of success.

Dreiser: *Evolution of a Financier*. After his observations of the lobster and the squid, what place would moral values have in the economic and political outlook of Frank Cowperwood? What does he think leads to success? What leads to failure? What is Dreiser's attitude toward Cowperwood? Does he consider Cowperwood a success or a failure? Do Max Weber's comments on the capitalistic rule of action help to explain Cowperwood's philosophy?

Dreiser: *The Titan and the Governor*. How do the philosophical assumptions about life that Cowperwood formed in the previous selection manifest themselves in this episode? What is the principal difference between the views of Swanson and Cowperwood? How does Dreiser indicate their mutual respect? Does Cowperwood conduct himself as though he regards his proposal as immoral, or merely amoral?

Dos Passos: *Main Chance, 1919*. What personal qualities of Richard Savage account for his rapid rise in rank? Is Savage pleased with himself? Why does the memory of Dirty Gertie's face linger with Savage? What values has he exchanged for rank and comfort? Is he consciously ambitious, or does he allow himself to be carried up on the basis of family reputation? Is he primarily a success or a failure?

Dos Passos: *The Big Money*. What characteristics of Richard Savage in the preceding selection are illustrated in this selection? What characteristics of E. R. Bingham suggest that Dos Passos might have deliberately modeled him after the pattern of the successful man described in Carnegie's essay and in Alger's stories? Is the portrait of Bingham a satirical one? Are there any suggestions of Bingham's hypocrisy? Do Bingham's ideas in any way resemble those of Frank Cowperwood?

Marquand: *A Promotion*. What, according to this selection, are the personal qualities necessary for success within a corporation? Why is Charles Gray preferred to Roger Blakesley for the opening? What does Marquand suggest when he says of Charley's success: "It was what he had dreamed of long ago and yet it was not the true texture of early dreams"? How does Charley define success? What is Marquand's attitude toward such a definition? Does Charley's situation illustrate the changes in business success discussed by Lerner and Mills?

Dissident Voices

Woolman: *A Plea for the Poor*. What are Woolman's objections to wealth? How does excessive attention to business make it difficult for one to lead a virtuous life? Why does Woolman object to "self-exaltation"? What is man's principal business, according to Woolman?

Cooper: *The Opportunist*. How do Bragg's table habits suggest his "go-ahead-ism"? How has Bragg's career demonstrated his concern with the main chance? How do his attitudes suggest his social vulgarity? In what ways do Cooper's attitudes toward the contrasts between Europe and America differ from Crèvecoeur's? How does the portrait of Bragg reflect the European attitude toward the "hard, practical, money-getting American democrat" described by Henry Adams in "American Ideals"?

Hawthorne: *The Great Stone Face*. In what way do Ernest's attitudes toward the responsibility of wealthy men parallel Woolman's statements? Why, in addition to the fact that Old Blood-and-Thunder does not resemble the Great Stone Face, does Ernest regard him as an unlikely person to fulfill the prophecy? What does Old Stony Phiz lack that the great man should possess? What definition of success is implicit in the story?

Emerson: *Success*. How does Emerson characterize the examples of success with which he opens his essay? In what way is egotism, according to Emerson, related to success? How does the example of Michelangelo contrast with what Emerson calls "shallow Americanism"? What, according to Emerson, constitutes success? In what ways can Emerson be regarded as a precursor of Norman Vincent Peale?

Emerson: *Days*. What type of success (as described in the preceding essay) is symbolized in the poem by "herbs and apples"? What gifts symbolize the more significant type of success? How, in the poem, is a person's relative success or failure determined?

Thoreau: *Life without Principle*. What does Thoreau consider to be the real business of living? What enterprizes does he consider worthwhile? What does he mean about embarking from his native port as soon as he came of age? How do the characters in the Cooper and Hawthorne selections reflect Thoreau's statements?

Whitman: *Four Poems*. In what specific statements or images does Whitman clarify his views about his own success or failure? How do these poems reveal that Whitman was an admirer of the writings of both Emerson and Thoreau?

Twain: *Story of the Bad Little Boy*. What generalizations about the "Sunday-school books" can you make on the basis of this story?

How do Twain's remarks about Jim's luck and his charmed life make a comment on the typical Alger story?

Bellamy: *The Coach of Capitalism*. Identify the elements of the allegory in terms of their economic and social counterparts. What economic condition is meant by a "specially bad piece of road"? What is the attitude of those in the coach toward those doing the toiling? What is the attitude of the coach riders toward themselves? What comment is Bellamy making about the effect of passing generations on social-class distinctions?

Lewis: *A Servant of Society*. For what reason is Babbitt in business? What are his goals? How is he revealed in the selection as a hypocrite, liar, fraud, and cheat? Is Babbitt portrayed as an individual or as a type? Does Lewis seem to be suggesting that the pursuit of economic success is necessarily a morally corrupting pursuit?

Dos Passos: *Emperor of the Caribbean*. At the end of the sketch, Dos Passos himself asks the most revealing questions about Minor C. Keith? What would be John Woolman's answer and the reasons for his answer?

Twain: *Millions and Millions*. What accounts for Colonel Sellers's failure? How does the supper-table setting provide an appropriate introduction to the chapter? What does Twain suggest about business success through his contrasting descriptions of Colonel Sellers and General Boswell?

Robinson: *Richard Cory*. What comment does this poem make about the value of riches and success? What do the townspeople have that Cory does not have?

Dreiser: "*Vanity, Vanity*," *Saith the Preacher*. What is X——'s definition of success? What are the characteristics of the period which the life of X—— "clearly and effectively" illustrates? What is Dreiser's attitude toward X——? Does X—— share the dream that Dreiser describes in "The City of My Dreams"?

Anderson: *The Egg*. How does Anderson account for his parents' "passion for getting up in the world"? In what way does Anderson suggest the danger of the American promise of success? What does he accomplish through his discussion of the grotesque chicks? Why does the father fail in his pursuit of success?

Fitzgerald: *The Crack-Up*. What were the ingredients of Fitzgerald's "infantile dream"? What led to its dissolution? What was the ultimate effect on Fitzgerald of his illness during college? What was Fitzgerald's attitude toward the rich? What had been his principal values? What caused their deterioration? What was his answer to his despair? What values did he substitute for the ones he had lost? Does he suggest that his state of mind is peculiar to him or that it is a common experience?

Cheever: *The Pot of Gold*. In what ways do Colonel Sellers and Ralph Whittemore, both of whom have visions of fortune, differ? Is

Cheever's treatment of Ralph and Laura satiric, as is Twain's portrait of Sellers? What is the tragedy in the lives of the Whittemores?

Cross Currents

Connell: *The Walls of Ávila*. Many features of this story have parallels in earlier selections. How, for instance, is Russell reminiscent of the characters in the stories by Anderson and Cheever? In what ways do Dave Zobrowski's attitudes and values reflect those basic to the Puritan ethic? What earlier characters or writers does J. D. resemble? How are his values similar to those of the transcendentalists? What is the attitude of the unnamed third friend, the narrator of the story, toward J. D.? How does he reveal that J. D., even in his youth, sought a type of fulfillment that popular goals could not satisfy? Does the contrast between American life and European life parallel the contrasts described by Henry Adams in "American Ideals"?

SUGGESTIONS FOR
FURTHER READING

In the first days of exploration America was recognized as a land of opportunity for men of industry. John Smith, in *A True Relation* (1608) and again in *A Description of New England* (1616), describes the new continent as a promising place for "men that have great spirits, and small means." Similar statements were found in the so-called "pamphlets of news" such as Francis Higginson's *New England's Plantation* (1630) and William Wood's *New England's Prospect* (1634). Public statements about opportunity as it existed on the American shores were often found in the writings from the continent. The fact of opportunity is a necessary corollary to the "noble savage" concept in the early-eighteenth-century literature of England or in the principles of Montesquieu or the idealizations of Chateaubriand, and it proves a starting point for the social philosophies of John Locke and Jean-Jacques Rousseau. Many European observers of American manners, however, saw dangers in the leveling process that they witnessed. Alexis de Tocqueville in his influential *Democracy in America* (1835, 1840), though sympathetic to what he realized the Americans were attempting, was nevertheless disturbed by evidence of vulgarizations of morals and manners, as was Michel Chevalier in *Society, Manners, and Politics in the United States: Being a Series of Letters on North America* (1834; Engl. transl. 1839). A convenient selection of observations of this kind may be found in Allan Nevins (ed.), *American Social History as Recorded by British Travellers* (1923). A German account is that of Ludwig Von Raumer, *America and Her People* (1846).

Frontier literature scarcely questioned the assumptions of open opportunity under which the frontier existed. The standard work describing its influence is Frederick Jackson Turner's *The Frontier in American History* (1920), a work supplemented by Walter Prescott Webb's *The Great Frontier* (1952). Of the works which challenge Turner's thesis, perhaps Henry Nash Smith's *Virgin Land* (1950) is the most valuable for the student of literature. Louis B. Wright's *Culture on the Moving Frontier* (1955) and Lucy L. Hazard's *The Frontier in American Literature* (1927) are important as general studies of the period. Dixon Wecter's *The Hero in America: A Chronicle of Hero-Worship* (1941) relies heavily on early frontier concepts of the hero.

Although the transcendentalist objected to the conventional materialistic goals of the American, his concept of man's goodness and potentiality is a direct outgrowth of the American concept of opportunity. Ralph Waldo Emerson uses these assumptions in "Self-Reliance" (1841), "Heroism" (1841), "The Transcendentalist" (1843), and in other of his early essays; Henry David Thoreau's glorification of man's potential in *Walden* (1854) is additional evidence of the ideal's strength. Walt Whitman's "Song of Myself" (1855) is the culmination of this kind of glorification of man.

Literature following the Civil War reflected a subtle change that occurred in the original optimism of the American ideal. The atmosphere of opportunity guided the satirical work of Mark Twain and Charles Dudley Warner in *The Gilded Age* (1873). The legends of Horatio Alger, Jr., and William T. Adams ("Oliver Optic") found their literary counterparts in the partially critical studies of William Dean Howells about opportunity, notably *The Rise of Silas Lapham* (1886), *A Hazard of New Fortunes* (1890), and *The World of Chance* (1893). The best-known representatives of big business in the works of Henry James, Christopher Newman of *The American* (1875), and Adam Verver of *The Golden Bowl* (1905), are mythical heroes from the land of opportunity. In the twentieth century, the atmosphere which promises success is the background for Dreiser's *The "Genius"* (1916) and becomes personal and literary for Thomas Wolfe in *Of Time and the River* (1935) and *The Web and the Rock* (1939).

Some early examples of the Puritan attitude toward business and money making, commonly referred to as the Puritan or Protestant ethic, may be seen in John Cotton's "Christian Calling," reprinted in *The American Puritans*, edited by Perry Miller (1956), in other selections of Cotton's *The Way of Life* (1641), reprinted in *The Puritans*, edited by Perry Miller and Thomas H. Johnson (1938), and Cotton Mather, *A Christian at His Calling* (1701). Griswold's notes cite bibliography through Franklin (see p. 19 ff.). Emerson's essays "Compensation" (1841) and "Wealth" (1860) show traces of the Protestant ethic. Andrew Carnegie's *Triumphant Democracy* (1893) and *The Gospel of Wealth and Other Essays* (1933) are useful as further illustrations of his ideas; interesting examples of the ethic at work in the 1920s is the study of a midwestern community, *Middletown* (1929), by Robert S. and Helen Merrell Lynd; Sherwood Anderson has examples in the character of Sam McPherson (in his early years of education) in *Windy McPherson's Son* (1916), in *Poor White* (1920), and in the character Jesse Bentley in one of his *Winesburg, Ohio* (1919) sketches;

George Babbitt in *Babbitt* (1922) is Sinclair Lewis's most prominent
example of the type; but we see others in *Main Street* (1920), *Arrowsmith* (1925), and *Elmer Gantry* (1927); the hero of *Marco's Millions*
(1927) is the best illustration we have in Eugene O'Neill's plays. A
vivid example of the final logical expression of the ethic, when the ethic
is taken quite literally, can be found in Bruce Barton's *The Man
Nobody Knows* (1925).

The self-made man, the person rising from lowly beginnings, has
been the figure of emulation in American popular literature. Political
figures, such as Andrew Jackson, William Henry Harrison, and Abraham
Lincoln carried the legend of their humble origins with them. The self-
made man of business appeared early. In colonial times we find John
Hull (eulogized in a sermon by Samuel Willard), a few years later John
Jacob Astor (described flatteringly in Washington Irving's *Astoria,*
1836), and in the period of industrialization Andrew Carnegie and
other business leaders. In the literature of the late eighteenth century
and throughout the nineteenth century, the figure was treated more or
less sympathetically—for instance, in the character Van Rough in
Royall Tyler's play *The Contrast* (1787) and Adam Trueman in Anna
Cora Mowatt's play *Fashion* (1850). In the latter part of the century
Howells's Silas Lapham in *The Rise of Silas Lapham* (1885) is the
honest merchant, although in *A Hazard of New Fortunes* (1890)
Howells treats his businessman, Dryfoos, less kindly. Frank Norris in
The Octopus (1901) reserves his contempt for the middleman agent of
the railroad, S. Behrman, rather than its president, Shelgrim, and in
The Pit (1903) creates a financier-hero in Curtis Jadwin. Robert
Herrick makes a successful and sympathetic study of the type in *The
Memoirs of an American Citizen* (1905). The best-known example of
this successful figure is Dreiser's Frank Cowperwood in *The Financier*
(1912), *The Titan* (1914), and *The Stoic* (1948). Later there was
Sherwood Anderson's Sam McPherson in *Windy McPherson's Son*
(1916). Andrew March of Floyd Dell's *Janet March* (1923) is treated as
a member of a disappearing species. Sinclair Lewis analyzes the
creative industrialist in *Dodsworth* (1929). In more recent times J. P.
Marquand has drawn a strong portrait of the type in *B. F.'s Daughter*
(1946). An extreme romanticist description is found in Ayn Rand's
Atlas Shrugged (1957).

Since 1900 the success figure has been described often in harsh
terms. Examples of condemnatory criticism of the successful businessmen are found in Upton Sinclair's *A Captain of Industry* (1906), *The
Metropolis* (1908), and his later works, *The Money Changers* (1926)
and *Oil!* (1927); Winston Churchill's *Mr. Crewe's Career* (1908); David
Graham Phillip's *The Master Rogue* (1903); and Edith Wharton's *The
Custom of the Country* (1913). Brief critical judgments about the type
are found in Sinclair Lewis's *Main Street* (1920) and *Arrowsmith*

(1925). John Dos Passos gives many critical and satirical examples in *U. S. A.* (1937).

In this bibliography the literature for the more popular market has scarcely been mentioned. In popular magazines and in books for the larger markets, success stories have always been plentiful. Analyses of these markets may lead the student to conclusions different from those in a success study of this nature. Audience identification may work on several levels. For instance, an important study in this area is the one by Leo Lowenthal, "Biographies in Popular Magazines," available in William Petersen, ed., *American Social Patterns* (1956). Lowenthal concludes that in the period 1900–1920 the mass reader ceased to identify with the business or political hero, as did the reader in the Horatio Alger, Jr., series, for instance, simply because the business hero was now too far beyond his hopes. According to this study, the reader now identifies with the movie or sports hero, and he looks now to the element of chance, rather than the old ideals of thrift and work, for the clue to his hero's achievements.

The problem of audience identification is, of course, important, but complicated by what one interprets as the audience. The sociologists such as David Riesman, Nathan Glazer, and Reuel Denney in *The Lonely Crowd* (1950), William H. Whyte, Jr., in *The Organization Man* (1956), and C. Wright Mills in *White Collar* (1956) are all concerned with the relationship between the individual and literary media. For further helpful bibliography in this area the reader can refer to the works listed in the essay by Max Lerner, "The Rise and Decline of the Titan." (See pp. 32–42).

Criticisms of the materialistic success goals can be divided conveniently into three groups: objections of moralists, objections of those who looked toward aristocratic ideals of behavior, and objections of those who felt that the individual is harmed in some manner because of the American people's obsession with success. Moral criticisms, similar to that of John Woolman, continued throughout the nineteenth century, particularly in the works of the transcendentalists: Emerson in some of his late essays, e.g., those in *Conduct of Life* (1860) and *Society and Solitude* (1870), strikes a moral tone. (The problem with Emerson is complicated because Emerson was intent on compromising between the necessities of the individual and society. Emerson gives what is perhaps his clearest definition of the successful man in the essay "Aristocracy," available conveniently in *The American Transcendentalists*, edited by Perry Miller [1957]—an essay which is, according to Miller in his introduction to the essay, "Emerson's most mature, though most inconclusive, discussion of the confrontation of self and society, Genius and the democracy.") Thoreau in "Life Without Principle," part of which is included here, shares many of Emerson's moral ideas.

Nathaniel Hawthorne touches the subject obliquely in the char-

acter of Judge Pyncheon in *The House of Seven Gables* (1851), and
Herman Melville comments on the American manifestation of man's
greed in *The Confidence Man: His Masquerade* (1857). From the Civil
War to 1900 the moral criticism of the success ethic was implicit in the
works of John William De Forest and Mark Twain and explicit in
Edward Bellamy's *Looking Backward, 2000–1887* (1888) and Howells's
utopian novels, *A Traveler from Altruria* (1894) and *Through the Eye
of the Needle* (1907). About the turn of the century the tone was
prominent in Hamlin Garland's descriptions of corruption in the midwest, *A Member of the Third House* (1892) and *The Spoils of Office*
(1892); Harold Frederic's *The Market-Place* (1898); David Graham
Phillips's works about Wall Street and the insurance trusts, *The Great
God Success* (1901), *The Master Rogue* (1903), *The Cost* (1904), *The
Plum Tree* (1905), and *The Light Fingered Gentry* (1907); Winston
Churchill's study of monopolies, *Mr. Crewe's Career* (1908), and of
politics, *Coniston* (1906); Upton Sinclair's studies of the business
world, *A Captain of Industry* (1906), *The Metropolis* (1908), *The
Money Changers* (1926), *Oil!* (1927), and *Boston* (1928); in Robert
Herrick's later works, *Waste* (1924) and *Chimes* (1926). Willa Cather
criticizes the means for obtaining success in "A Sculptor's Funeral"
(1905), *One of Ours* (1922), *A Lost Lady* (1923), and *The Professor's
House* (1925). Sinclair Lewis seems partially committed on the moral
level in *Elmer Gantry* (1927). John Dos Passos passes moral judgments
on the success characters in both his narratives and his profiles in the
trilogy *U. S. A.* (1937). One of the most unusual delineations of the
amorality of a success character is that of Flem Snopes in William
Faulkner's *The Hamlet* (1940), *The Town* (1957), and *The Mansion*
(1959).

The critics using values which, for the sake of convenience, may
be termed aristocratic ridiculed success figures on the score of vulgarity. In the early days of the Republic and throughout the eighteenth
century many European authors—Tocqueville to a degree; Frances
Trollope in *Domestic Manners of the Americans* (1832); and prominent English writers, Thomas Carlyle, Charles Dickens, and Matthew
Arnold among others—commented on the vulgarity of American manners, particularly as evidenced by the American's frank pursuit of
money. Washington Irving seems to condescend to have Ichabod
Crane of "The Legend of Sleepy Hollow" (1819–1820) assume a
modest success; James Fenimore Cooper in the satirical work *Monikins*
(1835) and the social studies *Homeward Bound* (1838) and *Home as
Found* (1838) criticizes the parvenus of the new society. Following the
Civil War Henry Adams reveals his own struggle to overcome his
prejudice against the type in *The Education of Henry Adams: An
Autobiography* (1907). Edith Wharton is partially divided in her
sympathies toward the type in *The House of Mirth* (1905), *The
Custom of the Country* (1913), *The Glimpses of the Moon* (1922),

Twilight Sleep (1927), *The Children* (1928), and *Hudson River Bracketed* (1929); Ellen Glasgow also is mixed in her attitude toward them in *The Romantic Comedians* (1926) and *They Stooped to Folly* (1928).

Other critics objected because of the apparent harm suffered by individuals within a success culture; for instance, Emerson and Thoreau felt that in the American's search for property and riches, values were distorted and energies dissipated. This objection is seen in Jack London's *Martin Eden* (1909), in Edgar Lee Masters's *Spoon River Anthology* (1915), *Songs and Satires* (1916), and *The New Spoon River* (1924). Sherwood Anderson accuses the money culture of disturbing the individual's psychic nature—his instinctual and sexual nature as well as his natural sympathy for other people. We find these ideas influencing *Windy McPherson's Son* (1916), *Winesburg, Ohio* (1919), many of his short stories, and stated explicitly in *Perhaps Women* (1931) and *Sherwood Anderson's Memoirs* (1942). Eugene O'Neill exploits this theme in *The Great God Brown* (1926) and *Strange Interlude* (1928). Other examples are Willa Cather's *One of Ours* (1922) and *The Professor's House* (1925); Floyd Dell in *Moon-Calf* (1921), *The Briary-Bush* (1921), and *Love without Money* (1931); Robert Herrick's *Waste* (1924) and *Chimes* (1926); Upton Sinclair in *Oil!* (1927); and John Dos Passos in *Manhattan Transfer* (1925) and *U. S. A.* (1937).

Accounts of the dream's corruption, of the disillusionment that came when the dream failed of its promise, began soon after the Civil War. Walt Whitman objected to the materialistic nature of the dream in *Democratic Vistas* (1871). Henry Adams in *Democracy—An American Novel* (1880) and John William De Forest in *Honest John Vane* (1875) and *Playing the Mischief* (1875) included pictures of the cynicism now attached to the dream. Frank Norris in *The Octopus* (1901) describes the betrayers of the promise. Jack London's Martin Eden in *Martin Eden* (1909) finds suicide the answer to the disillusioning reality of money success.

In the twentieth century Theodore Dreiser creates many characters affected in one or more ways by the success atmosphere: Hurstwood of *Sister Carrie* (1900), the narrator in the story "The Old Neighborhood" (1918), Mr. X—— in "'Vanity, Vanity,' Saith the Preacher" (in *Twelve Men*, 1919), Clyde Griffiths in *An American Tragedy* (1925). Sherwood Anderson pictures several failures in his works: Windy McPherson in *Windy McPherson's Son* (1916), Tom Willard in *Winesburg, Ohio* (1919), briefer portraits of failures in *Poor White* (1920). Sinclair Lewis caricatures the promise in *Babbitt* (1922) and *The Man Who Knew Coolidge* (1928); Gatsby in F. Scott Fitzgerald's *The Great Gatsby* (1925) is one of the most important of the victims in American literature; Willa Cather reveals her interest in the victim theme in her stories "The Sculptor's Funeral" (1905) and "Paul's Case" (1920), and in her novel *The Professor's House* (1925); John Dos

Passos uses the death of the dream as a central motif in *Manhattan Transfer* (1925) and the trilogy *U. S. A.* (1937). In plays, Clifford Odets in *Awake and Sing* (1935) and Arthur Miller in *Death of a Salesman* (1949) use the theme.

Secondary material about the success theme is limited in works treating the subject specifically but abundant in works that allude to the theme. A specialized study is that of Kenneth Lynn, *The Dream of Success* (1955), which analyzes the careers and works of Jack London, David Graham Phillips, Frank Norris, Robert Herrick, and Theodore Dreiser, seeking to prove that these writers' criticisms of American success must be viewed in the light of their commitment to their own desires for personal success. Most biographies and critical studies of the individual writers mentioned in this bibliography would be helpful. Many literary essayists—H. L. Mencken, Edmund Wilson, Lionel Trilling, to name only a few—have treated the subject significantly in their writing. Works by psychologists, in particular Erich Fromm, can prove valuable. There is, of course, a vast amount of sociological material about American success culture that is available.

NOTES ON THE AUTHORS

HENRY ADAMS: Member of a distinguished American family, Henry Adams (1838–1918) was a journalist, an editor, and a distinguished Harvard professor. In his voluminous writings on American history, as well as in *The Education of Henry Adams* (1918), he sought an understanding of the American past, which he hoped would help him to understand better the times he lived in.

HORATIO ALGER, JR.: The most popular, and perhaps the most influential, purveyor of the success mythology in the nineteenth century was Horatio Alger, Jr. (1832–1899). The son of a stern and narrow New England minister, Alger severed the spiritual strains that bound him to the New England past but held firm to its faith that a virtuous life, combined with hard work—and luck—led to success.

SHERWOOD ANDERSON: Born in Clyde, Ohio, the fourth of seven children, Sherwood Anderson (1876–1941) grew up on the edge of poverty, working as a child in livery stables and on farms. Later a modestly successful paint manufacturer, he left business for writing. Because of his own experiences he could understand the aspirations of the poor, living in the dream world of a commercial culture.

EDWARD BELLAMY: Few books in the last decades of the nineteenth century could claim the popularity of *Looking Backward* (1888), the utopian novel of Edward Bellamy (1850–1898). In his novel Bellamy looks forward to the year 2000 and sees a happy and prosperous America completely socialized. He sets up this "ideal" society as a striking contrast to the capitalistic economic structure of his native New England.

ANDREW CARNEGIE: Born in Scotland, Andrew Carnegie (1835–1919) came to America with his family and, at the age of ten, began his career as a bobbin-boy at twenty cents a day in a Pennsylvania cotton mill. By the age of thirty-three he had an annual income of fifty thousand dollars. He claimed that he owed his business success to virtuous and steady application and a mind alert to opportunity.

275

JOHN CHEEVER: John Cheever (b. 1912) has written hundreds of stories, most of them appearing in *The New Yorker* and some of them since re-published in two short-story collections. He found a larger audience with his popular study of a New England family, *The Wapshot Chronicle* (1957) —a story of various kinds of "successes."

EVAN S. CONNELL, JR.: According to one reviewer of the first volume of short stories by Evan S. Connell, Jr. (b. 1924), *The Anatomy Lesson and Other Stories* (1957), "Either the characters are distinctly American, or, scenically, they live on American ground and reveal modalities of Ameri-can thought." The definition of a successful man is one of the most promi-nent of these "modalities" of thought. Mr. Connell is the author of two short-story collections, two novels, and one book-length poem.

RUSSELL H. CONWELL: The rise from obscurity to material success was evident in the life of Russell H. Conwell (1842–1925); it was also the central message of his famous lecture "Acres of Diamonds." Born in Massachusetts, Conwell had a varied career as journalist, Baptist clergy-man, lawyer, and educator, principally in Philadelphia, where he was pastor of the Baptist Temple and founder of Temple University and the Samaritan Hospital.

JAMES FENIMORE COOPER: Although his popular fame is based upon his series of novels about the frontier, in his own time Cooper (1789–1851) was also well known for his essays and fiction about the American political and social structure. He viewed the opportunistic attitude of the common American as a threat to the cultural traditions in which he himself had been raised as the son of a wealthy landowner in Cooperstown, New York.

STEPHEN CRANE: Stephen Crane (1871–1900) is best known for his short stories and his novel *The Red Badge of Courage*, but his poems have at-tracted considerable attention, not only because of their stylistic experi-ments but for their assumptions—a view of man isolated in a Darwinian universe—which have placed them close to twentieth-century attitudes. Crane was no sentimentalist, but he did have a moral point of view, which helped to establish the irony in his poems.

MICHEL-GUILLAUME JEAN DE CRÈVECOEUR: Although born in France and educated in England, Crèvecoeur (1735–1813) was an American citizen not only by naturalization but also by temperament. In *Letters from an Ameri-can Farmer* (1782), he was one of the first to realize the importance of the role of individual success in the development of democratic ideals.

FLOYD DELL: In addition to editing leftist publications (editor of *Masses* from 1914 to 1917, *Liberator* from 1918 to 1924), Floyd Dell (b. 1887) pub-lished many novels describing psychological problems in a rapidly chang-ing social world. The heroine of *Janet March* (1923) seeks to adapt to her new emancipated role without rejecting her midwest heritage, represented in its best as well as its most rigid form by her Puritan grandfather, Andrew March.

JOHN DOS PASSOS: John Dos Passos (b. 1896) in his trilogy, *U. S. A.* (*42nd Parallel*, 1930; *Nineteen Nineteen*, 1932; and *The Big Money*, 1936), presents a detailed picture of the American cultural scene from about 1912 to 1930, a culture dominated by commercial success values. The characters included in this anthology furnish a telling commentary on the destructive moral and social effects of these values.

THEODORE DREISER: In his childhood in Indiana Theodore Dreiser (1871–1945) knew poverty and lived under the shadow of his father's failure. As a journalist in Chicago, St. Louis, Pittsburgh, and New York, he struggled, often in poverty, for his own fame and fortune, eventually gaining a success as a New York editor, finally as a writer. His experiences in an economic dog-eat-dog world directly influenced his social philosophy, which uniquely combined social Darwinism and Nietzscheanism to produce a naturalism with its successes (Frank Cowperwood of *The Financier*, 1912, and *The Titan*, 1914) and its failures (Hurstwood of *Sister Carrie*, 1900; X—— of *Twelve Men*, 1919; and Clyde Griffiths of *An American Tragedy*, 1925).

RALPH WALDO EMERSON: The leading spokesman of the American transcendentalists, Emerson (1803–1882) had a double heritage: an almost unrestrained optimism about man and the universe, and a high moral purpose. In his major essays, such as "The American Scholar" and "Self-Reliance," Emerson calls upon the individual to rise above a dependence on the past, on society, and on wealth and property, to rely upon his inner resources, and to insist upon the sacredness of his own integrity.

F. SCOTT FITZGERALD: No writer understood the polar experiences of success and failure as thoroughly as did F. Scott Fitzgerald (1896–1940). In his most important novel, *The Great Gatsby* (1925), and in his later autobiographical work, "The Crack-Up" (1934, 1936), Fitzgerald reveals valuable insights into the nature of American material aspirations. Like Dick Diver, the hero of his later novel *Tender Is the Night* (1934), Fitzgerald himself had sought to live the dream and had found both himself and the dream to be failures.

BENJAMIN FRANKLIN: At the age of seventeen Benjamin Franklin (1706–1790) arrived as an almost penniless printer in Philadelphia. Twenty-five years later he was able to retire, or, as he says in his *Autobiography*, "disengage . . . from private business." His career as an organizer, a diplomat, a scientist, an inventor, and a soldier is indelibly recorded in the history of eighteenth-century America. To later generations Franklin has become a symbol of industriousness and success.

HORACE GREELEY: As editor of the New York *Tribune* from 1841 to his death, Horace Greeley (1811–1872) was able to exert significant influence on public attitudes. Through such statements as "Go West, young man, and grow up with the country," he gave expression to popular idealistic aspirations at a time when opportunity on all frontiers—whether in the West, the city, or the small town—seemed boundless.

ALFRED WHITNEY GRISWOLD: Alfred Whitney Griswold (1906–1963), historian and former president of Yale University, in his study of the close relationship between Puritan doctrine and mercantile practice is following the general arguments of Max Weber. His essay on the three Puritans is one of the first published formal studies of American success.

NATHANIEL HAWTHORNE: Nathaniel Hawthorne (1804–1864), great-grandson of a judge at the Salem witchcraft trials and descendant of a long line of Puritans, was deeply involved emotionally in the tradition of his ancestors—a tradition that linked spiritual and worldly success. Despite his artistic successes, he believed that his ancestors would have regarded him a failure: "No aim, that I have ever cherished, would they recognize as laudable; no success of mine . . . would they deem otherwise than worthless, if not positively disgraceful."

WILLIAM DEAN HOWELLS: William Dean Howells (1837–1920) was at the beginning of his influential literary career when he wrote his campaign biography of Abraham Lincoln. In the *Life* (1860) he seldom rose above the conventional phrases used in the current campaign biographies. He did, however, realize the political value in Lincoln's humble origin, and he admirably capitalized on an already established legend of the success story, of course unaware that he was writing the story of the man who would become the prototype of that legend.

MAX LERNER: In *America as a Civilization* (1957) Max Lerner (b. 1902) goes back in history to explain the close relationship between American institutions and contemporary American thought. Mr. Lerner has a reputation as a newspaper columnist, editor (*Nation,* 1936 to 1939), and teacher. He is the author of many articles and books on the contemporary scene.

SINCLAIR LEWIS: In his novels of the 1920s Sinclair Lewis (1885–1951) became widely known for his incisive interpretations of the American business scene with his portraits of the small and large businessman in *Main Street* (1920), *Babbitt* (1922), *Arrowsmith* (1925), and *Dodsworth* (1929). For all of his businessmen characters, "success" means money; but, as with George F. Babbitt's "ideals and visions," rationalizations always accompanied the money search.

ABRAHAM LINCOLN: See pages 94–98.

JOHN P. MARQUAND: John P. Marquand (1893–1960), himself a descendant of New England Puritans, is best known for his novels about the New England upper echelon, the latter-day Puritans, notably *The Late George Apley* (1937) and *H. M. Pulham, Esq.* (1941). In *Point of No Return* (1949) he contributes to success literature in his portrait of the new "organization man," who seemingly has rejected the Puritan individualistic ethic in favor of society and security.

C. WRIGHT MILLS: C. Wright Mills (1915–1962), sociologist and teacher, felt that sociology has a particular obligation to fulfill, that of educating the American citizen to the nature of American society, specifically its corporate structure and the places of power within the structure. *White Collar* (1951) examines the changing role of the middle-class laborer in a restrictive society.

NORMAN VINCENT PEALE: Dr. Norman Vincent Peale (b. 1898) is the author of several widely read books on the art of living. *The Power of Positive Thinking* has sold over two million copies in the hard-cover edition alone since its publication in 1952. Since 1932 Dr. Peale has been pastor at the Marble Collegiate Reformed Church in New York City.

EDWIN ARLINGTON ROBINSON: Edwin Arlington Robinson (1869–1935) left his hometown of Gardiner, Maine, when he was twenty-seven and settled in New York City for a life of poetry and disappointment. Many of Robinson's early poems were written about the inhabitants of "Tilbury Town," a town similar in striking respects to Gardiner. Robinson was from the beginning interested in the fates of the obscure people of this town and in the psychological reaction of these people to the pressures of a large social world.

HENRY DAVID THOREAU: Like Emerson, his neighbor, close friend, and mentor, Henry David Thoreau (1817–1862) advocated the unhurried and reflective life, not the "restless, nervous, bustling, trivial Nineteenth Century" he observed about him. His masterpiece is *Walden* (1854), a record of his more than two years at Walden Pond (near Concord, Massachusetts) and a classic statement of the spirit of individualism.

MAX WEBER: Max Weber (1864–1920), a German sociologist and politi- newspaper reporter, journalist, and Western miner, Mark Twain (1835–1910) was a keen observer of mankind. His conclusions about success in life did not conform to those of Alger, a contemporary, or of the even more anemic tales in the Sunday School weeklies. In an age of the entrepeneur, he had often witnessed rascals exchange their rags for riches— without benefit of the Alger formula.

MAX WEBER: Max Weber (1864–1920), a German sociologist and political economist, was a pioneer in a comprehensive approach to cultural history. In his best-known work, *The Protestant Ethic and the Spirit of Capitalism* (1904–1905), he established the influential thesis that capitalism carried with it a new set of ethical standards to which Protestantism adapted itself. One factor in this adaptation was the new interest in worldly success.

WALT WHITMAN: In his long poems Walt Whitman (1819–1892) attempted to be a spokesman for a young, vigorous America, certain of its leading role in the world as the peak of political and social democracy scientific development, and spiritual progress. In many of his shorter—and often more personal—poems, however, he contrasts the public concept of success and his belief in the ultimate value of friendship, love, and beauty.

JOHN WOOLMAN: At the age of thirty-six John Woolman (1720–1772) was a successful tailor and merchant in Mount Holly, New Jersey. He could not, he found, reconcile his success in merchandising and his desire to live the life of a Christian. Though he continued to practice his trade as a tailor, he gave up selling goods that he felt were items of luxury and devoted his life to preaching to the settlements of Friends in the colonies and to practicing the life of a plain Quaker and a lover of mankind.